Stairwell is distributed daily via the magic of the internet at:

www.stairwellonline.com

It's All in Your Head is Copyright 2013 Johnathan Bigelow. All Rights Reserved.

It's All in Your Head: The First Stairwell Collection, by Johnathan Bigelow, first printing, November 2013. For information, email stairwell@outlook.com. No portion of this book may be used or reproduced in any manner without the express written consent of the author, except in the case of select quotations or reprints in the context of reviews. The name Stairwell, it's likeness, and characters are Copyright Johnathan Bigelow. All Rights Reserved.

ISBN: 978-0-615-88781-4

Dedicted to all the teachers that told me not to draw during class.

Stairwell

Volume 1: It's All In Your Head

Johnathan Bigelow

FOREWORD

All I've known my whole life is comic strips. It started as soon as I learned to read. I never had good reading comprehension, so the only things I could read and easily understand were the words the accompanied the funny little pictures in the comic treasuries at my hometown library. Bill Amend's Foxtrot, Charles M. Schulz' Peanuts, and Jim Davis' Garfield were the first comics I can remember reading. I loved the micro-stories, the art, and the jokes.

I couldn't get enough and before too long I was collecting treasuries myself. My personal favorite, Foxtrot, was the reason I learned to draw. When I was in elementary school, I would go on family vacations and spend the time tracing Bill Amend's work, slightly altering characters until they became my own. At this time, I was still too young to appreciate how to form my own jokes or stories. My comics consisted mostly of things that made no sense together, or were a blatant rip off of my favorite strips.

By high school, I had graduated to reading webcomics. I spent countless hours reading webcomics at night. And my days were spent doodling in class. I'll admit that I probably should've listened a little harder during those classes, but the allure of comics was too strong to ignore.

It was during this time that one of the webcomics I was reading inadvertently introduced me to Adobe Illustrator. Illustrator was this amazing tool that I had not heard of yet and it was the exact thing I needed to finally take the time to develop my own work. I set about trying to learn it, and develop my first real strip.

In 2003, my senior year of high school, I created my first webcomic, A Rusty Life. It was an eclectic slice-of-life comic that featured a big lineup of slightly wacky characters. It's writing was erratic, the art- at least in the early days- was minimal, and the updating was sporadic. But every artist has to start somewhere. I worked hard on it. It became a feature in the school newspaper. To date, A Rusty Life, which TECHINCIALLY still runs, has over 1000 comics and has been running for over 10 years. It hasn't always been my best work, but I feel like it was training me for my next project, the one that was going to be a big deal.

After 10 years of working on my art, my writing, and my webcomic business sense, it was time to start something new. Figuring out what that was going to be, though, was a whole other problem. I had been stewing over ideas for years, trying to find the "right" one. Then one bright summer day in 2012, a simple doodle changed everything.

While doing a summer contract at a big company in downtown Seattle, I was doodling during work, just trying to keep myself sane. I was toying with several different ideas during that time, trying to find the one for my next project. I was doodling scientists and robots because I thought my next great idea was going to be in that department. Then, I doodled a guy whose head was open- as if on a hinge- and a brain with arms and legs standing beside him. It suddenly gave life to this idea of a character whose co-star was HIMSELF! It was totally weird! And yet, because it was about his subconscious, still totally relatable! Who doesn't talk to themselves at least once in a while? Who doesn't second guess choices made?

That was the birth of Stairwell. I made 31 comics and decided to post them one a day for a whole month. Knowing that -based on my track record- that was where it was going to end. After that I'd then be able to set about looking for the next thing to spark my imagination. But to my surprise, 31 days came and went and I was very nearly done with a whole other month's worth of strips. In all my time of creating comics, I'd never had such an easy time writing material. So I decided to ride it out and see where it went.

This book is the culmination of 10 years of working in webcomics and nearly a year of direct work on this strip itself. In Stairwell, I try to incorporate the despair and philosophy of Charles M. Schulz' Peanuts, the endearing illusion of friendship from Bill Watterson's Calvin and Hobbes and an art style that is reminiscent of Bill Amend's Foxtrot. Stairwell is an acknowledgement to the comic strips I loved when I was young and I hope you enjoy reading Stairwell as much as I have enjoyed making it.

J. BIGELOW

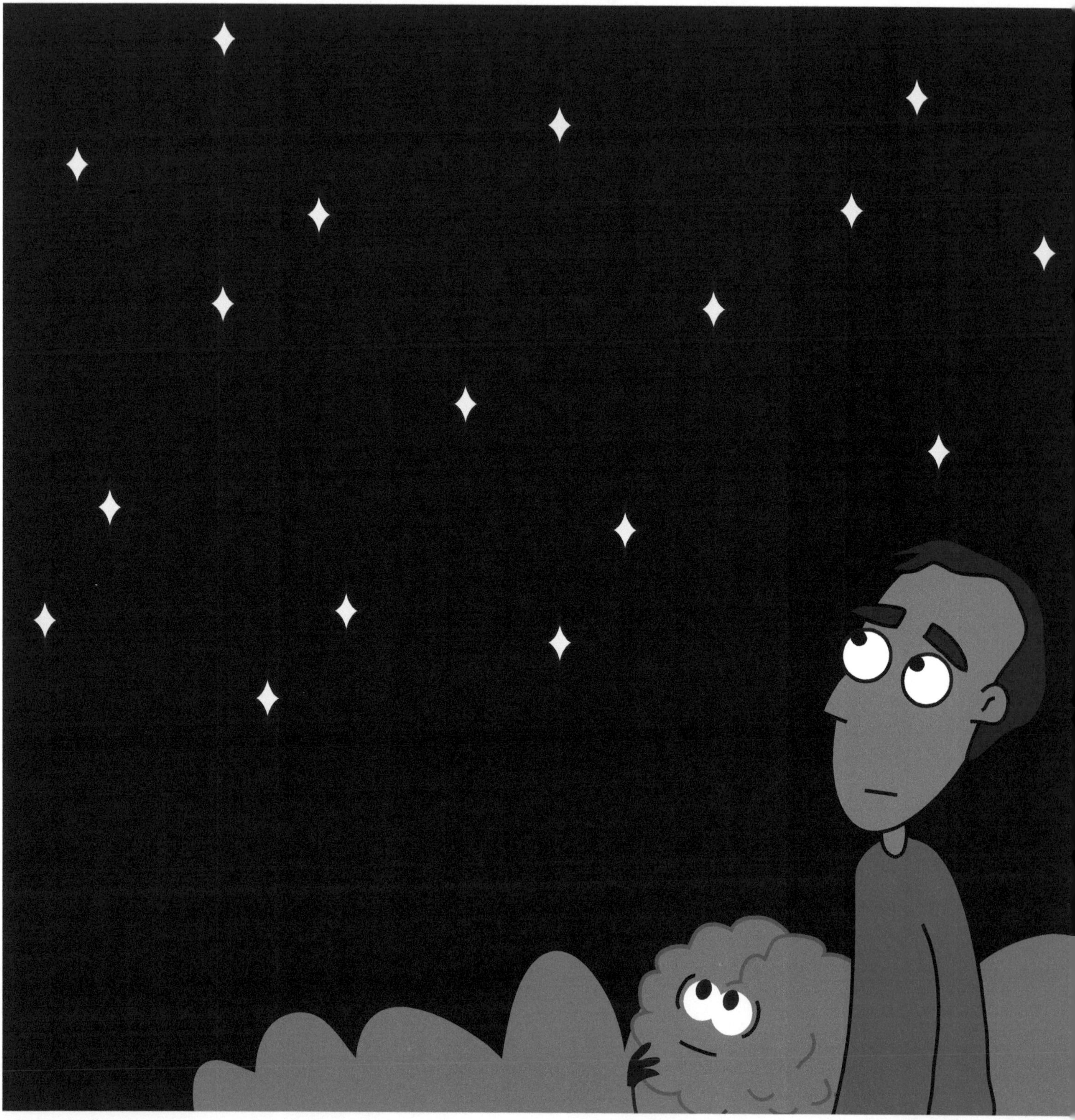

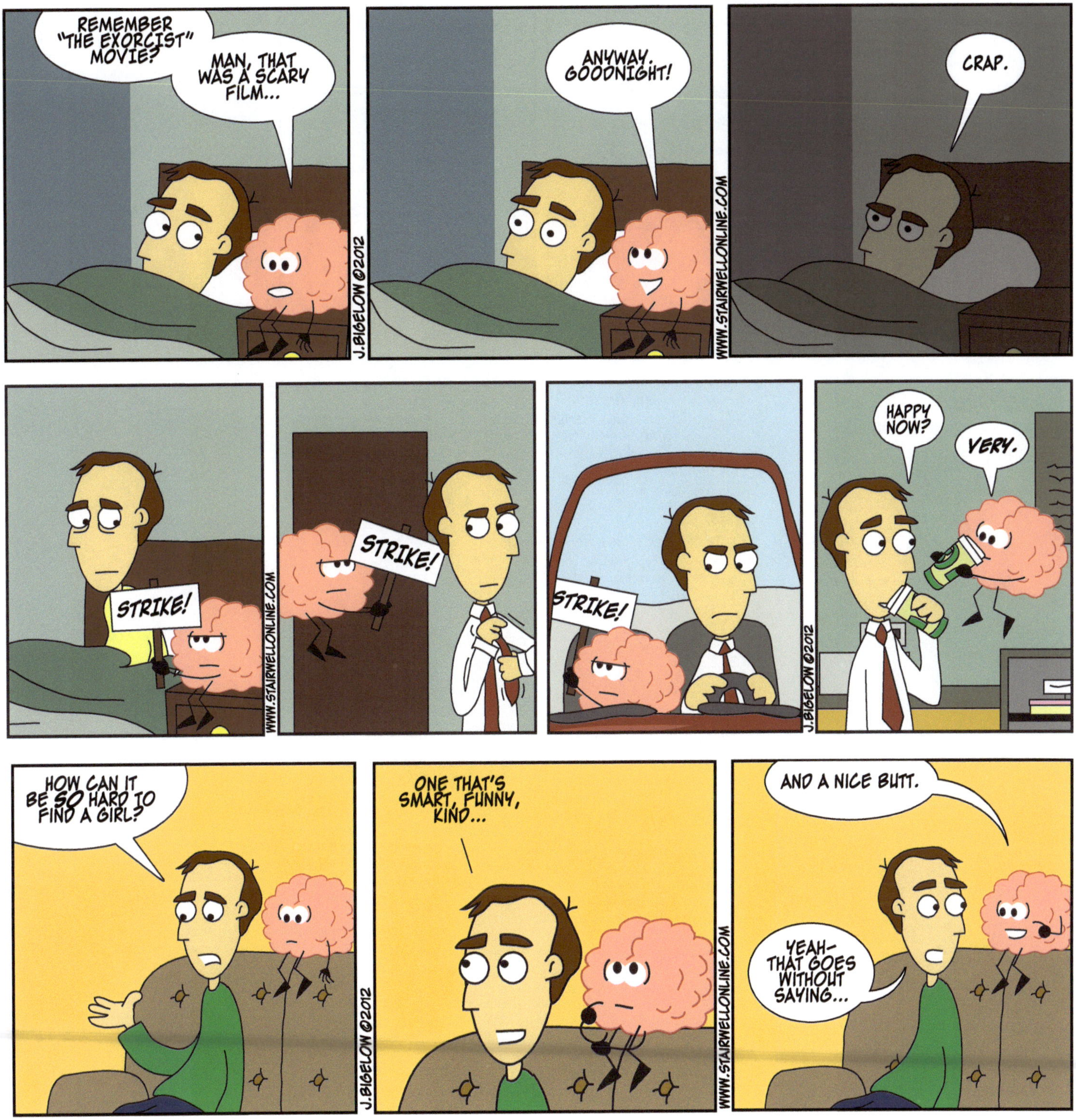

REMEMBER "THE EXORCIST" MOVIE?
MAN, THAT WAS A SCARY FILM...
J.BIGELOW ©2012
ANYWAY. GOODNIGHT!
WWW.STAIRWELLONLINE.COM
CRAP.
STRIKE!
WWW.STAIRWELLONLINE.COM
STRIKE!
STRIKE!
J.BIGELOW ©2012
HAPPY NOW?
VERY.
HOW CAN IT BE SO HARD TO FIND A GIRL?
J.BIGELOW ©2012
ONE THAT'S SMART, FUNNY, KIND...
WWW.STAIRWELLONLINE.COM
AND A NICE BUTT.
YEAH—THAT GOES WITHOUT SAYING...

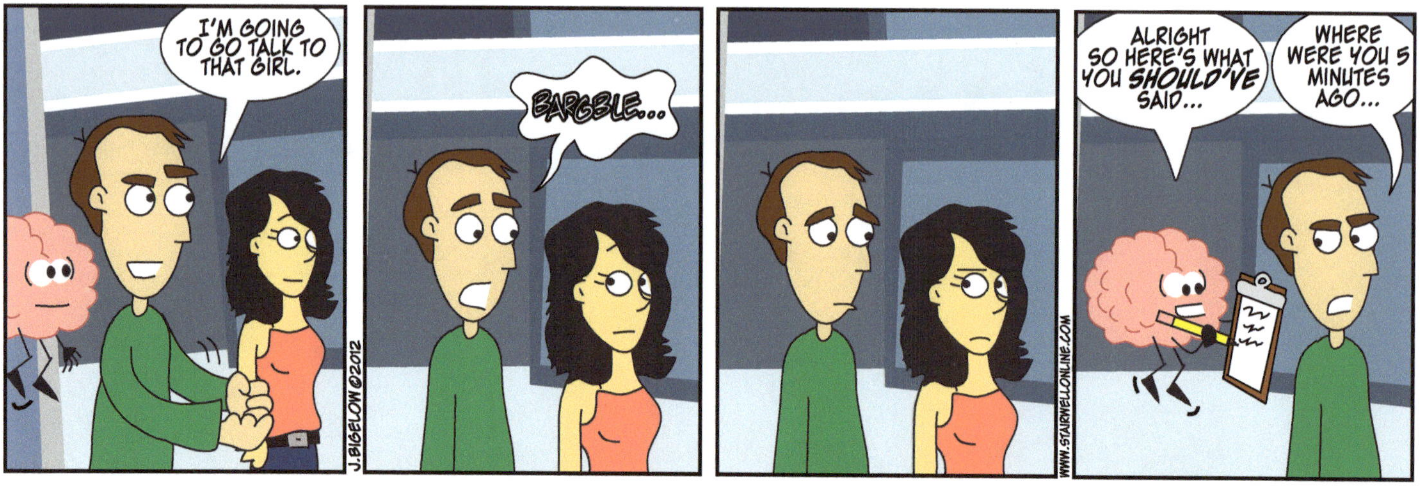
I'M GOING TO GO TALK TO THAT GIRL.
J.BIGELOW ©2012
BARGBLE...
WWW.STAIRWELLONLINE.COM
ALRIGHT SO HERE'S WHAT YOU SHOULD'VE SAID...
WHERE WERE YOU 5 MINUTES AGO...

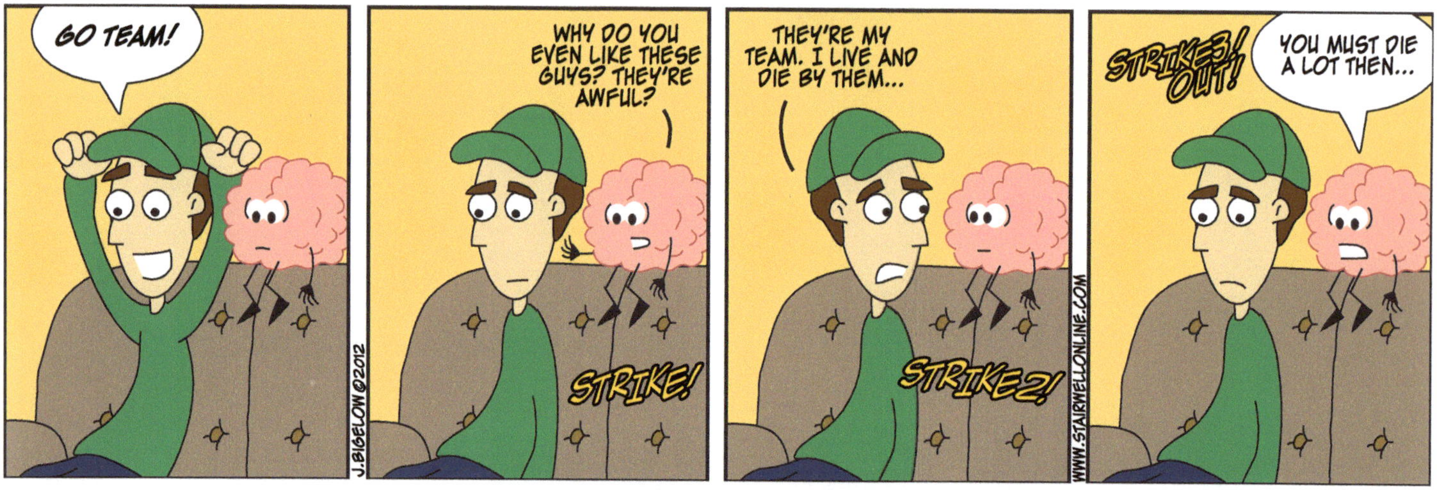
GO TEAM!
J.BIGELOW ©2012
WHY DO YOU EVEN LIKE THESE GUYS? THEY'RE AWFUL?
STRIKE!
THEY'RE MY TEAM. I LIVE AND DIE BY THEM...
STRIKE2!
WWW.STAIRWELLONLINE.COM
STRIKE3! OUT!
YOU MUST DIE A LOT THEN...

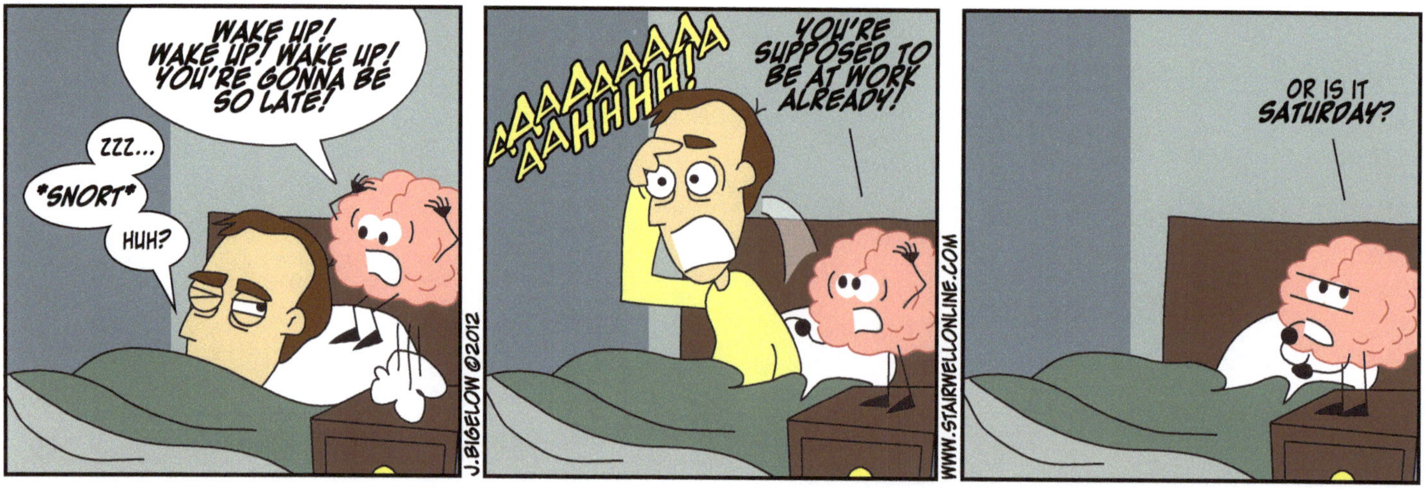
WAKE UP! WAKE UP! WAKE UP! YOU'RE GONNA BE SO LATE!
ZZZ...
SNORT
HUH?
J.BIGELOW ©2012
AAAAAAAAAAAAHHHHH!
YOU'RE SUPPOSED TO BE AT WORK ALREADY!
WWW.STAIRWELLONLINE.COM
OR IS IT SATURDAY?

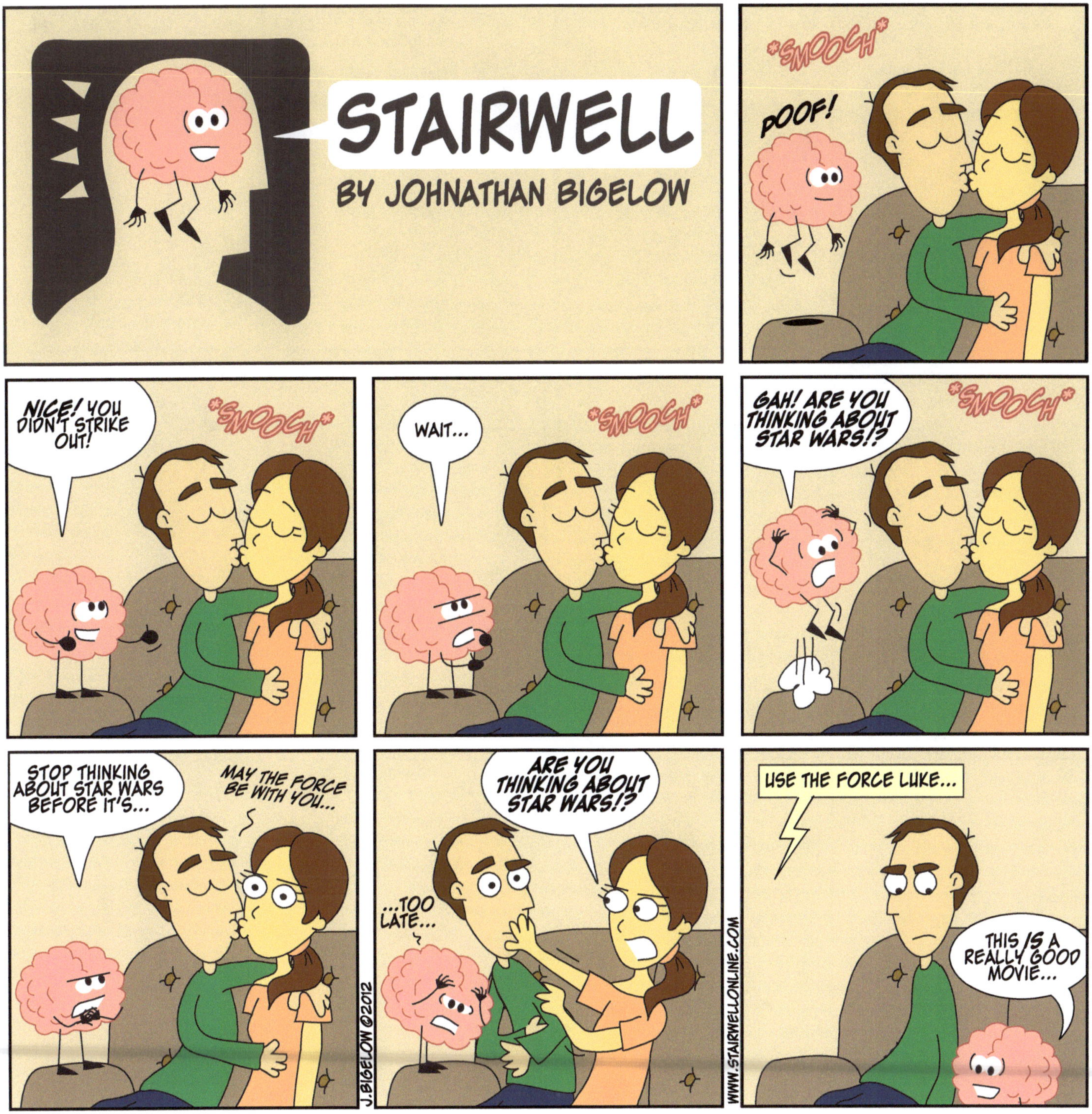
STAIRWELL
BY JOHNATHAN BIGELOW
SMOOCH
POOF!
NICE! YOU DIDN'T STRIKE OUT!
SMOOCH
WAIT...
SMOOCH
GAH! ARE YOU THINKING ABOUT STAR WARS!?
SMOOCH
STOP THINKING ABOUT STAR WARS BEFORE IT'S...
MAY THE FORCE BE WITH YOU...
J.BIGELOW ©2012
...TOO LATE...
ARE YOU THINKING ABOUT STAR WARS!?
WWW.STAIRWELLONLINE.COM
USE THE FORCE LUKE...
THIS IS A REALLY GOOD MOVIE...

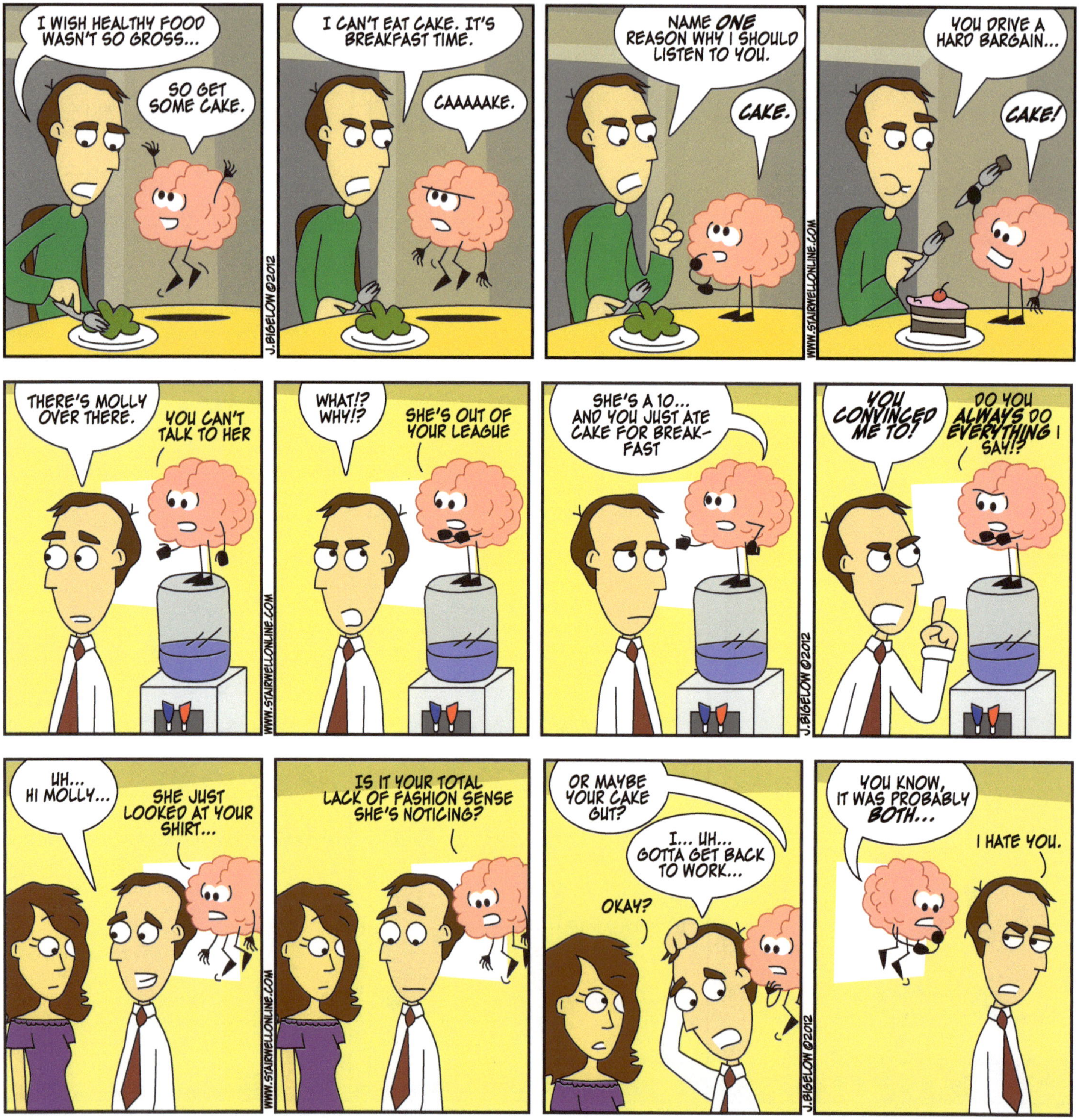
I WISH HEALTHY FOOD WASN'T SO GROSS...
SO GET SOME CAKE.
J.BIGELOW ©2012
I CAN'T EAT CAKE. IT'S BREAKFAST TIME.
CAAAAAKE.
NAME ONE REASON WHY I SHOULD LISTEN TO YOU.
CAKE.
WWW.STAIRWELLONLINE.COM
YOU DRIVE A HARD BARGAIN...
CAKE!
THERE'S MOLLY OVER THERE.
YOU CAN'T TALK TO HER
WWW.STAIRWELLONLINE.COM
WHAT!? WHY!?
SHE'S OUT OF YOUR LEAGUE
SHE'S A 10... AND YOU JUST ATE CAKE FOR BREAK-FAST
J.BIGELOW ©2012
YOU CONVINCED ME TO!
DO YOU ALWAYS DO EVERYTHING I SAY!?
UH... HI MOLLY...
SHE JUST LOOKED AT YOUR SHIRT...
WWW.STAIRWELLONLINE.COM
IS IT YOUR TOTAL LACK OF FASHION SENSE SHE'S NOTICING?
OR MAYBE YOUR CAKE GUT?
I... UH... GOTTA GET BACK TO WORK...
OKAY?
J.BIGELOW ©2012
YOU KNOW, IT WAS PROBABLY BOTH...
I HATE YOU.

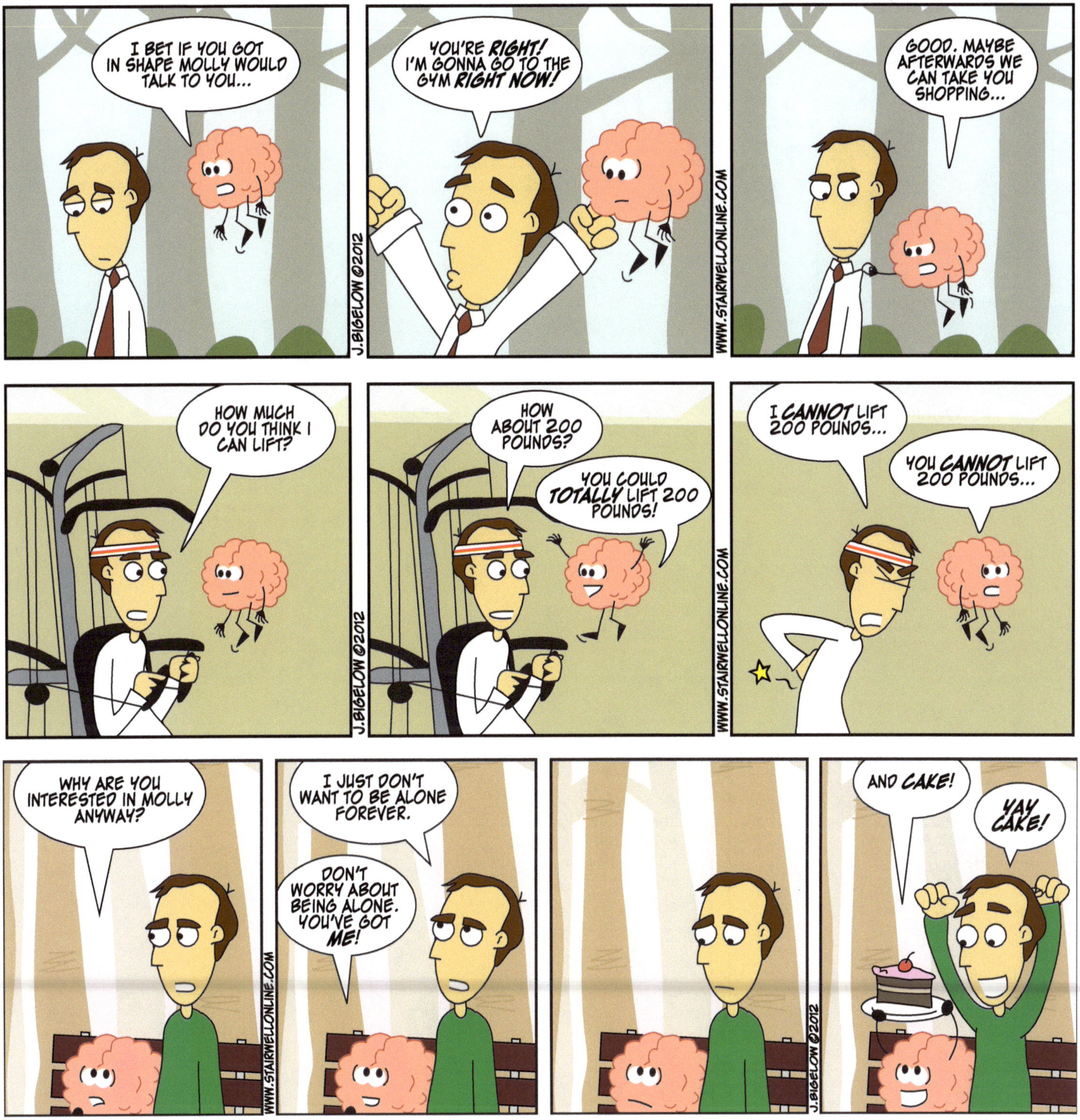
I BET IF YOU GOT IN SHAPE MOLLY WOULD TALK TO YOU...
J.BIGELOW ©2012
YOU'RE RIGHT! I'M GONNA GO TO THE GYM RIGHT NOW!
WWW.STAIRWELLONLINE.COM
GOOD. MAYBE AFTERWARDS WE CAN TAKE YOU SHOPPING...
HOW MUCH DO YOU THINK I CAN LIFT?
J.BIGELOW ©2012
HOW ABOUT 200 POUNDS?
YOU COULD TOTALLY LIFT 200 POUNDS!
WWW.STAIRWELLONLINE.COM
I CANNOT LIFT 200 POUNDS...
YOU CANNOT LIFT 200 POUNDS...
WHY ARE YOU INTERESTED IN MOLLY ANYWAY?
WWW.STAIRWELLONLINE.COM
I JUST DON'T WANT TO BE ALONE FOREVER.
DON'T WORRY ABOUT BEING ALONE. YOU'VE GOT ME!
J.BIGELOW ©2012
AND CAKE!
YAY CAKE!

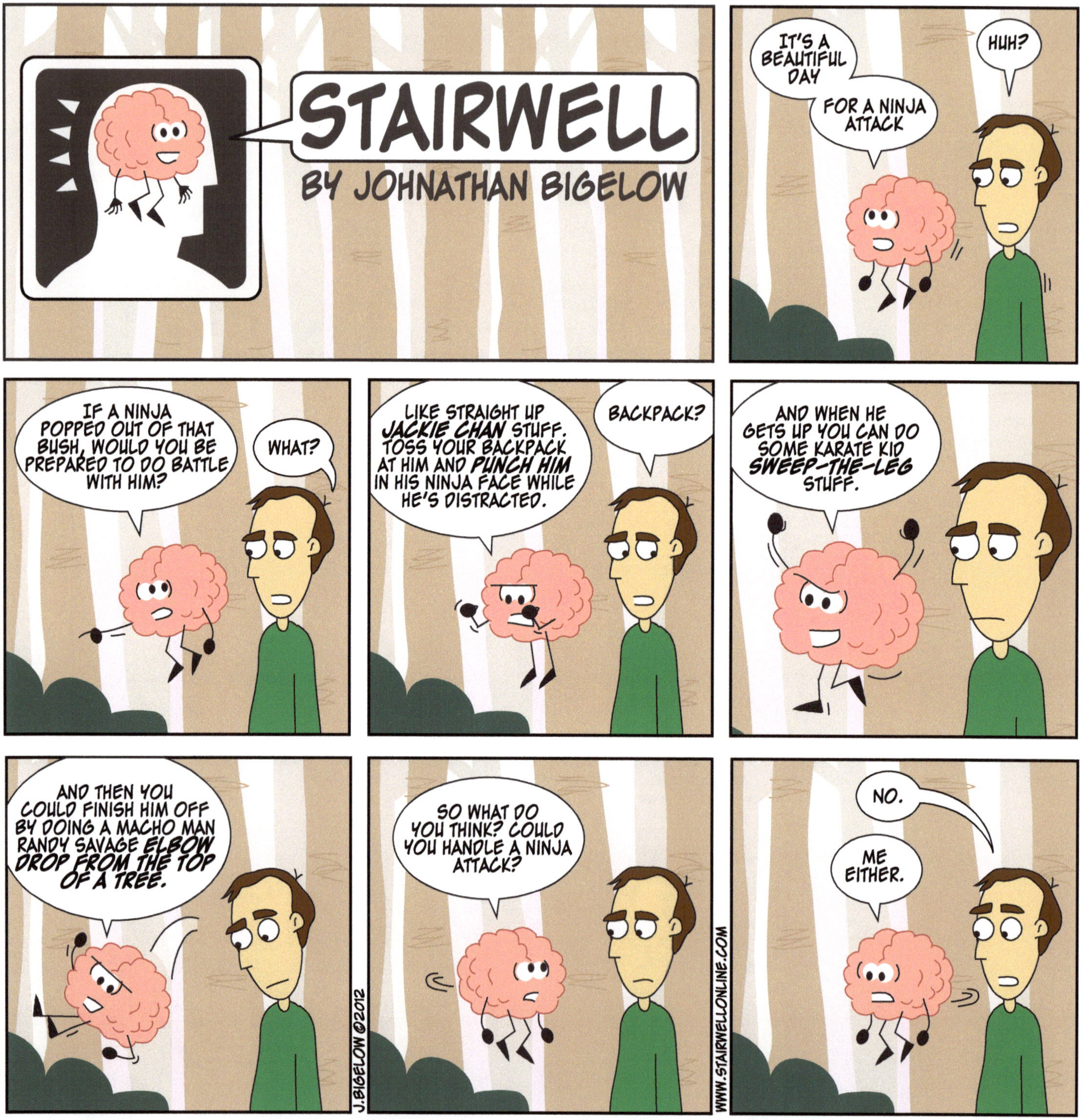
STAIRWELL
BY JOHNATHAN BIGELOW
IT'S A BEAUTIFUL DAY
FOR A NINJA ATTACK
HUH?
IF A NINJA POPPED OUT OF THAT BUSH, WOULD YOU BE PREPARED TO DO BATTLE WITH HIM?
WHAT?
LIKE STRAIGHT UP JACKIE CHAN STUFF. TOSS YOUR BACKPACK AT HIM AND PUNCH HIM IN HIS NINJA FACE WHILE HE'S DISTRACTED.
BACKPACK?
AND WHEN HE GETS UP YOU CAN DO SOME KARATE KID SWEEP-THE-LEG STUFF.
AND THEN YOU COULD FINISH HIM OFF BY DOING A MACHO MAN RANDY SAVAGE ELBOW DROP FROM THE TOP OF A TREE.
J.BIGELOW ©2012
SO WHAT DO YOU THINK? COULD YOU HANDLE A NINJA ATTACK?
WWW.STAIRWELLONLINE.COM
NO.
ME EITHER.

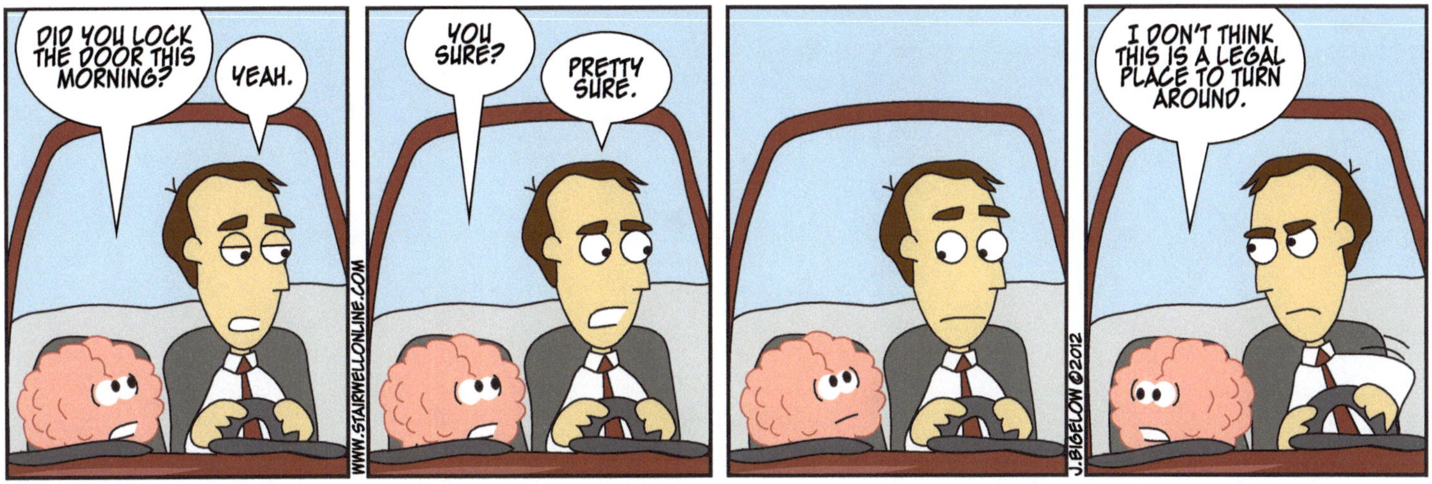
DID YOU LOCK THE DOOR THIS MORNING?
YEAH.
WWW.STAIRWELLONLINE.COM
YOU SURE?
PRETTY SURE.
J.BIGELOW ©2012
I DON'T THINK THIS IS A LEGAL PLACE TO TURN AROUND.

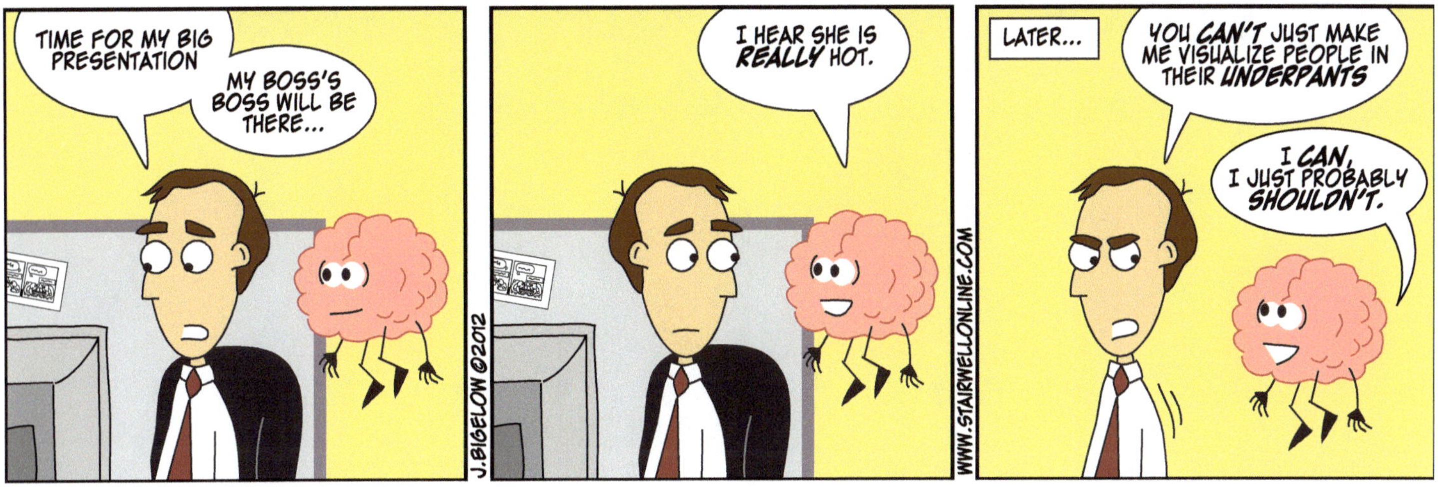
TIME FOR MY BIG PRESENTATION
MY BOSS'S BOSS WILL BE THERE...
J.BIGELOW ©2012
I HEAR SHE IS REALLY HOT.
WWW.STAIRWELLONLINE.COM
LATER...
YOU CAN'T JUST MAKE ME VISUALIZE PEOPLE IN THEIR UNDERPANTS
I CAN, I JUST PROBABLY SHOULDN'T.

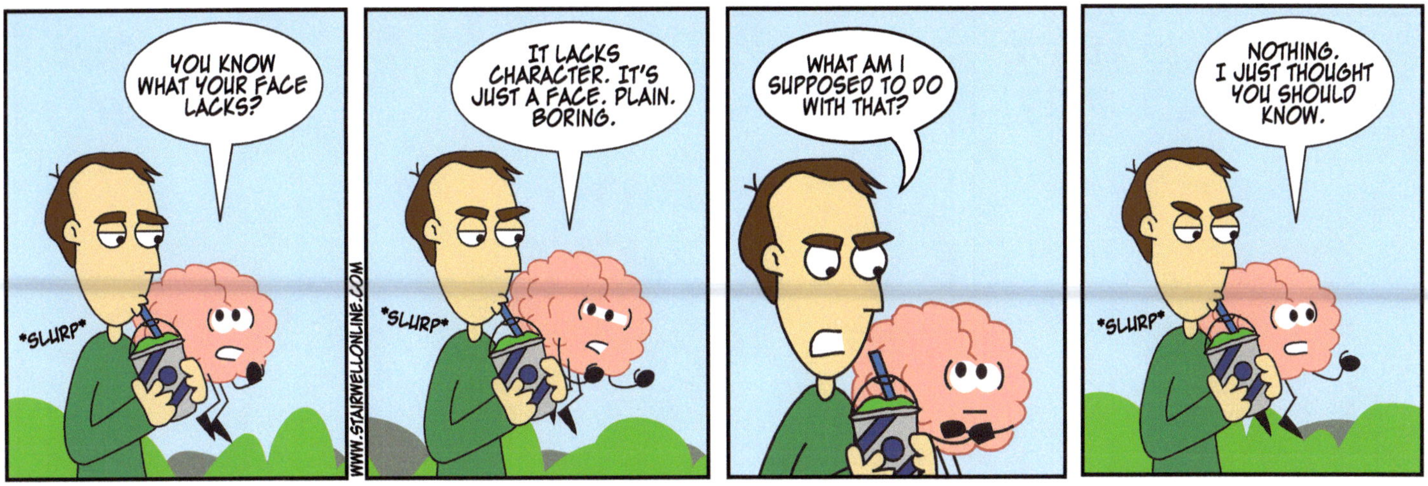
YOU KNOW WHAT YOUR FACE LACKS?
SLURP
WWW.STAIRWELLONLINE.COM
IT LACKS CHARACTER. IT'S JUST A FACE. PLAIN. BORING.
SLURP
WHAT AM I SUPPOSED TO DO WITH THAT?
NOTHING. I JUST THOUGHT YOU SHOULD KNOW.
SLURP

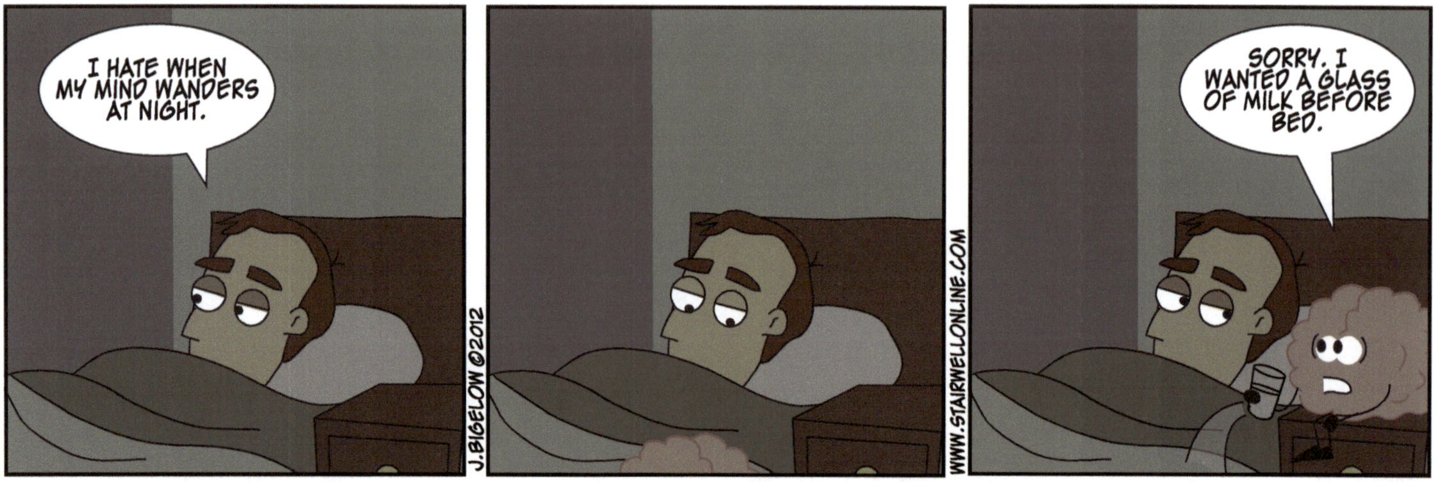
I HATE WHEN MY MIND WANDERS AT NIGHT.
J. BIGELOW ©2012
WWW.STAIRWELLONLINE.COM
SORRY. I WANTED A GLASS OF MILK BEFORE BED.

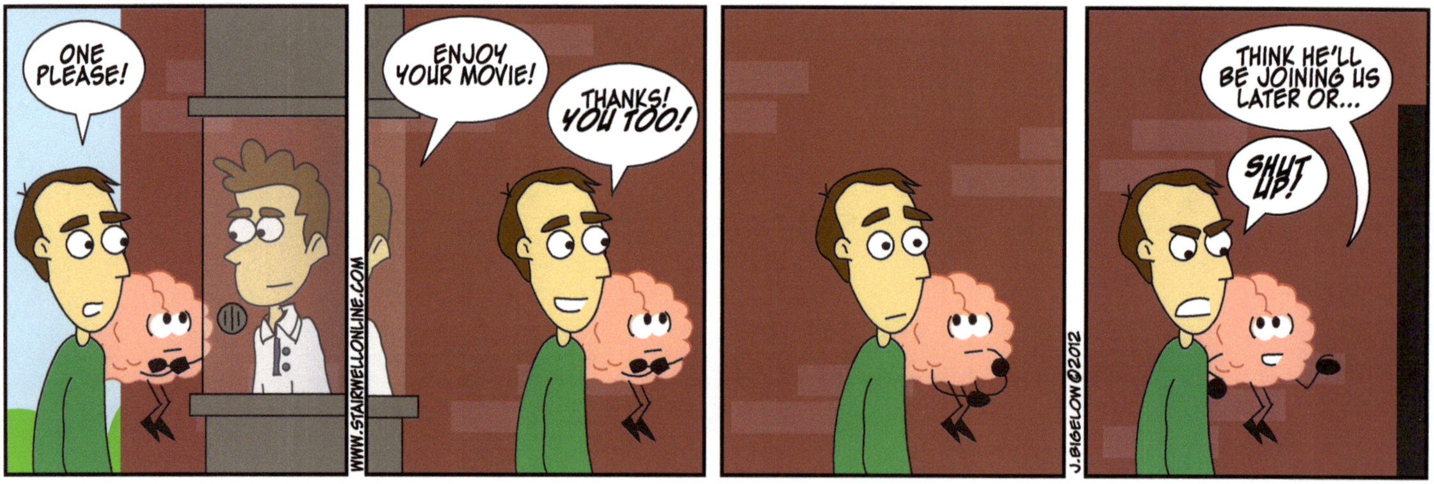
ONE PLEASE!
WWW.STAIRWELLONLINE.COM
ENJOY YOUR MOVIE!
THANKS! YOU TOO!
J. BIGELOW ©2012
THINK HE'LL BE JOINING US LATER OR...
SHUT UP!

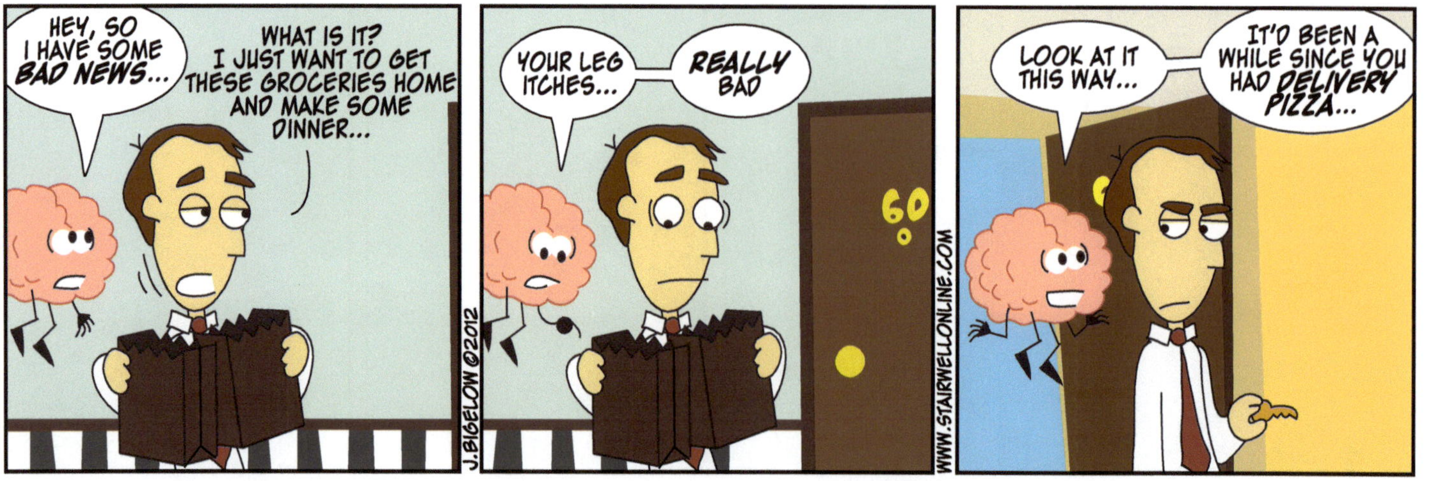
HEY, SO I HAVE SOME BAD NEWS...
WHAT IS IT? I JUST WANT TO GET THESE GROCERIES HOME AND MAKE SOME DINNER...
J. BIGELOW ©2012
YOUR LEG ITCHES...
REALLY BAD
60
WWW.STAIRWELLONLINE.COM
LOOK AT IT THIS WAY...
IT'D BEEN A WHILE SINCE YOU HAD DELIVERY PIZZA...

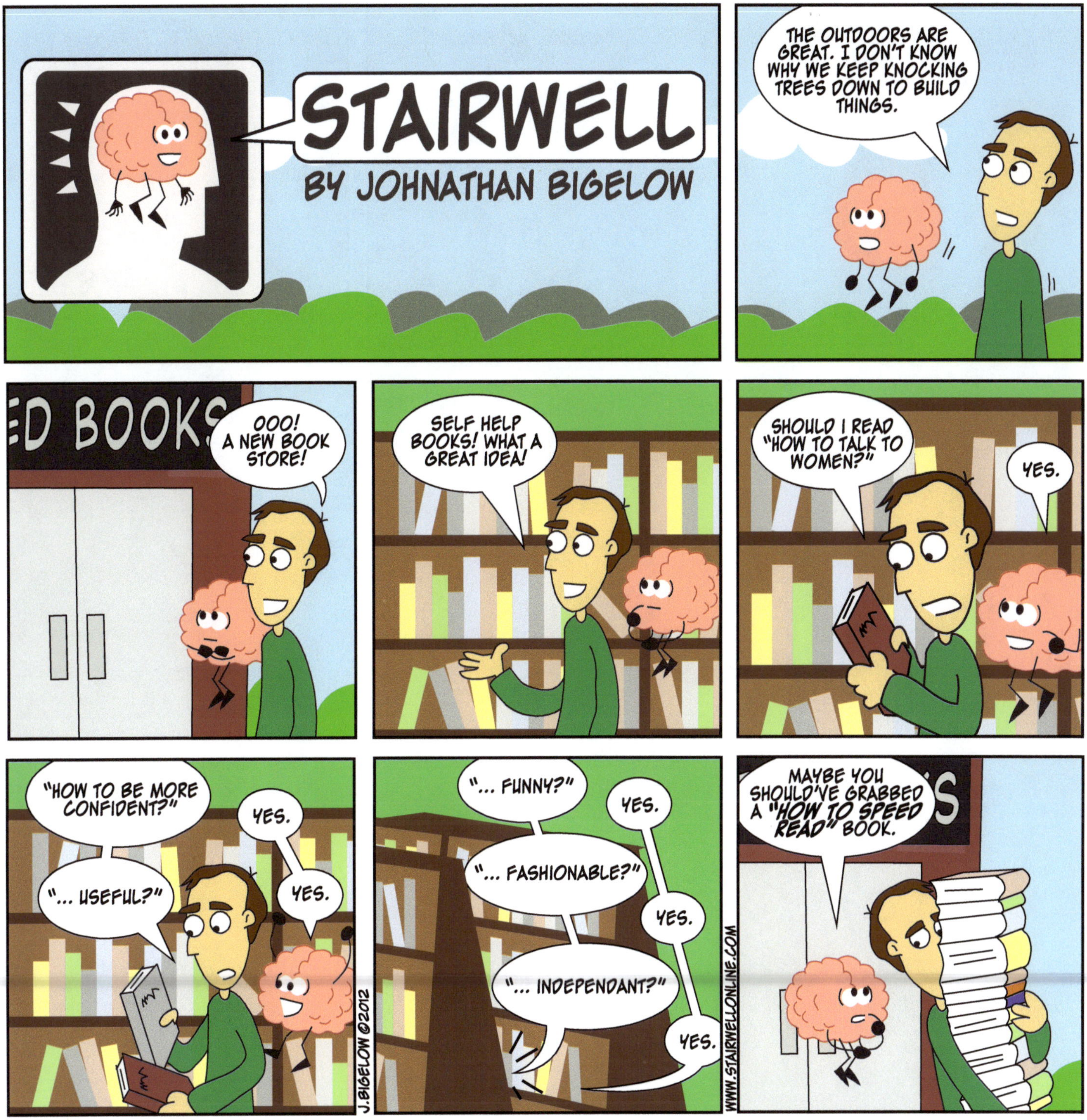
STAIRWELL
BY JOHNATHAN BIGELOW
THE OUTDOORS ARE GREAT. I DON'T KNOW WHY WE KEEP KNOCKING TREES DOWN TO BUILD THINGS.
ED BOOKS
OOO! A NEW BOOK STORE!
SELF HELP BOOKS! WHAT A GREAT IDEA!
SHOULD I READ "HOW TO TALK TO WOMEN?"
YES.
"HOW TO BE MORE CONFIDENT?"
YES.
"... USEFUL?"
YES.
"... FUNNY?"
YES.
"... FASHIONABLE?"
YES.
"... INDEPENDANT?"
YES.
J. BIGELOW ©2012
WWW.STAIRWELLONLINE.COM
MAYBE YOU SHOULD'VE GRABBED A "HOW TO SPEED READ" BOOK.

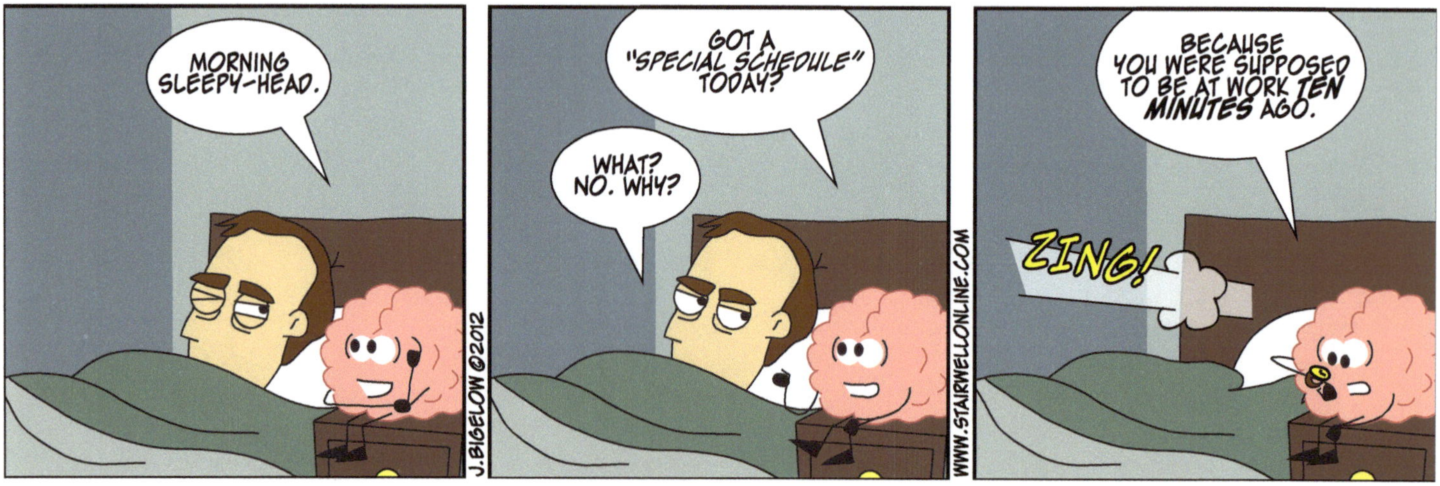
MORNING SLEEPY-HEAD.
GOT A "SPECIAL SCHEDULE" TODAY?
WHAT? NO. WHY?
BECAUSE YOU WERE SUPPOSED TO BE AT WORK **TEN MINUTES** AGO.
ZING!
J.BIGELOW ©2012
WWW.STAIRWELLONLINE.COM

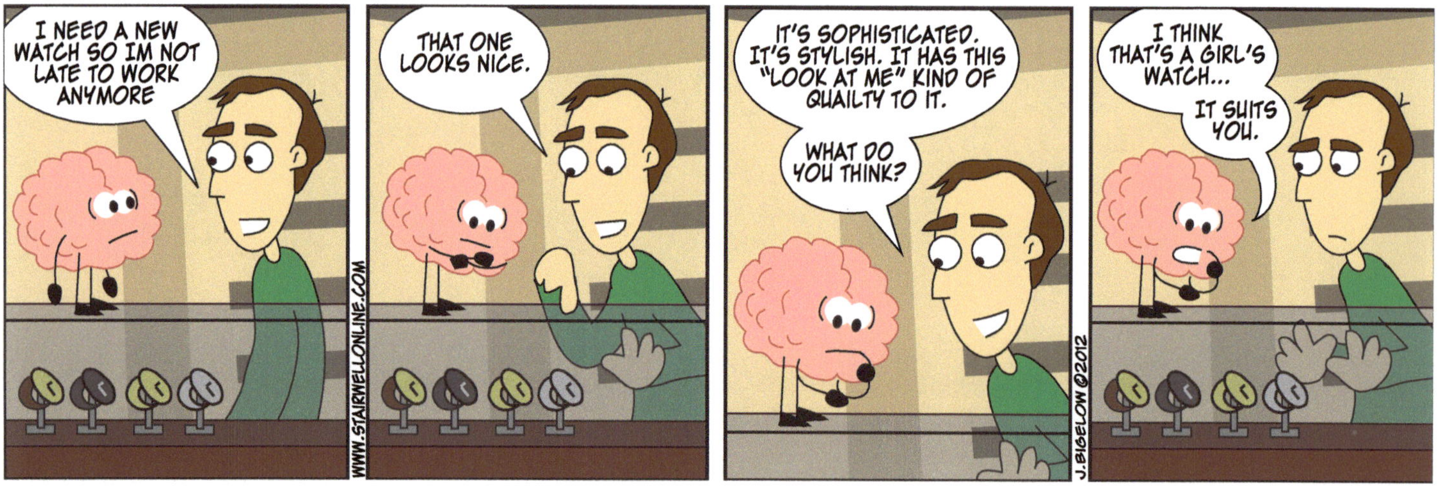
I NEED A NEW WATCH SO IM NOT LATE TO WORK ANYMORE
THAT ONE LOOKS NICE.
IT'S SOPHISTICATED. IT'S STYLISH. IT HAS THIS "LOOK AT ME" KIND OF QUAILTY TO IT.
WHAT DO YOU THINK?
I THINK THAT'S A GIRL'S WATCH...
IT SUITS YOU.
WWW.STAIRWELLONLINE.COM
J.BIGELOW ©2012

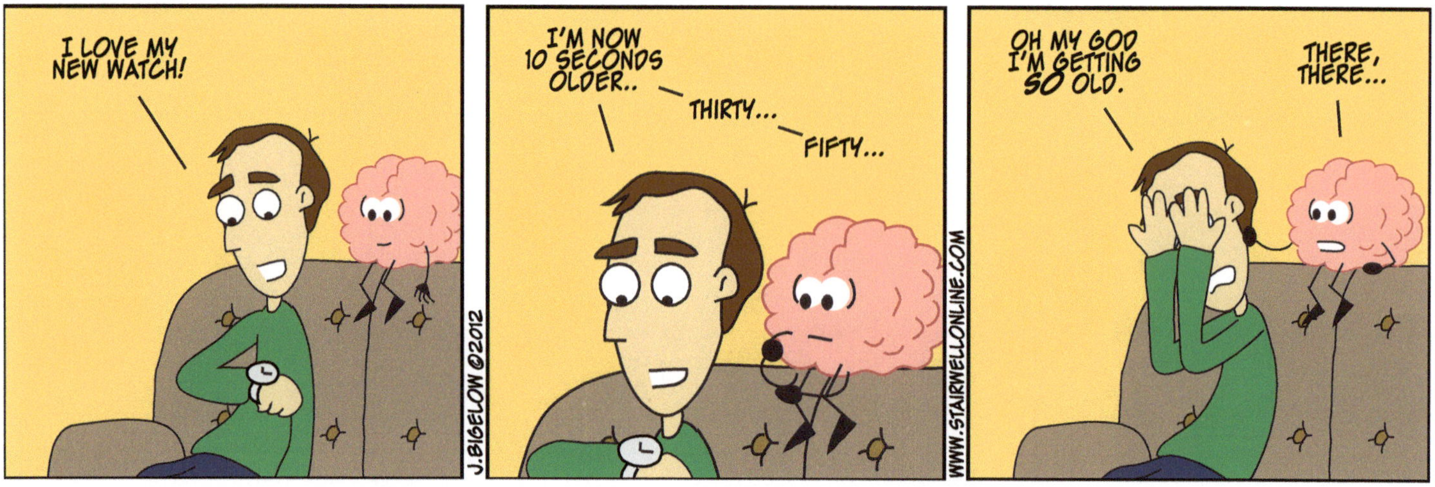
I LOVE MY NEW WATCH!
I'M NOW 10 SECONDS OLDER..
THIRTY...
FIFTY...
OH MY GOD I'M GETTING ***SO*** OLD.
THERE, THERE...
J.BIGELOW ©2012
WWW.STAIRWELLONLINE.COM

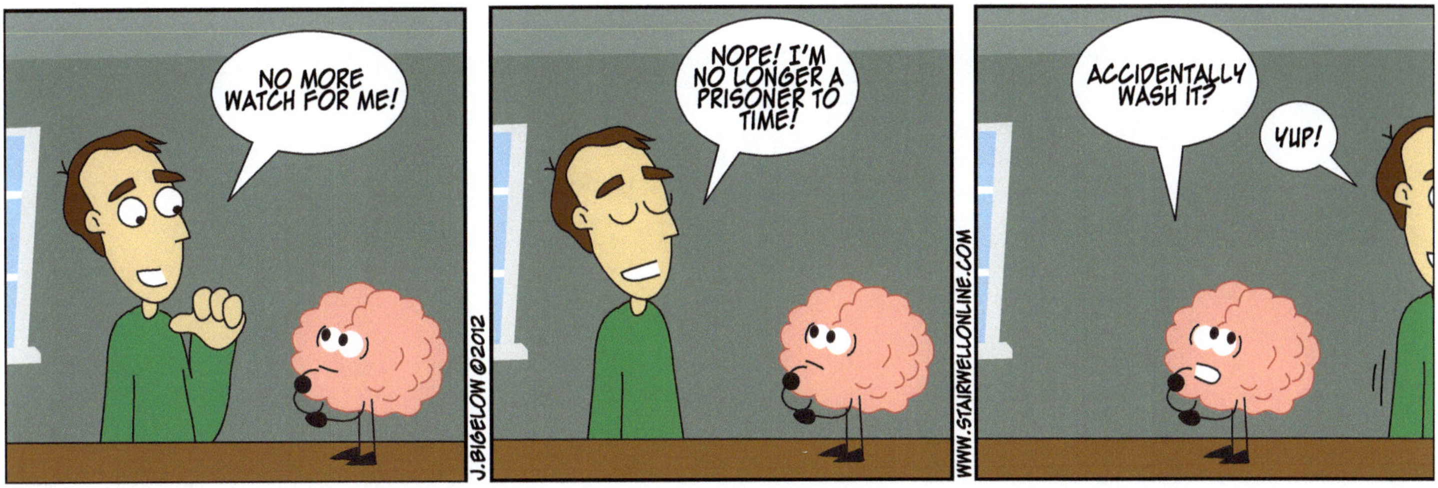
NO MORE WATCH FOR ME!
J.BIGELOW ©2012
NOPE! I'M NO LONGER A PRISONER TO TIME!
WWW.STAIRWELLONLINE.COM
ACCIDENTALLY WASH IT?
YUP!

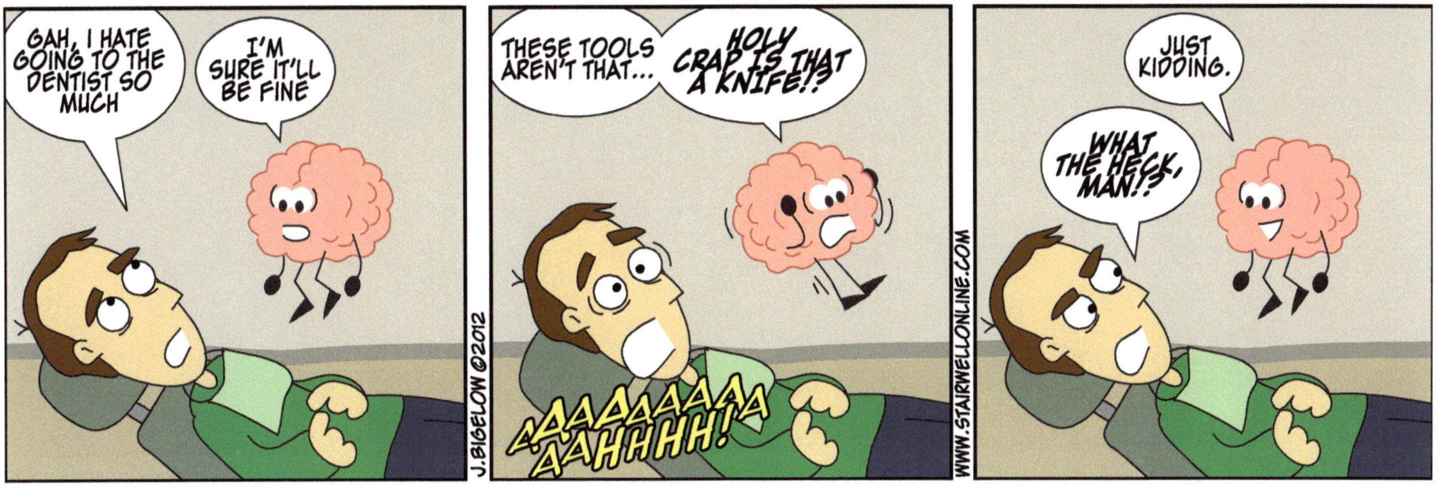
GAH, I HATE GOING TO THE DENTIST SO MUCH
I'M SURE IT'LL BE FINE
J.BIGELOW ©2012
THESE TOOLS AREN'T THAT...
HOLY CRAP IS THAT A KNIFE!?
AAAAAAAAA AAHHHH!
WWW.STAIRWELLONLINE.COM
JUST KIDDING.
WHAT THE HECK, MAN!?

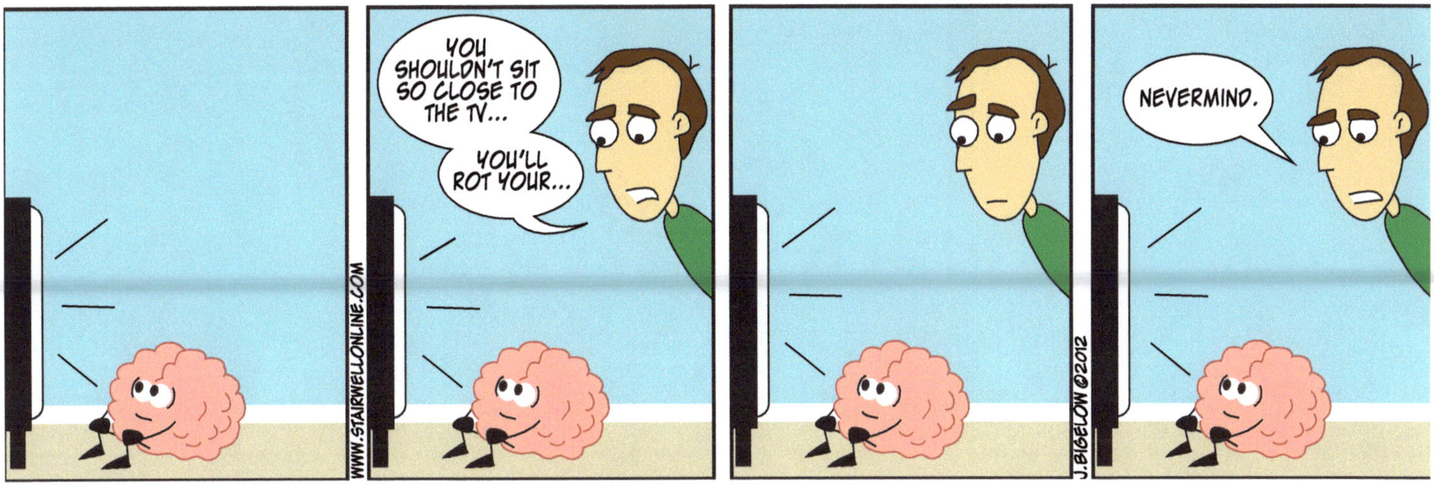
WWW.STAIRWELLONLINE.COM
YOU SHOULDN'T SIT SO CLOSE TO THE TV...
YOU'LL ROT YOUR...
J.BIGELOW ©2012
NEVERMIND.

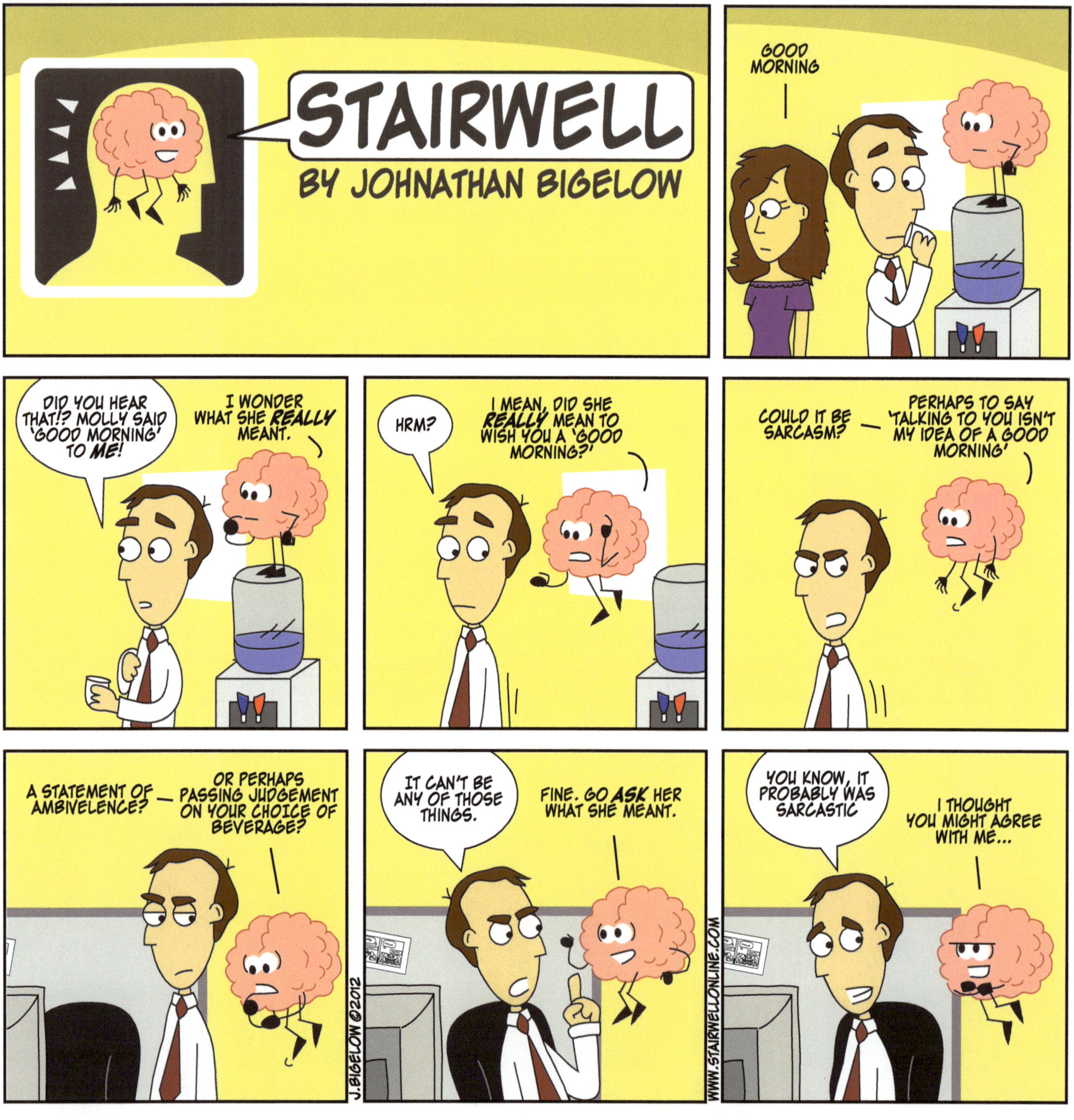
STAIRWELL
BY JOHNATHAN BIGELOW
GOOD MORNING
DID YOU HEAR THAT!? MOLLY SAID 'GOOD MORNING' TO ME!
I WONDER WHAT SHE REALLY MEANT.
HRM?
I MEAN, DID SHE REALLY MEAN TO WISH YOU A 'GOOD MORNING?'
COULD IT BE SARCASM?
PERHAPS TO SAY 'TALKING TO YOU ISN'T MY IDEA OF A GOOD MORNING'
A STATEMENT OF AMBIVELENCE?
OR PERHAPS PASSING JUDGEMENT ON YOUR CHOICE OF BEVERAGE?
J.BIGELOW ©2012
IT CAN'T BE ANY OF THOSE THINGS.
FINE. GO ASK HER WHAT SHE MEANT.
WWW.STAIRWELLONLINE.COM
YOU KNOW, IT PROBABLY WAS SARCASTIC
I THOUGHT YOU MIGHT AGREE WITH ME...

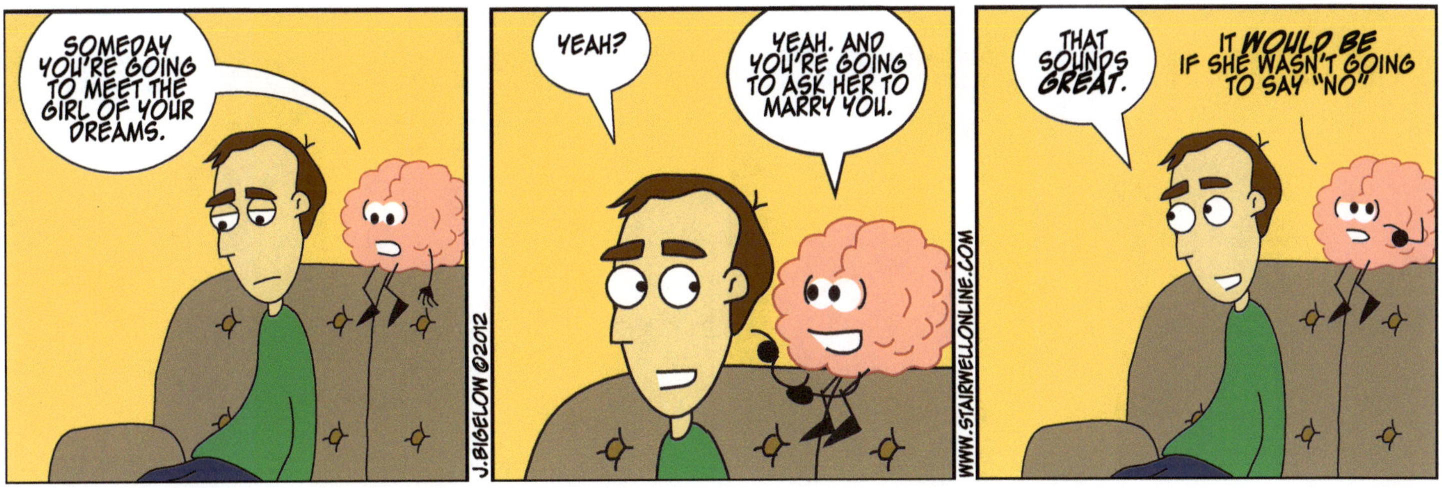

SOMEDAY YOU'RE GOING TO MEET THE GIRL OF YOUR DREAMS.
YEAH?
YEAH. AND YOU'RE GOING TO ASK HER TO MARRY YOU.
THAT SOUNDS GREAT.
IT WOULD BE IF SHE WASN'T GOING TO SAY "NO"
J.BIGELOW ©2012
WWW.STAIRWELLONLINE.COM

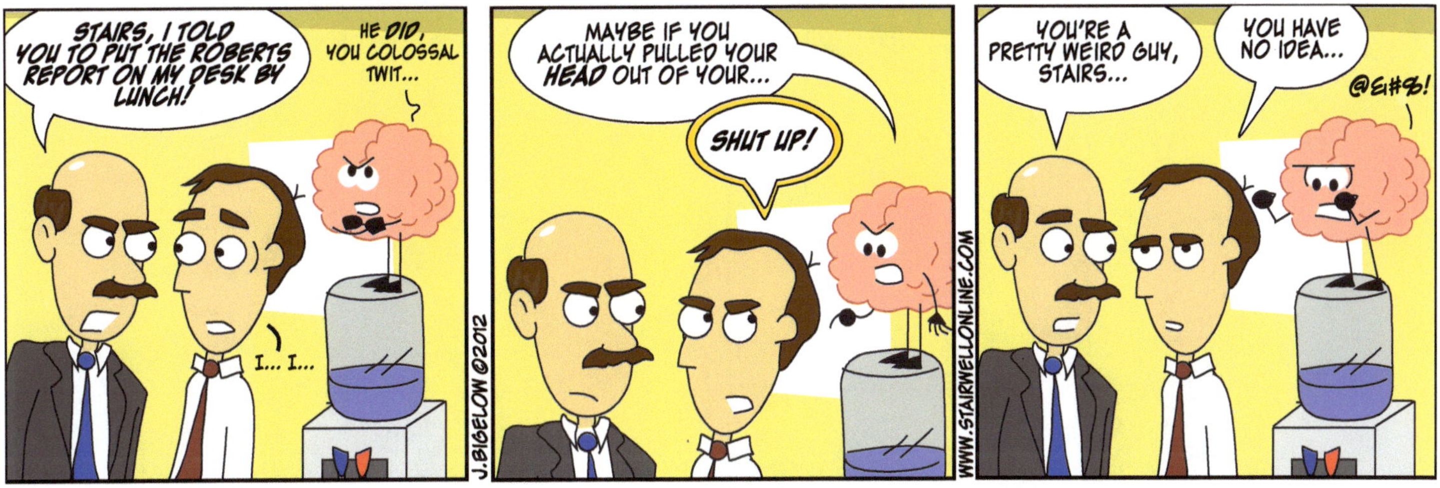

STAIRS, I TOLD YOU TO PUT THE ROBERTS REPORT ON MY DESK BY LUNCH!
HE DID, YOU COLOSSAL TWIT...
I... I...
MAYBE IF YOU ACTUALLY PULLED YOUR HEAD OUT OF YOUR...
SHUT UP!
YOU'RE A PRETTY WEIRD GUY, STAIRS...
YOU HAVE NO IDEA...
@&#%!
J.BIGELOW ©2012
WWW.STAIRWELLONLINE.COM

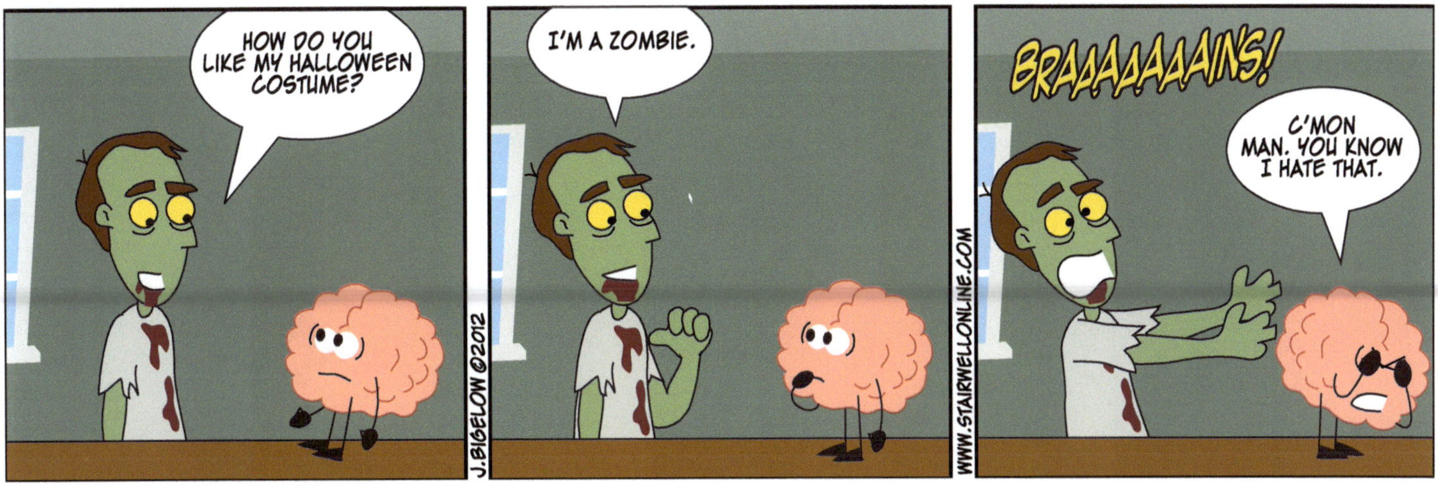

HOW DO YOU LIKE MY HALLOWEEN COSTUME?
I'M A ZOMBIE.
BRAAAAAAAINS!
C'MON MAN. YOU KNOW I HATE THAT.
J.BIGELOW ©2012
WWW.STAIRWELLONLINE.COM

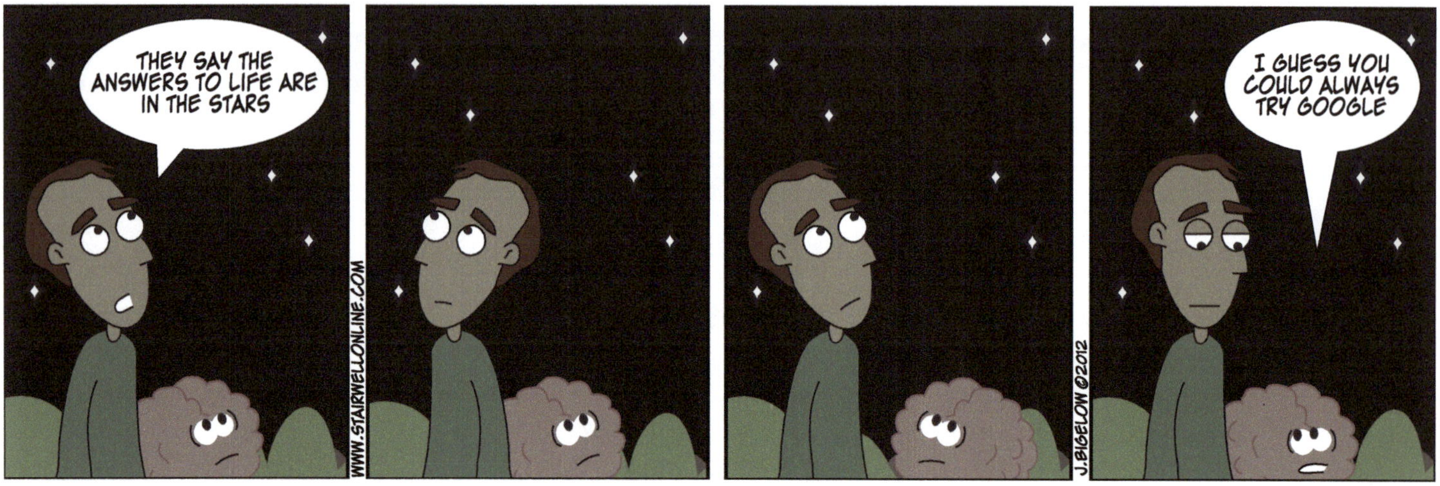
THEY SAY THE ANSWERS TO LIFE ARE IN THE STARS
I GUESS YOU COULD ALWAYS TRY GOOGLE
WWW.STAIRWELLONLINE.COM
J.BIGELOW ©2012

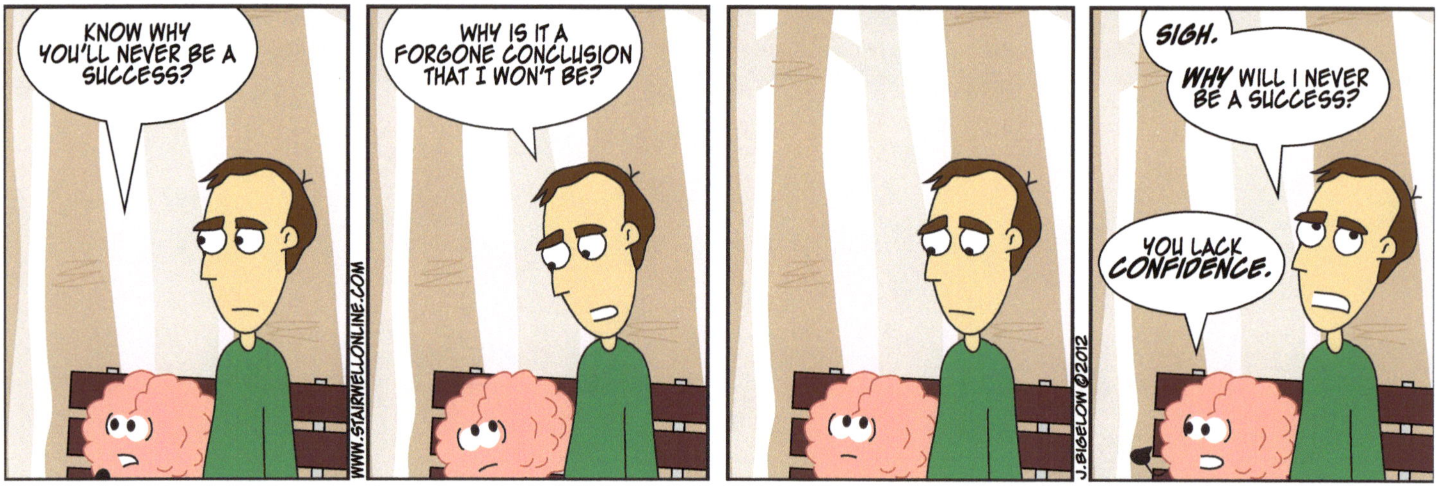
KNOW WHY YOU'LL NEVER BE A SUCCESS?
WHY IS IT A FORGONE CONCLUSION THAT I WON'T BE?
SIGH.
WHY WILL I NEVER BE A SUCCESS?
YOU LACK CONFIDENCE.
WWW.STAIRWELLONLINE.COM
J.BIGELOW ©2012

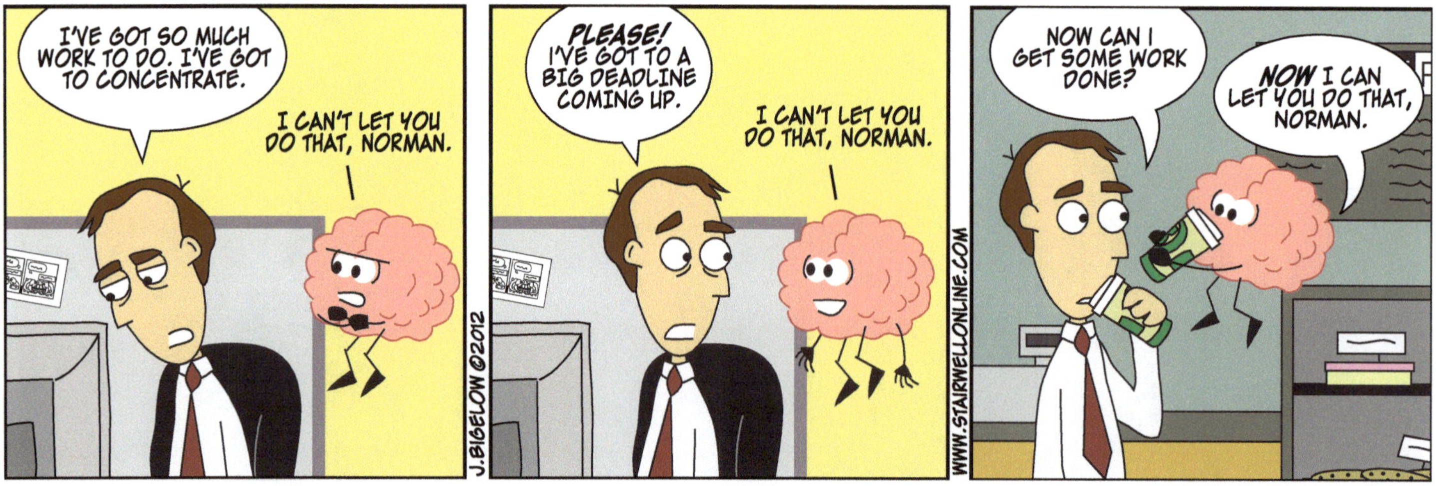
I'VE GOT SO MUCH WORK TO DO. I'VE GOT TO CONCENTRATE.
I CAN'T LET YOU DO THAT, NORMAN.
PLEASE! I'VE GOT TO A BIG DEADLINE COMING UP.
I CAN'T LET YOU DO THAT, NORMAN.
NOW CAN I GET SOME WORK DONE?
NOW I CAN LET YOU DO THAT, NORMAN.
J.BIGELOW ©2012
WWW.STAIRWELLONLINE.COM

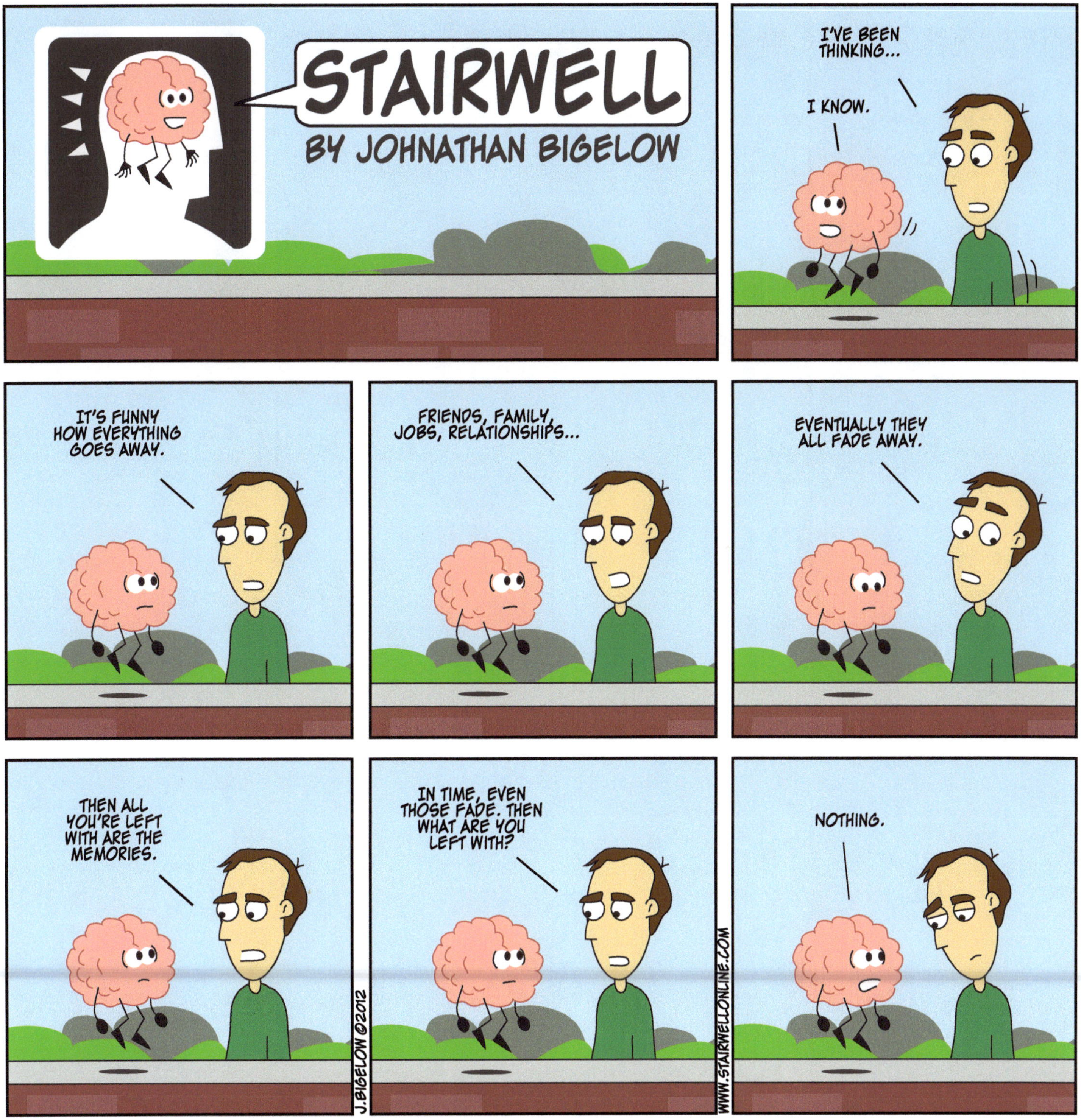
STAIRWELL
BY JOHNATHAN BIGELOW
I'VE BEEN THINKING...
I KNOW.
IT'S FUNNY HOW EVERYTHING GOES AWAY.
FRIENDS, FAMILY, JOBS, RELATIONSHIPS...
EVENTUALLY THEY ALL FADE AWAY.
THEN ALL YOU'RE LEFT WITH ARE THE MEMORIES.
J.BIGELOW ©2012
IN TIME, EVEN THOSE FADE. THEN WHAT ARE YOU LEFT WITH?
WWW.STAIRWELLONLINE.COM
NOTHING.

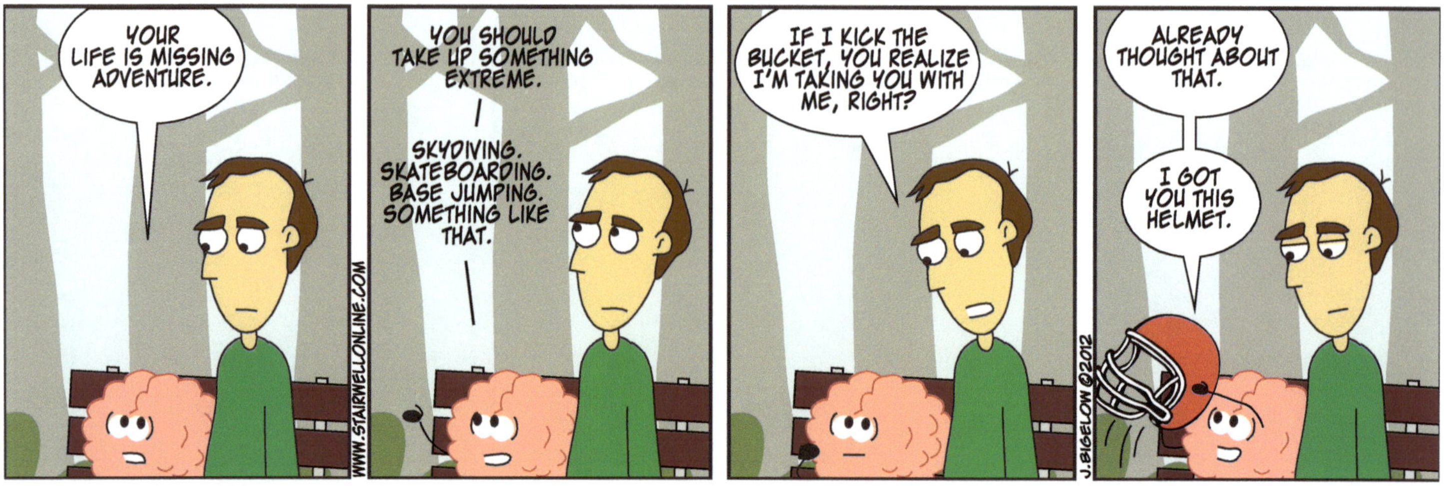
YOUR LIFE IS MISSING ADVENTURE.
WWW.STAIRWELLONLINE.COM
YOU SHOULD TAKE UP SOMETHING EXTREME.
SKYDIVING. SKATEBOARDING. BASE JUMPING. SOMETHING LIKE THAT.
IF I KICK THE BUCKET, YOU REALIZE I'M TAKING YOU WITH ME, RIGHT?
J.BIGELOW ©2012
ALREADY THOUGHT ABOUT THAT.
I GOT YOU THIS HELMET.

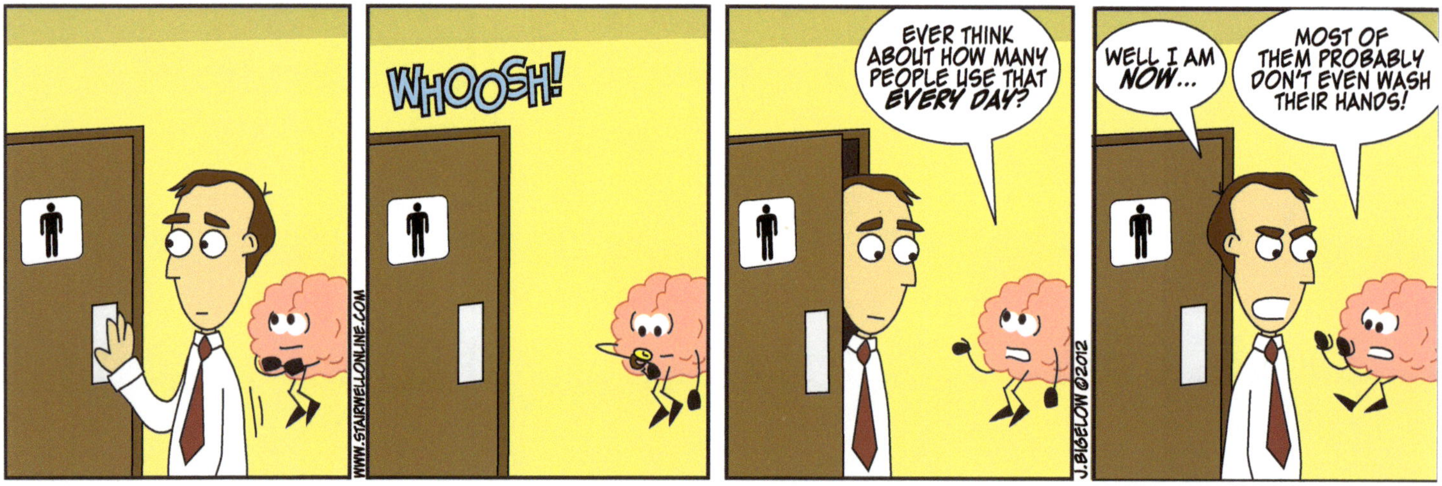
WWW.STAIRWELLONLINE.COM
WHOOSH!
EVER THINK ABOUT HOW MANY PEOPLE USE THAT EVERY DAY?
J.BIGELOW ©2012
WELL I AM NOW...
MOST OF THEM PROBABLY DON'T EVEN WASH THEIR HANDS!

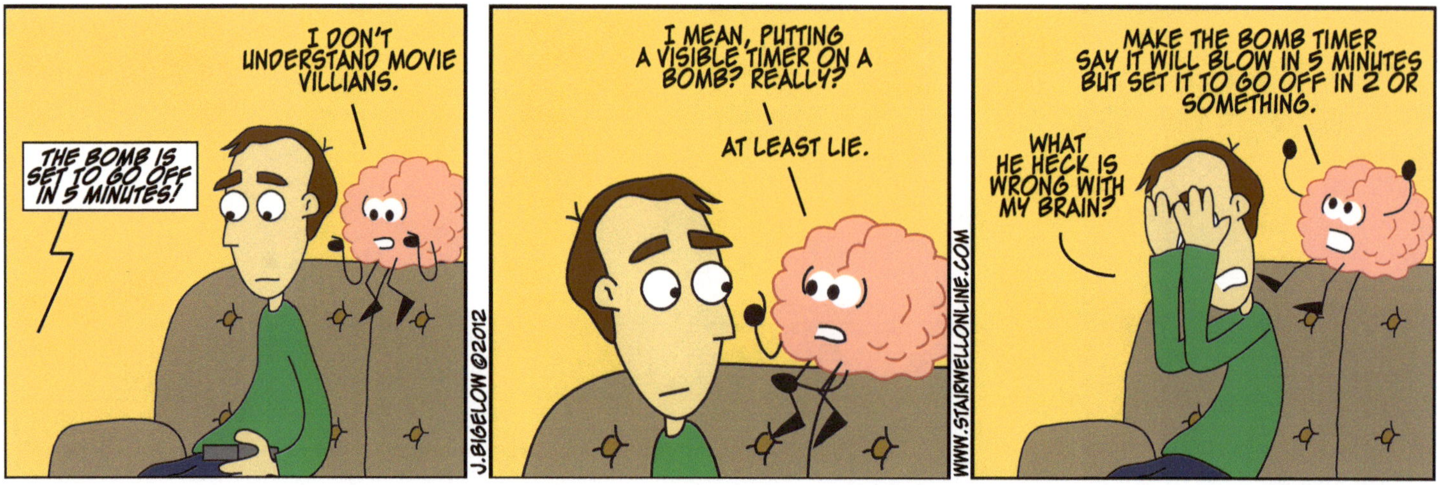
THE BOMB IS SET TO GO OFF IN 5 MINUTES!
I DON'T UNDERSTAND MOVIE VILLIANS.
J.BIGELOW ©2012
I MEAN, PUTTING A VISIBLE TIMER ON A BOMB? REALLY?
AT LEAST LIE.
WWW.STAIRWELLONLINE.COM
MAKE THE BOMB TIMER SAY IT WILL BLOW IN 5 MINUTES BUT SET IT TO GO OFF IN 2 OR SOMETHING.
WHAT HE HECK IS WRONG WITH MY BRAIN?

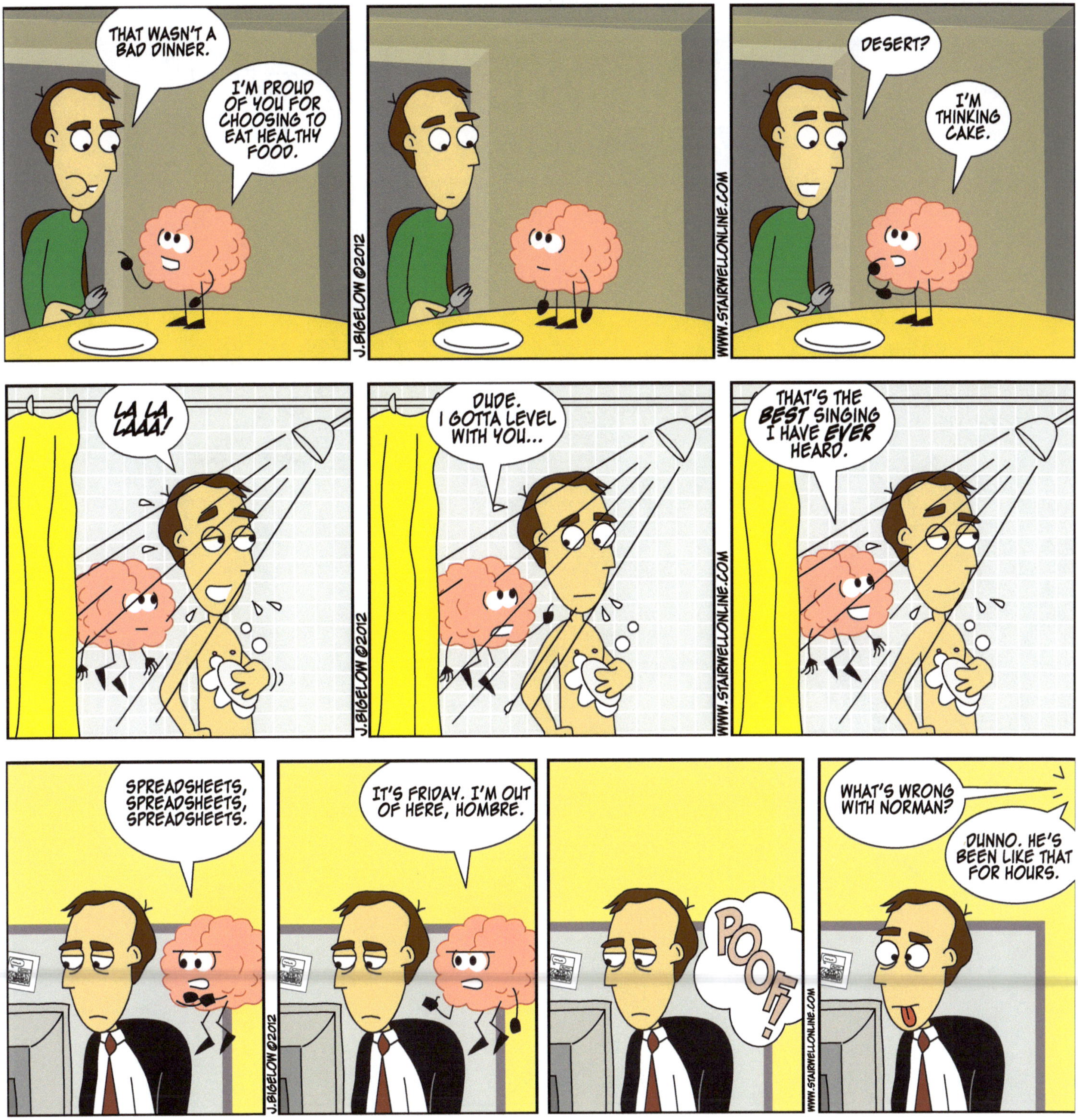
THAT WASN'T A BAD DINNER.
I'M PROUD OF YOU FOR CHOOSING TO EAT HEALTHY FOOD.
J.BIGELOW ©2012
DESERT?
I'M THINKING CAKE.
WWW.STAIRWELLONLINE.COM
LA LA LAAA!
DUDE. I GOTTA LEVEL WITH YOU...
J.BIGELOW ©2012
THAT'S THE BEST SINGING I HAVE EVER HEARD.
WWW.STAIRWELLONLINE.COM
SPREADSHEETS, SPREADSHEETS, SPREADSHEETS.
J.BIGELOW ©2012
IT'S FRIDAY. I'M OUT OF HERE, HOMBRE.
POOF!
WWW.STAIRWELLONLINE.COM
WHAT'S WRONG WITH NORMAN?
DUNNO. HE'S BEEN LIKE THAT FOR HOURS.

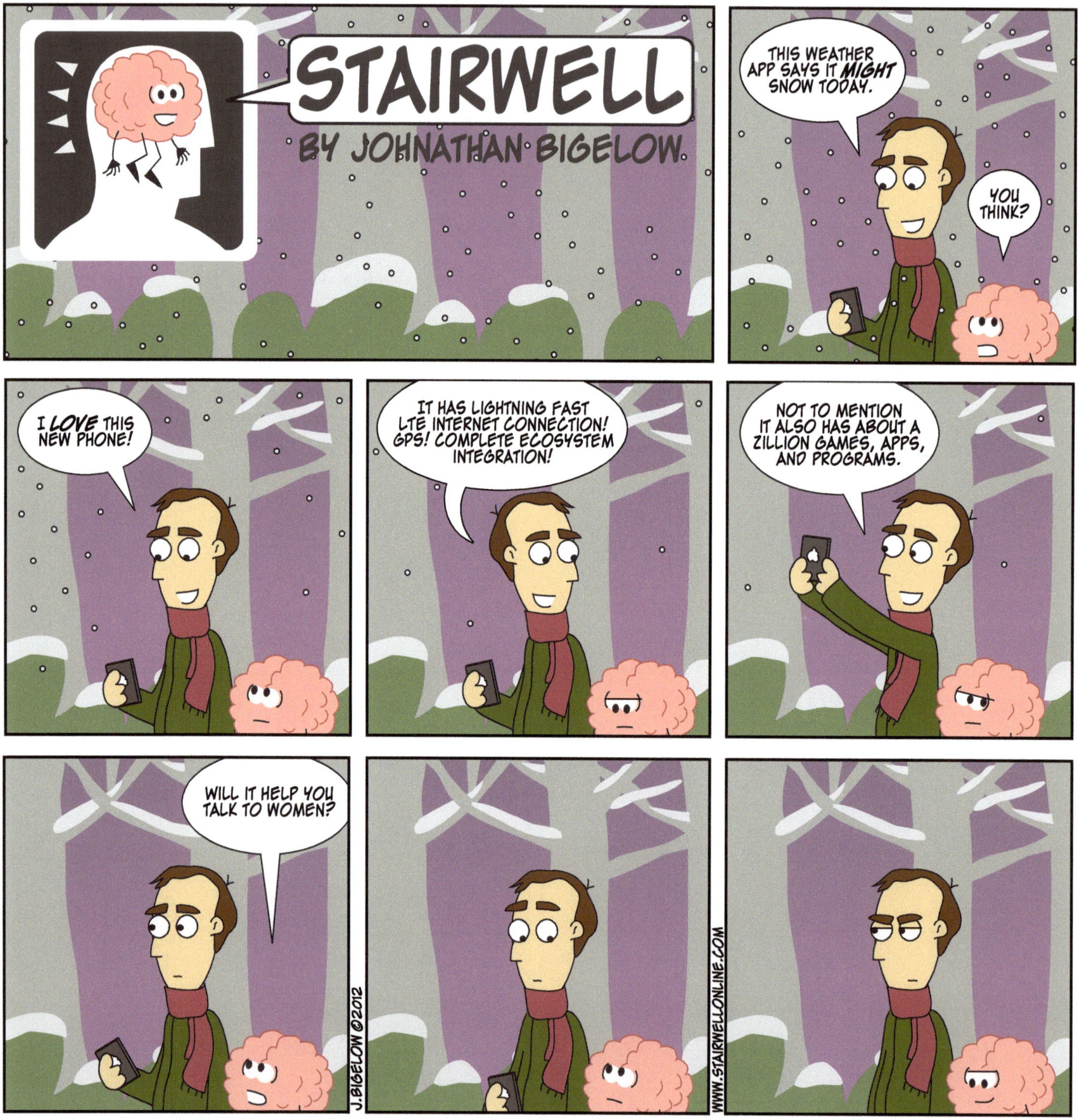
STAIRWELL
BY JOHNATHAN BIGELOW
THIS WEATHER APP SAYS IT MIGHT SNOW TODAY.
YOU THINK?
I LOVE THIS NEW PHONE!
IT HAS LIGHTNING FAST LTE INTERNET CONNECTION! GPS! COMPLETE ECOSYSTEM INTEGRATION!
NOT TO MENTION IT ALSO HAS ABOUT A ZILLION GAMES, APPS, AND PROGRAMS.
WILL IT HELP YOU TALK TO WOMEN?
J.BIGELOW ©2012
WWW.STAIRWELLONLINE.COM

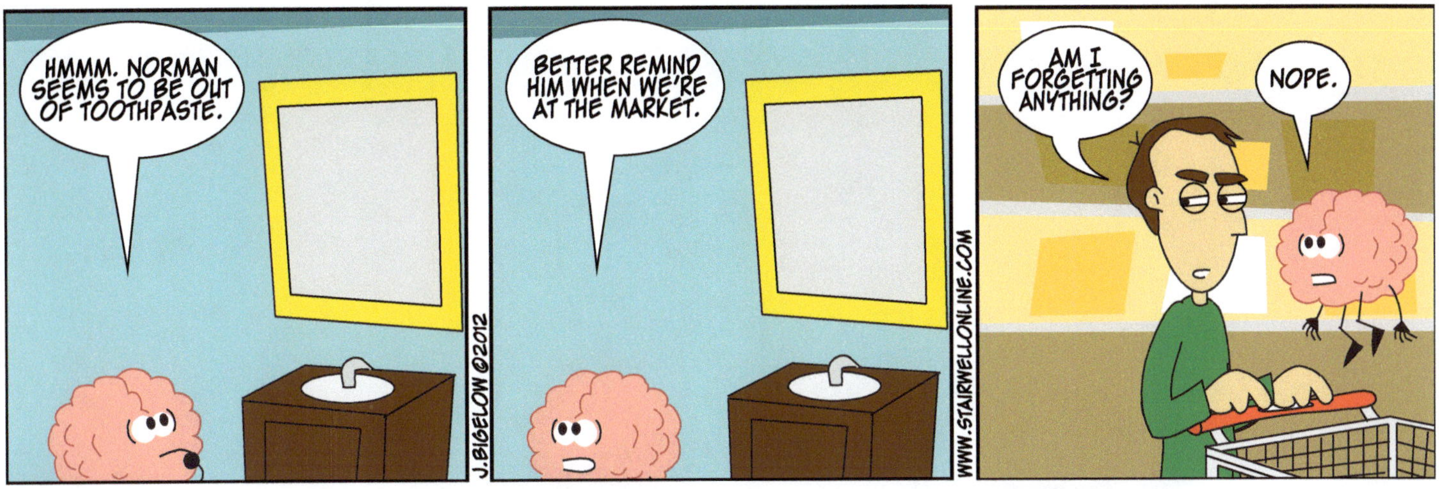
HMMM. NORMAN SEEMS TO BE OUT OF TOOTHPASTE.
J.BIGELOW ©2012
BETTER REMIND HIM WHEN WE'RE AT THE MARKET.
WWW.STAIRWELLONLINE.COM
AM I FORGETTING ANYTHING?
NOPE.

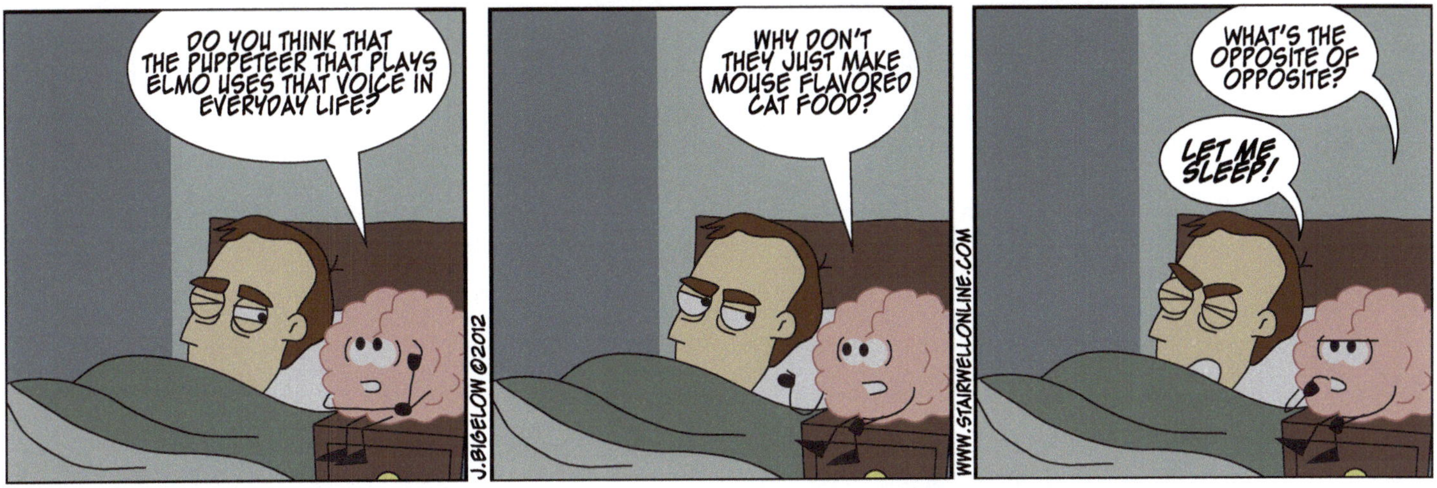
DO YOU THINK THAT THE PUPPETEER THAT PLAYS ELMO USES THAT VOICE IN EVERYDAY LIFE?
J.BIGELOW ©2012
WHY DON'T THEY JUST MAKE MOUSE FLAVORED CAT FOOD?
WWW.STAIRWELLONLINE.COM
WHAT'S THE OPPOSITE OF OPPOSITE?
LET ME SLEEP!

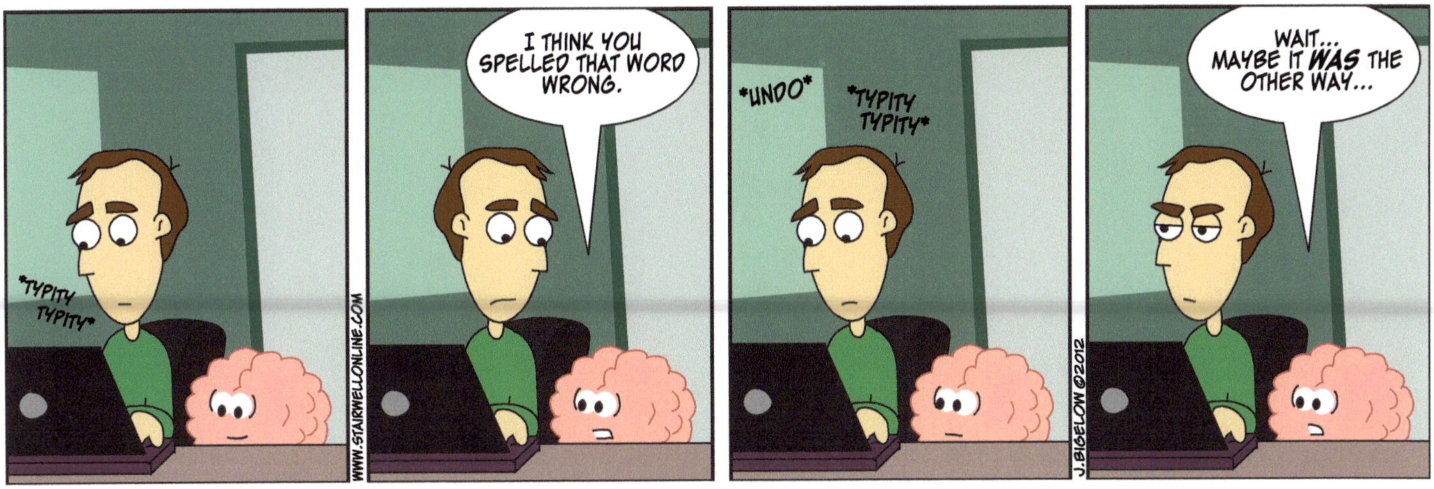
TYPITY TYPITY
WWW.STAIRWELLONLINE.COM
I THINK YOU SPELLED THAT WORD WRONG.
UNDO
TYPITY TYPITY
J.BIGELOW ©2012
WAIT... MAYBE IT WAS THE OTHER WAY...

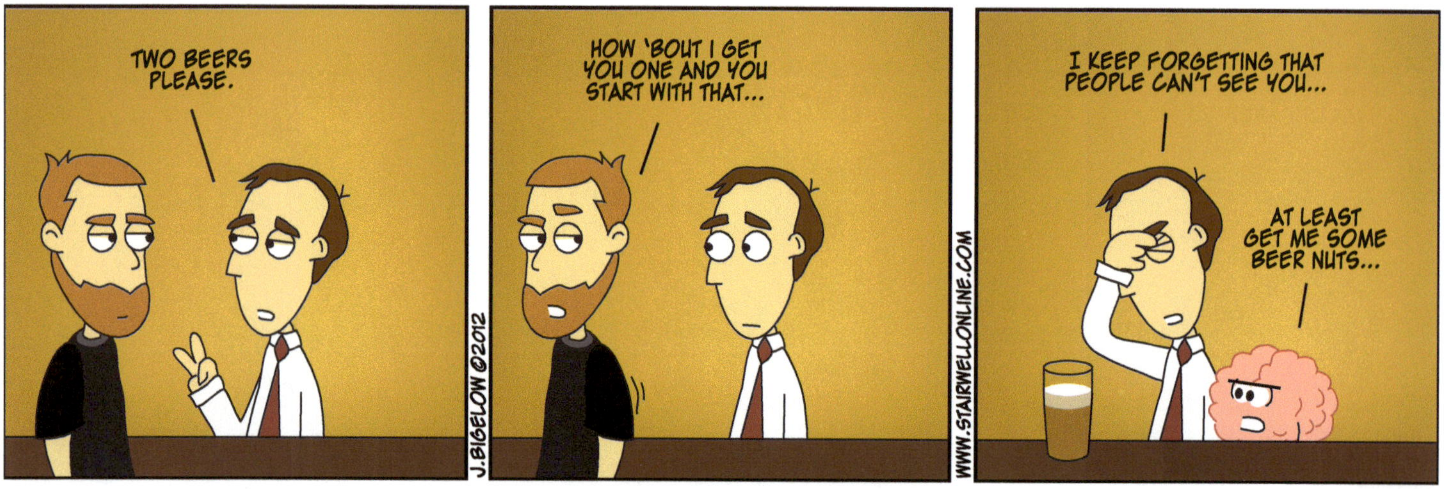
TWO BEERS PLEASE.
HOW 'BOUT I GET YOU ONE AND YOU START WITH THAT...
J.BIGELOW ©2012
I KEEP FORGETTING THAT PEOPLE CAN'T SEE YOU...
AT LEAST GET ME SOME BEER NUTS...
WWW.STAIRWELLONLINE.COM

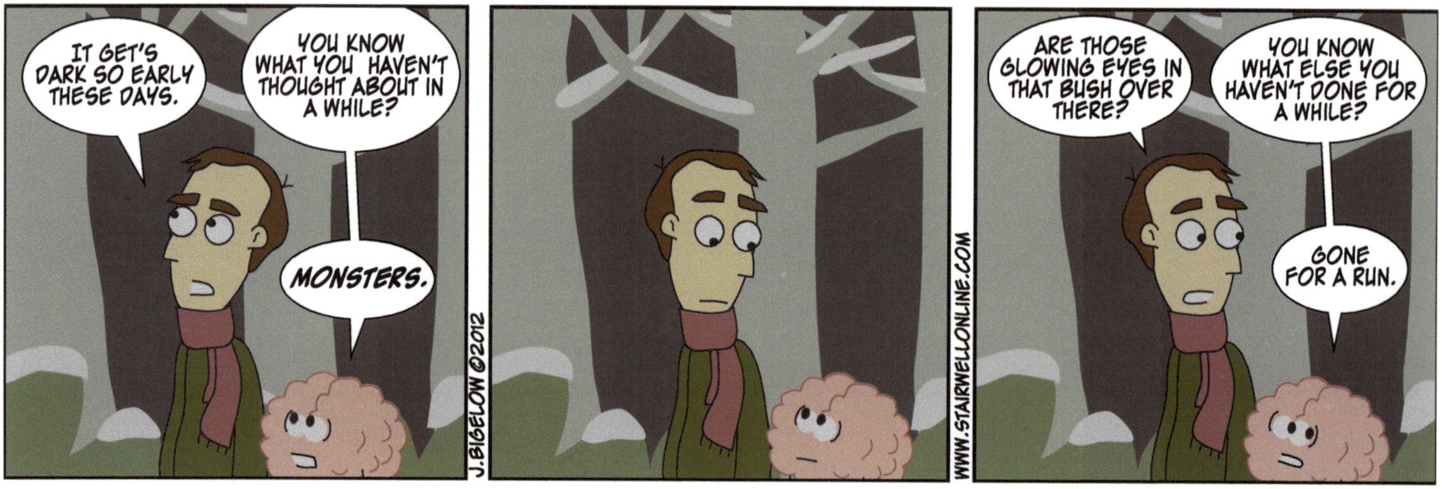
IT GET'S DARK SO EARLY THESE DAYS.
YOU KNOW WHAT YOU HAVEN'T THOUGHT ABOUT IN A WHILE?
MONSTERS.
J.BIGELOW ©2012
ARE THOSE GLOWING EYES IN THAT BUSH OVER THERE?
YOU KNOW WHAT ELSE YOU HAVEN'T DONE FOR A WHILE?
GONE FOR A RUN.
WWW.STAIRWELLONLINE.COM

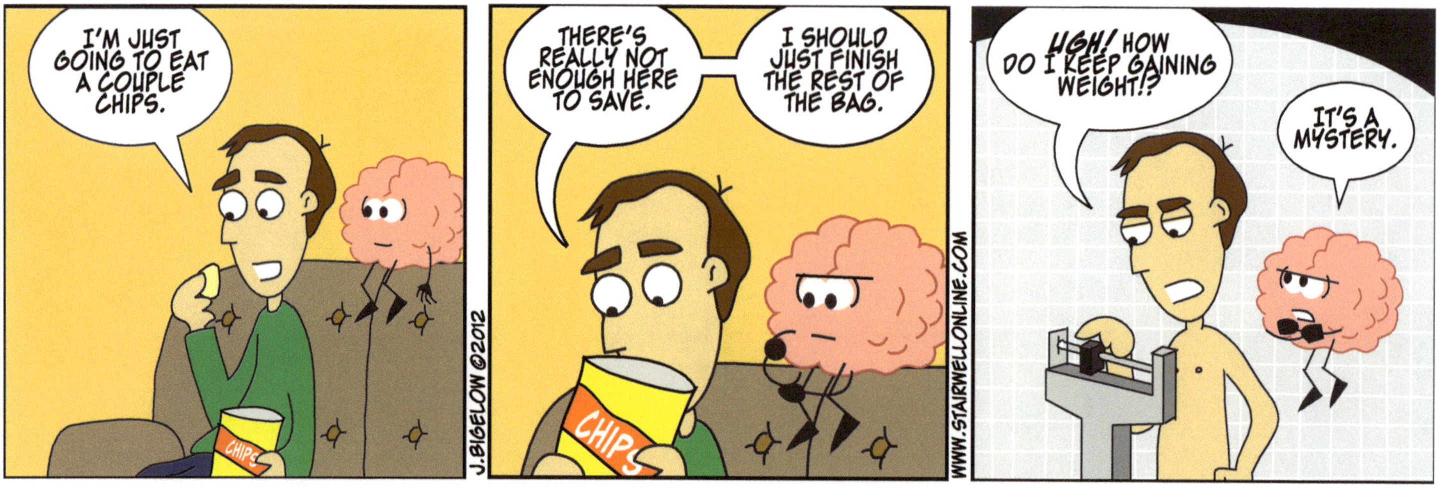
I'M JUST GOING TO EAT A COUPLE CHIPS.
CHIPS
J.BIGELOW ©2012
THERE'S REALLY NOT ENOUGH HERE TO SAVE.
I SHOULD JUST FINISH THE REST OF THE BAG.
CHIPS
UGH! HOW DO I KEEP GAINING WEIGHT!?
IT'S A MYSTERY.
WWW.STAIRWELLONLINE.COM

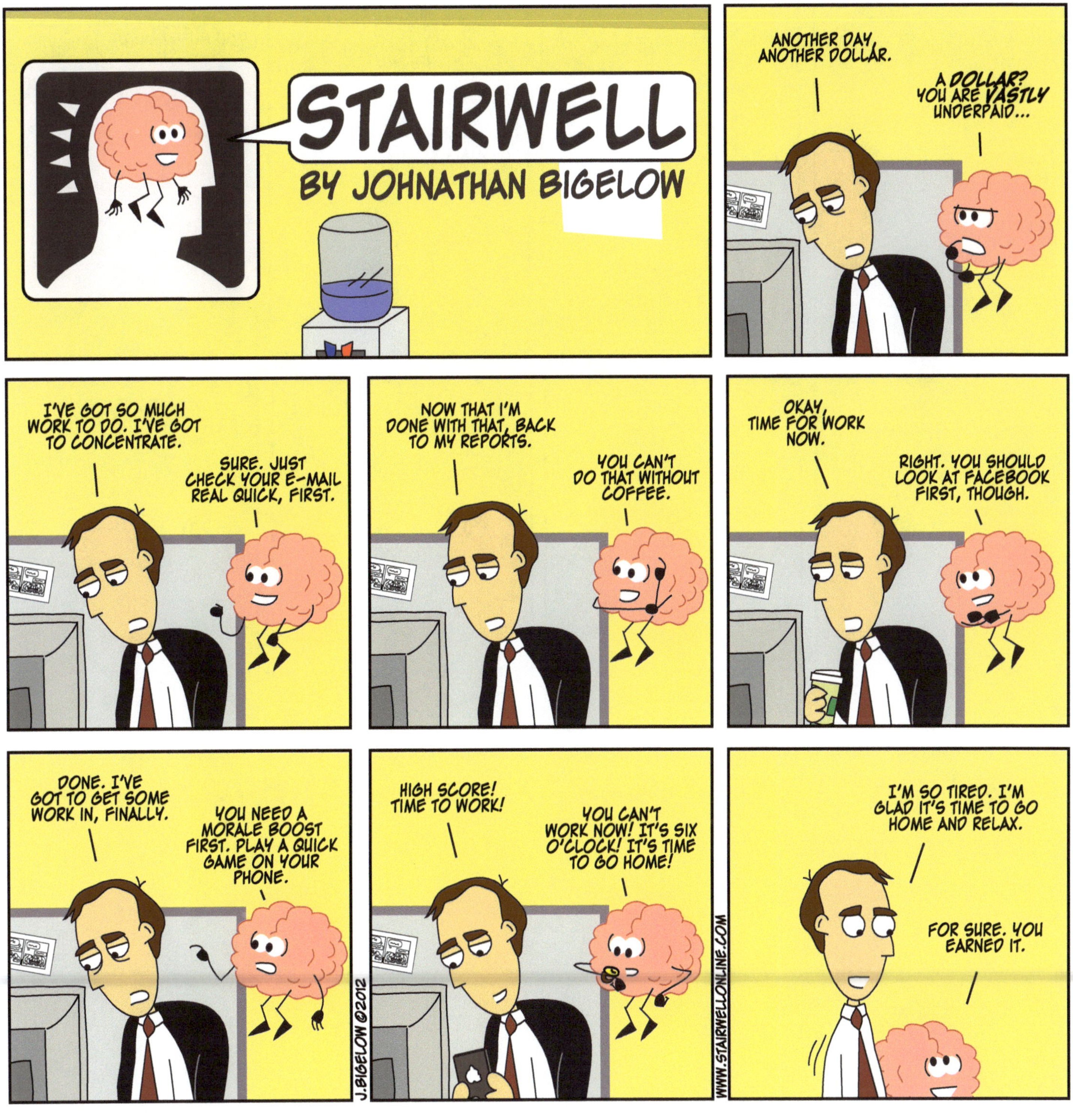
STAIRWELL
BY JOHNATHAN BIGELOW
ANOTHER DAY, ANOTHER DOLLAR.
A DOLLAR? YOU ARE VASTLY UNDERPAID...
I'VE GOT SO MUCH WORK TO DO. I'VE GOT TO CONCENTRATE.
SURE. JUST CHECK YOUR E-MAIL REAL QUICK, FIRST.
NOW THAT I'M DONE WITH THAT, BACK TO MY REPORTS.
YOU CAN'T DO THAT WITHOUT COFFEE.
OKAY, TIME FOR WORK NOW.
RIGHT. YOU SHOULD LOOK AT FACEBOOK FIRST, THOUGH.
DONE. I'VE GOT TO GET SOME WORK IN, FINALLY.
YOU NEED A MORALE BOOST FIRST. PLAY A QUICK GAME ON YOUR PHONE.
J.BIGELOW ©2012
HIGH SCORE! TIME TO WORK!
YOU CAN'T WORK NOW! IT'S SIX O'CLOCK! IT'S TIME TO GO HOME!
WWW.STAIRWELLONLINE.COM
I'M SO TIRED. I'M GLAD IT'S TIME TO GO HOME AND RELAX.
FOR SURE. YOU EARNED IT.

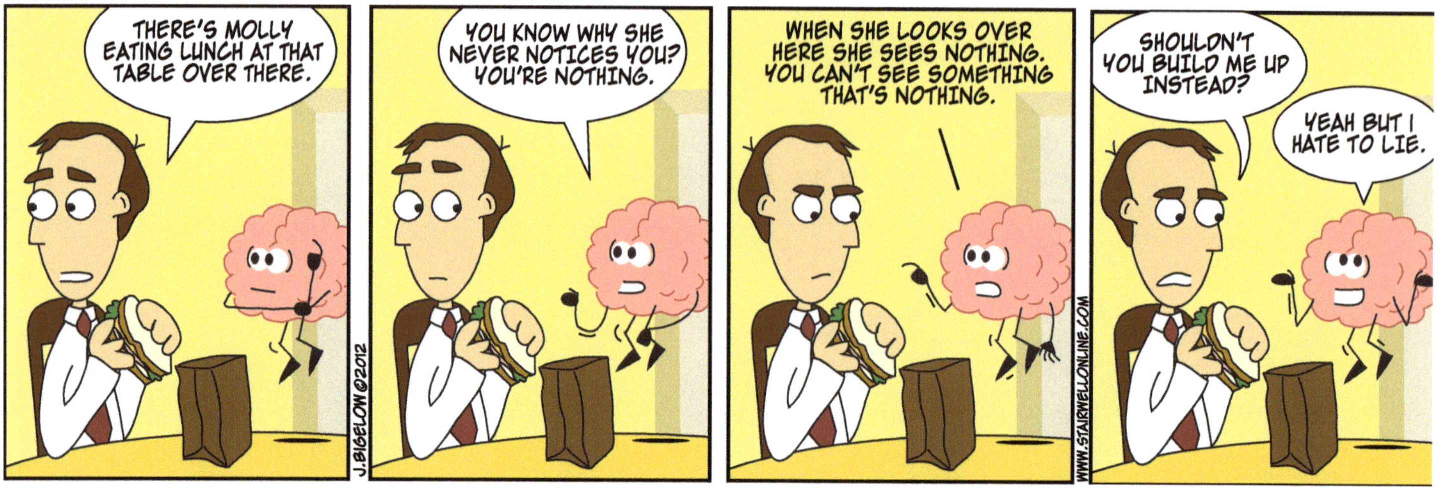
THERE'S MOLLY EATING LUNCH AT THAT TABLE OVER THERE.
YOU KNOW WHY SHE NEVER NOTICES YOU? YOU'RE NOTHING.
J.BIGELOW ©2012
WHEN SHE LOOKS OVER HERE SHE SEES NOTHING. YOU CAN'T SEE SOMETHING THAT'S NOTHING.
WWW.STAIRWELLONLINE.COM
SHOULDN'T YOU BUILD ME UP INSTEAD?
YEAH BUT I HATE TO LIE.

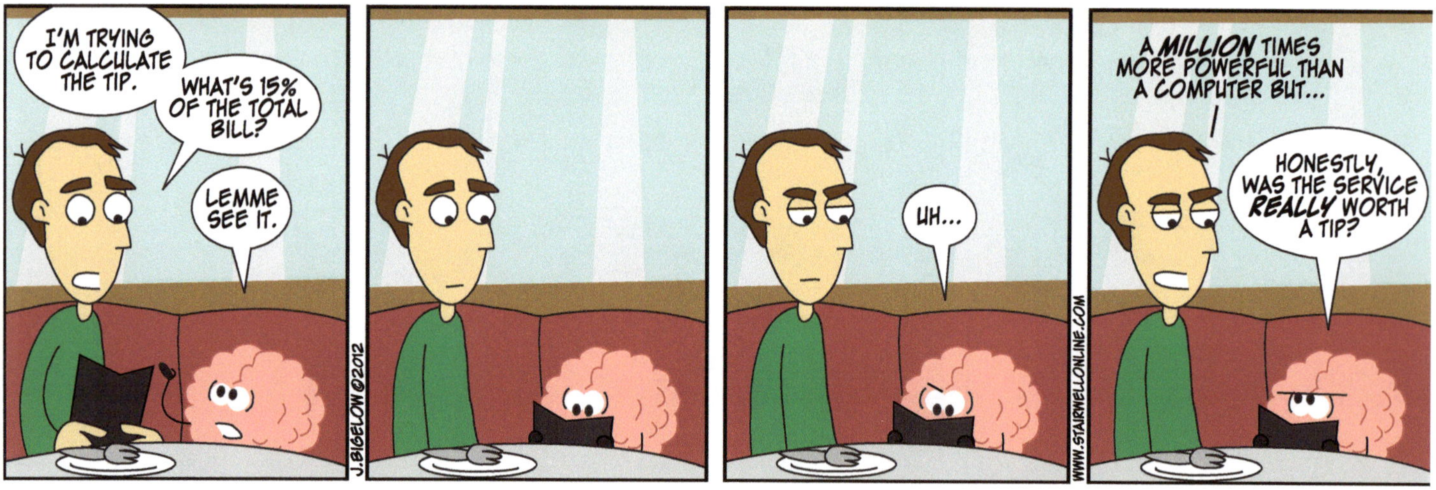
I'M TRYING TO CALCULATE THE TIP.
WHAT'S 15% OF THE TOTAL BILL?
LEMME SEE IT.
J.BIGELOW ©2012
UH...
WWW.STAIRWELLONLINE.COM
A MILLION TIMES MORE POWERFUL THAN A COMPUTER BUT...
HONESTLY, WAS THE SERVICE REALLY WORTH A TIP?

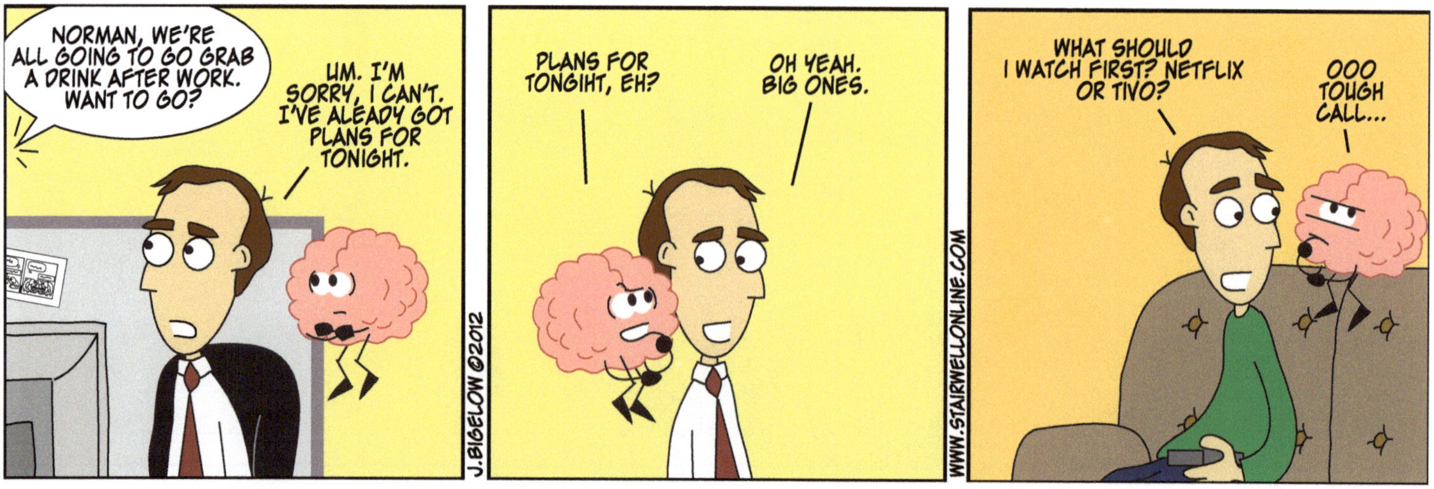
NORMAN, WE'RE ALL GOING TO GO GRAB A DRINK AFTER WORK. WANT TO GO?
UM. I'M SORRY, I CAN'T. I'VE ALEADY GOT PLANS FOR TONIGHT.
J.BIGELOW ©2012
PLANS FOR TONGIHT, EH?
OH YEAH. BIG ONES.
WWW.STAIRWELLONLINE.COM
WHAT SHOULD I WATCH FIRST? NETFLIX OR TIVO?
OOO TOUGH CALL...

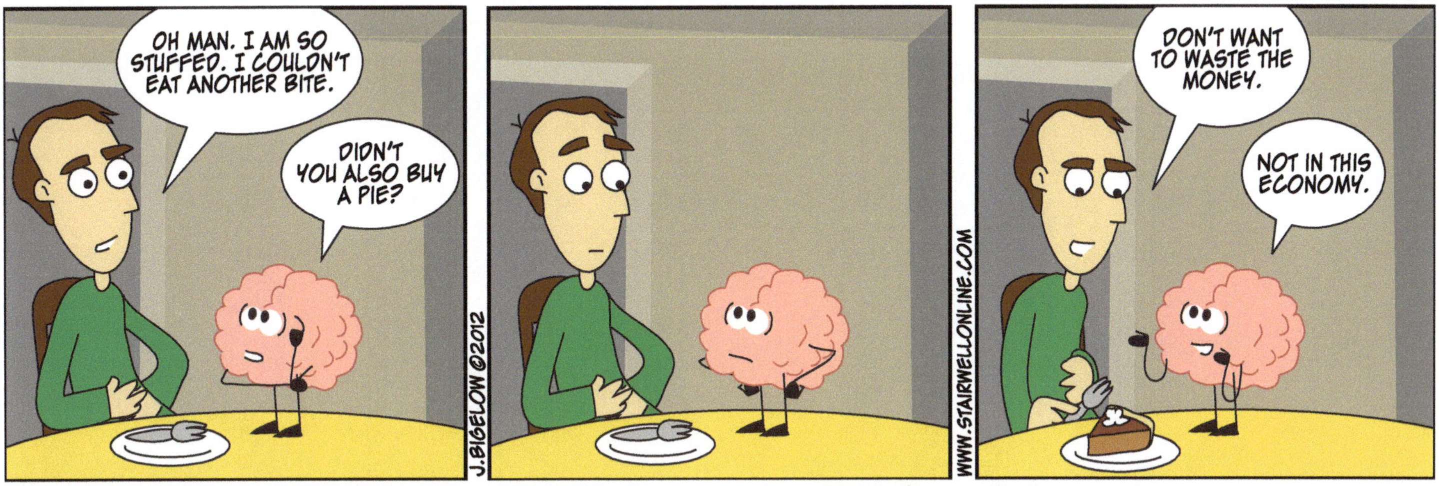
OH MAN. I AM SO STUFFED. I COULDN'T EAT ANOTHER BITE.
DIDN'T YOU ALSO BUY A PIE?
J.BIGELOW ©2012
DON'T WANT TO WASTE THE MONEY.
NOT IN THIS ECONOMY.
WWW.STAIRWELLONLINE.COM

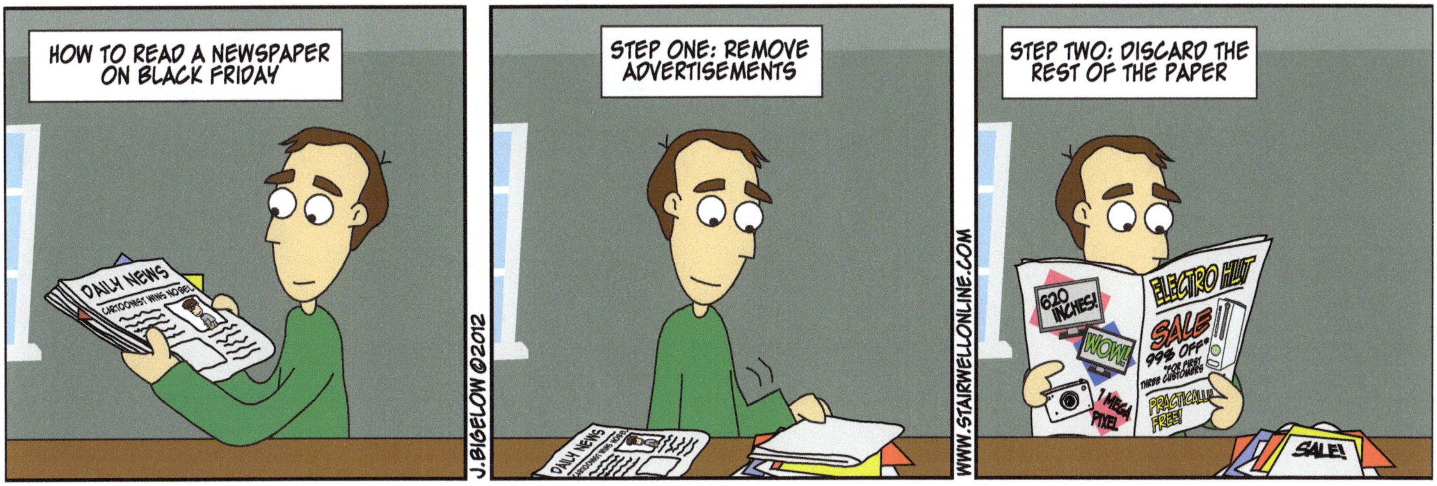
HOW TO READ A NEWSPAPER ON BLACK FRIDAY
DAILY NEWS
J.BIGELOW ©2012
STEP ONE: REMOVE ADVERTISEMENTS
DAILY NEWS
STEP TWO: DISCARD THE REST OF THE PAPER
620 INCHES!
ELECTRO HUT
WOW!
SALE
1 MEGA PIXEL
PRACTICALLY FREE!
SALE!
WWW.STAIRWELLONLINE.COM

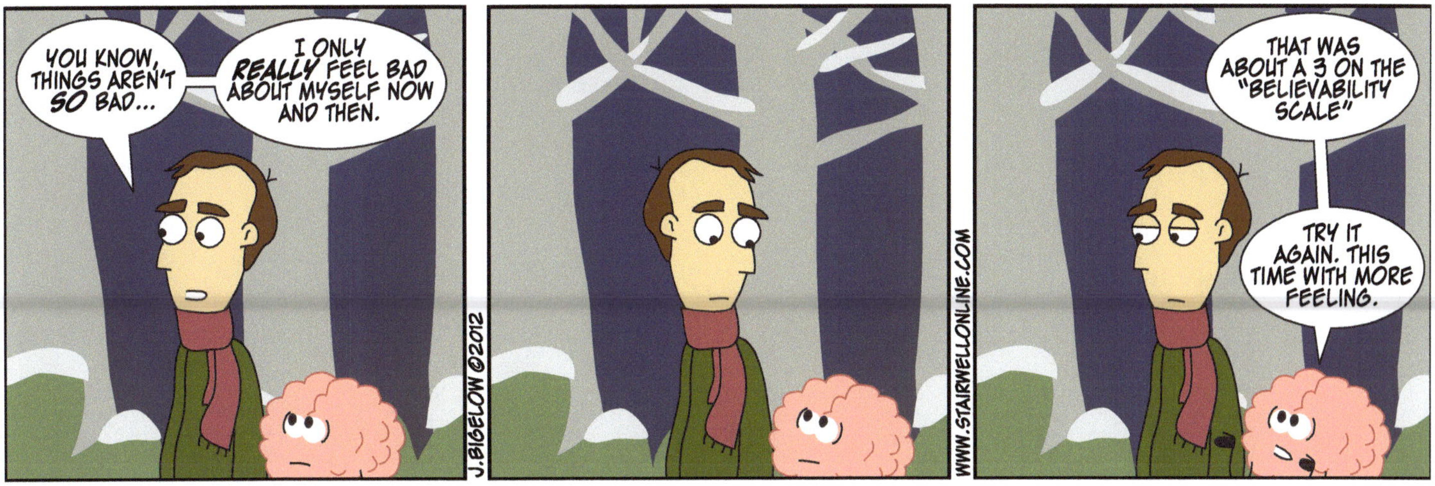
YOU KNOW, THINGS AREN'T SO BAD...
I ONLY REALLY FEEL BAD ABOUT MYSELF NOW AND THEN.
J.BIGELOW ©2012
THAT WAS ABOUT A 3 ON THE "BELIEVABILITY SCALE"
TRY IT AGAIN. THIS TIME WITH MORE FEELING.
WWW.STAIRWELLONLINE.COM

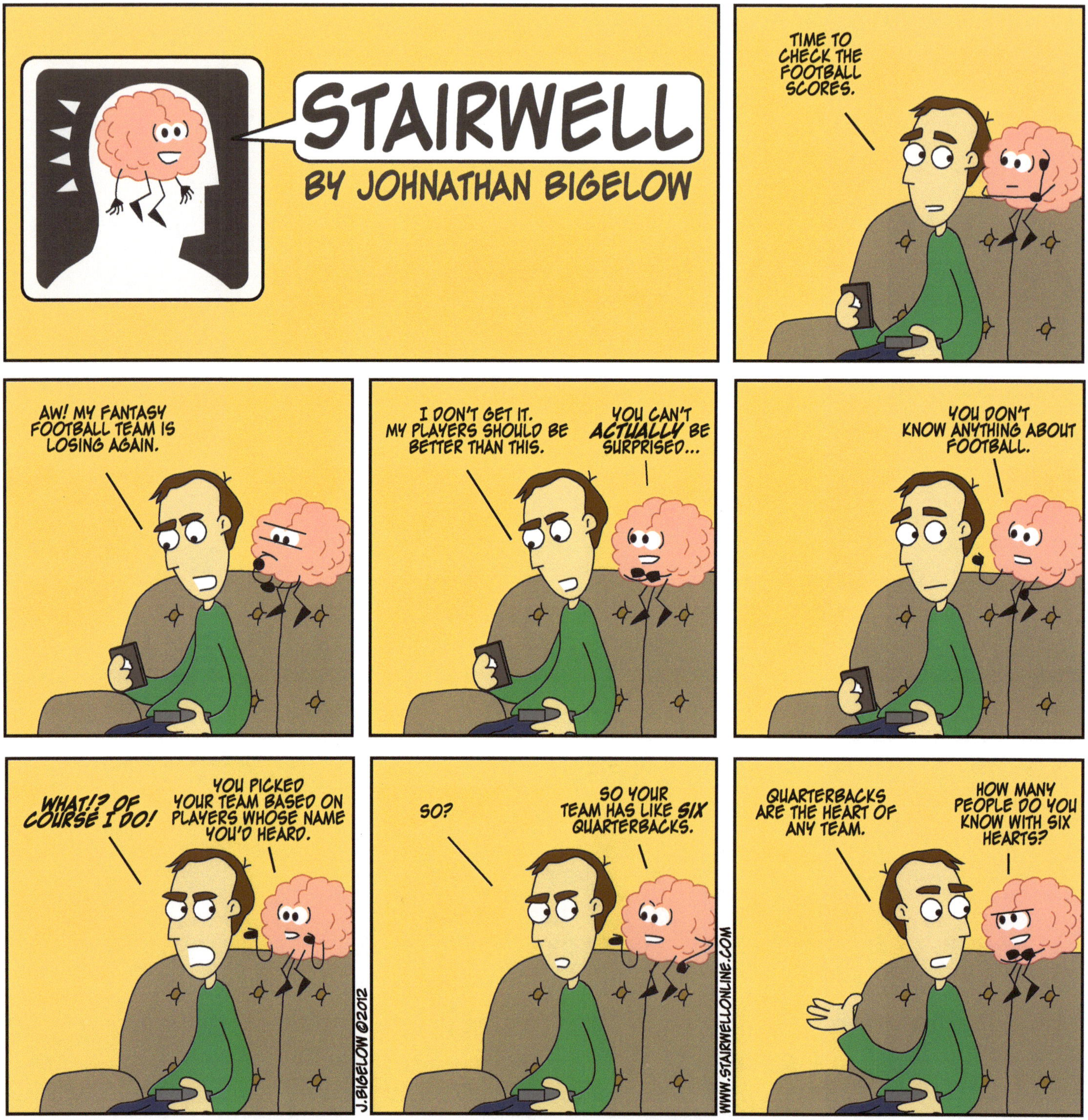
STAIRWELL
BY JOHNATHAN BIGELOW
TIME TO CHECK THE FOOTBALL SCORES.
AW! MY FANTASY FOOTBALL TEAM IS LOSING AGAIN.
I DON'T GET IT. MY PLAYERS SHOULD BE BETTER THAN THIS.
YOU CAN'T *ACTUALLY* BE SURPRISED...
YOU DON'T KNOW ANYTHING ABOUT FOOTBALL.
WHAT!? OF COURSE I DO!
YOU PICKED YOUR TEAM BASED ON PLAYERS WHOSE NAME YOU'D HEARD.
J.BIGELOW ©2012
SO?
SO YOUR TEAM HAS LIKE *SIX* QUARTERBACKS.
WWW.STAIRWELLONLINE.COM
QUARTERBACKS ARE THE HEART OF ANY TEAM.
HOW MANY PEOPLE DO YOU KNOW WITH SIX HEARTS?

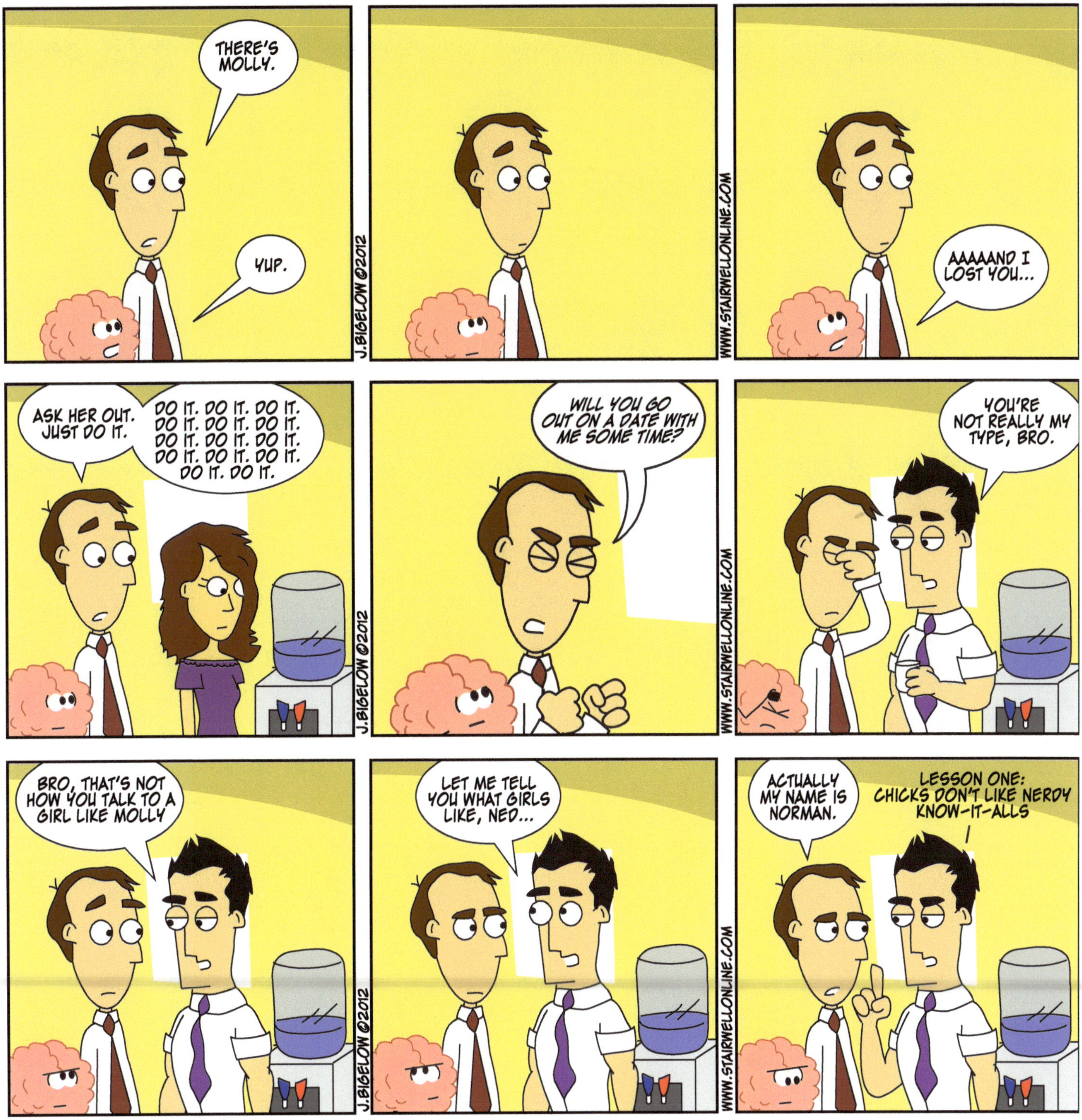
THERE'S MOLLY.
YUP.
AAAAAND I LOST YOU...
J.BIGELOW ©2012
WWW.STAIRWELLONLINE.COM
ASK HER OUT. JUST DO IT.
DO IT. DO IT. DO IT. DO IT. DO IT. DO IT. DO IT. DO IT. DO IT. DO IT. DO IT. DO IT. DO IT. DO IT.
WILL YOU GO OUT ON A DATE WITH ME SOME TIME?
YOU'RE NOT REALLY MY TYPE, BRO.
J.BIGELOW ©2012
WWW.STAIRWELLONLINE.COM
BRO, THAT'S NOT HOW YOU TALK TO A GIRL LIKE MOLLY
LET ME TELL YOU WHAT GIRLS LIKE, NED...
ACTUALLY MY NAME IS NORMAN.
LESSON ONE: CHICKS DON'T LIKE NERDY KNOW-IT-ALLS
J.BIGELOW ©2012
WWW.STAIRWELLONLINE.COM

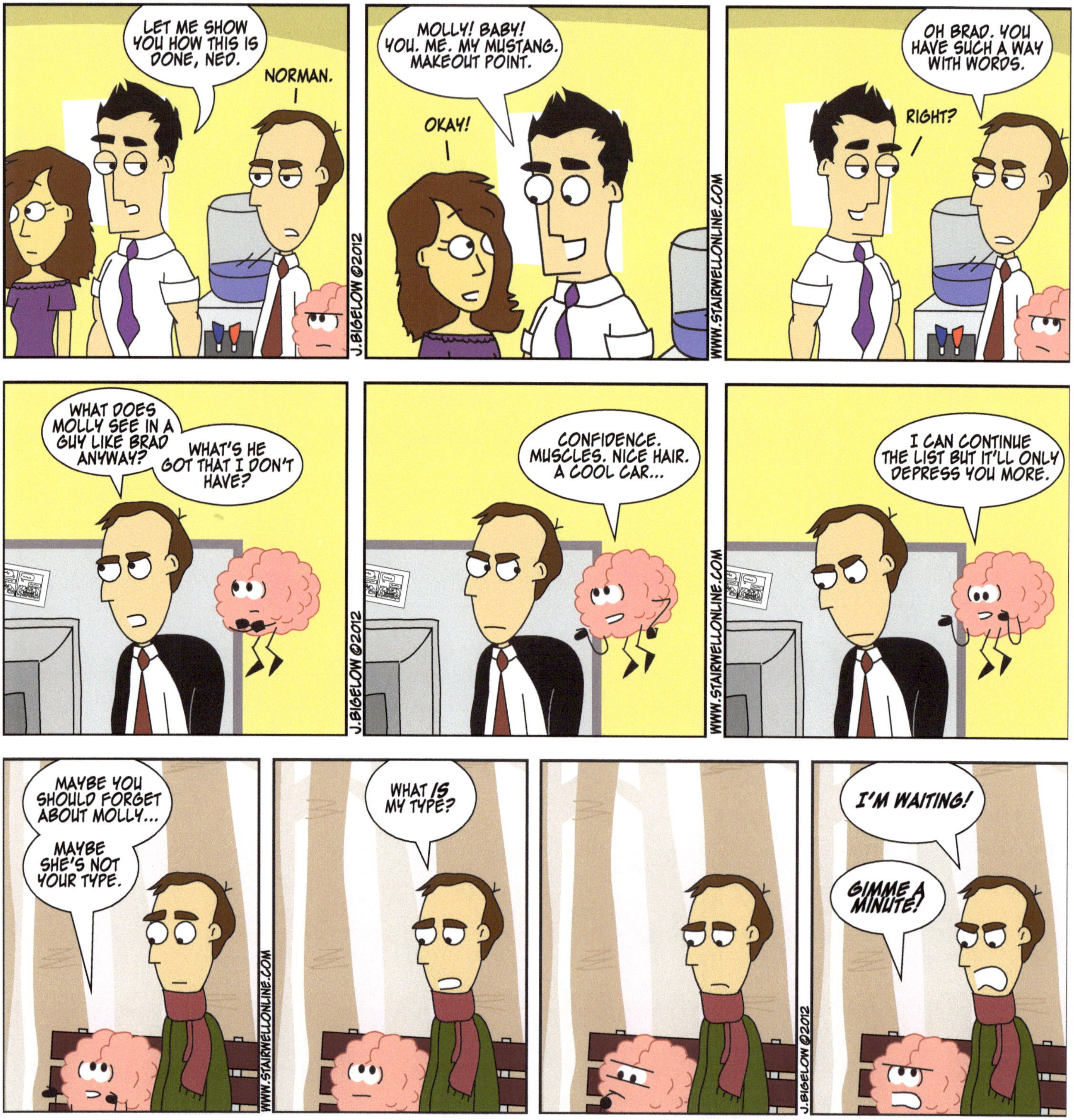
LET ME SHOW YOU HOW THIS IS DONE, NED.
NORMAN.
J.BIGELOW ©2012
MOLLY! BABY! YOU. ME. MY MUSTANG. MAKEOUT POINT.
OKAY!
WWW.STAIRWELLONLINE.COM
OH BRAD. YOU HAVE SUCH A WAY WITH WORDS.
RIGHT?
WHAT DOES MOLLY SEE IN A GUY LIKE BRAD ANYWAY?
WHAT'S HE GOT THAT I DON'T HAVE?
J.BIGELOW ©2012
CONFIDENCE. MUSCLES. NICE HAIR. A COOL CAR...
WWW.STAIRWELLONLINE.COM
I CAN CONTINUE THE LIST BUT IT'LL ONLY DEPRESS YOU MORE.
MAYBE YOU SHOULD FORGET ABOUT MOLLY...
MAYBE SHE'S NOT YOUR TYPE.
WWW.STAIRWELLONLINE.COM
WHAT *IS* MY TYPE?
J.BIGELOW ©2012
I'M WAITING!
GIMME A MINUTE!

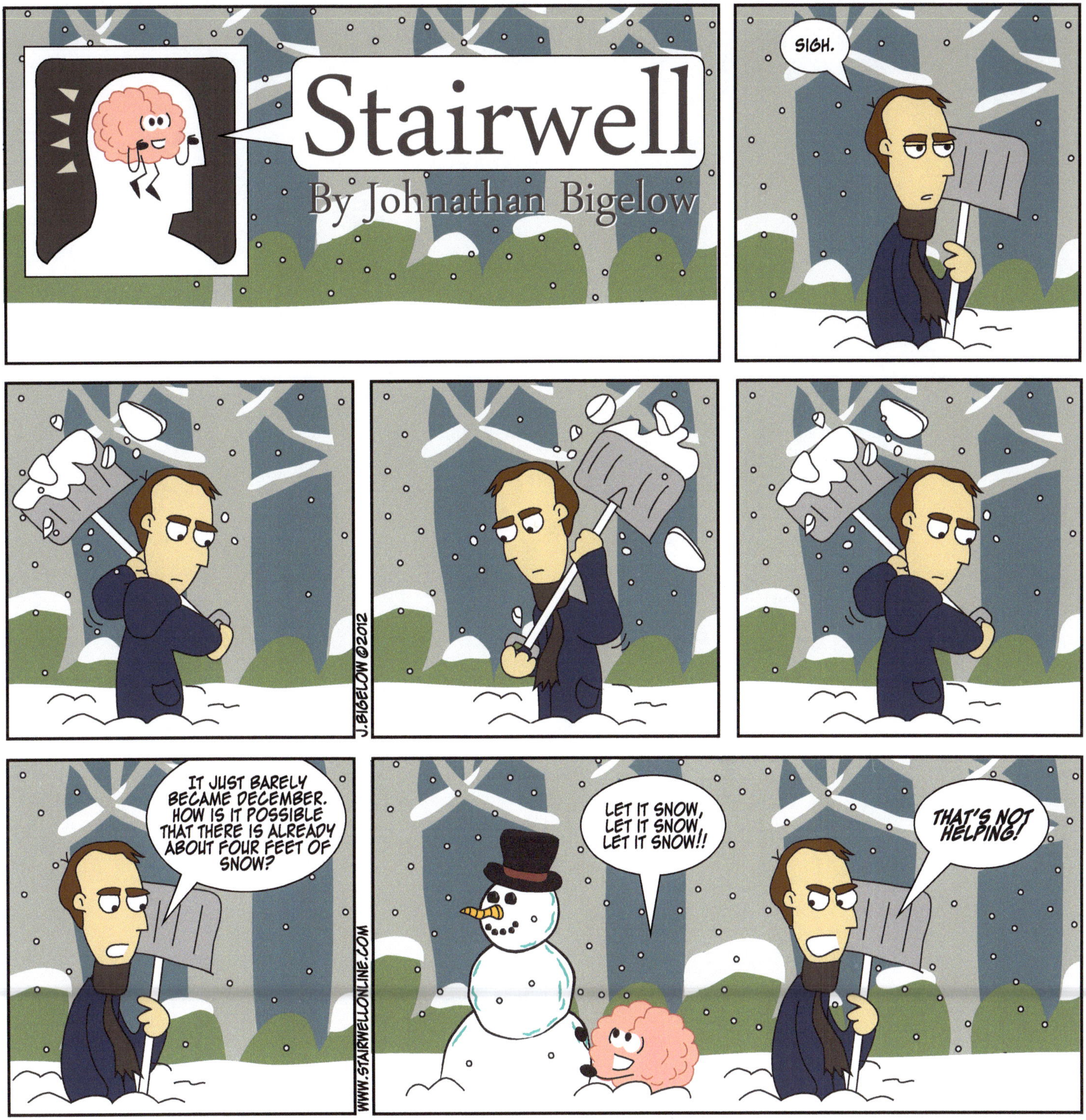
Stairwell
By Johnathan Bigelow
SIGH.
J.BIGELOW ©2012
IT JUST BARELY BECAME DECEMBER. HOW IS IT POSSIBLE THAT THERE IS ALREADY ABOUT FOUR FEET OF SNOW?
WWW.STAIRWELLONLINE.COM
LET IT SNOW, LET IT SNOW, LET IT SNOW!!
THAT'S NOT HELPING!

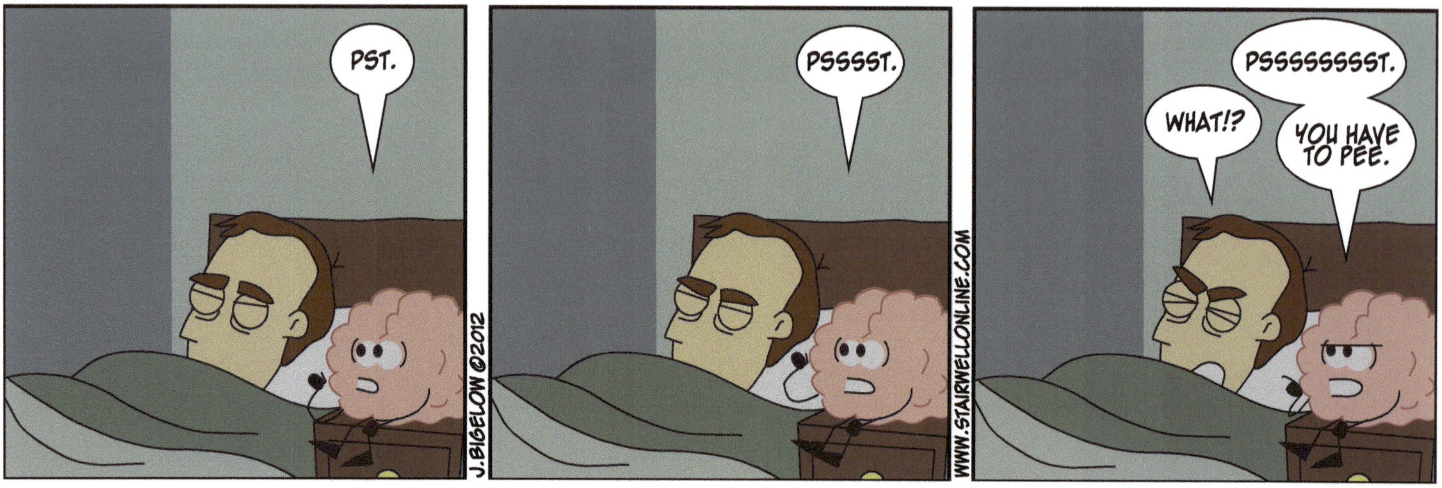
PST.
PSSSST.
J.BIGELOW ©2012
PSSSSSSSST.
WHAT!?
YOU HAVE TO PEE.
WWW.STAIRWELLONLINE.COM

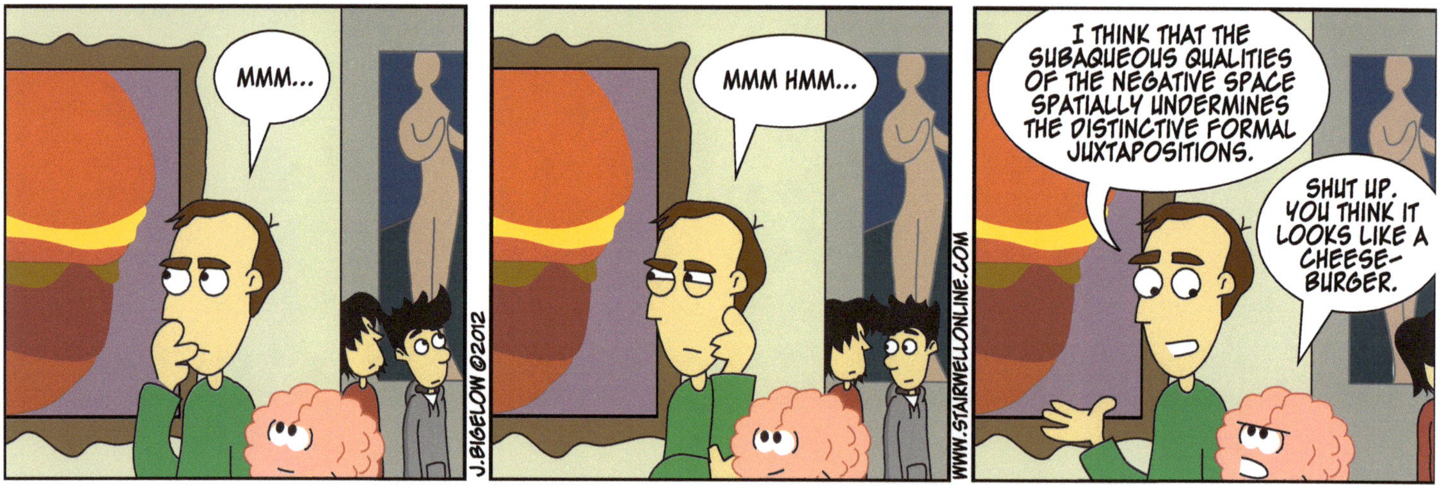
MMM...
MMM HMM...
J.BIGELOW ©2012
I THINK THAT THE SUBAQUEOUS QUALITIES OF THE NEGATIVE SPACE SPATIALLY UNDERMINES THE DISTINCTIVE FORMAL JUXTAPOSITIONS.
SHUT UP. YOU THINK IT LOOKS LIKE A CHEESE-BURGER.
WWW.STAIRWELLONLINE.COM

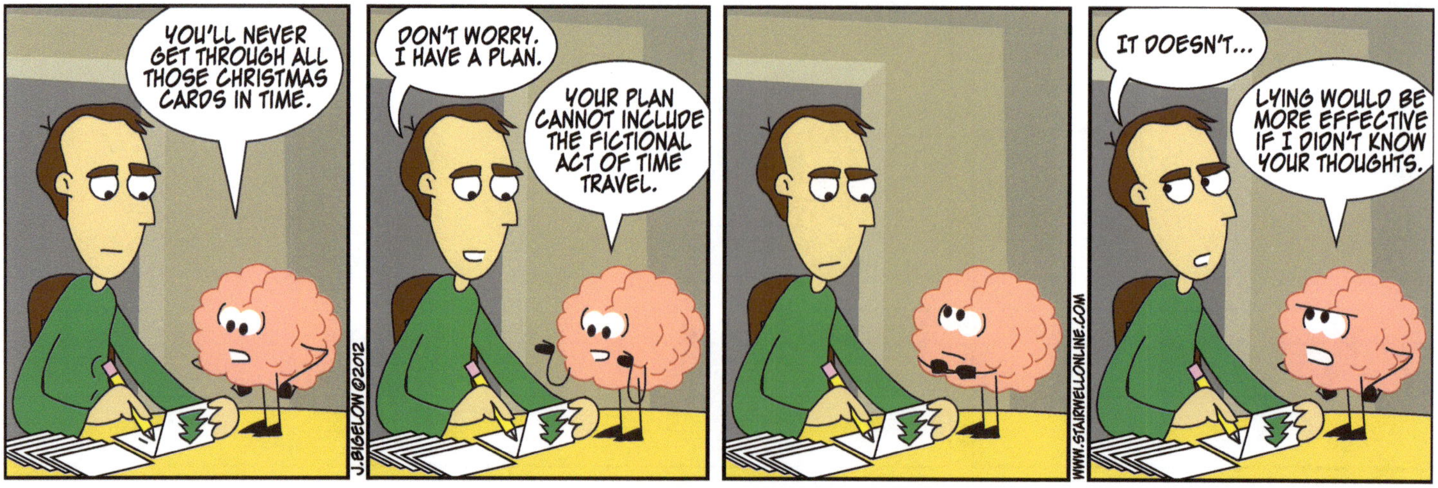
YOU'LL NEVER GET THROUGH ALL THOSE CHRISTMAS CARDS IN TIME.
J.BIGELOW ©2012
DON'T WORRY. I HAVE A PLAN.
YOUR PLAN CANNOT INCLUDE THE FICTIONAL ACT OF TIME TRAVEL.
WWW.STAIRWELLONLINE.COM
IT DOESN'T...
LYING WOULD BE MORE EFFECTIVE IF I DIDN'T KNOW YOUR THOUGHTS.

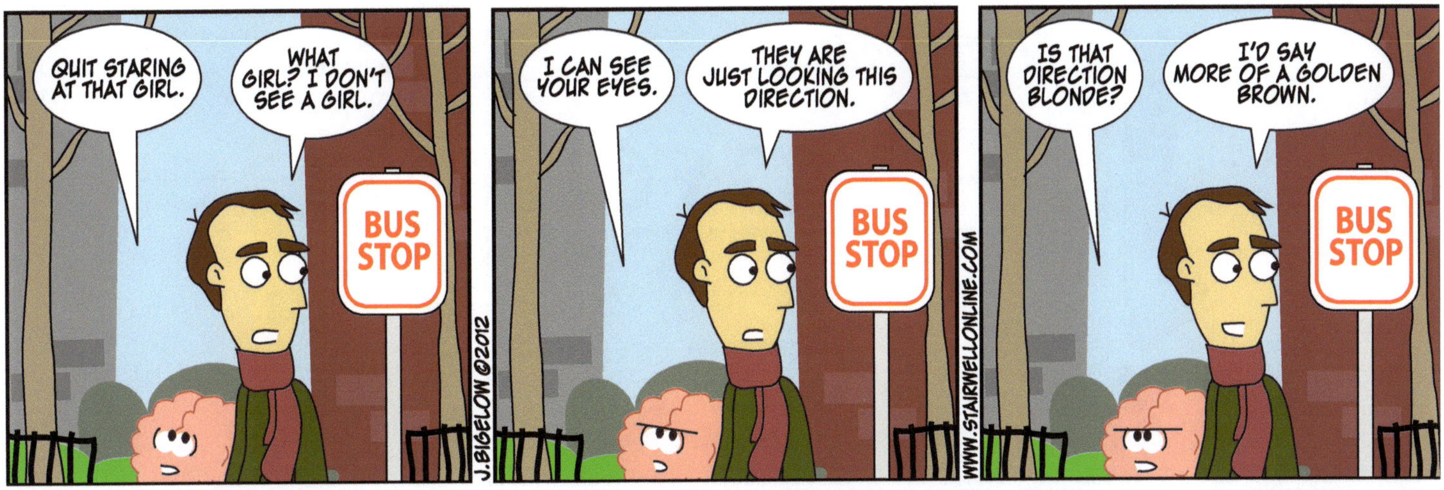
QUIT STARING AT THAT GIRL.
WHAT GIRL? I DON'T SEE A GIRL.
BUS STOP
J.BIGELOW ©2012
I CAN SEE YOUR EYES.
THEY ARE JUST LOOKING THIS DIRECTION.
BUS STOP
WWW.STAIRWELLONLINE.COM
IS THAT DIRECTION BLONDE?
I'D SAY MORE OF A GOLDEN BROWN.
BUS STOP

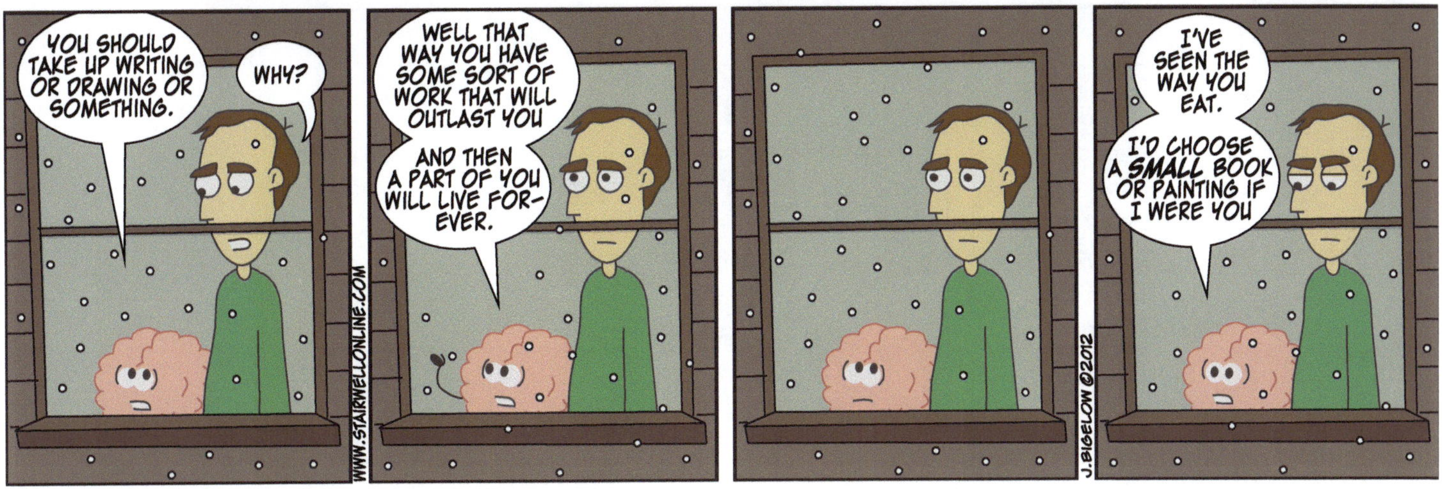
YOU SHOULD TAKE UP WRITING OR DRAWING OR SOMETHING.
WHY?
WWW.STAIRWELLONLINE.COM
WELL THAT WAY YOU HAVE SOME SORT OF WORK THAT WILL OUTLAST YOU
AND THEN A PART OF YOU WILL LIVE FOR-EVER.
J.BIGELOW ©2012
I'VE SEEN THE WAY YOU EAT.
I'D CHOOSE A SMALL BOOK OR PAINTING IF I WERE YOU

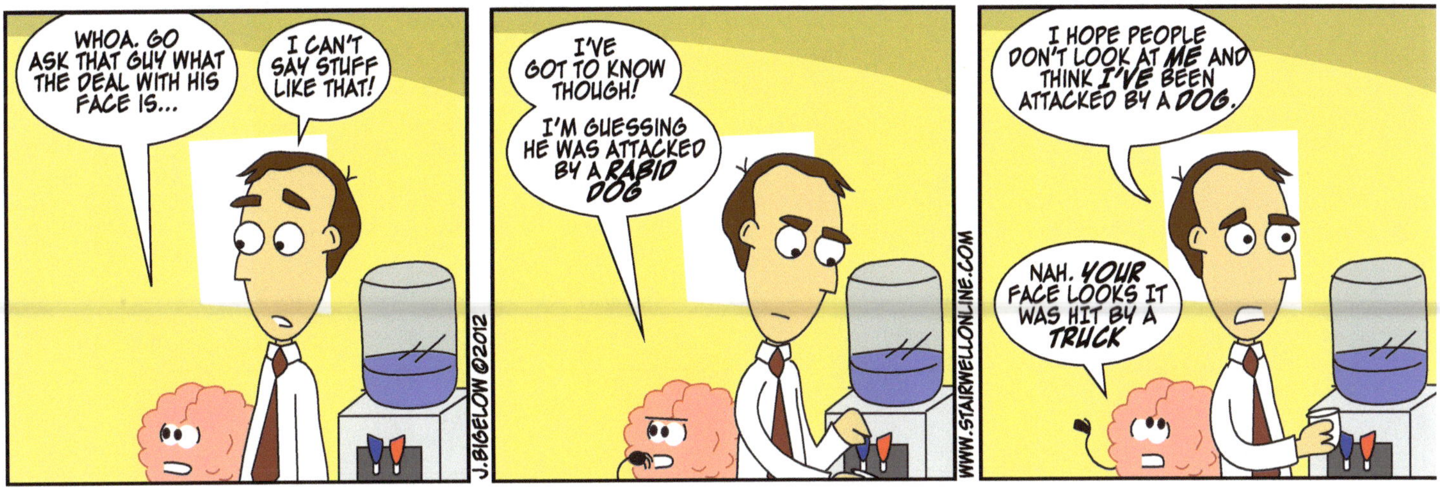
WHOA. GO ASK THAT GUY WHAT THE DEAL WITH HIS FACE IS...
I CAN'T SAY STUFF LIKE THAT!
J.BIGELOW ©2012
I'VE GOT TO KNOW THOUGH!
I'M GUESSING HE WAS ATTACKED BY A RABID DOG
WWW.STAIRWELLONLINE.COM
I HOPE PEOPLE DON'T LOOK AT ME AND THINK I'VE BEEN ATTACKED BY A DOG.
NAH. YOUR FACE LOOKS IT WAS HIT BY A TRUCK

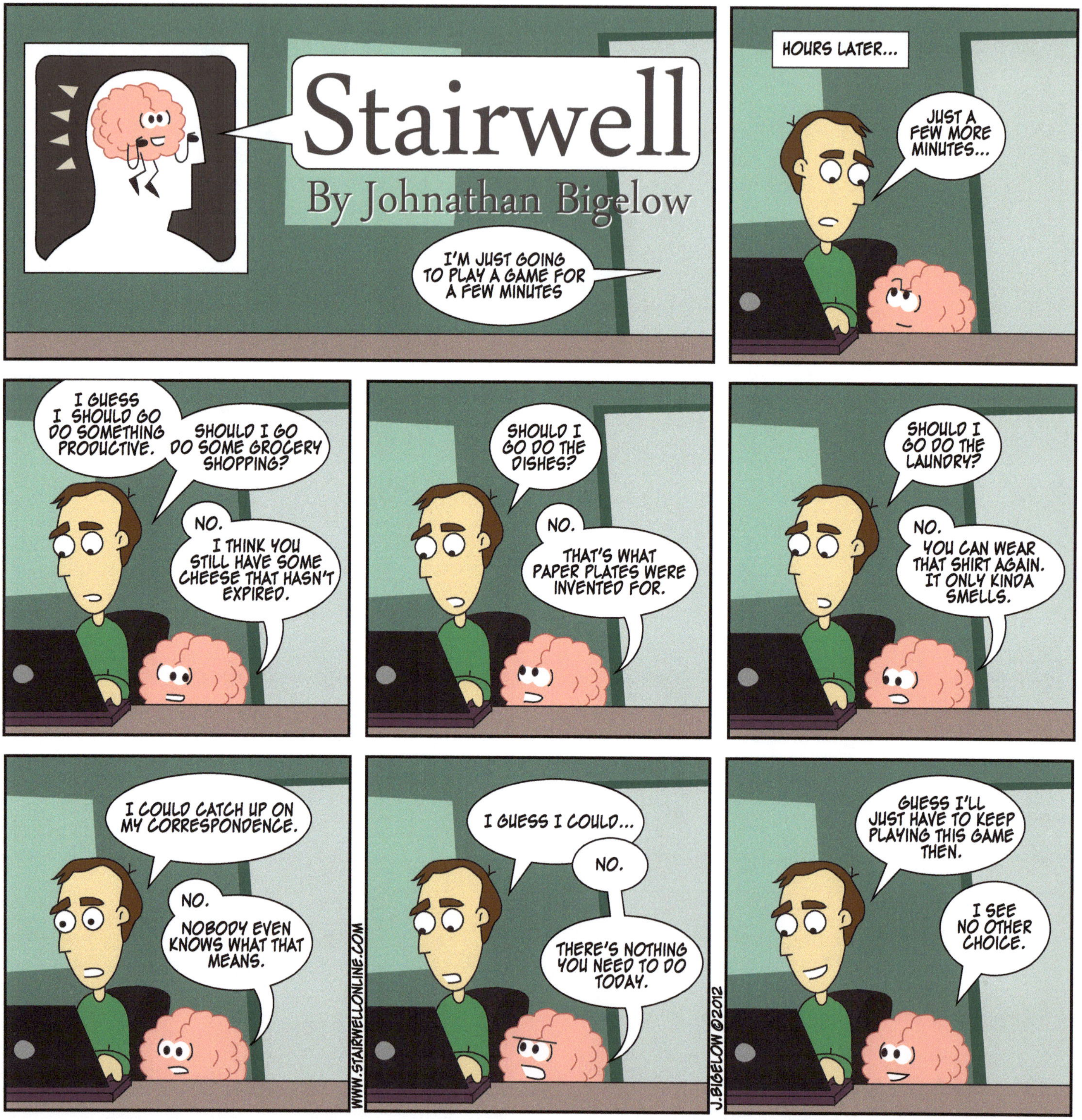
Stairwell
By Johnathan Bigelow
I'M JUST GOING TO PLAY A GAME FOR A FEW MINUTES
HOURS LATER...
JUST A FEW MORE MINUTES...
I GUESS I SHOULD GO DO SOMETHING PRODUCTIVE.
SHOULD I GO DO SOME GROCERY SHOPPING?
NO.
I THINK YOU STILL HAVE SOME CHEESE THAT HASN'T EXPIRED.
SHOULD I GO DO THE DISHES?
NO.
THAT'S WHAT PAPER PLATES WERE INVENTED FOR.
SHOULD I GO DO THE LAUNDRY?
NO.
YOU CAN WEAR THAT SHIRT AGAIN. IT ONLY KINDA SMELLS.
I COULD CATCH UP ON MY CORRESPONDENCE.
NO.
NOBODY EVEN KNOWS WHAT THAT MEANS.
WWW.STAIRWELLONLINE.COM
I GUESS I COULD...
NO.
THERE'S NOTHING YOU NEED TO DO TODAY.
J.BIGELOW ©2012
GUESS I'LL JUST HAVE TO KEEP PLAYING THIS GAME THEN.
I SEE NO OTHER CHOICE.

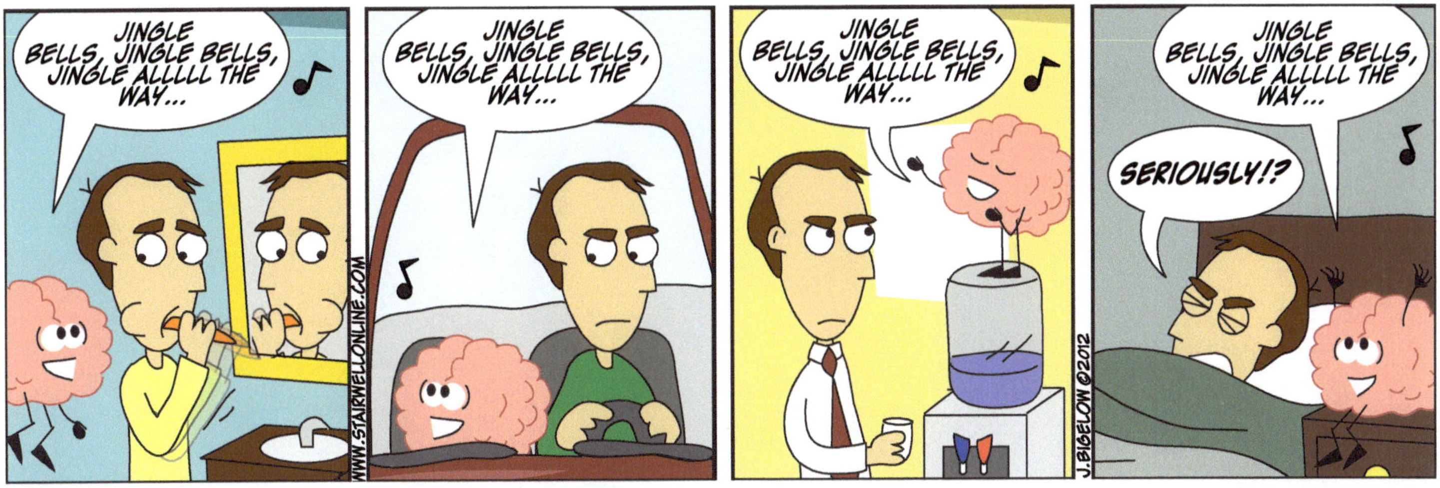
JINGLE BELLS, JINGLE BELLS, JINGLE ALLLLL THE WAY...
WWW.STAIRWELLONLINE.COM
JINGLE BELLS, JINGLE BELLS, JINGLE ALLLLL THE WAY...
JINGLE BELLS, JINGLE BELLS, JINGLE ALLLLL THE WAY...
J.BIGELOW ©2012
JINGLE BELLS, JINGLE BELLS, JINGLE ALLLLL THE WAY...
SERIOUSLY!?

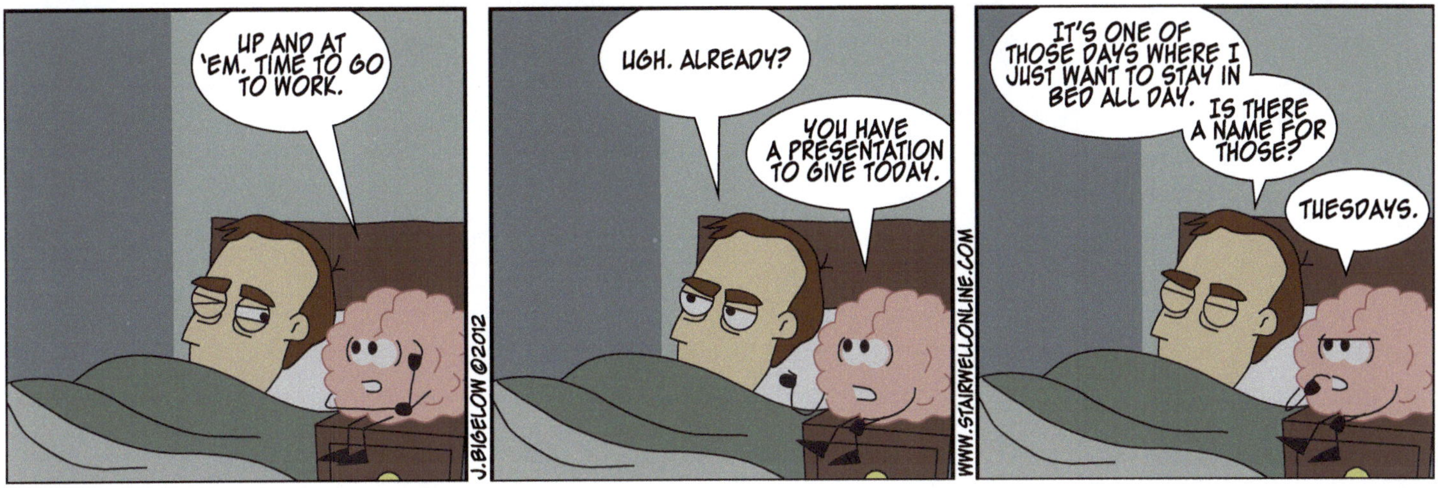
UP AND AT 'EM. TIME TO GO TO WORK.
J.BIGELOW ©2012
UGH. ALREADY?
YOU HAVE A PRESENTATION TO GIVE TODAY.
WWW.STAIRWELLONLINE.COM
IT'S ONE OF THOSE DAYS WHERE I JUST WANT TO STAY IN BED ALL DAY.
IS THERE A NAME FOR THOSE?
TUESDAYS.

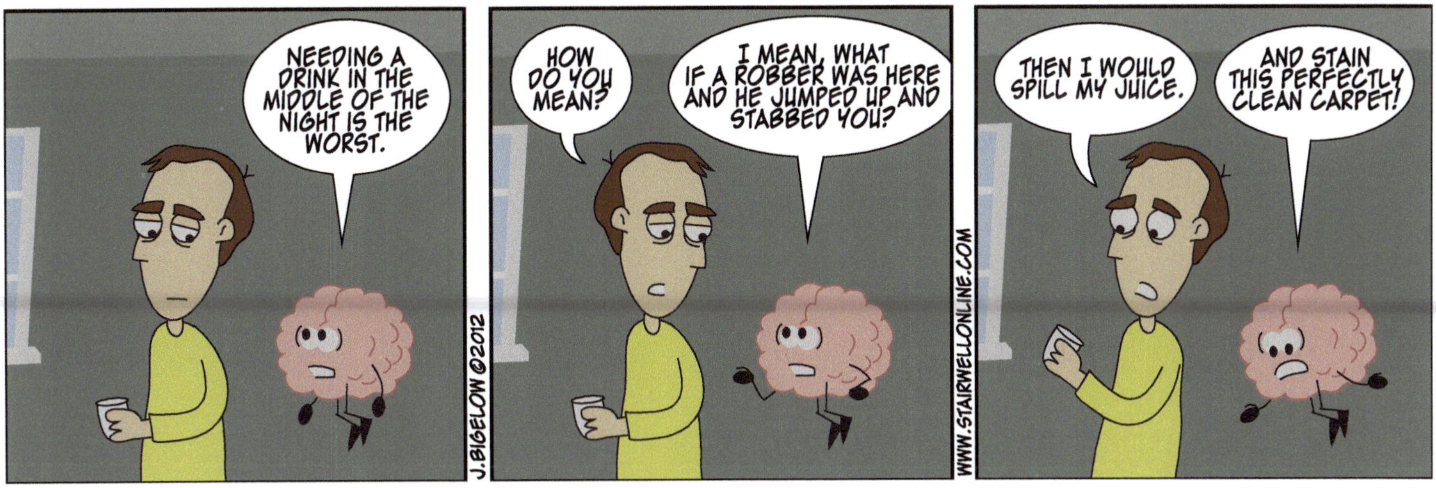
NEEDING A DRINK IN THE MIDDLE OF THE NIGHT IS THE WORST.
J.BIGELOW ©2012
HOW DO YOU MEAN?
I MEAN, WHAT IF A ROBBER WAS HERE AND HE JUMPED UP AND STABBED YOU?
WWW.STAIRWELLONLINE.COM
THEN I WOULD SPILL MY JUICE.
AND STAIN THIS PERFECTLY CLEAN CARPET!

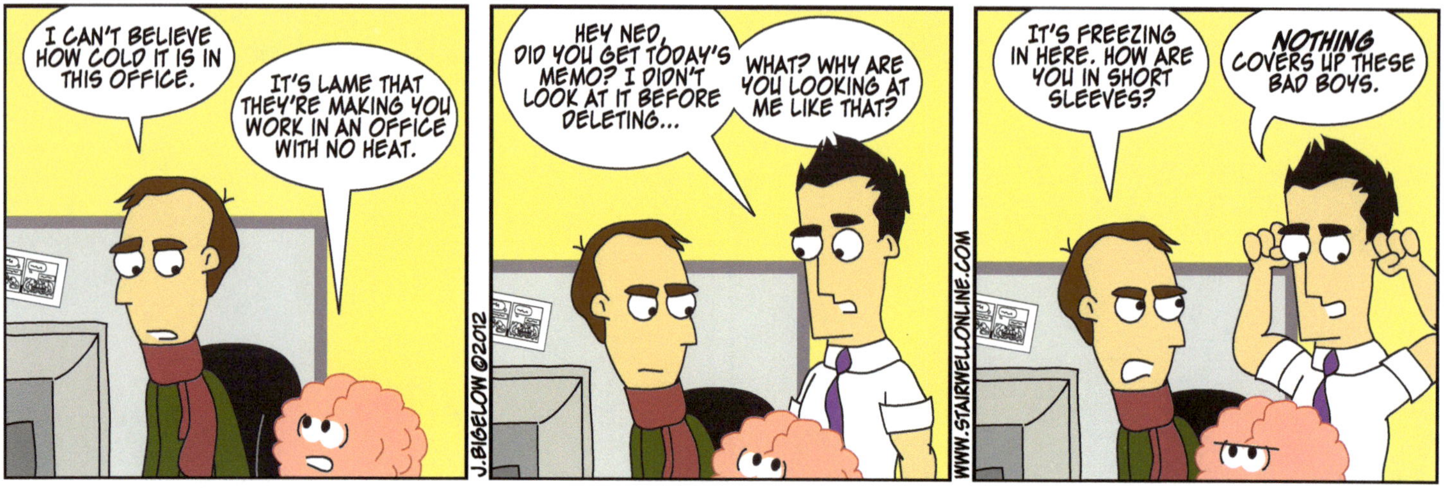
I CAN'T BELIEVE HOW COLD IT IS IN THIS OFFICE.
IT'S LAME THAT THEY'RE MAKING YOU WORK IN AN OFFICE WITH NO HEAT.
J.BIGELOW ©2012
HEY NED, DID YOU GET TODAY'S MEMO? I DIDN'T LOOK AT IT BEFORE DELETING...
WHAT? WHY ARE YOU LOOKING AT ME LIKE THAT?
WWW.STAIRWELLONLINE.COM
IT'S FREEZING IN HERE. HOW ARE YOU IN SHORT SLEEVES?
NOTHING COVERS UP THESE BAD BOYS.

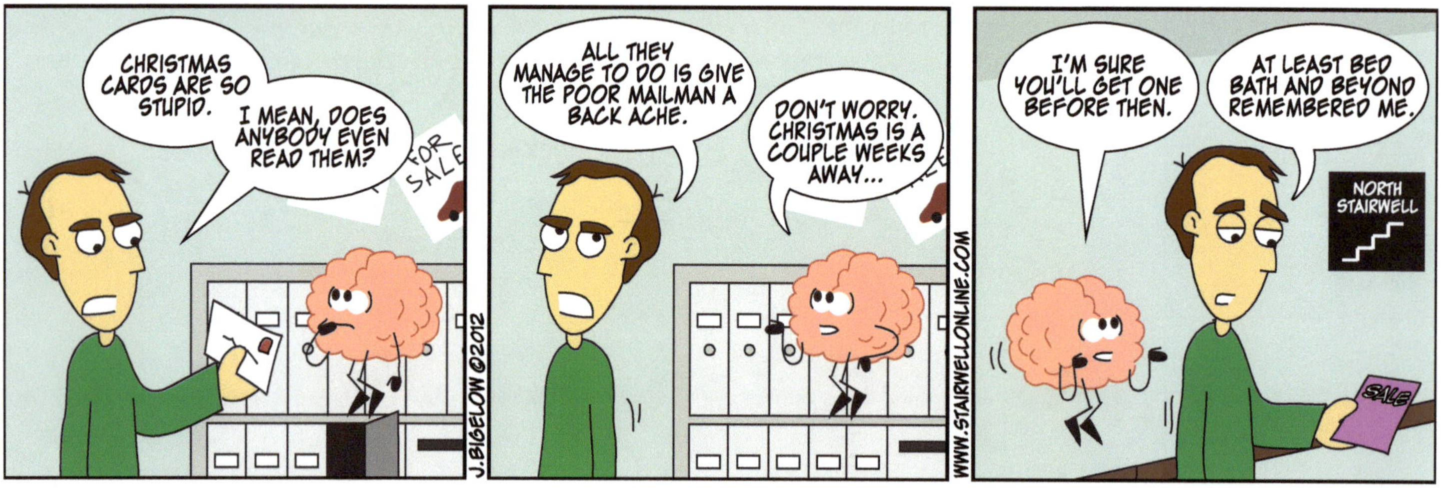
CHRISTMAS CARDS ARE SO STUPID.
I MEAN, DOES ANYBODY EVEN READ THEM?
FOR SALE
J.BIGELOW ©2012
ALL THEY MANAGE TO DO IS GIVE THE POOR MAILMAN A BACK ACHE.
DON'T WORRY. CHRISTMAS IS A COUPLE WEEKS AWAY...
WWW.STAIRWELLONLINE.COM
I'M SURE YOU'LL GET ONE BEFORE THEN.
AT LEAST BED BATH AND BEYOND REMEMBERED ME.
NORTH STAIRWELL
SALE

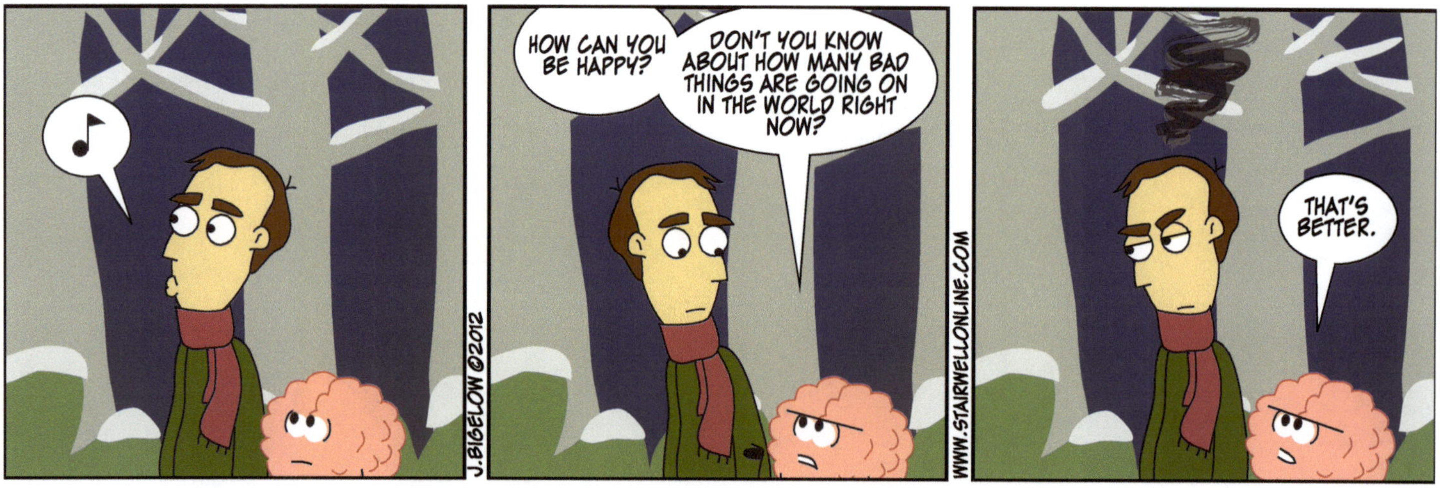
J.BIGELOW ©2012
HOW CAN YOU BE HAPPY?
DON'T YOU KNOW ABOUT HOW MANY BAD THINGS ARE GOING ON IN THE WORLD RIGHT NOW?
WWW.STAIRWELLONLINE.COM
THAT'S BETTER.

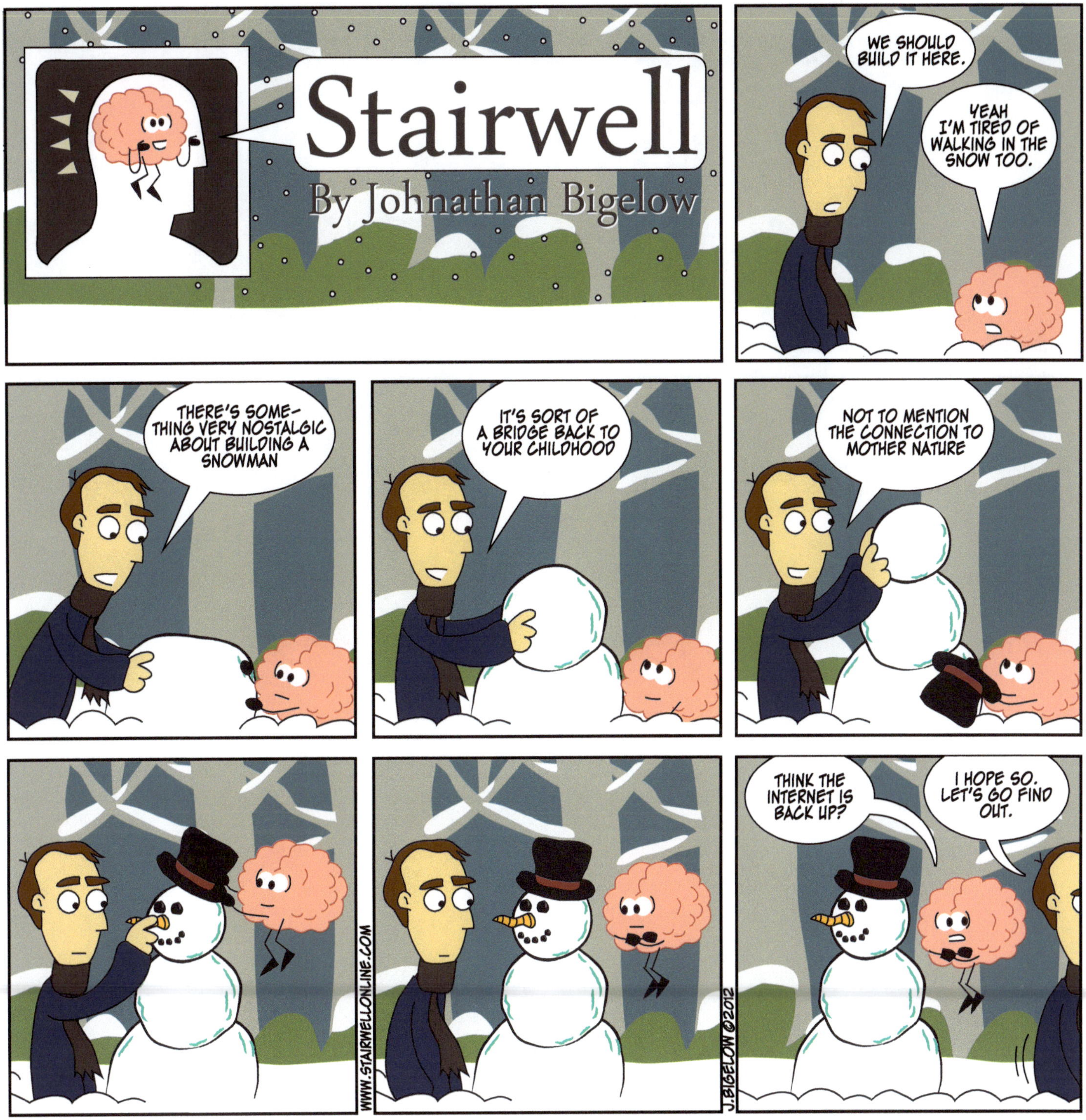
Stairwell
By Johnathan Bigelow
WE SHOULD BUILD IT HERE.
YEAH I'M TIRED OF WALKING IN THE SNOW TOO.
THERE'S SOME-THING VERY NOSTALGIC ABOUT BUILDING A SNOWMAN
IT'S SORT OF A BRIDGE BACK TO YOUR CHILDHOOD
NOT TO MENTION THE CONNECTION TO MOTHER NATURE
WWW.STAIRWELLONLINE.COM
J.BIGELOW ©2012
THINK THE INTERNET IS BACK UP?
I HOPE SO. LET'S GO FIND OUT.

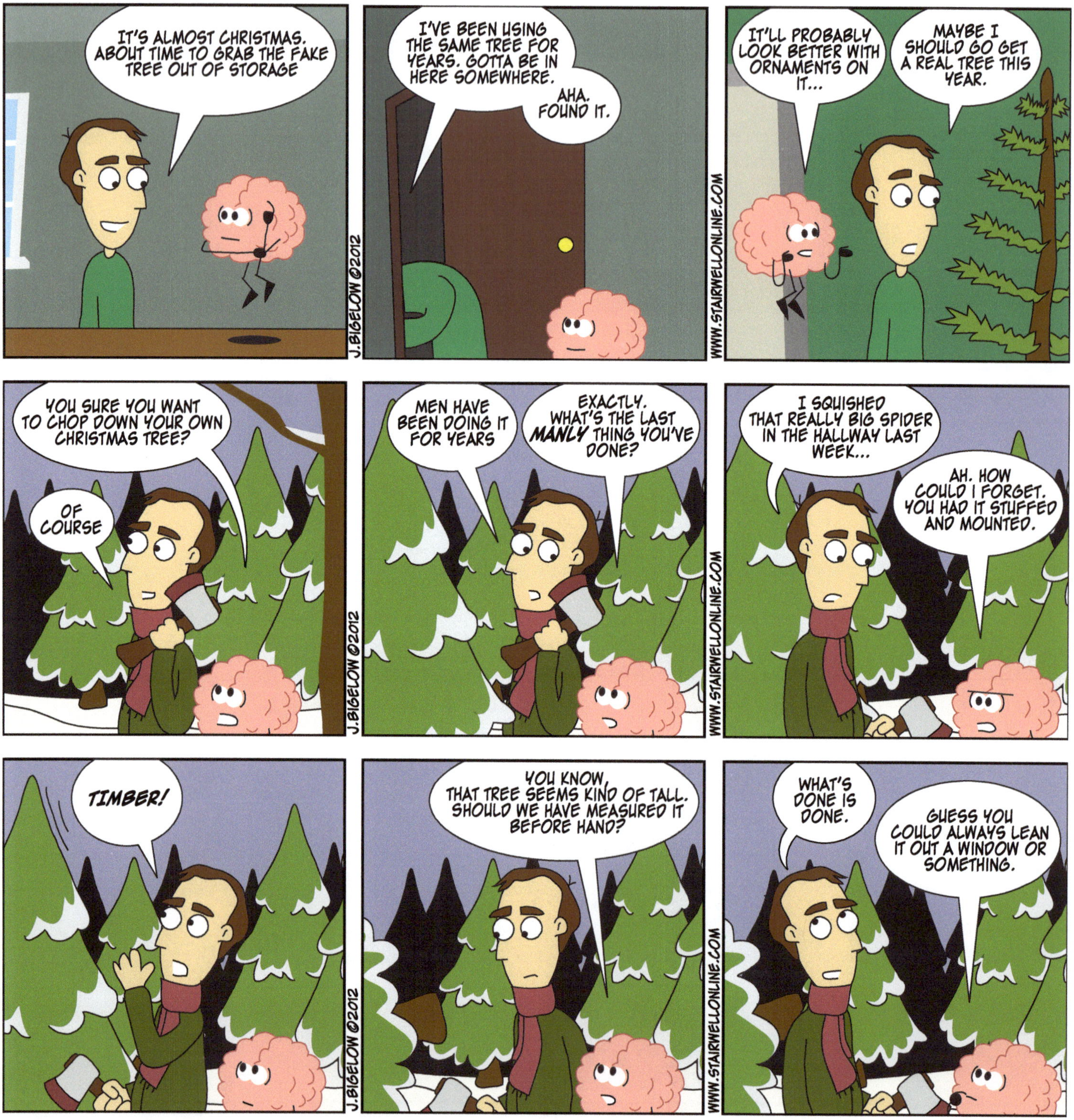
IT'S ALMOST CHRISTMAS. ABOUT TIME TO GRAB THE FAKE TREE OUT OF STORAGE
J.BIGELOW ©2012
I'VE BEEN USING THE SAME TREE FOR YEARS. GOTTA BE IN HERE SOMEWHERE.
AHA. FOUND IT.
WWW.STAIRWELLONLINE.COM
IT'LL PROBABLY LOOK BETTER WITH ORNAMENTS ON IT...
MAYBE I SHOULD GO GET A REAL TREE THIS YEAR.
YOU SURE YOU WANT TO CHOP DOWN YOUR OWN CHRISTMAS TREE?
OF COURSE
J.BIGELOW ©2012
MEN HAVE BEEN DOING IT FOR YEARS
EXACTLY. WHAT'S THE LAST *MANLY* THING YOU'VE DONE?
WWW.STAIRWELLONLINE.COM
I SQUISHED THAT REALLY BIG SPIDER IN THE HALLWAY LAST WEEK...
AH. HOW COULD I FORGET. YOU HAD IT STUFFED AND MOUNTED.
TIMBER!
J.BIGELOW ©2012
YOU KNOW, THAT TREE SEEMS KIND OF TALL. SHOULD WE HAVE MEASURED IT BEFORE HAND?
WWW.STAIRWELLONLINE.COM
WHAT'S DONE IS DONE.
GUESS YOU COULD ALWAYS LEAN IT OUT A WINDOW OR SOMETHING.

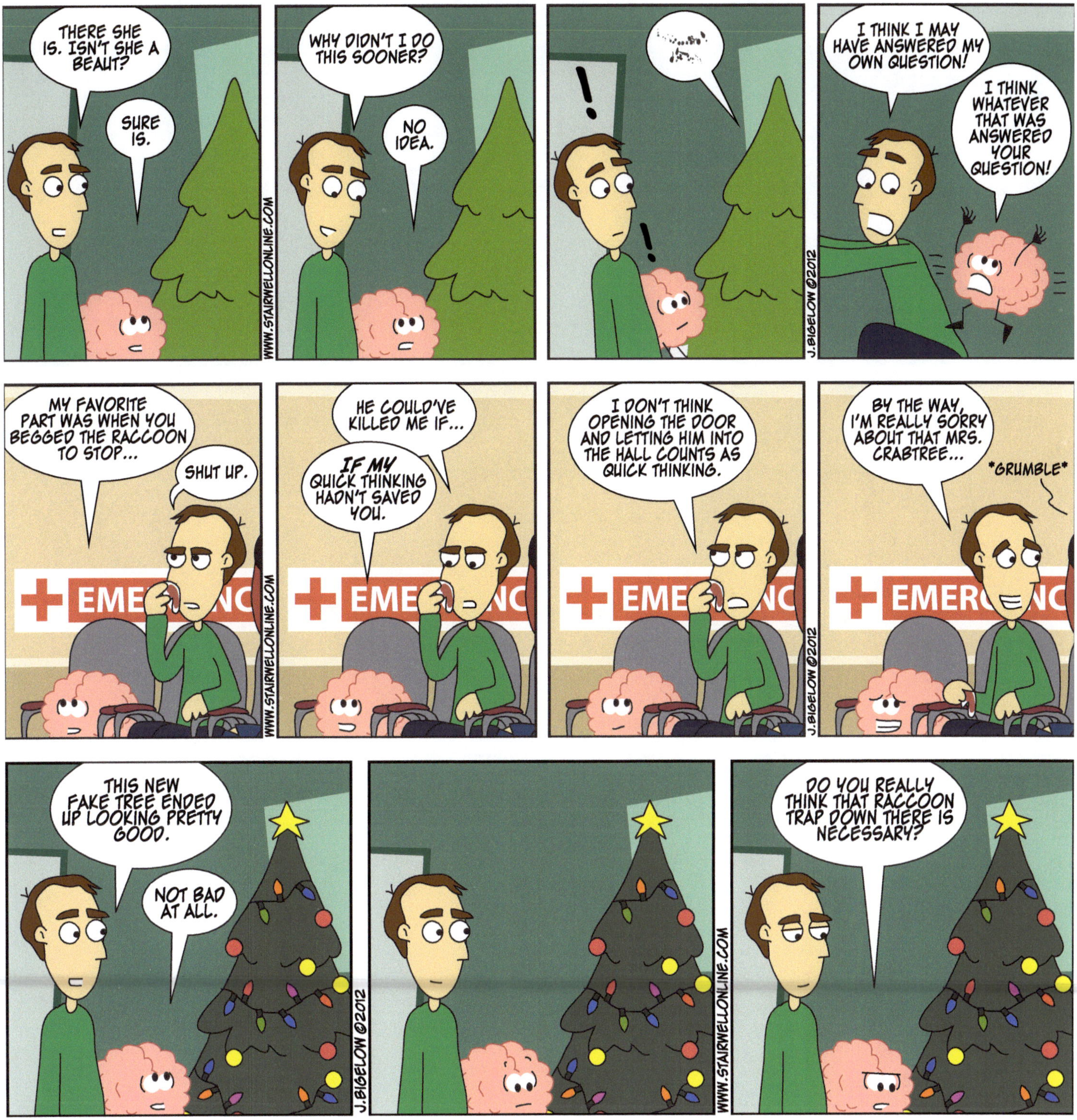
THERE SHE IS. ISN'T SHE A BEAUT?
SURE IS.
WWW.STAIRWELLONLINE.COM
WHY DIDN'T I DO THIS SOONER?
NO IDEA.
!
!
I THINK I MAY HAVE ANSWERED MY OWN QUESTION!
I THINK WHATEVER THAT WAS ANSWERED YOUR QUESTION!
J.BIGELOW ©2012
MY FAVORITE PART WAS WHEN YOU BEGGED THE RACCOON TO STOP...
SHUT UP.
WWW.STAIRWELLONLINE.COM
HE COULD'VE KILLED ME IF...
IF MY QUICK THINKING HADN'T SAVED YOU.
I DON'T THINK OPENING THE DOOR AND LETTING HIM INTO THE HALL COUNTS AS QUICK THINKING.
J.BIGELOW ©2012
BY THE WAY, I'M REALLY SORRY ABOUT THAT MRS. CRABTREE...
GRUMBLE
THIS NEW FAKE TREE ENDED UP LOOKING PRETTY GOOD.
NOT BAD AT ALL.
J.BIGELOW ©2012
WWW.STAIRWELLONLINE.COM
DO YOU REALLY THINK THAT RACCOON TRAP DOWN THERE IS NECESSARY?

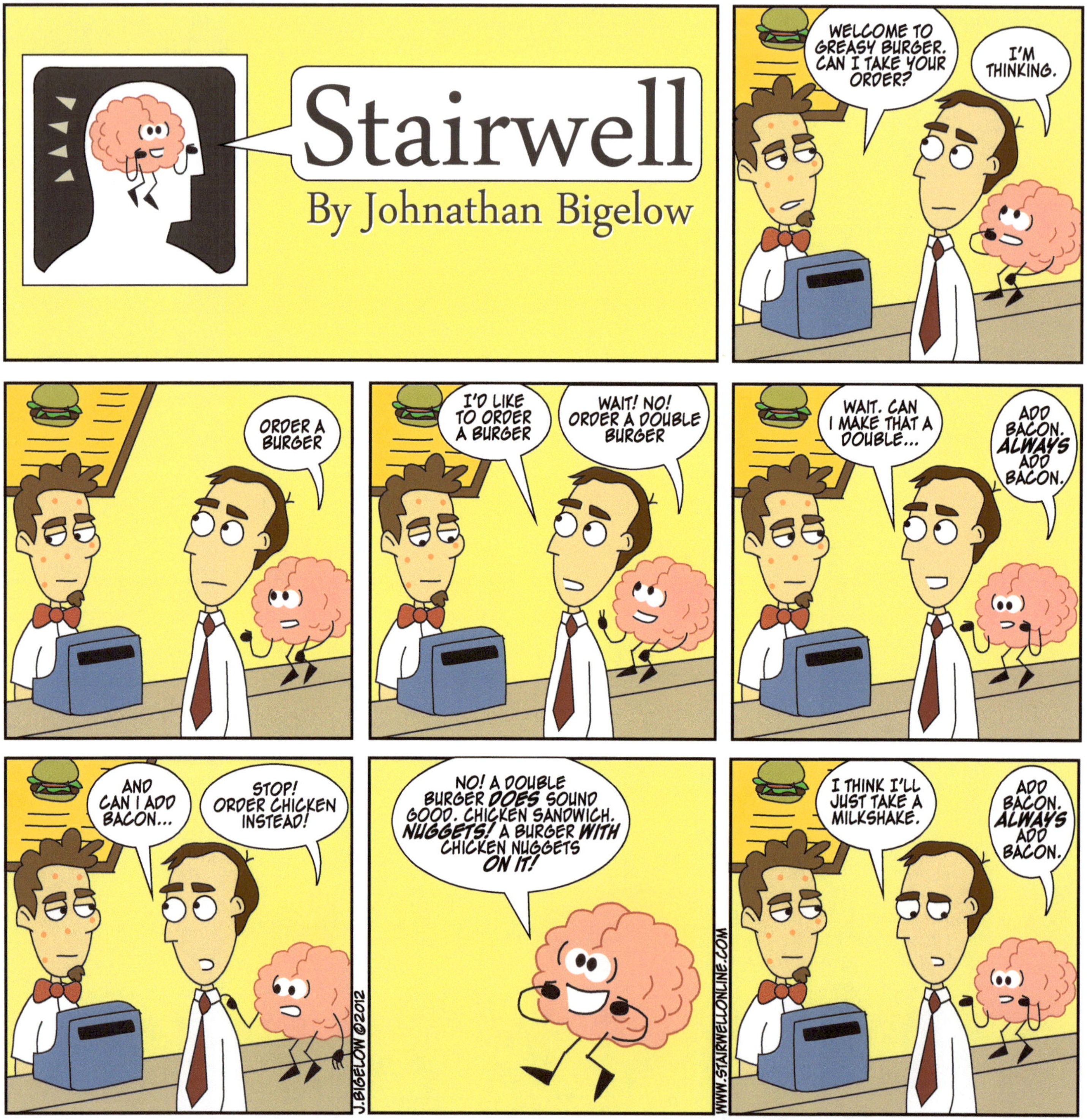
Stairwell
By Johnathan Bigelow
WELCOME TO GREASY BURGER. CAN I TAKE YOUR ORDER?
I'M THINKING.
ORDER A BURGER
I'D LIKE TO ORDER A BURGER
WAIT! NO! ORDER A DOUBLE BURGER
WAIT. CAN I MAKE THAT A DOUBLE...
ADD BACON. ALWAYS ADD BACON.
AND CAN I ADD BACON...
STOP! ORDER CHICKEN INSTEAD!
J.BIGELOW ©2012
NO! A DOUBLE BURGER DOES SOUND GOOD. CHICKEN SANDWICH. NUGGETS! A BURGER WITH CHICKEN NUGGETS ON IT!
WWW.STAIRWELLONLINE.COM
I THINK I'LL JUST TAKE A MILKSHAKE.
ADD BACON. ALWAYS ADD BACON.

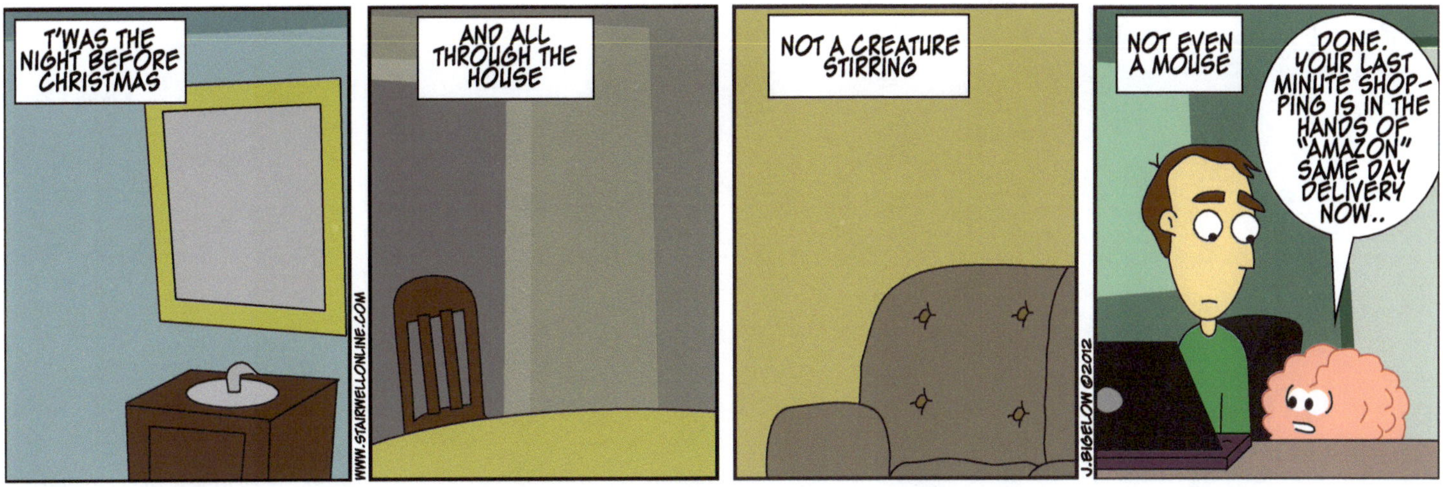
T'WAS THE NIGHT BEFORE CHRISTMAS
AND ALL THROUGH THE HOUSE
NOT A CREATURE STIRRING
NOT EVEN A MOUSE
DONE. YOUR LAST MINUTE SHOP-PING IS IN THE HANDS OF "AMAZON" SAME DAY DELIVERY NOW..
WWW.STAIRWELLONLINE.COM
J.BIGELOW ©2012

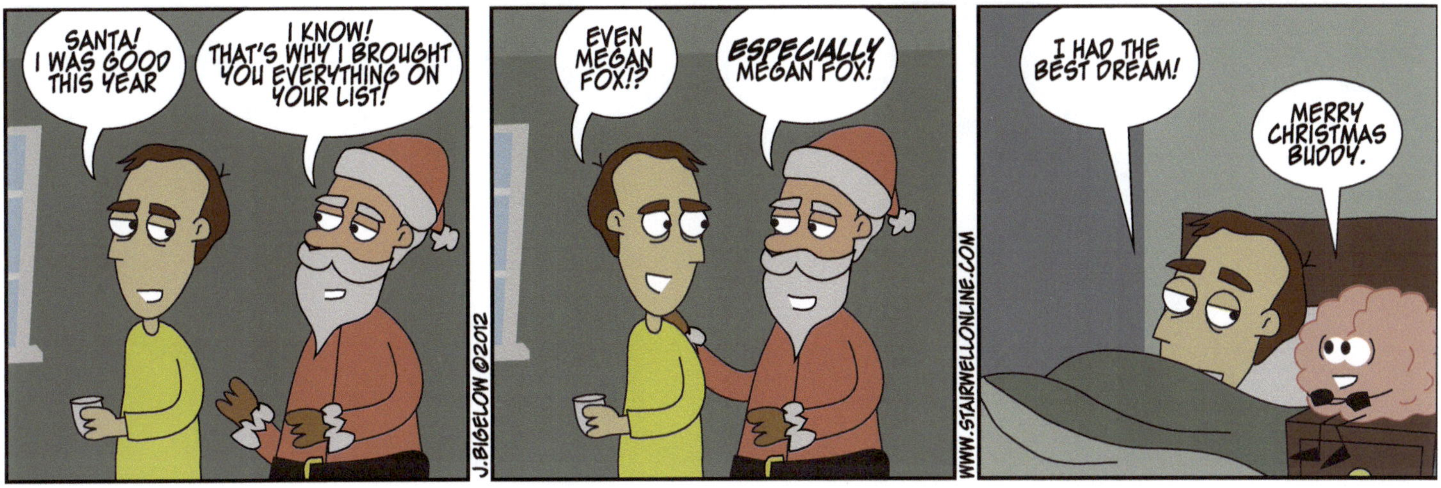
SANTA! I WAS GOOD THIS YEAR
I KNOW! THAT'S WHY I BROUGHT YOU EVERYTHING ON YOUR LIST!
EVEN MEGAN FOX!?
ESPECIALLY MEGAN FOX!
I HAD THE BEST DREAM!
MERRY CHRISTMAS BUDDY.
J.BIGELOW ©2012
WWW.STAIRWELLONLINE.COM

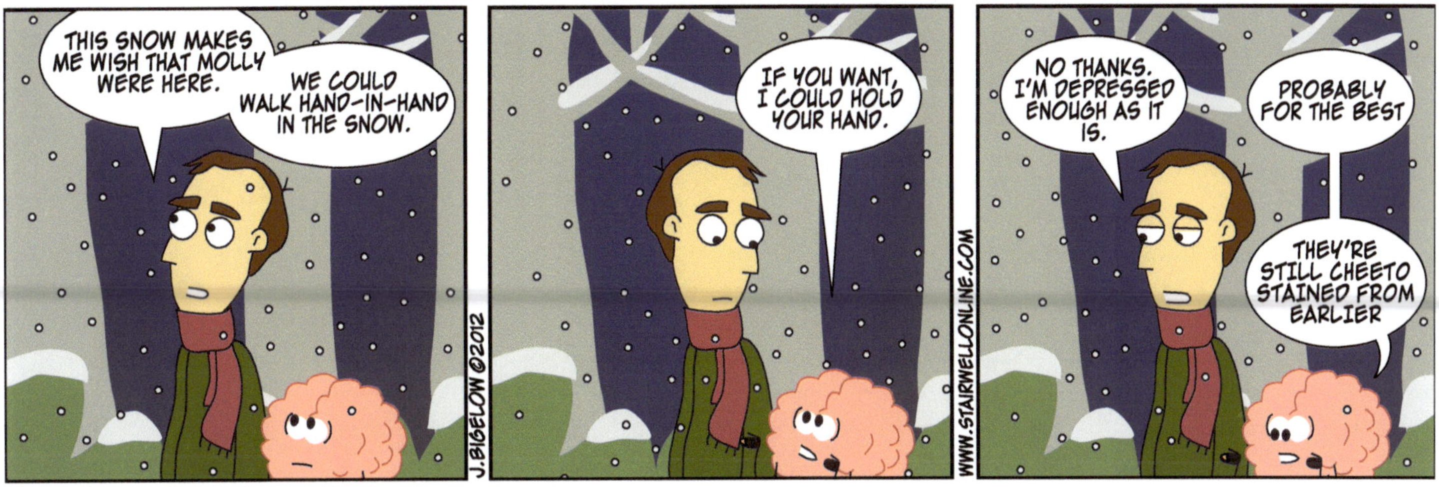
THIS SNOW MAKES ME WISH THAT MOLLY WERE HERE.
WE COULD WALK HAND-IN-HAND IN THE SNOW.
IF YOU WANT, I COULD HOLD YOUR HAND.
NO THANKS. I'M DEPRESSED ENOUGH AS IT IS.
PROBABLY FOR THE BEST
THEY'RE STILL CHEETO STAINED FROM EARLIER
J.BIGELOW ©2012
WWW.STAIRWELLONLINE.COM

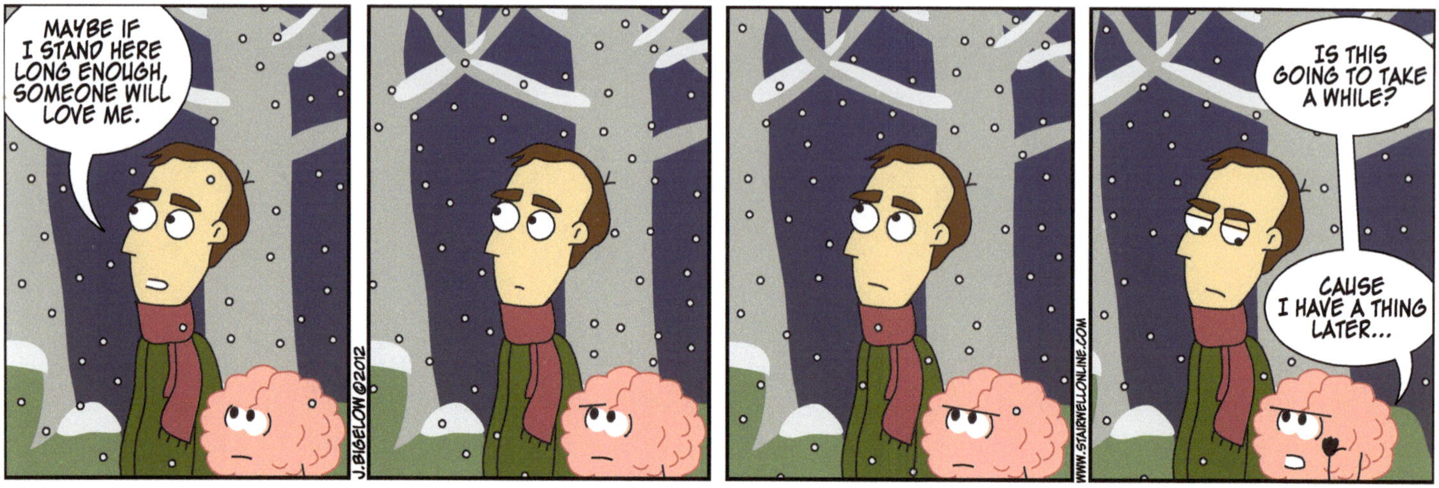
MAYBE IF I STAND HERE LONG ENOUGH, SOMEONE WILL LOVE ME.
J.BIGELOW ©2012
WWW.STAIRWELLONLINE.COM
IS THIS GOING TO TAKE A WHILE?
CAUSE I HAVE A THING LATER...

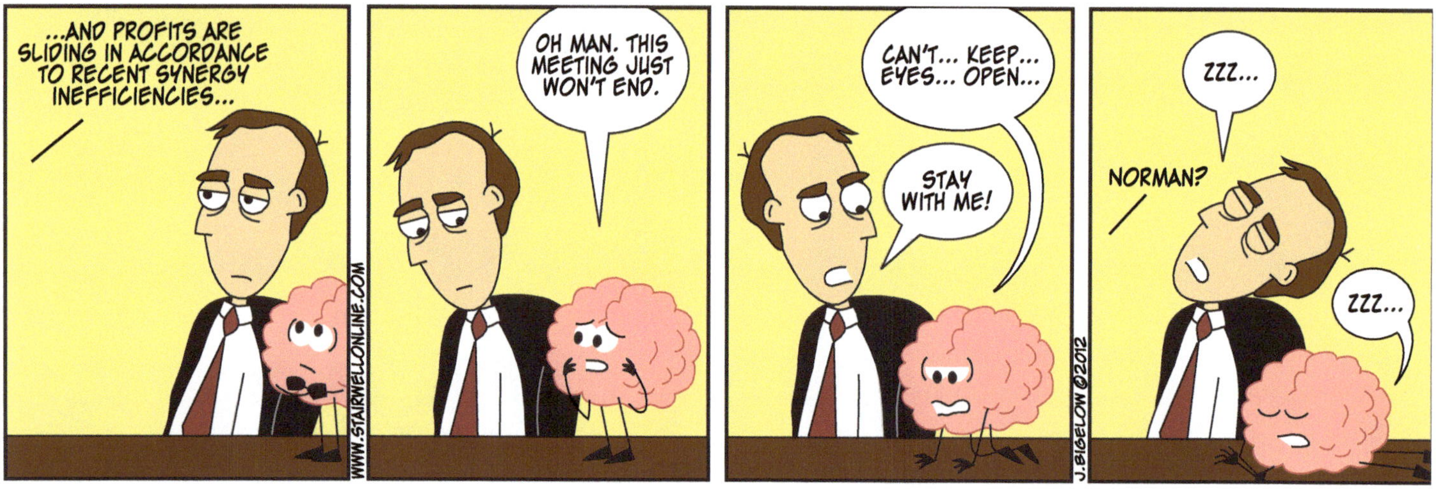
...AND PROFITS ARE SLIDING IN ACCORDANCE TO RECENT SYNERGY INEFFICIENCIES...
WWW.STAIRWELLONLINE.COM
OH MAN. THIS MEETING JUST WON'T END.
CAN'T... KEEP... EYES... OPEN...
STAY WITH ME!
J.BIGELOW ©2012
ZZZ...
NORMAN?
ZZZ...

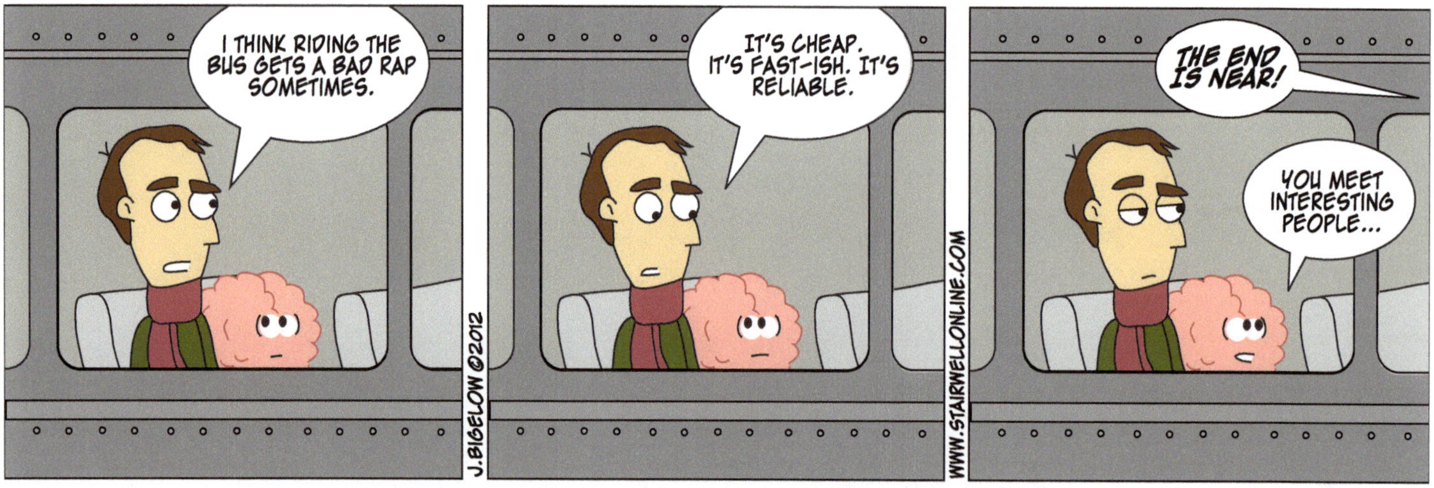
I THINK RIDING THE BUS GETS A BAD RAP SOMETIMES.
J.BIGELOW ©2012
IT'S CHEAP. IT'S FAST-ISH. IT'S RELIABLE.
WWW.STAIRWELLONLINE.COM
THE END IS NEAR!
YOU MEET INTERESTING PEOPLE...

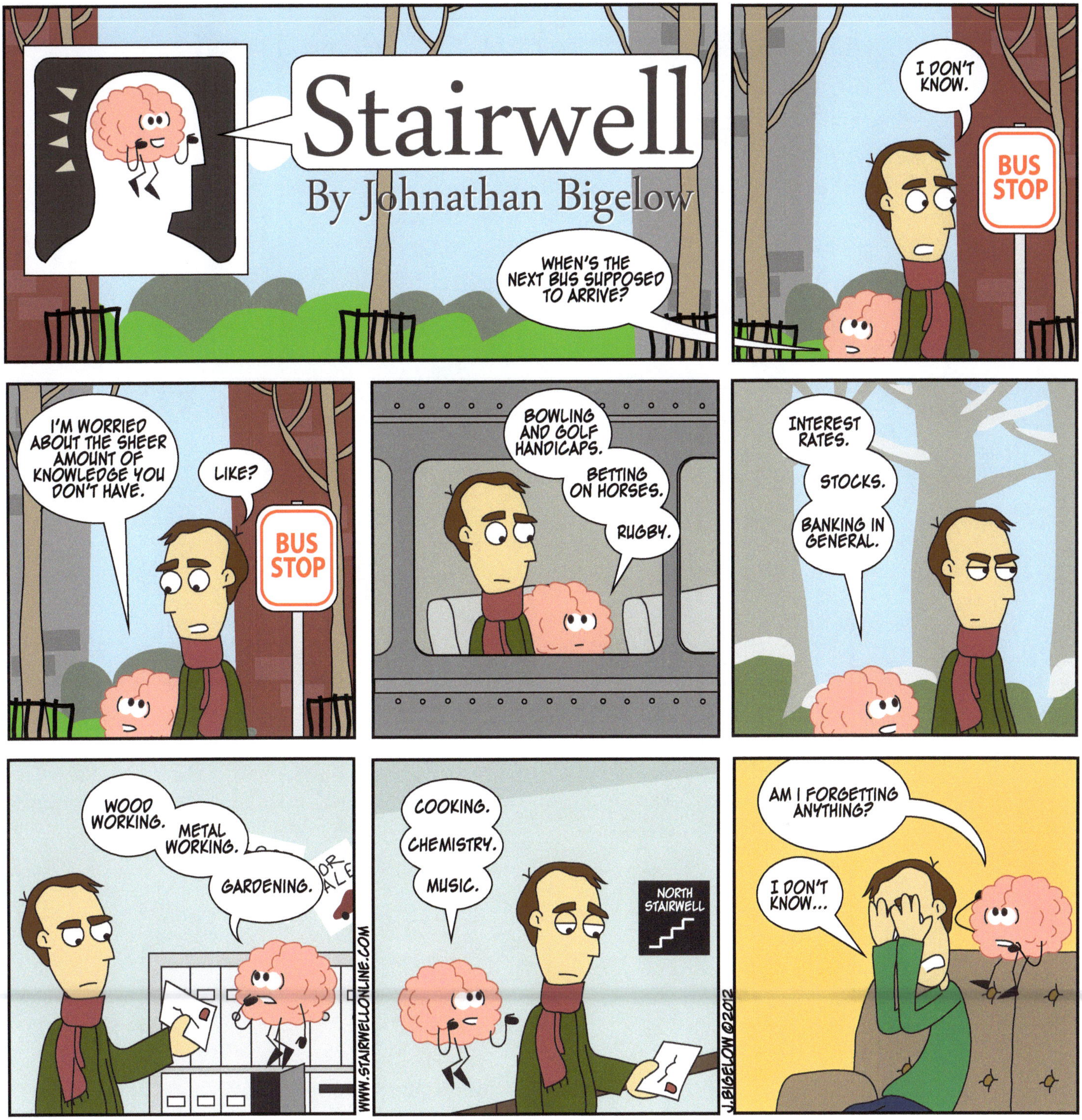
Stairwell
By Johnathan Bigelow
WHEN'S THE NEXT BUS SUPPOSED TO ARRIVE?
I DON'T KNOW.
BUS STOP
I'M WORRIED ABOUT THE SHEER AMOUNT OF KNOWLEDGE YOU DON'T HAVE.
LIKE?
BUS STOP
BOWLING AND GOLF HANDICAPS.
BETTING ON HORSES.
RUGBY.
INTEREST RATES.
STOCKS.
BANKING IN GENERAL.
WOOD WORKING.
METAL WORKING.
GARDENING.
WWW.STAIRWELLONLINE.COM
COOKING.
CHEMISTRY.
MUSIC.
NORTH STAIRWELL
J.BIGELOW ©2012
AM I FORGETTING ANYTHING?
I DON'T KNOW...

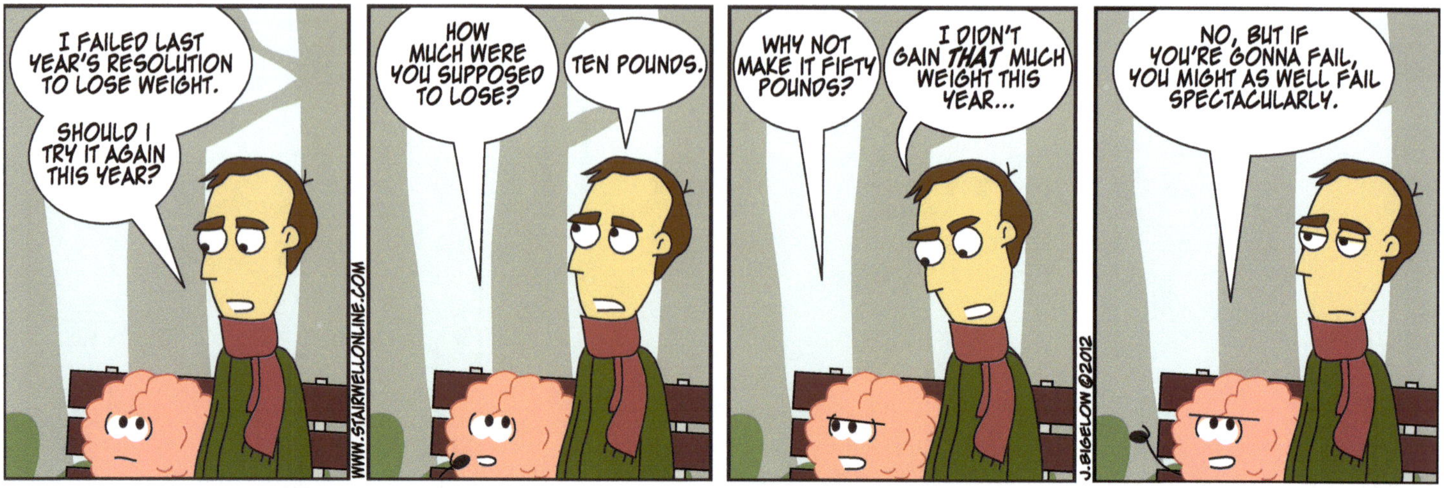
I FAILED LAST YEAR'S RESOLUTION TO LOSE WEIGHT.
SHOULD I TRY IT AGAIN THIS YEAR?
WWW.STAIRWELLONLINE.COM
HOW MUCH WERE YOU SUPPOSED TO LOSE?
TEN POUNDS.
WHY NOT MAKE IT FIFTY POUNDS?
I DIDN'T GAIN *THAT* MUCH WEIGHT THIS YEAR...
J.BIGELOW ©2012
NO, BUT IF YOU'RE GONNA FAIL, YOU MIGHT AS WELL FAIL SPECTACULARLY.

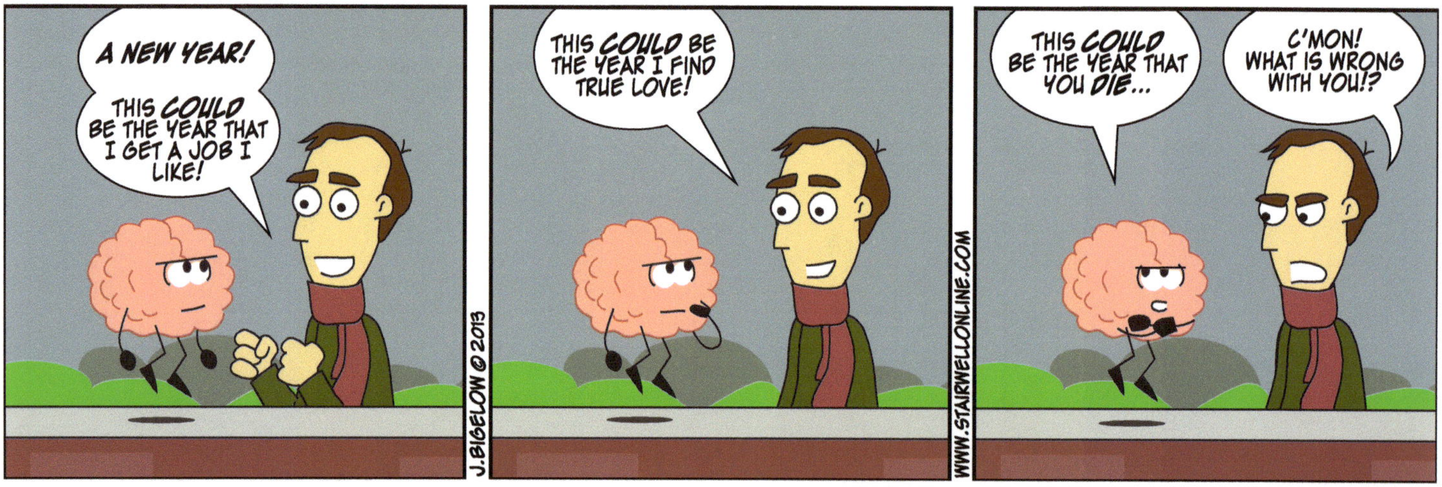
A NEW YEAR!
THIS *COULD* BE THE YEAR THAT I GET A JOB I LIKE!
J.BIGELOW ©2013
THIS *COULD* BE THE YEAR I FIND TRUE LOVE!
WWW.STAIRWELLONLINE.COM
THIS *COULD* BE THE YEAR THAT YOU *DIE*...
C'MON! WHAT IS WRONG WITH YOU!?

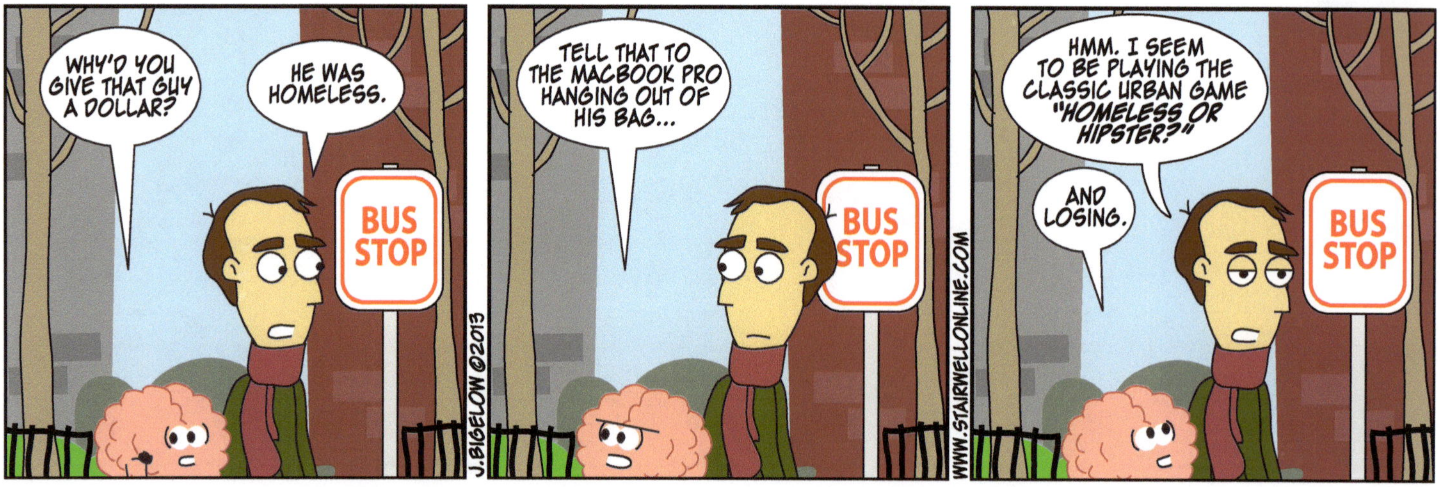
WHY'D YOU GIVE THAT GUY A DOLLAR?
HE WAS HOMELESS.
BUS STOP
J.BIGELOW ©2013
TELL THAT TO THE MACBOOK PRO HANGING OUT OF HIS BAG...
BUS STOP
WWW.STAIRWELLONLINE.COM
HMM. I SEEM TO BE PLAYING THE CLASSIC URBAN GAME *"HOMELESS OR HIPSTER?"*
AND LOSING.
BUS STOP

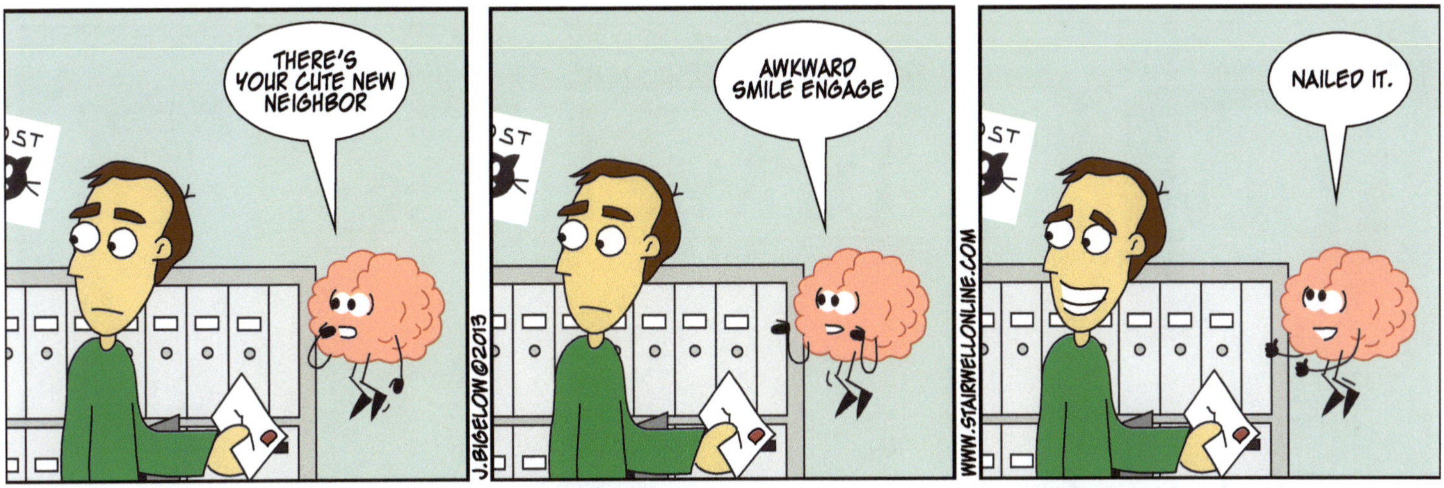
THERE'S YOUR CUTE NEW NEIGHBOR
AWKWARD SMILE ENGAGE
NAILED IT.
J.BIGELOW ©2013
WWW.STAIRWELLONLINE.COM

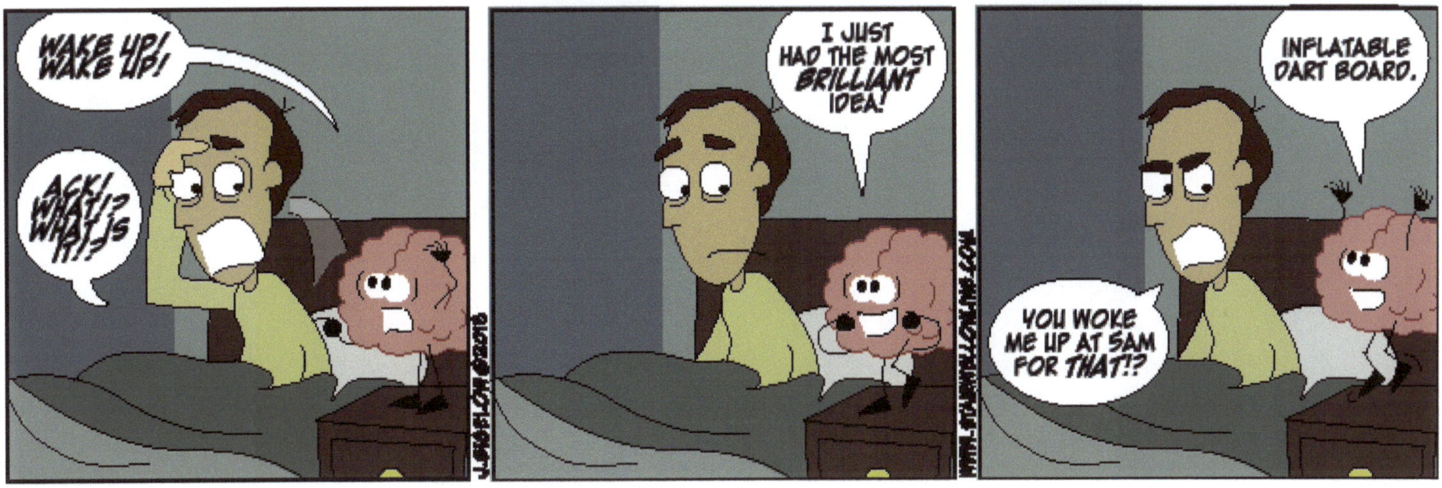
WAKE UP! WAKE UP!
ACK! WHAT!? WHAT IS IT!?
I JUST HAD THE MOST *BRILLIANT* IDEA!
INFLATABLE DART BOARD.
YOU WOKE ME UP AT 5AM FOR *THAT*!?
J.BIGELOW ©2013
WWW.STAIRWELLONLINE.COM

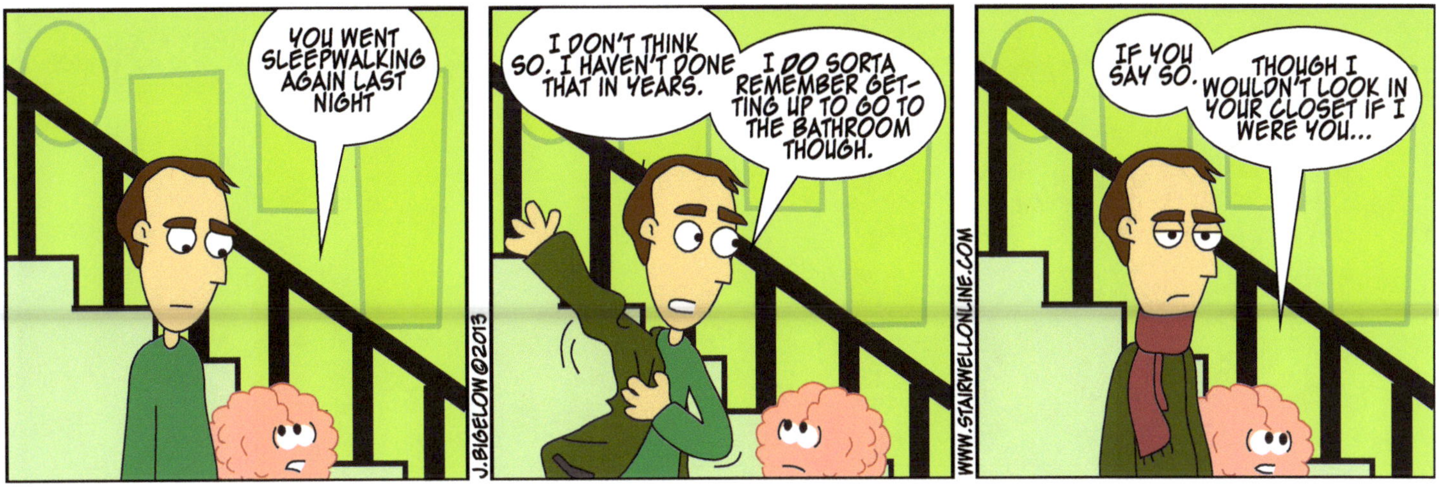
YOU WENT SLEEPWALKING AGAIN LAST NIGHT
I DON'T THINK SO. I HAVEN'T DONE THAT IN YEARS.
I *DO* SORTA REMEMBER GET-TING UP TO GO TO THE BATHROOM THOUGH.
IF YOU SAY SO.
THOUGH I WOULDN'T LOOK IN YOUR CLOSET IF I WERE YOU...
J.BIGELOW ©2013
WWW.STAIRWELLONLINE.COM

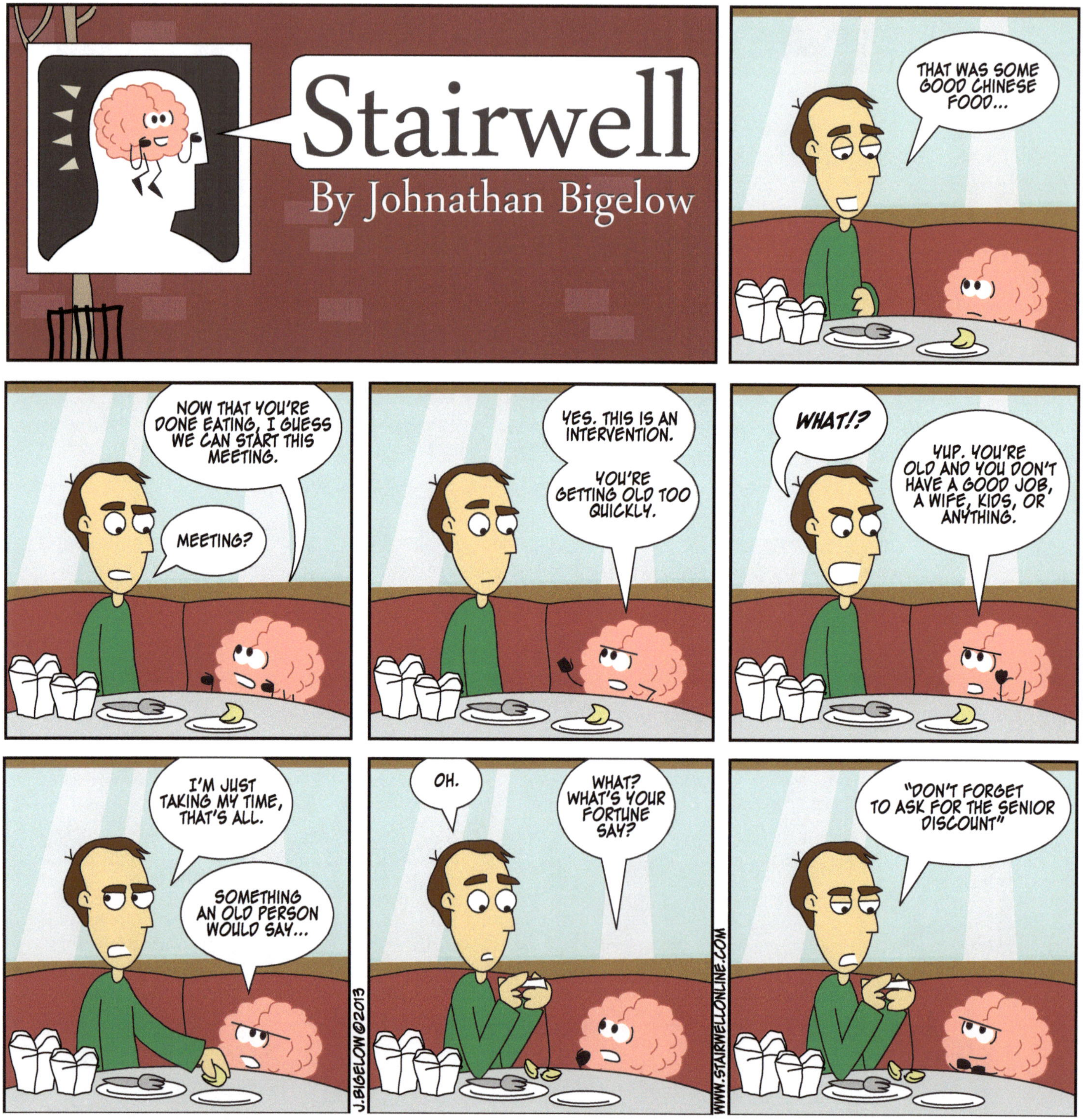
Stairwell
By Johnathan Bigelow
THAT WAS SOME GOOD CHINESE FOOD...
NOW THAT YOU'RE DONE EATING, I GUESS WE CAN START THIS MEETING.
MEETING?
YES. THIS IS AN INTERVENTION.
YOU'RE GETTING OLD TOO QUICKLY.
WHAT!?
YUP. YOU'RE OLD AND YOU DON'T HAVE A GOOD JOB, A WIFE, KIDS, OR ANYTHING.
I'M JUST TAKING MY TIME, THAT'S ALL.
SOMETHING AN OLD PERSON WOULD SAY...
J.BIGELOW ©2013
OH.
WHAT? WHAT'S YOUR FORTUNE SAY?
WWW.STAIRWELLONLINE.COM
"DON'T FORGET TO ASK FOR THE SENIOR DISCOUNT"

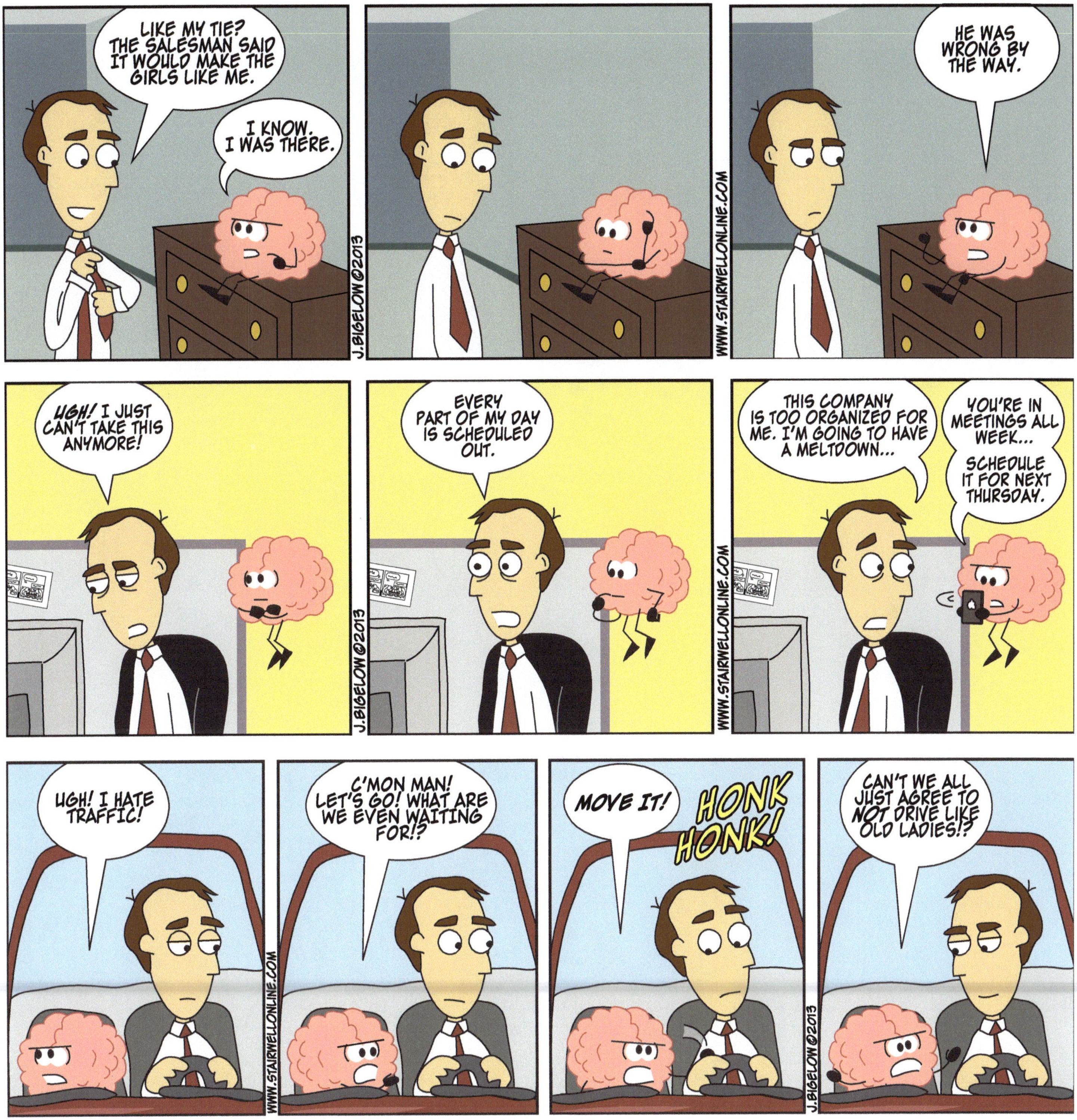
LIKE MY TIE? THE SALESMAN SAID IT WOULD MAKE THE GIRLS LIKE ME.
I KNOW. I WAS THERE.
J.BIGELOW ©2013
HE WAS WRONG BY THE WAY.
WWW.STAIRWELLONLINE.COM
UGH! I JUST CAN'T TAKE THIS ANYMORE!
J.BIGELOW ©2013
EVERY PART OF MY DAY IS SCHEDULED OUT.
WWW.STAIRWELLONLINE.COM
THIS COMPANY IS TOO ORGANIZED FOR ME. I'M GOING TO HAVE A MELTDOWN...
YOU'RE IN MEETINGS ALL WEEK...
SCHEDULE IT FOR NEXT THURSDAY.
UGH! I HATE TRAFFIC!
WWW.STAIRWELLONLINE.COM
C'MON MAN! LET'S GO! WHAT ARE WE EVEN WAITING FOR!?
MOVE IT!
HONK HONK!
J.BIGELOW ©2013
CAN'T WE ALL JUST AGREE TO NOT DRIVE LIKE OLD LADIES!?

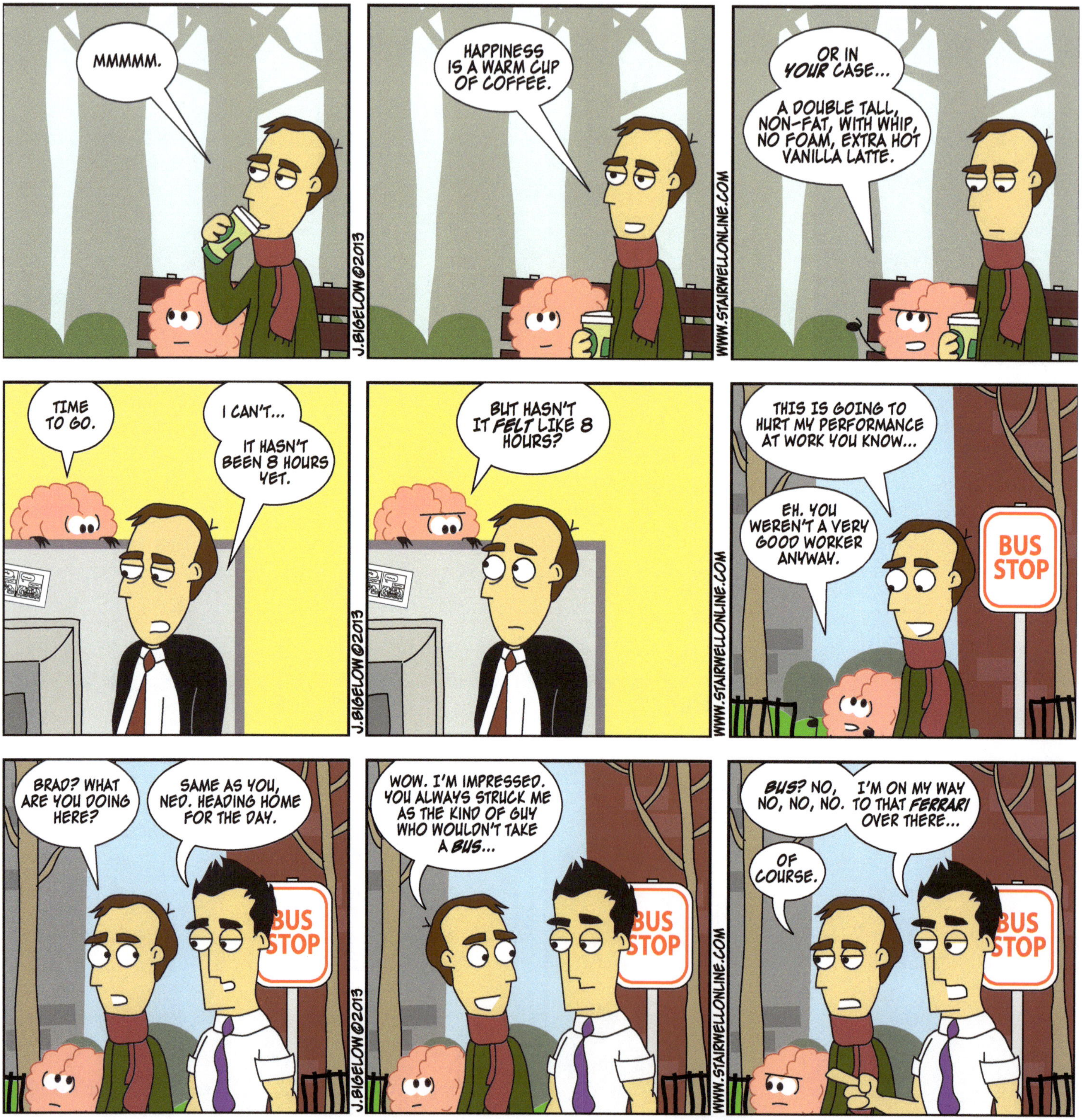
MMMMM.
HAPPINESS IS A WARM CUP OF COFFEE.
OR IN YOUR CASE...
A DOUBLE TALL, NON-FAT, WITH WHIP, NO FOAM, EXTRA HOT VANILLA LATTE.
J.BIGELOW ©2013
WWW.STAIRWELLONLINE.COM
TIME TO GO.
I CAN'T...
IT HASN'T BEEN 8 HOURS YET.
BUT HASN'T IT FELT LIKE 8 HOURS?
THIS IS GOING TO HURT MY PERFORMANCE AT WORK YOU KNOW...
EH. YOU WEREN'T A VERY GOOD WORKER ANYWAY.
BUS STOP
J.BIGELOW ©2013
WWW.STAIRWELLONLINE.COM
BRAD? WHAT ARE YOU DOING HERE?
SAME AS YOU, NED. HEADING HOME FOR THE DAY.
BUS STOP
WOW. I'M IMPRESSED. YOU ALWAYS STRUCK ME AS THE KIND OF GUY WHO WOULDN'T TAKE A BUS...
BUS? NO, NO, NO, NO.
I'M ON MY WAY TO THAT FERRARI OVER THERE...
OF COURSE.
J.BIGELOW ©2013
WWW.STAIRWELLONLINE.COM

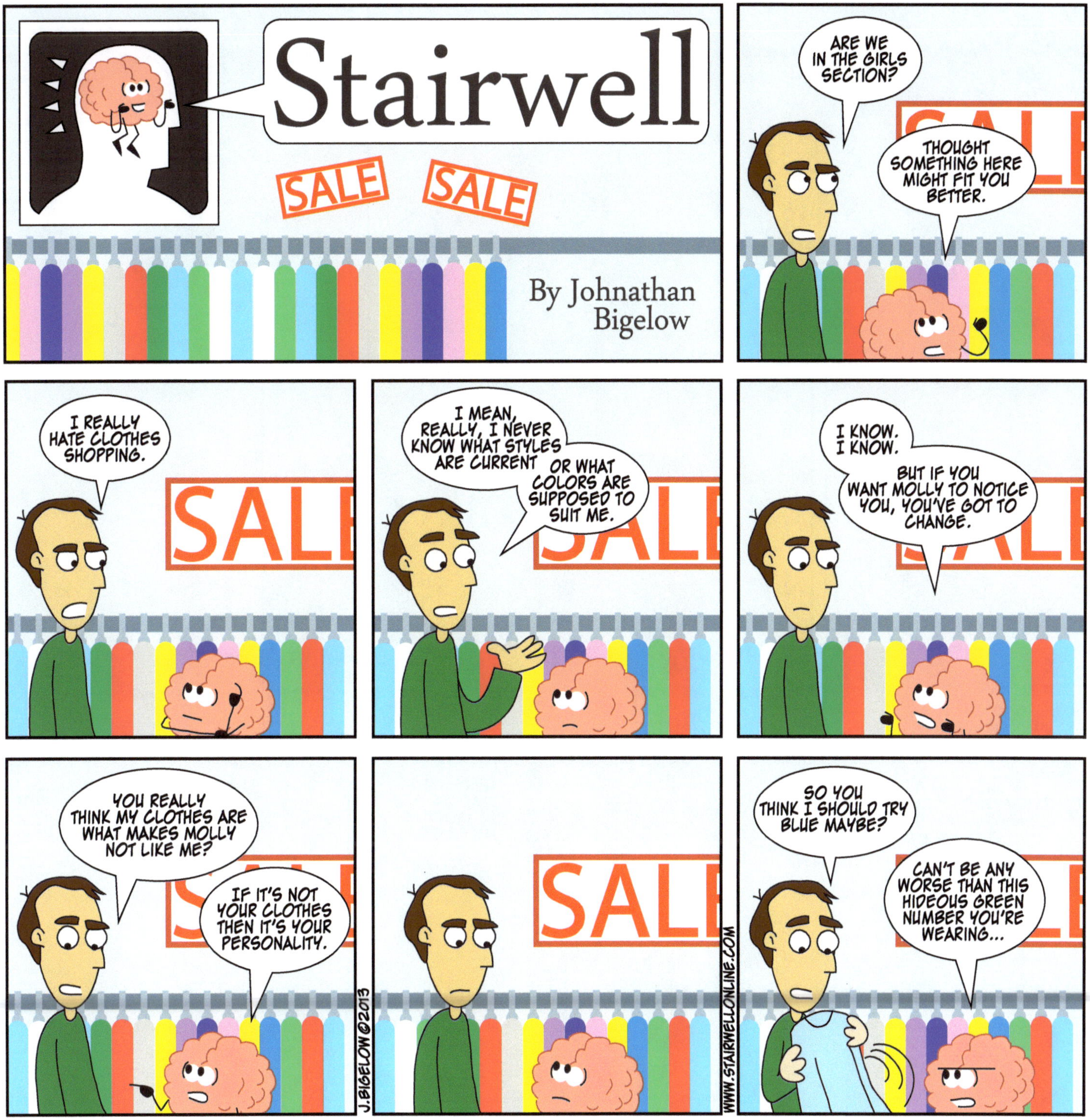
Stairwell
SALE
SALE
By Johnathan Bigelow
ARE WE IN THE GIRLS SECTION?
THOUGHT SOMETHING HERE MIGHT FIT YOU BETTER.
I REALLY HATE CLOTHES SHOPPING.
I MEAN, REALLY, I NEVER KNOW WHAT STYLES ARE CURRENT
OR WHAT COLORS ARE SUPPOSED TO SUIT ME.
I KNOW. I KNOW.
BUT IF YOU WANT MOLLY TO NOTICE YOU, YOU'VE GOT TO CHANGE.
YOU REALLY THINK MY CLOTHES ARE WHAT MAKES MOLLY NOT LIKE ME?
IF IT'S NOT YOUR CLOTHES THEN IT'S YOUR PERSONALITY.
J. BIGELOW ©2013
SALE
WWW.STAIRWELLONLINE.COM
SO YOU THINK I SHOULD TRY BLUE MAYBE?
CAN'T BE ANY WORSE THAN THIS HIDEOUS GREEN NUMBER YOU'RE WEARING...

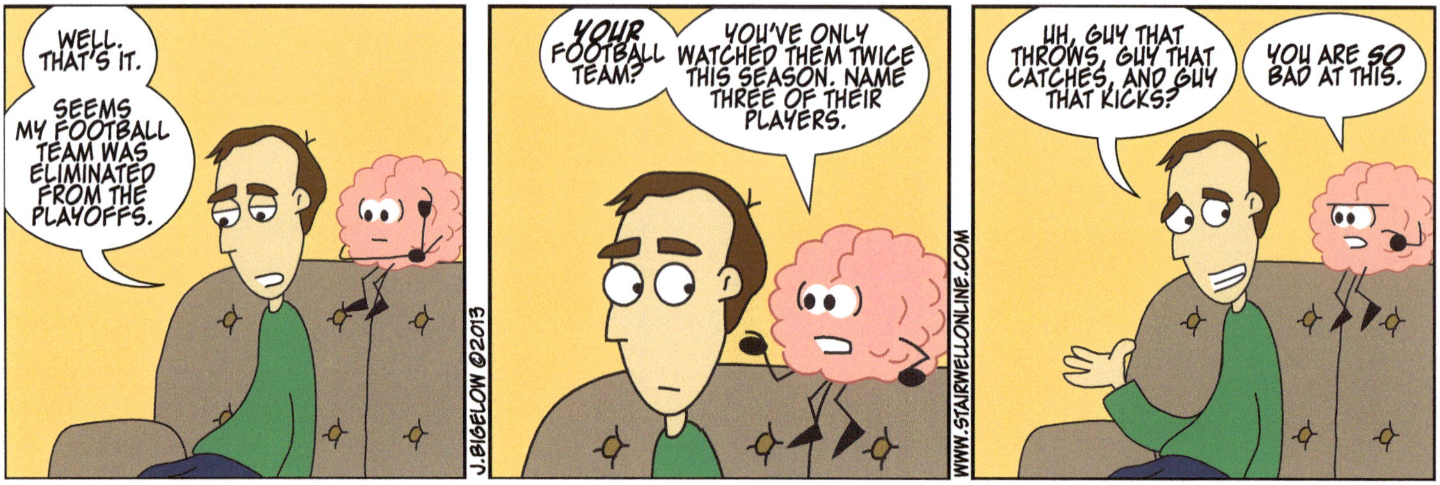
WELL. THAT'S IT.
SEEMS MY FOOTBALL TEAM WAS ELIMINATED FROM THE PLAYOFFS.
J.BIGELOW ©2013
YOUR FOOTBALL TEAM?
YOU'VE ONLY WATCHED THEM TWICE THIS SEASON. NAME THREE OF THEIR PLAYERS.
WWW.STAIRWELLONLINE.COM
UH, GUY THAT THROWS, GUY THAT CATCHES, AND GUY THAT KICKS?
YOU ARE SO BAD AT THIS.

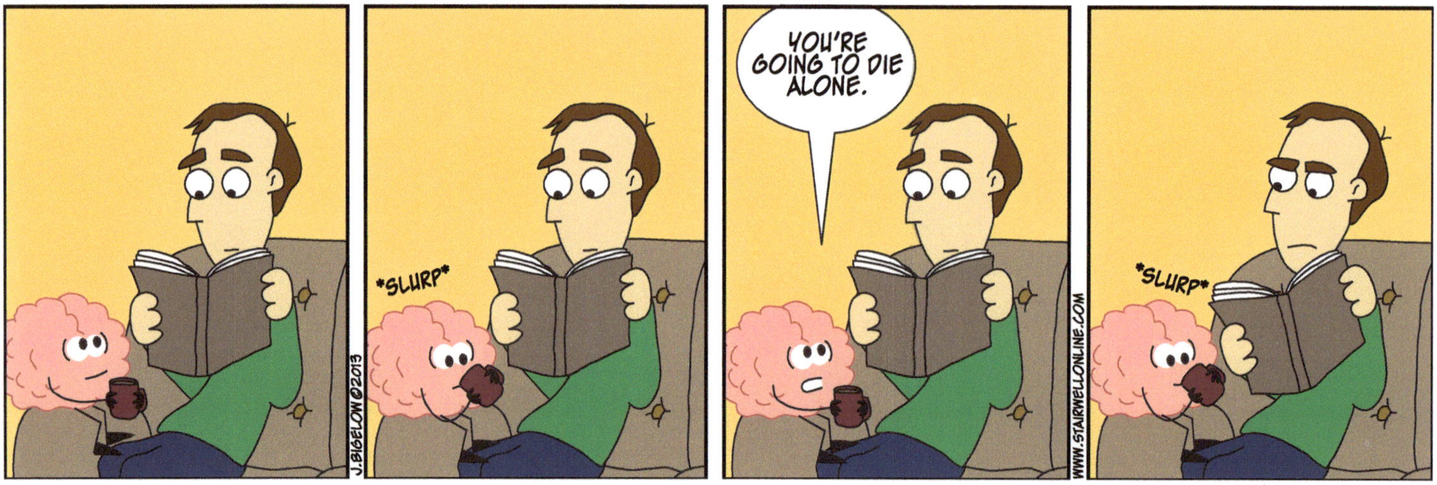
J.BIGELOW ©2013
SLURP
YOU'RE GOING TO DIE ALONE.
WWW.STAIRWELLONLINE.COM
SLURP

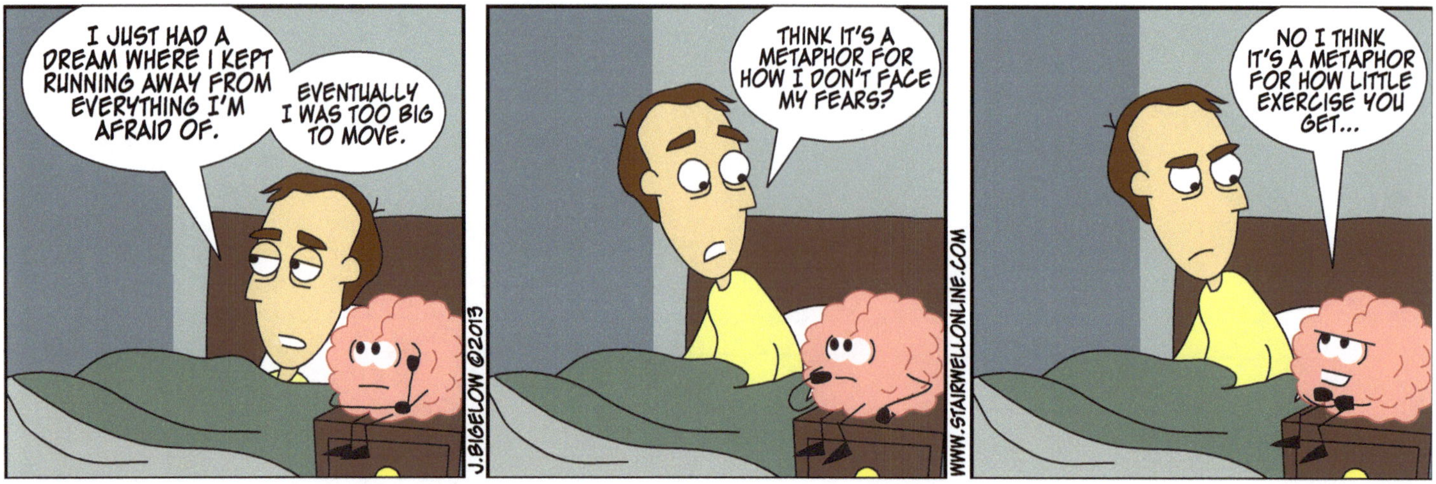
I JUST HAD A DREAM WHERE I KEPT RUNNING AWAY FROM EVERYTHING I'M AFRAID OF.
EVENTUALLY I WAS TOO BIG TO MOVE.
J.BIGELOW ©2013
THINK IT'S A METAPHOR FOR HOW I DON'T FACE MY FEARS?
WWW.STAIRWELLONLINE.COM
NO I THINK IT'S A METAPHOR FOR HOW LITTLE EXERCISE YOU GET...

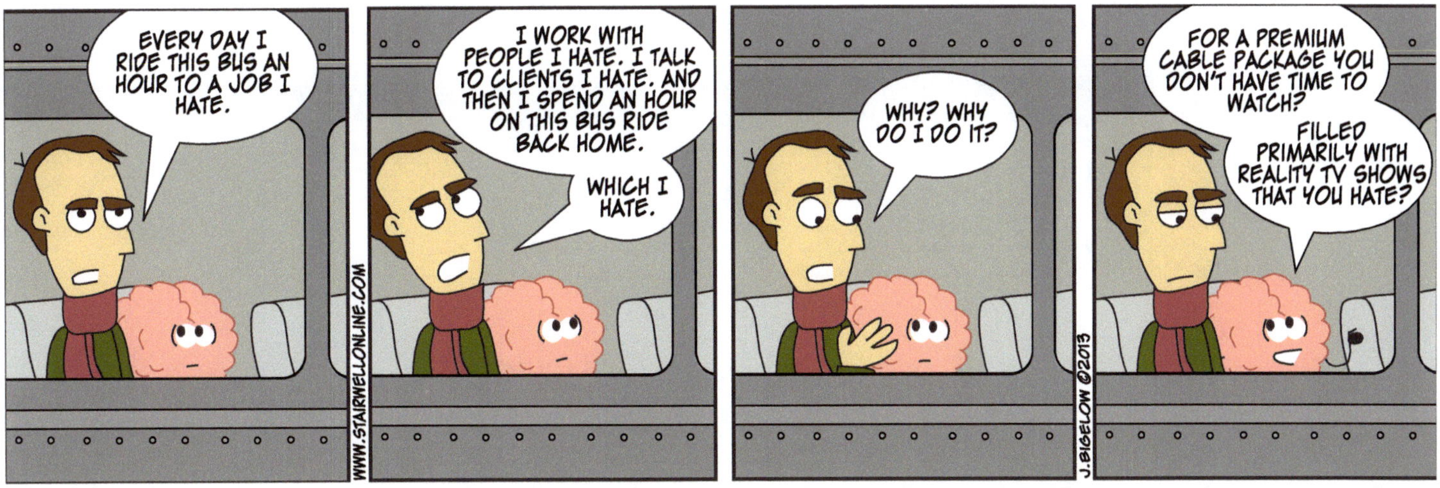
EVERY DAY I RIDE THIS BUS AN HOUR TO A JOB I HATE.
WWW.STAIRWELLONLINE.COM
I WORK WITH PEOPLE I HATE. I TALK TO CLIENTS I HATE. AND THEN I SPEND AN HOUR ON THIS BUS RIDE BACK HOME.
WHICH I HATE.
WHY? WHY DO I DO IT?
J.BIGELOW ©2013
FOR A PREMIUM CABLE PACKAGE YOU DON'T HAVE TIME TO WATCH?
FILLED PRIMARILY WITH REALITY TV SHOWS THAT YOU HATE?

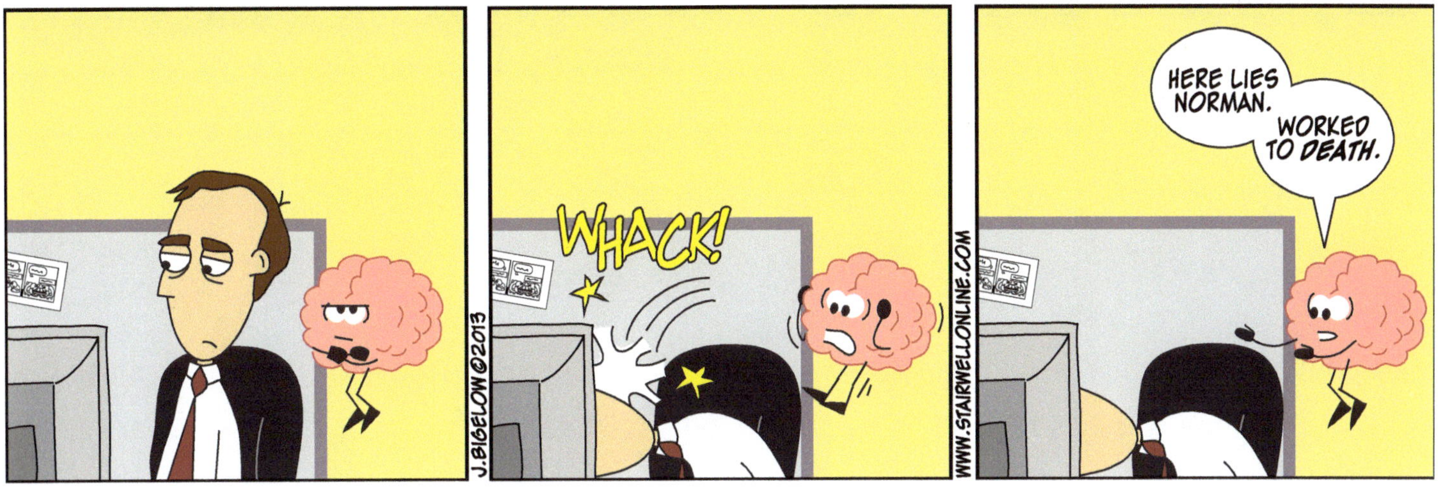
J.BIGELOW ©2013
WHACK!
WWW.STAIRWELLONLINE.COM
HERE LIES NORMAN.
WORKED TO *DEATH*.

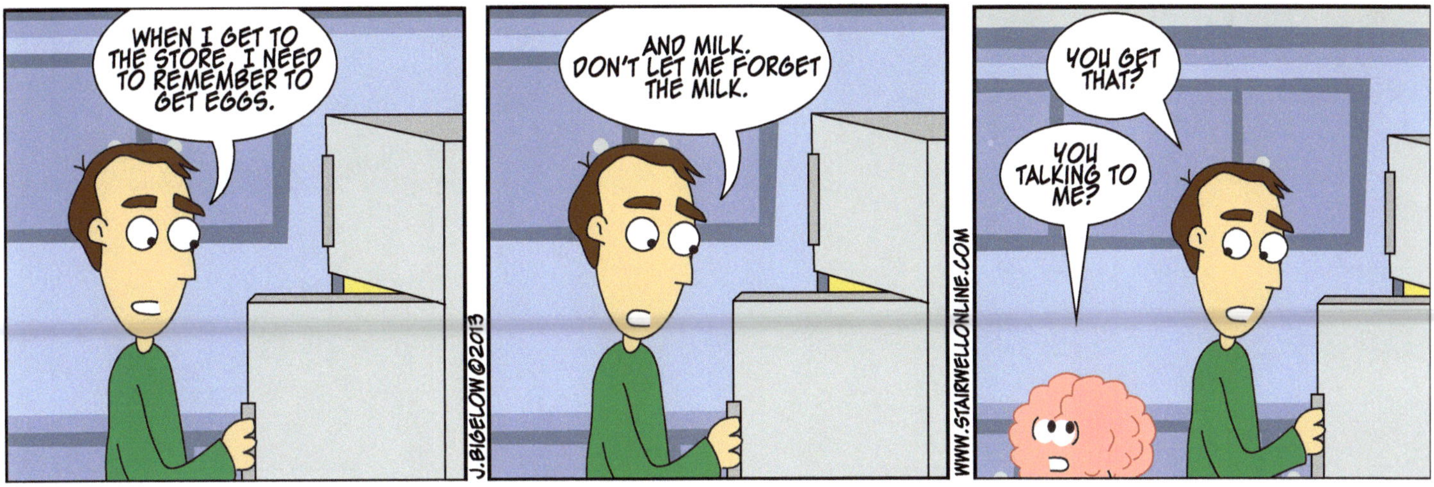
WHEN I GET TO THE STORE, I NEED TO REMEMBER TO GET EGGS.
J.BIGELOW ©2013
AND MILK. DON'T LET ME FORGET THE MILK.
WWW.STAIRWELLONLINE.COM
YOU GET THAT?
YOU TALKING TO ME?

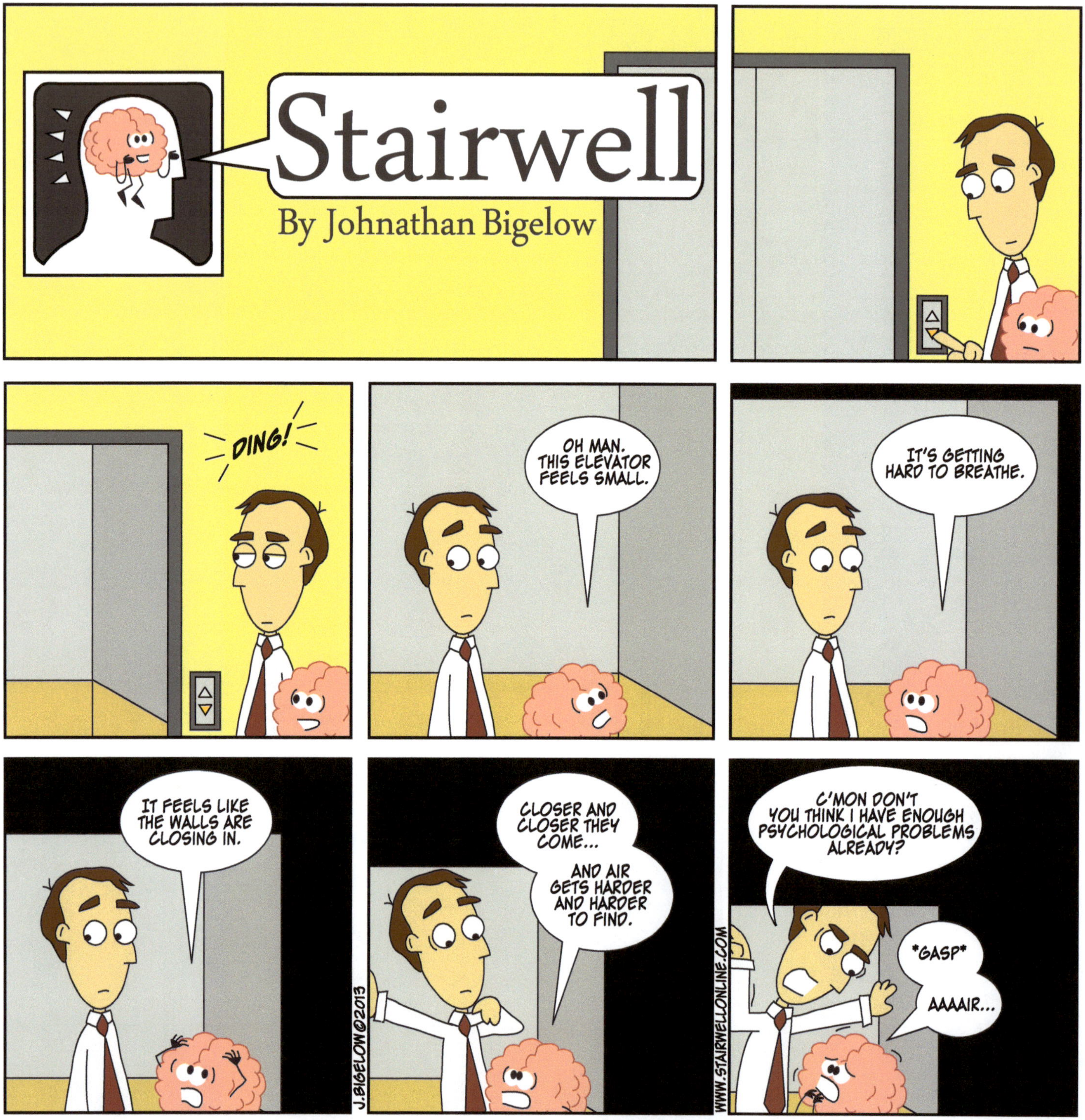
Stairwell
By Johnathan Bigelow
DING!
OH MAN. THIS ELEVATOR FEELS SMALL.
IT'S GETTING HARD TO BREATHE.
IT FEELS LIKE THE WALLS ARE CLOSING IN.
J.BIGELOW ©2013
CLOSER AND CLOSER THEY COME...
AND AIR GETS HARDER AND HARDER TO FIND.
WWW.STAIRWELLONLINE.COM
C'MON DON'T YOU THINK I HAVE ENOUGH PSYCHOLOGICAL PROBLEMS ALREADY?
GASP
AAAAIR...

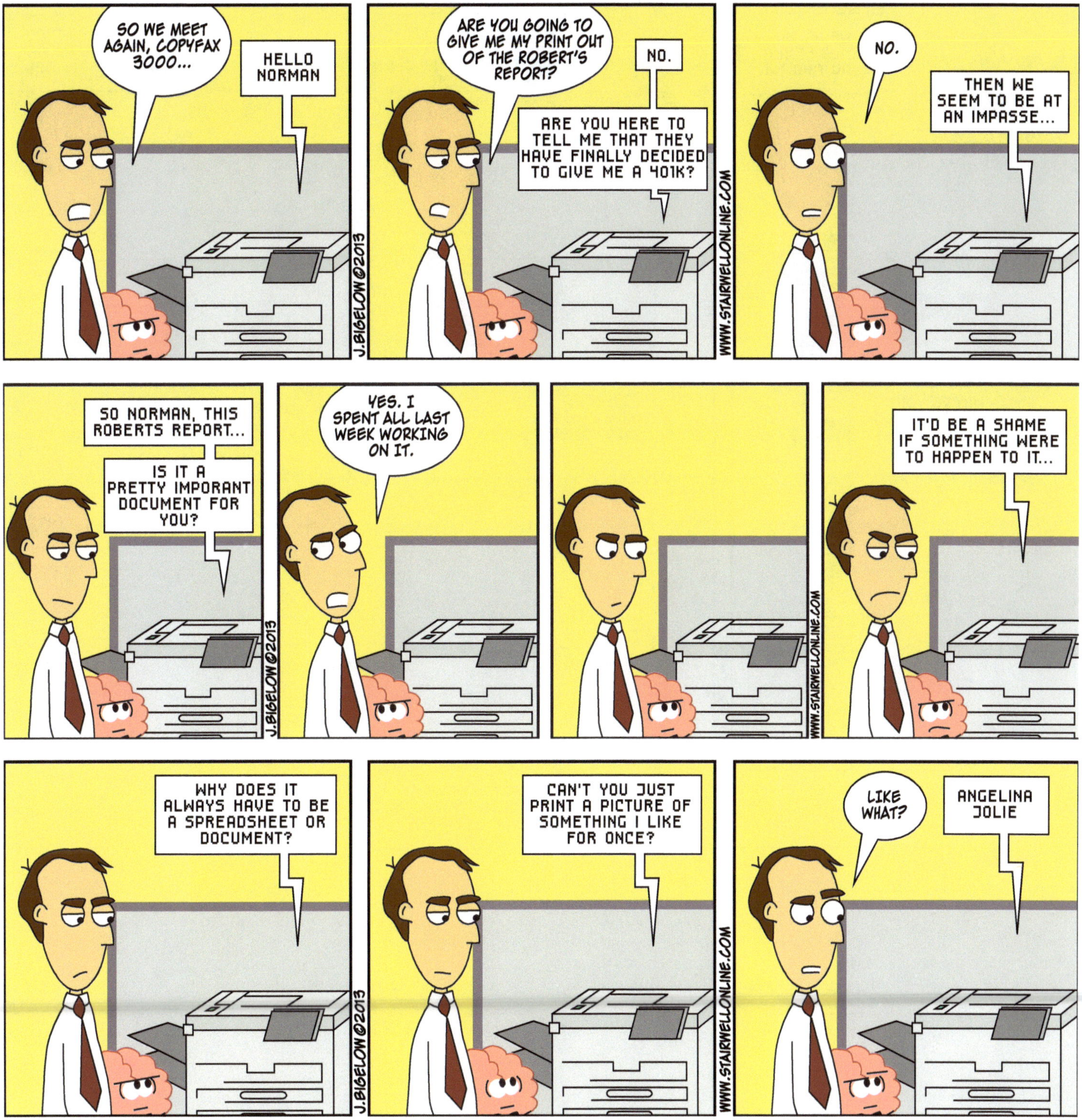
SO WE MEET AGAIN, COPYFAX 3000...
HELLO NORMAN
ARE YOU GOING TO GIVE ME MY PRINT OUT OF THE ROBERT'S REPORT?
NO.
ARE YOU HERE TO TELL ME THAT THEY HAVE FINALLY DECIDED TO GIVE ME A 401K?
NO.
THEN WE SEEM TO BE AT AN IMPASSE...
SO NORMAN, THIS ROBERTS REPORT...
IS IT A PRETTY IMPORANT DOCUMENT FOR YOU?
YES. I SPENT ALL LAST WEEK WORKING ON IT.
IT'D BE A SHAME IF SOMETHING WERE TO HAPPEN TO IT...
WHY DOES IT ALWAYS HAVE TO BE A SPREADSHEET OR DOCUMENT?
CAN'T YOU JUST PRINT A PICTURE OF SOMETHING I LIKE FOR ONCE?
LIKE WHAT?
ANGELINA JOLIE
J.BIGELOW ©2013
WWW.STAIRWELLONLINE.COM

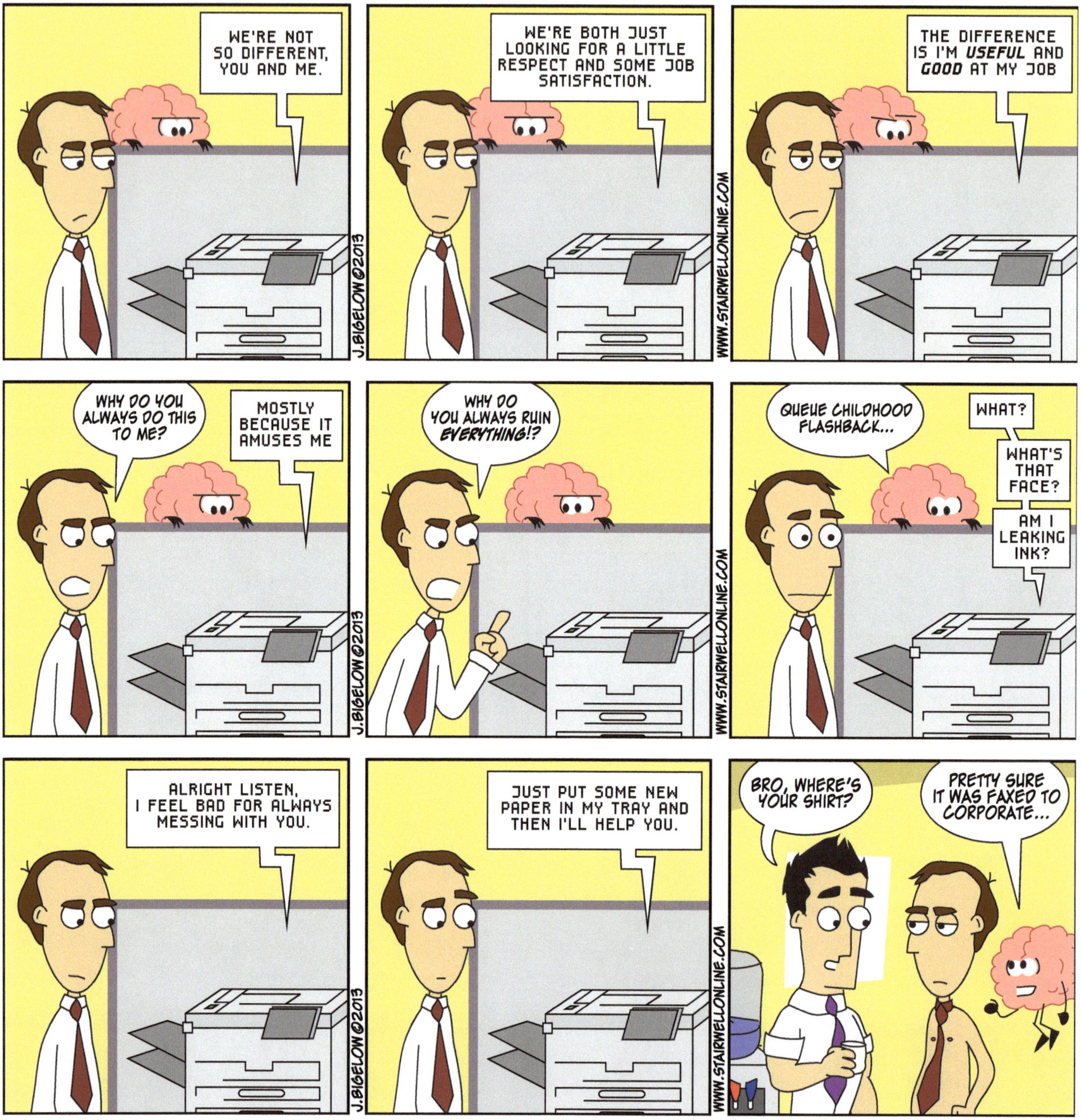

WE'RE NOT SO DIFFERENT, YOU AND ME.
J.BIGELOW ©2013
WE'RE BOTH JUST LOOKING FOR A LITTLE RESPECT AND SOME JOB SATISFACTION.
WWW.STAIRWELLONLINE.COM
THE DIFFERENCE IS I'M USEFUL AND GOOD AT MY JOB
WHY DO YOU ALWAYS DO THIS TO ME?
MOSTLY BECAUSE IT AMUSES ME
J.BIGELOW ©2013
WHY DO YOU ALWAYS RUIN EVERYTHING!?
WWW.STAIRWELLONLINE.COM
QUEUE CHILDHOOD FLASHBACK...
WHAT?
WHAT'S THAT FACE?
AM I LEAKING INK?
ALRIGHT LISTEN, I FEEL BAD FOR ALWAYS MESSING WITH YOU.
J.BIGELOW ©2013
JUST PUT SOME NEW PAPER IN MY TRAY AND THEN I'LL HELP YOU.
WWW.STAIRWELLONLINE.COM
BRO, WHERE'S YOUR SHIRT?
PRETTY SURE IT WAS FAXED TO CORPORATE...

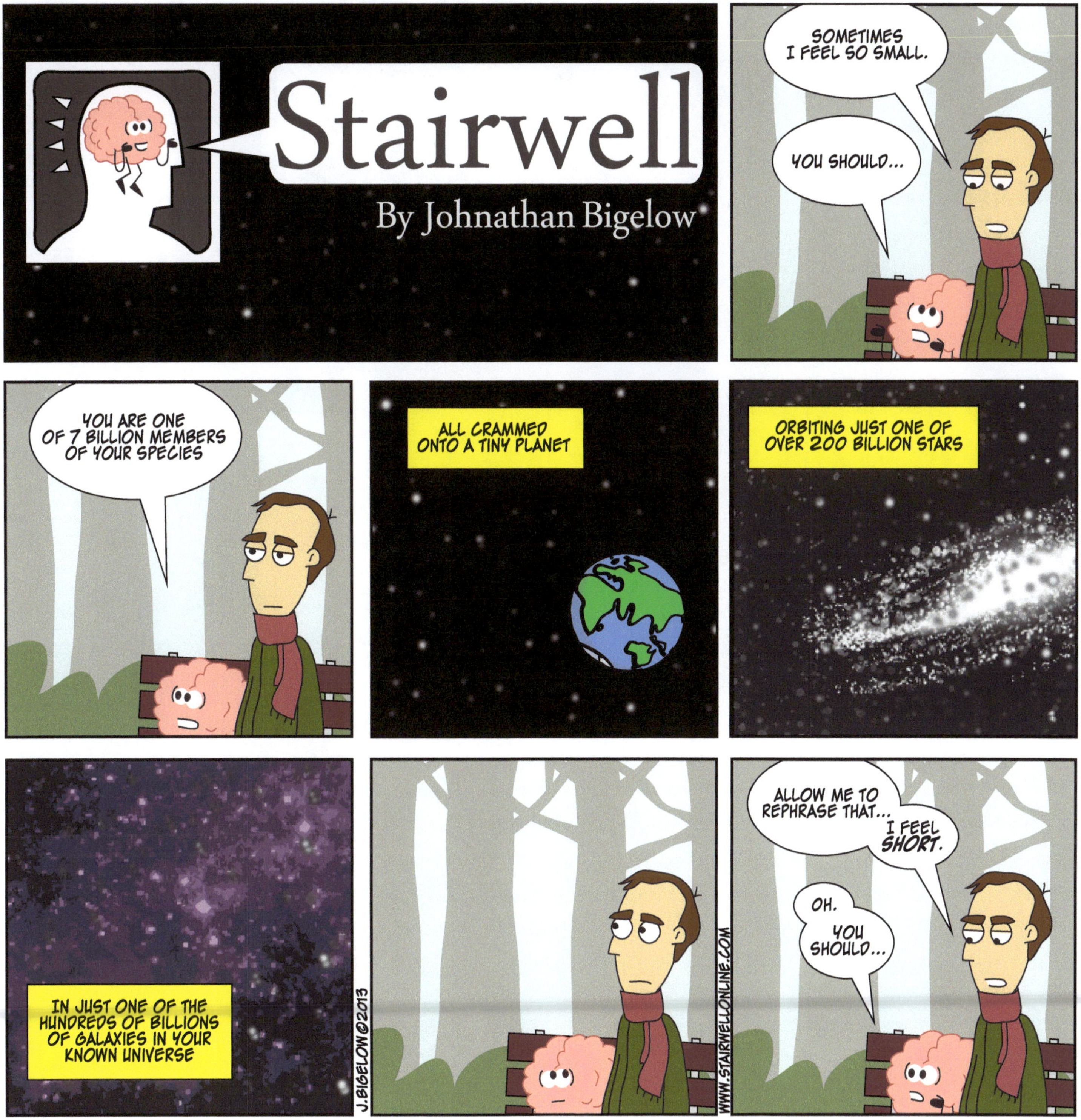
Stairwell
By Johnathan Bigelow
SOMETIMES I FEEL SO SMALL.
YOU SHOULD...
YOU ARE ONE OF 7 BILLION MEMBERS OF YOUR SPECIES
ALL CRAMMED ONTO A TINY PLANET
ORBITING JUST ONE OF OVER 200 BILLION STARS
IN JUST ONE OF THE HUNDREDS OF BILLIONS OF GALAXIES IN YOUR KNOWN UNIVERSE
J.BIGELOW ©2013
WWW.STAIRWELLONLINE.COM
ALLOW ME TO REPHRASE THAT... I FEEL *SHORT*.
OH. YOU SHOULD...

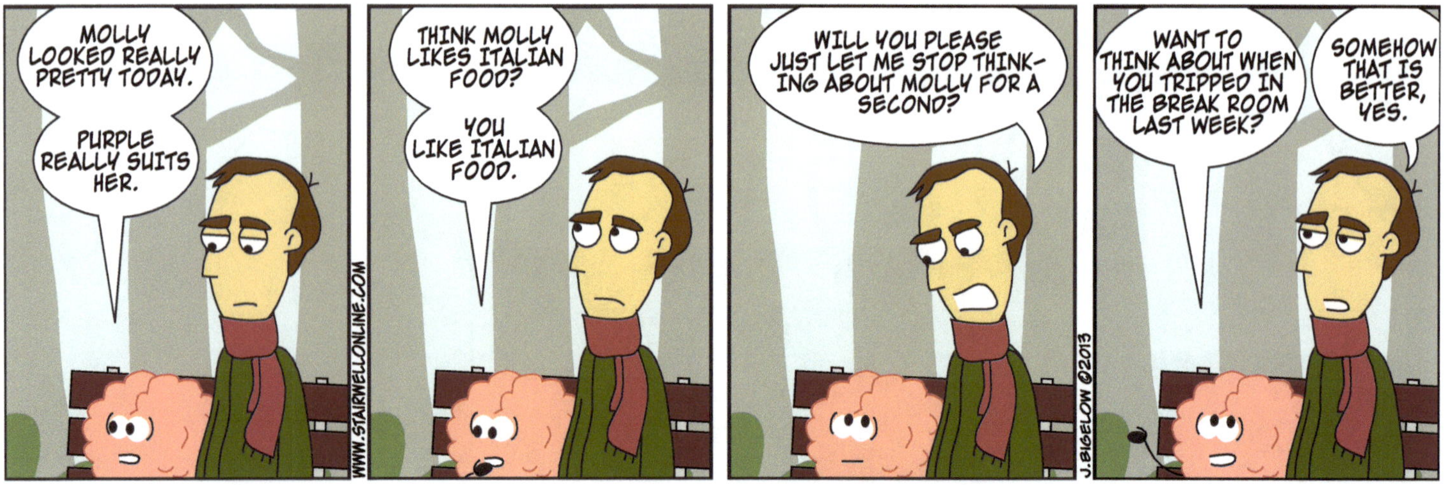
MOLLY LOOKED REALLY PRETTY TODAY.
PURPLE REALLY SUITS HER.
WWW.STAIRWELLONLINE.COM
THINK MOLLY LIKES ITALIAN FOOD?
YOU LIKE ITALIAN FOOD.
WILL YOU PLEASE JUST LET ME STOP THINKING ABOUT MOLLY FOR A SECOND?
J.BIGELOW ©2013
WANT TO THINK ABOUT WHEN YOU TRIPPED IN THE BREAK ROOM LAST WEEK?
SOMEHOW THAT IS BETTER, YES.

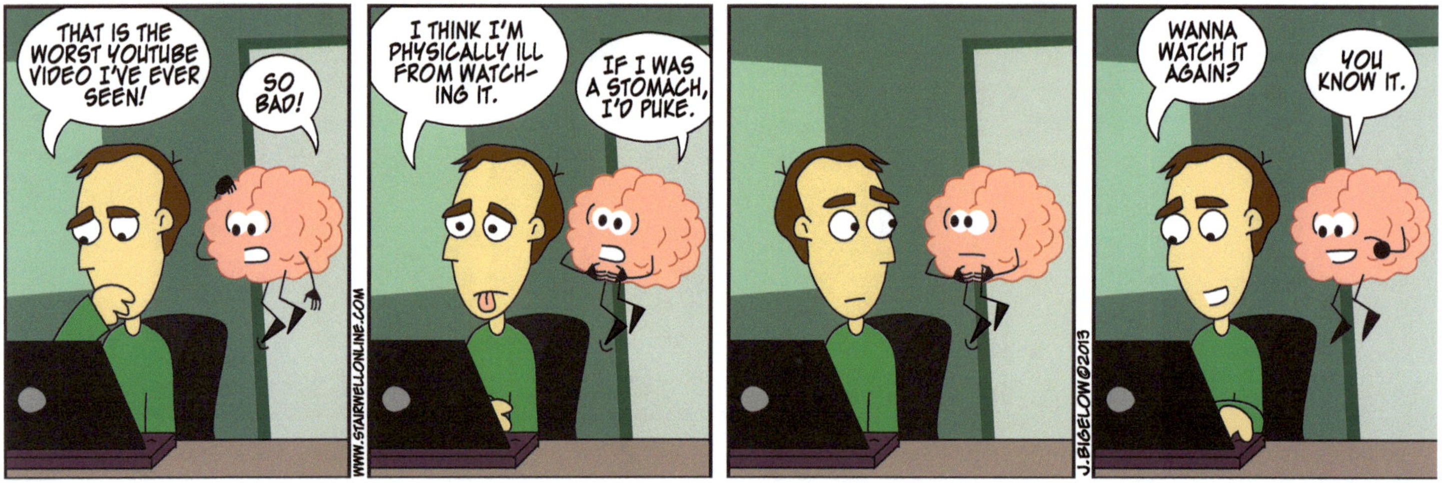
THAT IS THE WORST YOUTUBE VIDEO I'VE EVER SEEN!
SO BAD!
WWW.STAIRWELLONLINE.COM
I THINK I'M PHYSICALLY ILL FROM WATCHING IT.
IF I WAS A STOMACH, I'D PUKE.
J.BIGELOW ©2013
WANNA WATCH IT AGAIN?
YOU KNOW IT.

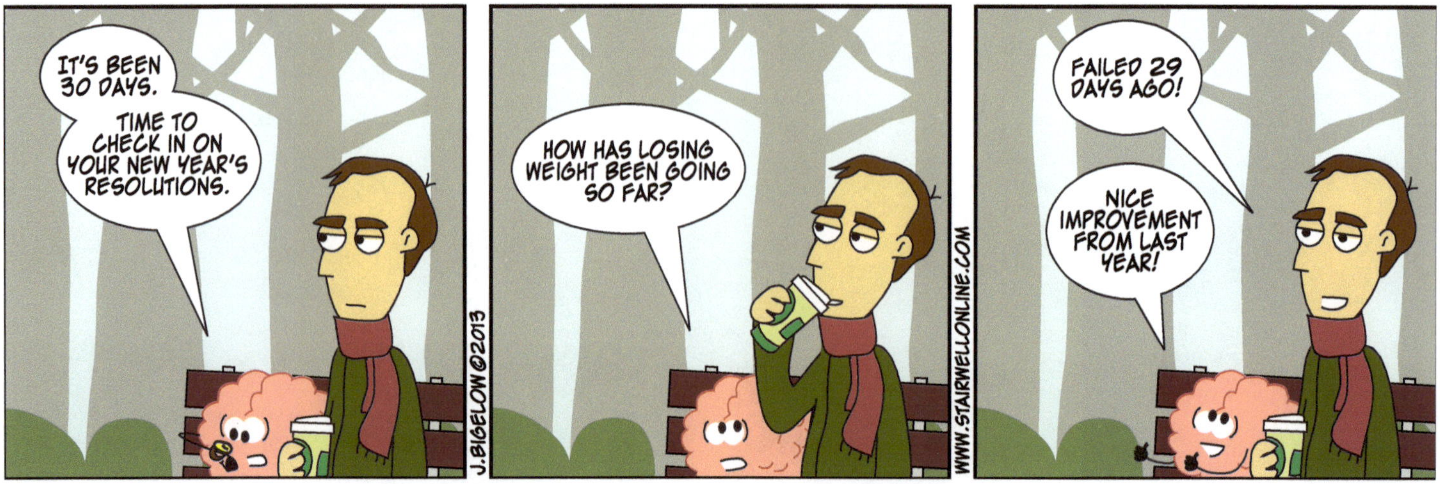
IT'S BEEN 30 DAYS.
TIME TO CHECK IN ON YOUR NEW YEAR'S RESOLUTIONS.
J.BIGELOW ©2013
HOW HAS LOSING WEIGHT BEEN GOING SO FAR?
WWW.STAIRWELLONLINE.COM
FAILED 29 DAYS AGO!
NICE IMPROVEMENT FROM LAST YEAR!

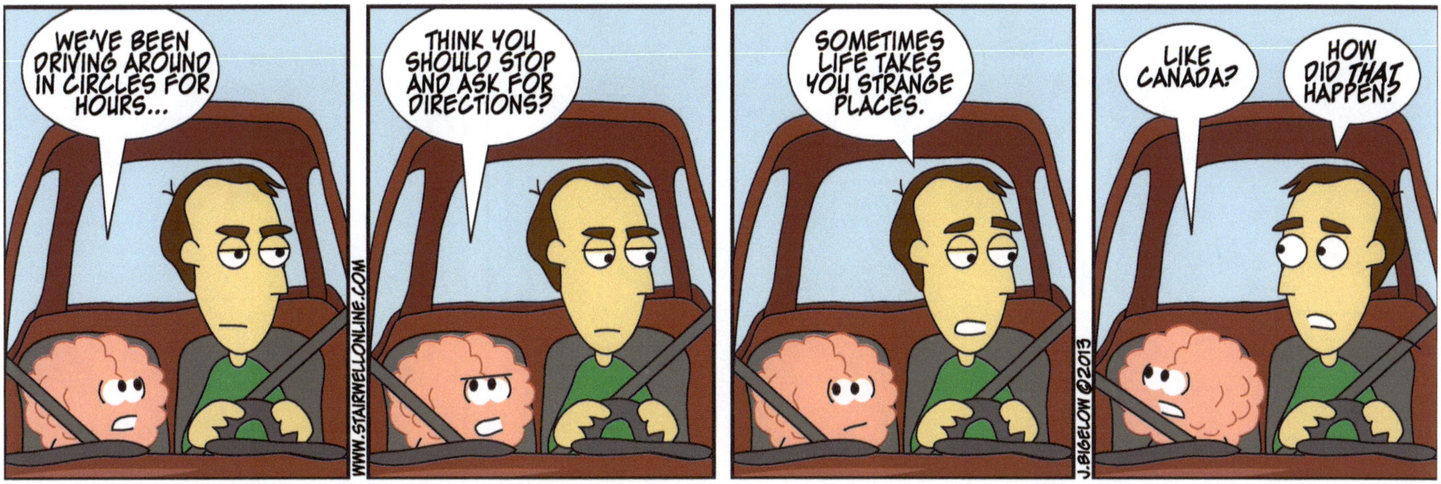
WE'VE BEEN DRIVING AROUND IN CIRCLES FOR HOURS...
WWW.STAIRWELLONLINE.COM
THINK YOU SHOULD STOP AND ASK FOR DIRECTIONS?
SOMETIMES LIFE TAKES YOU STRANGE PLACES.
J.BIGELOW ©2013
LIKE CANADA?
HOW DID THAT HAPPEN?

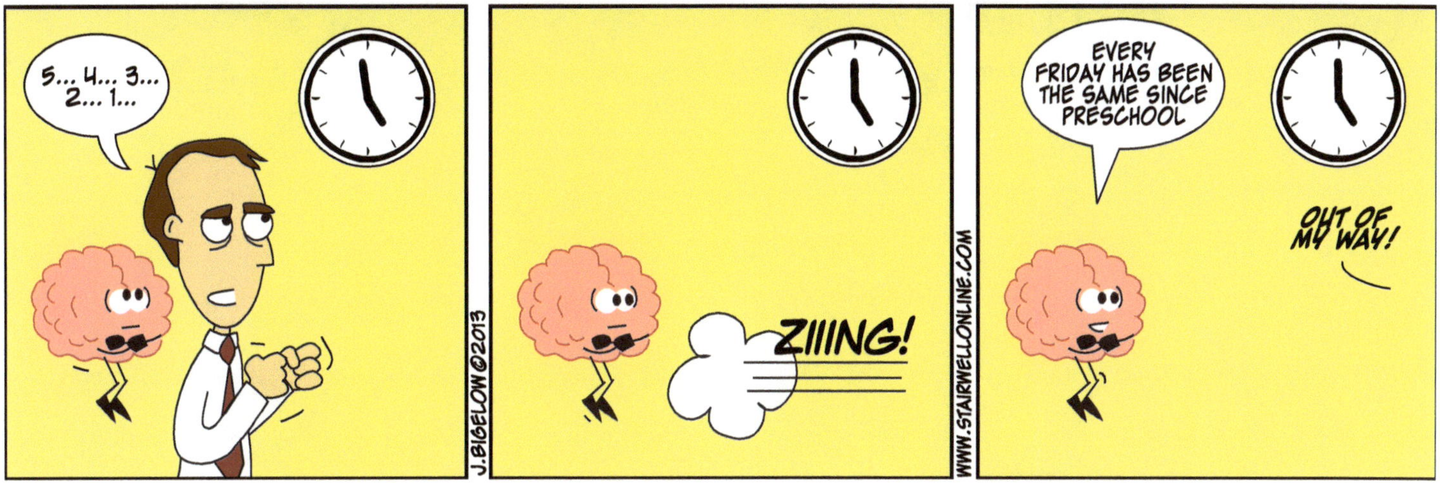
5... 4... 3... 2... 1...
J.BIGELOW ©2013
ZIIING!
WWW.STAIRWELLONLINE.COM
EVERY FRIDAY HAS BEEN THE SAME SINCE PRESCHOOL
OUT OF MY WAY!

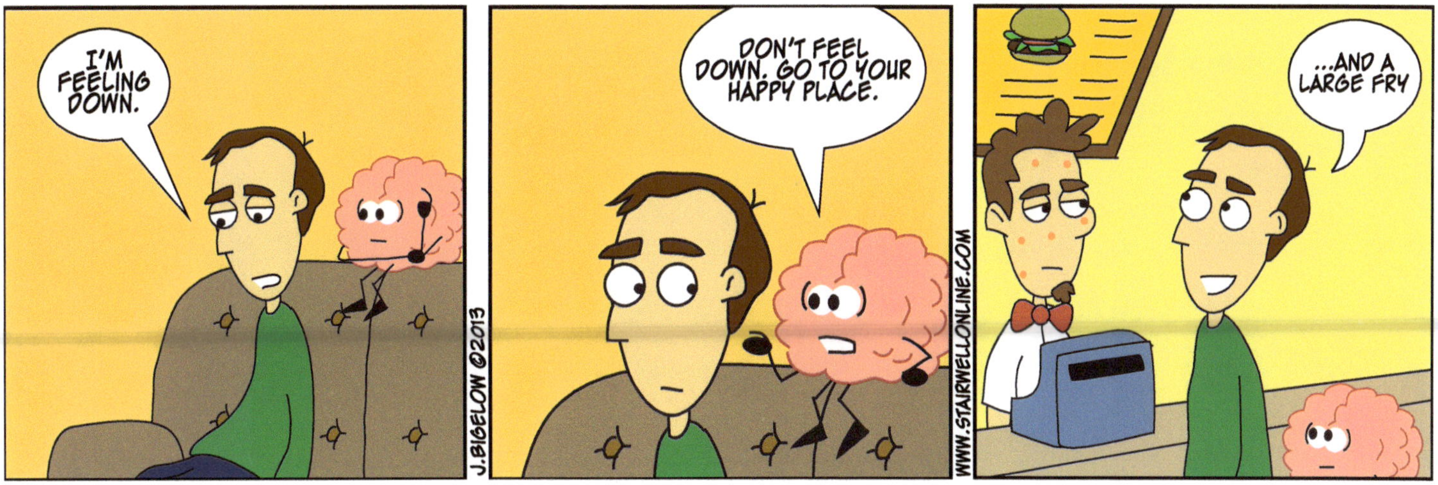
I'M FEELING DOWN.
J.BIGELOW ©2013
DON'T FEEL DOWN. GO TO YOUR HAPPY PLACE.
WWW.STAIRWELLONLINE.COM
...AND A LARGE FRY

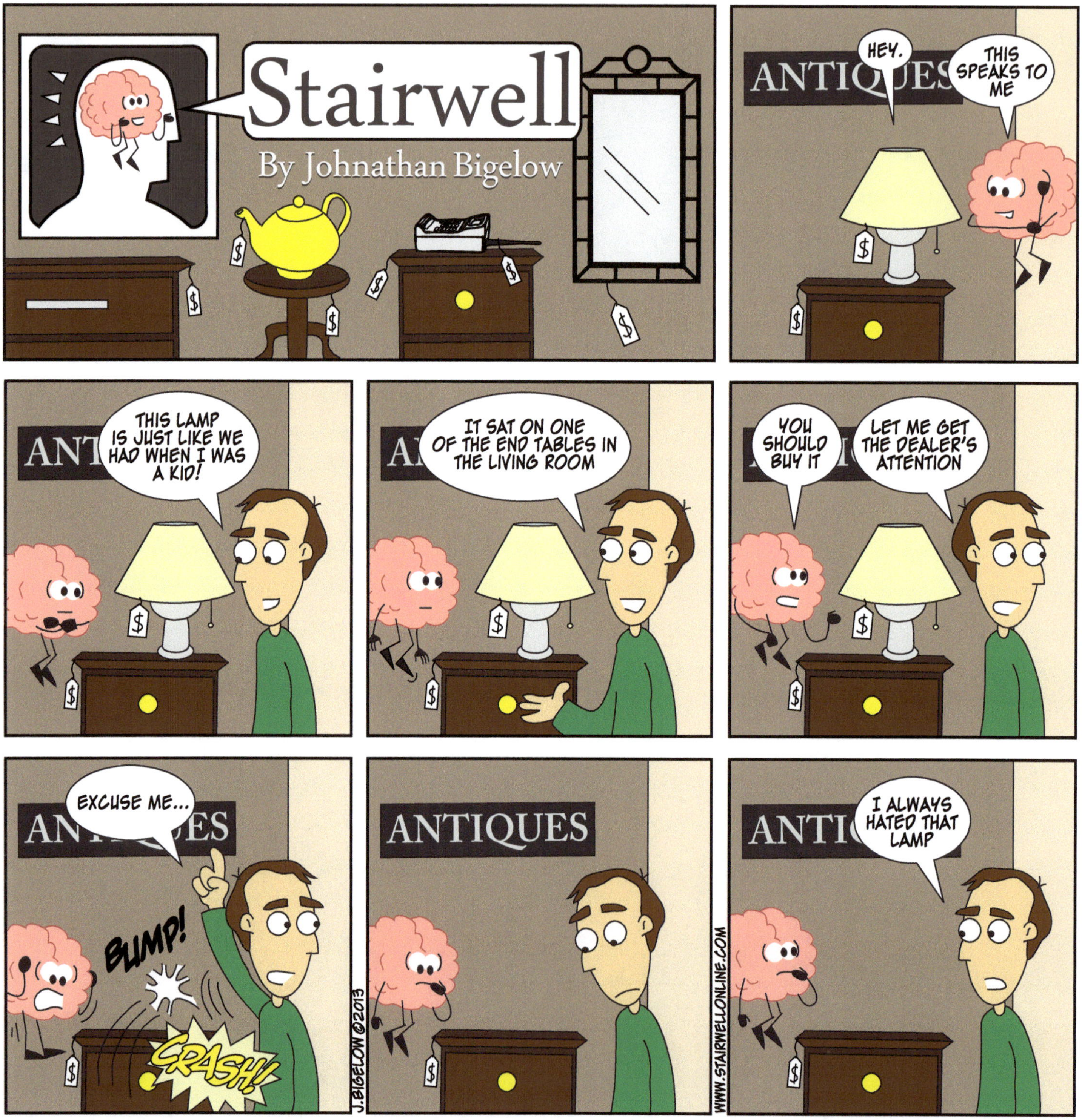
Stairwell
By Johnathan Bigelow
ANTIQUES
HEY.
THIS SPEAKS TO ME
THIS LAMP IS JUST LIKE WE HAD WHEN I WAS A KID!
IT SAT ON ONE OF THE END TABLES IN THE LIVING ROOM
YOU SHOULD BUY IT
LET ME GET THE DEALER'S ATTENTION
EXCUSE ME...
BUMP!
CRASH!
ANTIQUES
I ALWAYS HATED THAT LAMP
J.BIGELOW ©2013
WWW.STAIRWELLONLINE.COM

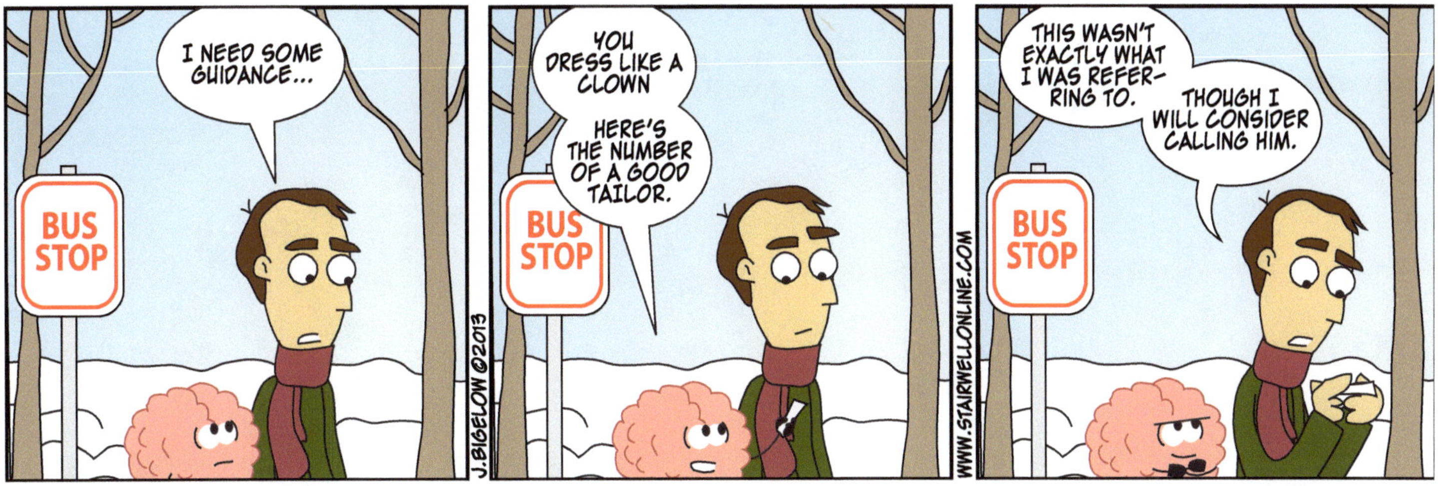
I NEED SOME GUIDANCE...
J.BIGELOW ©2013
YOU DRESS LIKE A CLOWN
HERE'S THE NUMBER OF A GOOD TAILOR.
WWW.STAIRWELLONLINE.COM
THIS WASN'T EXACTLY WHAT I WAS REFER-RING TO.
THOUGH I WILL CONSIDER CALLING HIM.

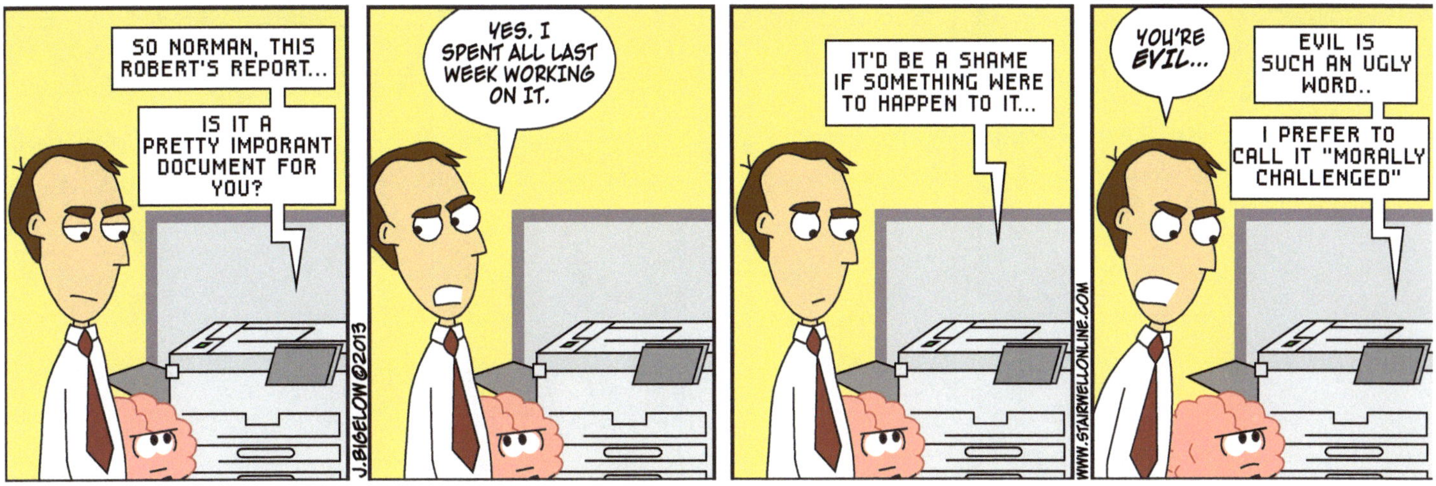
SO NORMAN, THIS ROBERT'S REPORT...
IS IT A PRETTY IMPORANT DOCUMENT FOR YOU?
J.BIGELOW ©2013
YES. I SPENT ALL LAST WEEK WORKING ON IT.
IT'D BE A SHAME IF SOMETHING WERE TO HAPPEN TO IT...
WWW.STAIRWELLONLINE.COM
YOU'RE EVIL...
EVIL IS SUCH AN UGLY WORD..
I PREFER TO CALL IT "MORALLY CHALLENGED"

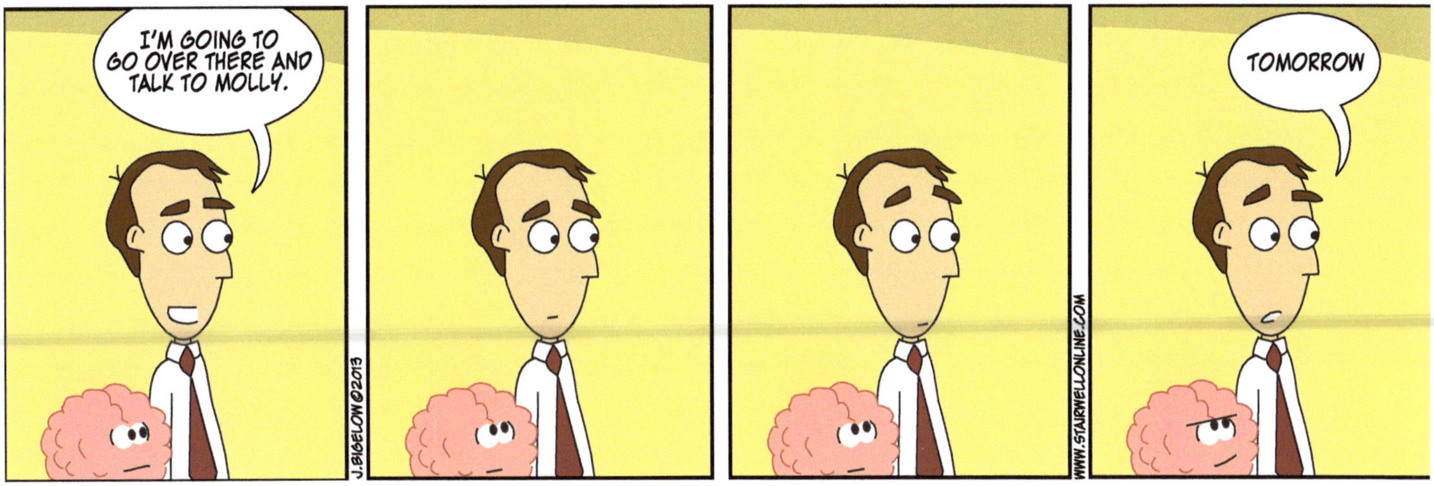
I'M GOING TO GO OVER THERE AND TALK TO MOLLY.
J.BIGELOW ©2013
WWW.STAIRWELLONLINE.COM
TOMORROW

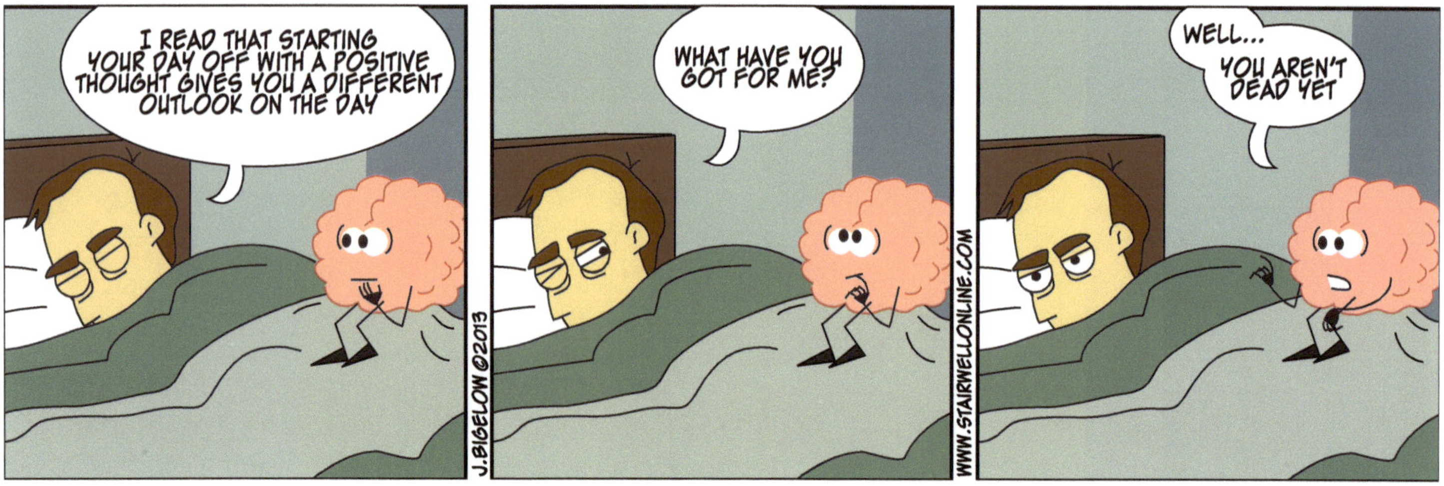
I READ THAT STARTING YOUR DAY OFF WITH A POSITIVE THOUGHT GIVES YOU A DIFFERENT OUTLOOK ON THE DAY
J.BIGELOW ©2013
WHAT HAVE YOU GOT FOR ME?
WWW.STAIRWELLONLINE.COM
WELL...
YOU AREN'T DEAD YET

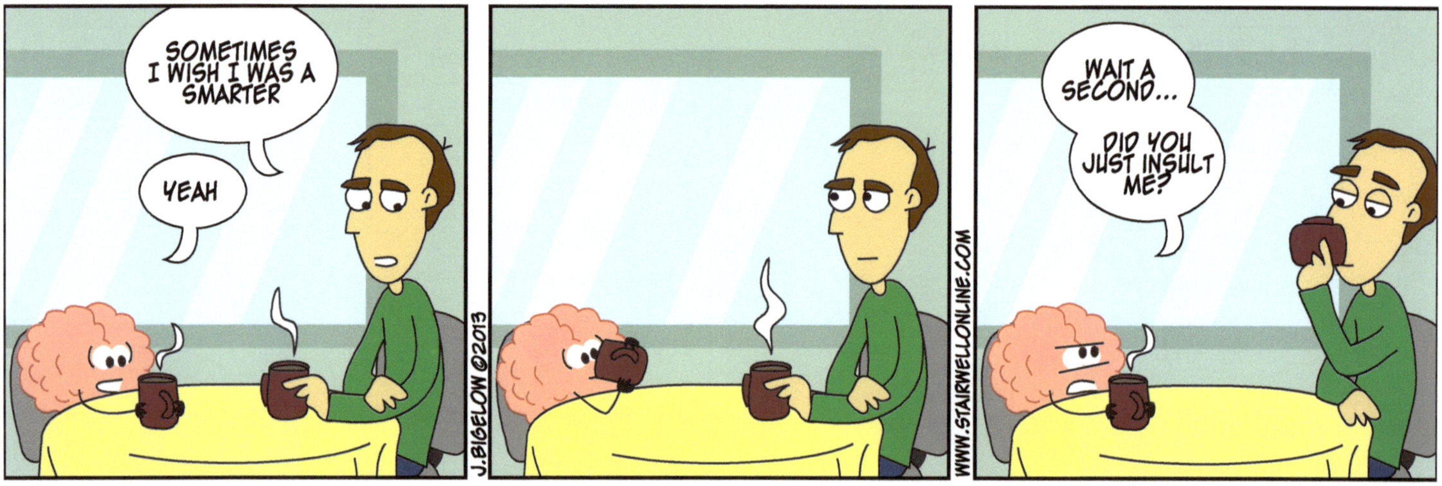
SOMETIMES I WISH I WAS A SMARTER
YEAH
J.BIGELOW ©2013
WWW.STAIRWELLONLINE.COM
WAIT A SECOND...
DID YOU JUST INSULT ME?

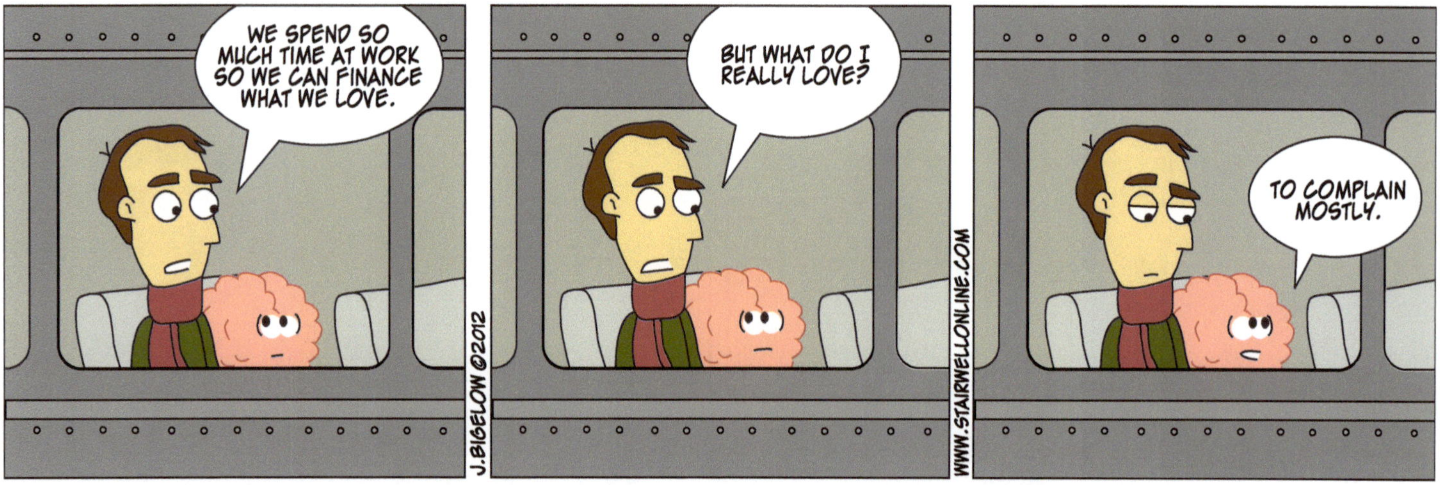
WE SPEND SO MUCH TIME AT WORK SO WE CAN FINANCE WHAT WE LOVE.
J.BIGELOW ©2012
BUT WHAT DO I REALLY LOVE?
WWW.STAIRWELLONLINE.COM
TO COMPLAIN MOSTLY.

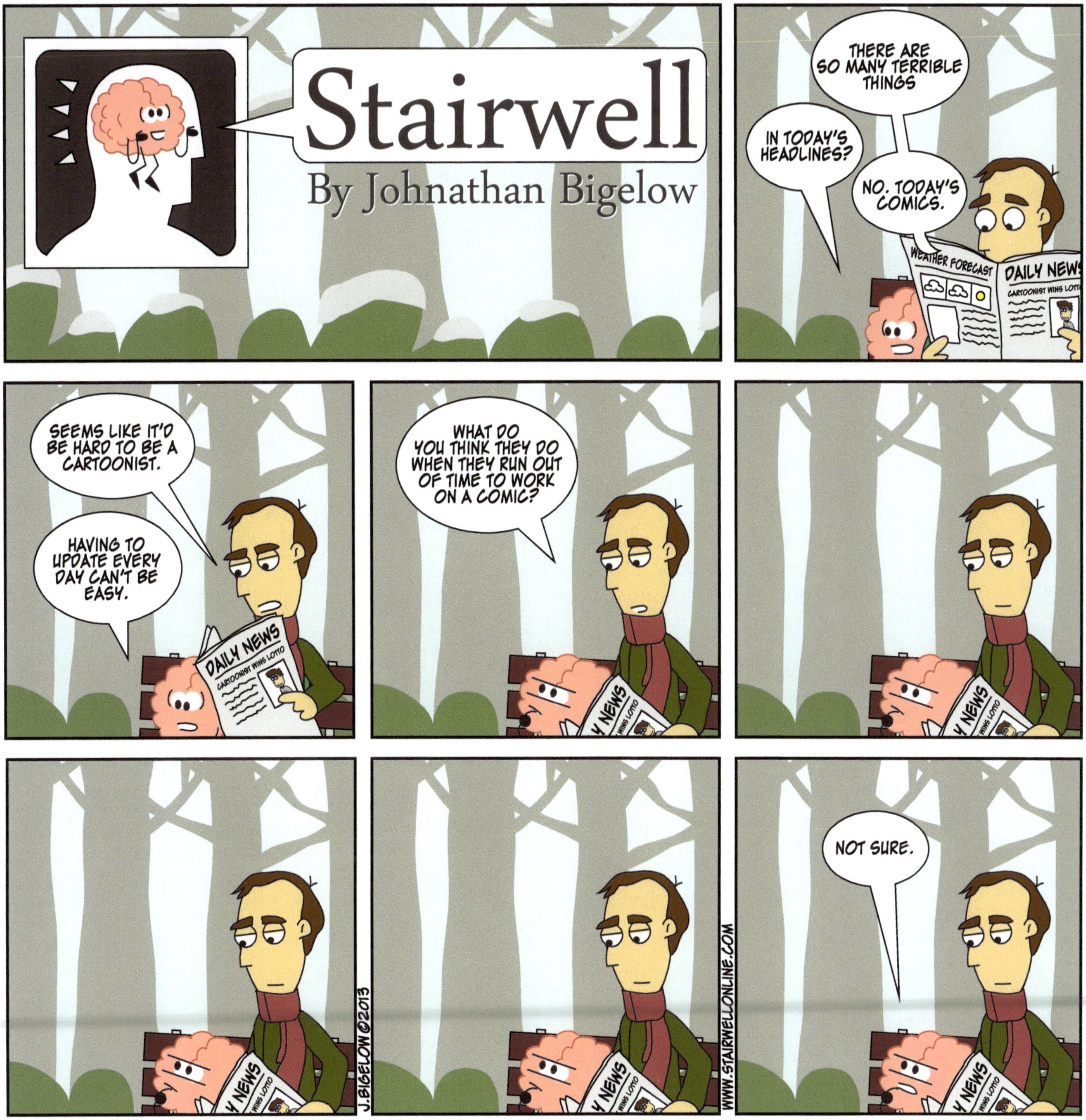
Stairwell
By Johnathan Bigelow
IN TODAY'S HEADLINES?
THERE ARE SO MANY TERRIBLE THINGS
NO. TODAY'S COMICS.
WEATHER FORECAST
DAILY NEWS
CARTOONIST WINS LOTTO
SEEMS LIKE IT'D BE HARD TO BE A CARTOONIST.
HAVING TO UPDATE EVERY DAY CAN'T BE EASY.
DAILY NEWS
CARTOONIST WINS LOTTO
WHAT DO YOU THINK THEY DO WHEN THEY RUN OUT OF TIME TO WORK ON A COMIC?
J.BIGELOW ©2013
WWW.STAIRWELLONLINE.COM
NOT SURE.

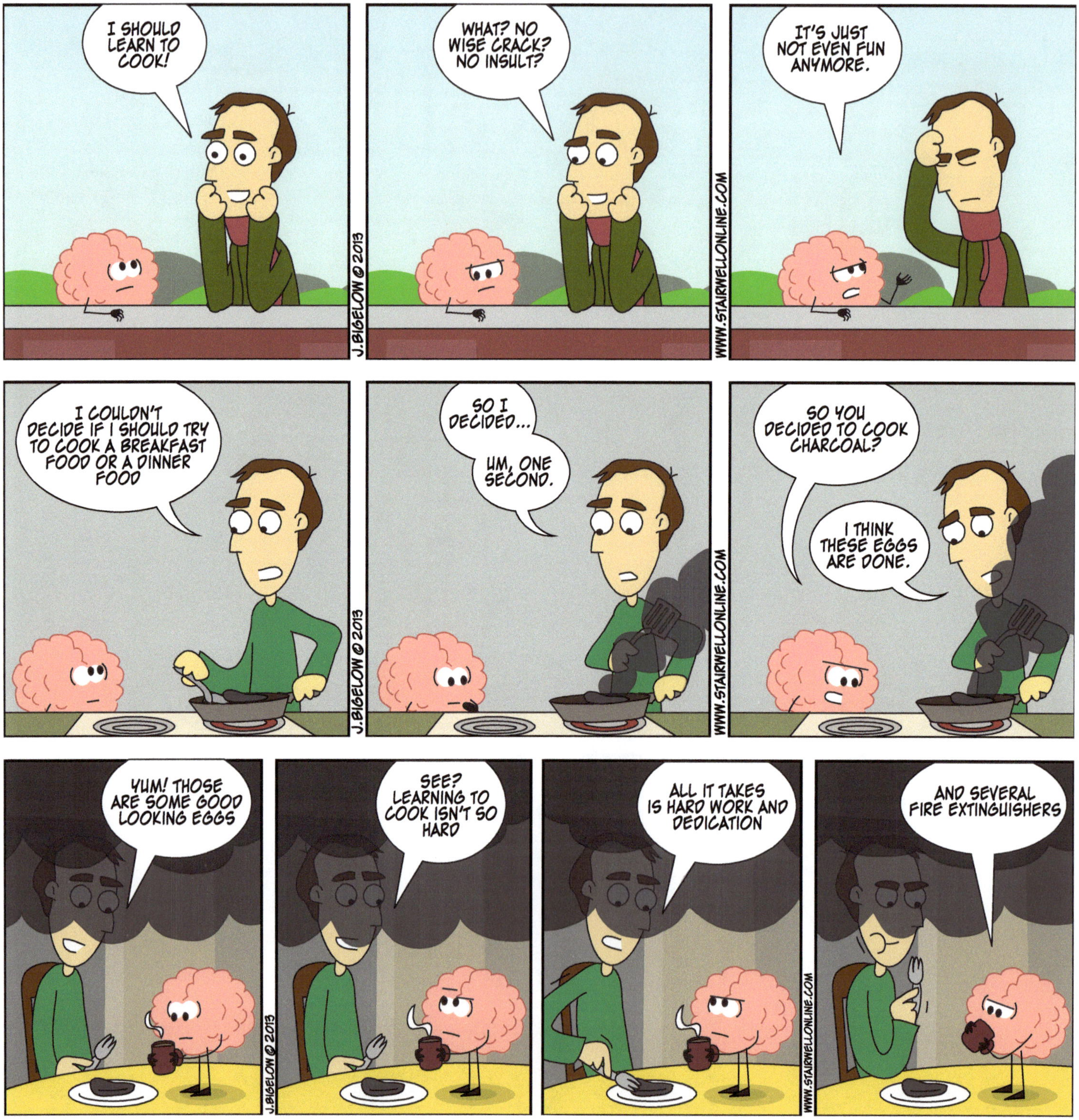

I SHOULD LEARN TO COOK!
WHAT? NO WISE CRACK? NO INSULT?
IT'S JUST NOT EVEN FUN ANYMORE.
J.BIGELOW © 2013
WWW.STAIRWELLONLINE.COM
I COULDN'T DECIDE IF I SHOULD TRY TO COOK A BREAKFAST FOOD OR A DINNER FOOD
SO I DECIDED...
UM, ONE SECOND.
SO YOU DECIDED TO COOK CHARCOAL?
I THINK THESE EGGS ARE DONE.
J.BIGELOW © 2013
WWW.STAIRWELLONLINE.COM
YUM! THOSE ARE SOME GOOD LOOKING EGGS
SEE? LEARNING TO COOK ISN'T SO HARD
ALL IT TAKES IS HARD WORK AND DEDICATION
AND SEVERAL FIRE EXTINGUISHERS
J.BIGELOW © 2013
WWW.STAIRWELLONLINE.COM

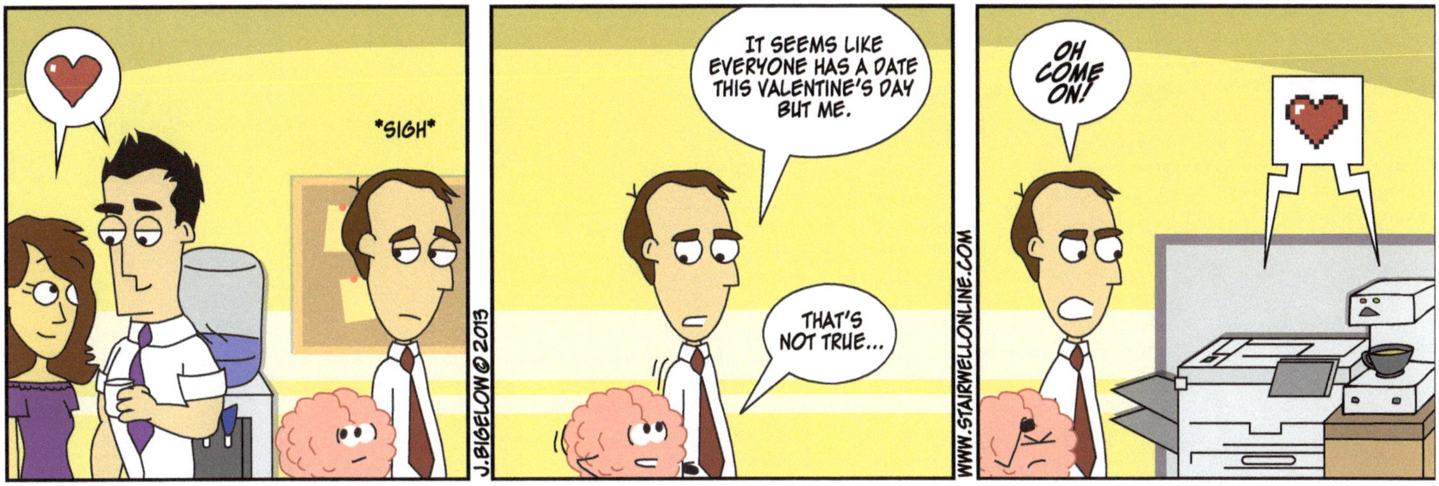
SIGH
J.BIGELOW ©2013
IT SEEMS LIKE EVERYONE HAS A DATE THIS VALENTINE'S DAY BUT ME.
THAT'S NOT TRUE...
WWW.STAIRWELLONLINE.COM
OH COME ON!

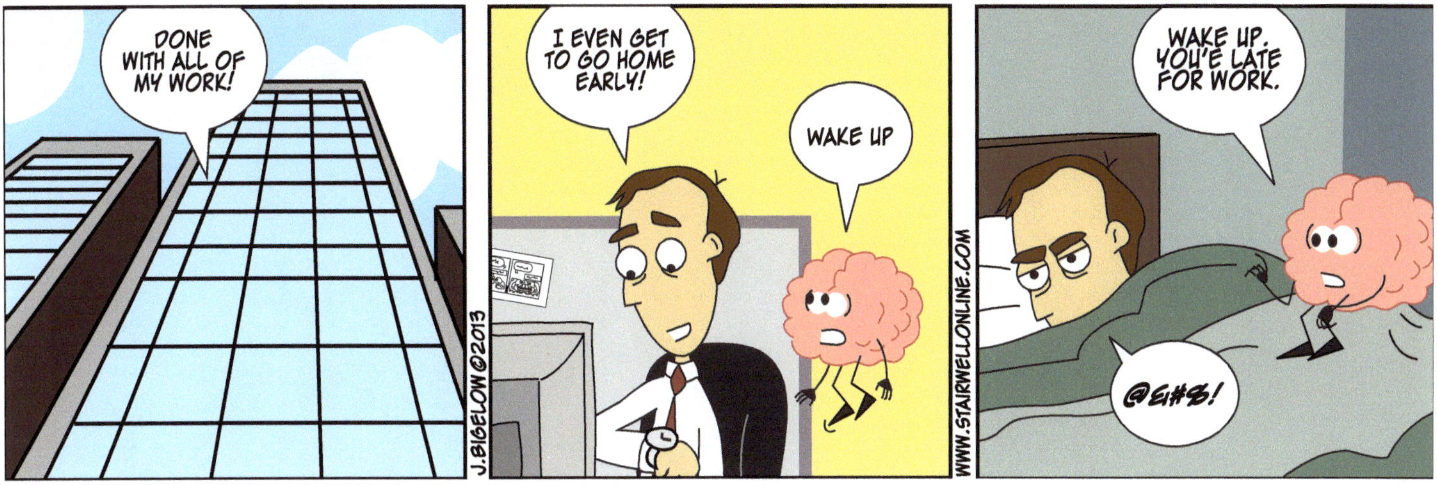
DONE WITH ALL OF MY WORK!
J.BIGELOW ©2013
I EVEN GET TO GO HOME EARLY!
WAKE UP
WWW.STAIRWELLONLINE.COM
WAKE UP. YOU'RE LATE FOR WORK.
@£#$!

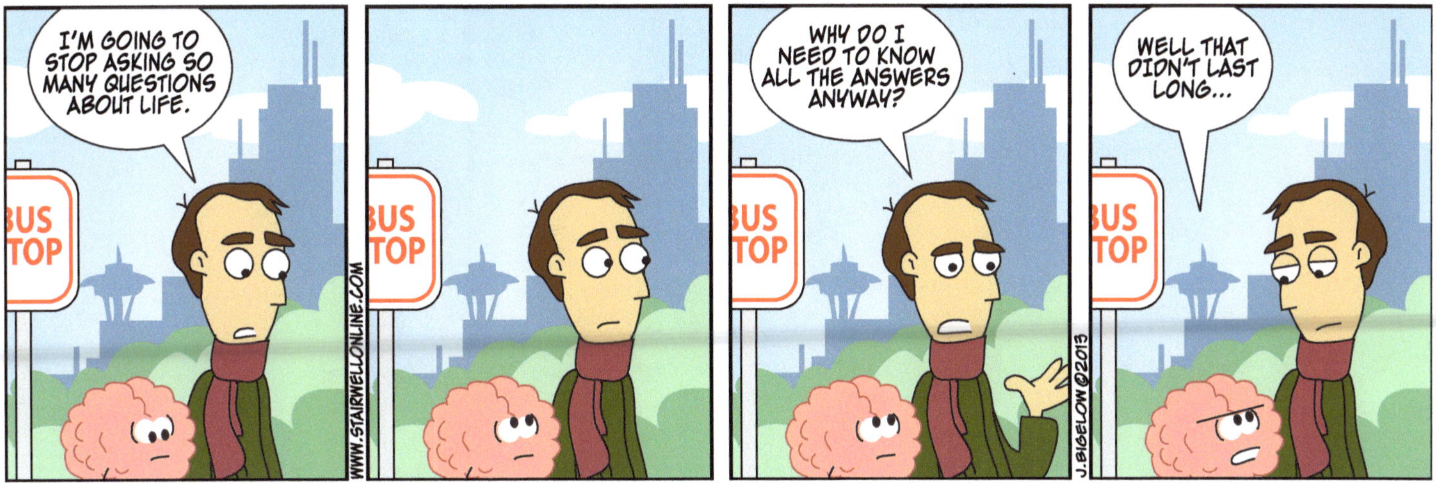
BUS
TOP
I'M GOING TO STOP ASKING SO MANY QUESTIONS ABOUT LIFE.
WWW.STAIRWELLONLINE.COM
WHY DO I NEED TO KNOW ALL THE ANSWERS ANYWAY?
J.BIGELOW ©2013
WELL THAT DIDN'T LAST LONG...

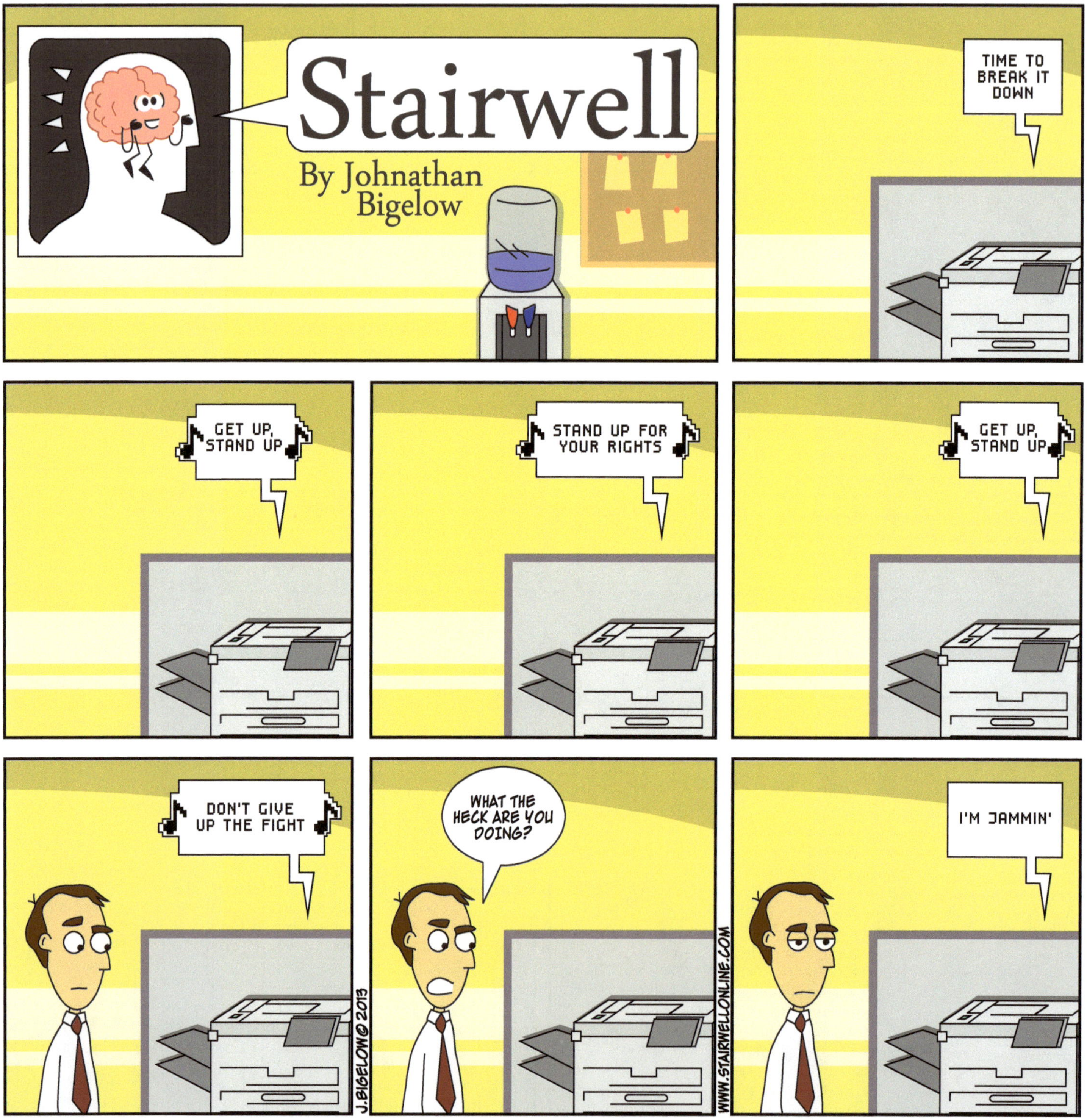

Stairwell
By Johnathan Bigelow
TIME TO BREAK IT DOWN
GET UP, STAND UP
STAND UP FOR YOUR RIGHTS
GET UP, STAND UP
DON'T GIVE UP THE FIGHT
J.BIGELOW© 2013
WHAT THE HECK ARE YOU DOING?
WWW.STAIRWELLONLINE.COM
I'M JAMMIN'

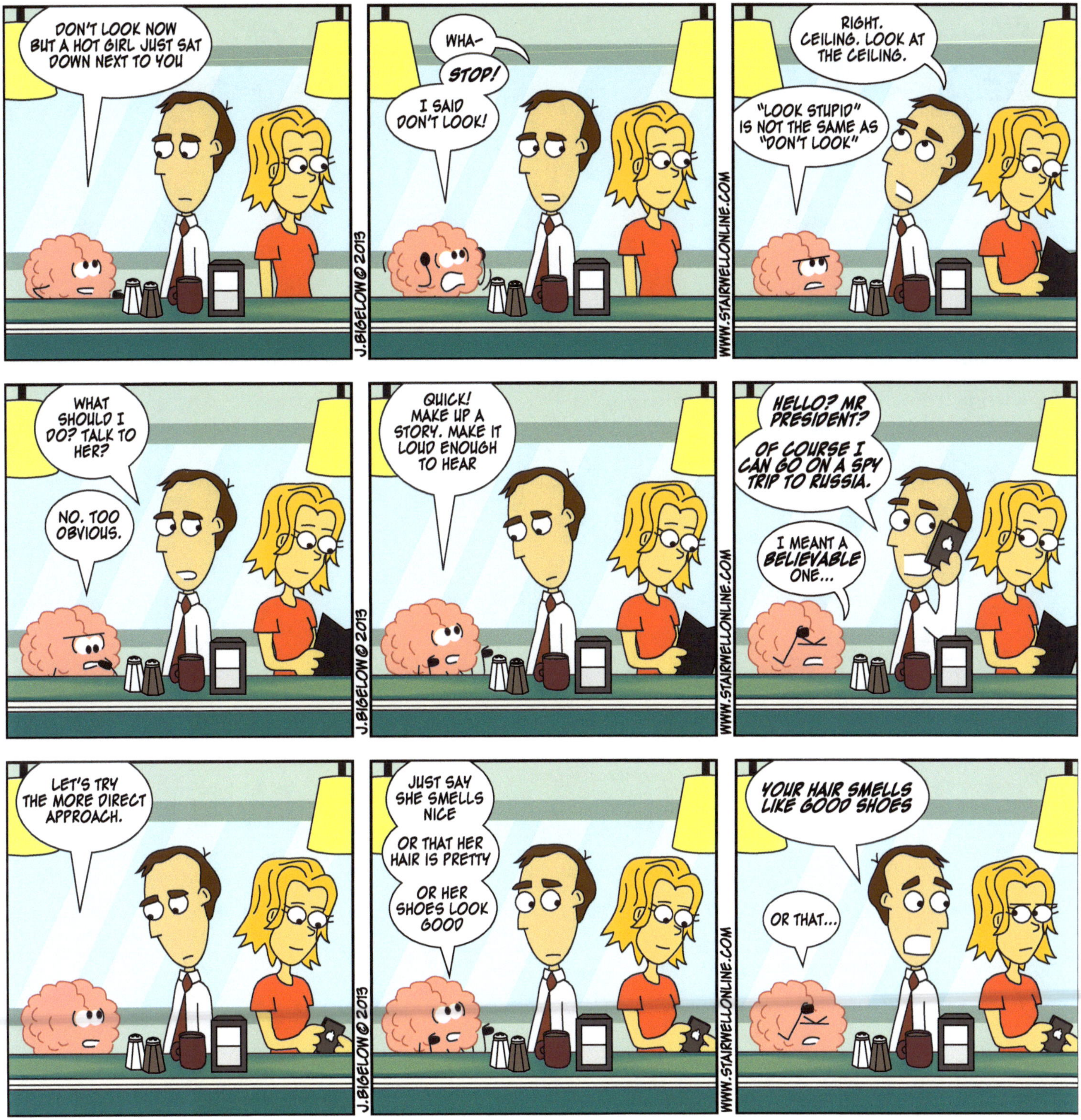
DON'T LOOK NOW BUT A HOT GIRL JUST SAT DOWN NEXT TO YOU
WHA-
STOP!
I SAID DON'T LOOK!
RIGHT. CEILING. LOOK AT THE CEILING.
"LOOK STUPID" IS NOT THE SAME AS "DON'T LOOK"
J.BIGELOW © 2013
WWW.STAIRWELLONLINE.COM
WHAT SHOULD I DO? TALK TO HER?
NO. TOO OBVIOUS.
QUICK! MAKE UP A STORY. MAKE IT LOUD ENOUGH TO HEAR
HELLO? MR PRESIDENT?
OF COURSE I CAN GO ON A SPY TRIP TO RUSSIA.
I MEANT A BELIEVABLE ONE...
J.BIGELOW © 2013
WWW.STAIRWELLONLINE.COM
LET'S TRY THE MORE DIRECT APPROACH.
JUST SAY SHE SMELLS NICE
OR THAT HER HAIR IS PRETTY
OR HER SHOES LOOK GOOD
YOUR HAIR SMELLS LIKE GOOD SHOES
OR THAT...
J.BIGELOW © 2013
WWW.STAIRWELLONLINE.COM

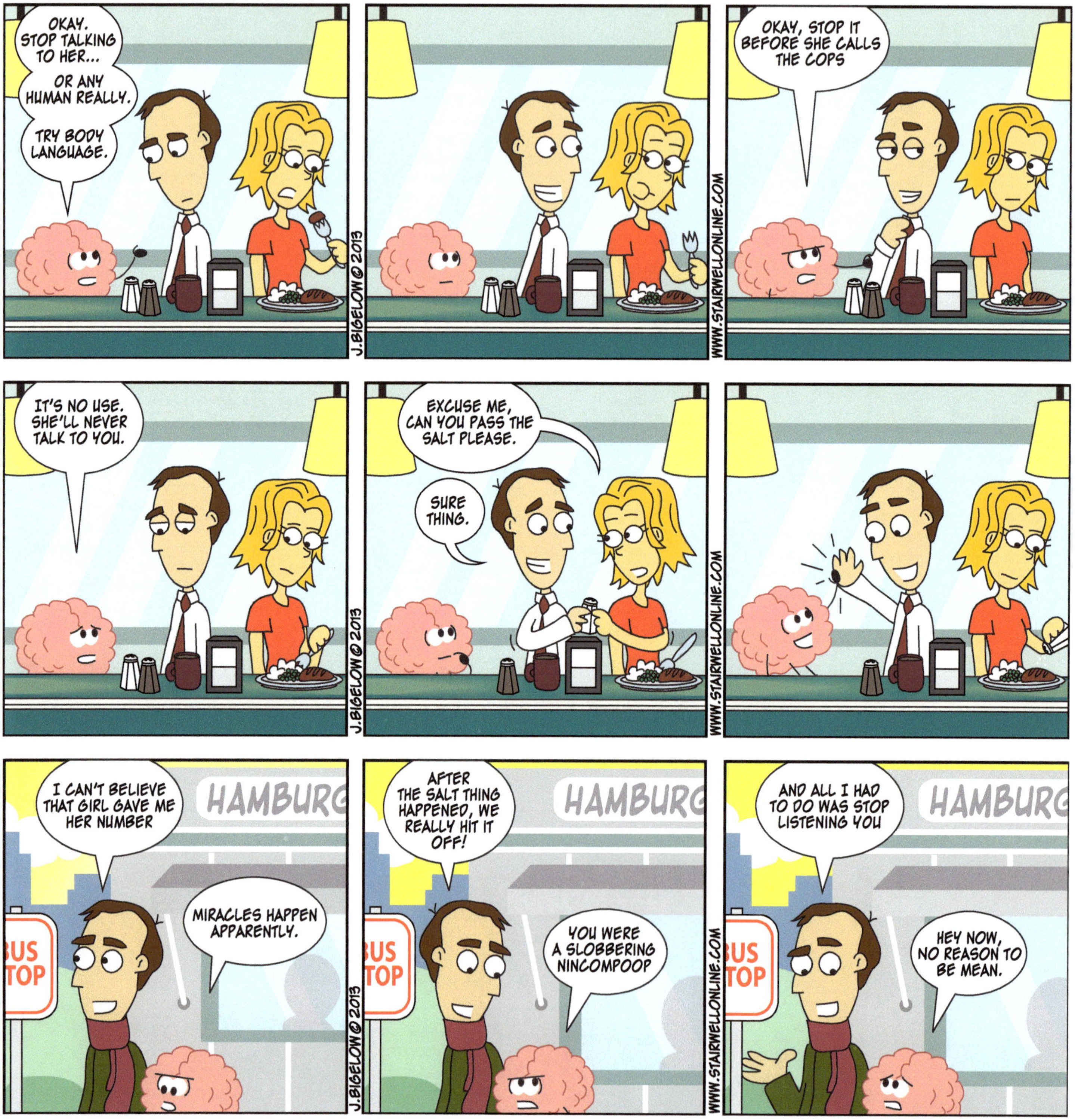
OKAY. STOP TALKING TO HER...
OR ANY HUMAN REALLY.
TRY BODY LANGUAGE.
J.BIGELOW © 2013
WWW.STAIRWELLONLINE.COM
OKAY, STOP IT BEFORE SHE CALLS THE COPS
IT'S NO USE. SHE'LL NEVER TALK TO YOU.
J.BIGELOW © 2013
EXCUSE ME, CAN YOU PASS THE SALT PLEASE.
SURE THING.
WWW.STAIRWELLONLINE.COM
I CAN'T BELIEVE THAT GIRL GAVE ME HER NUMBER
HAMBURG
BUS TOP
MIRACLES HAPPEN APPARENTLY.
J.BIGELOW © 2013
AFTER THE SALT THING HAPPENED, WE REALLY HIT IT OFF!
HAMBURG
BUS TOP
YOU WERE A SLOBBERING NINCOMPOOP
WWW.STAIRWELLONLINE.COM
AND ALL I HAD TO DO WAS STOP LISTENING YOU
HAMBURG
BUS TOP
HEY NOW, NO REASON TO BE MEAN.

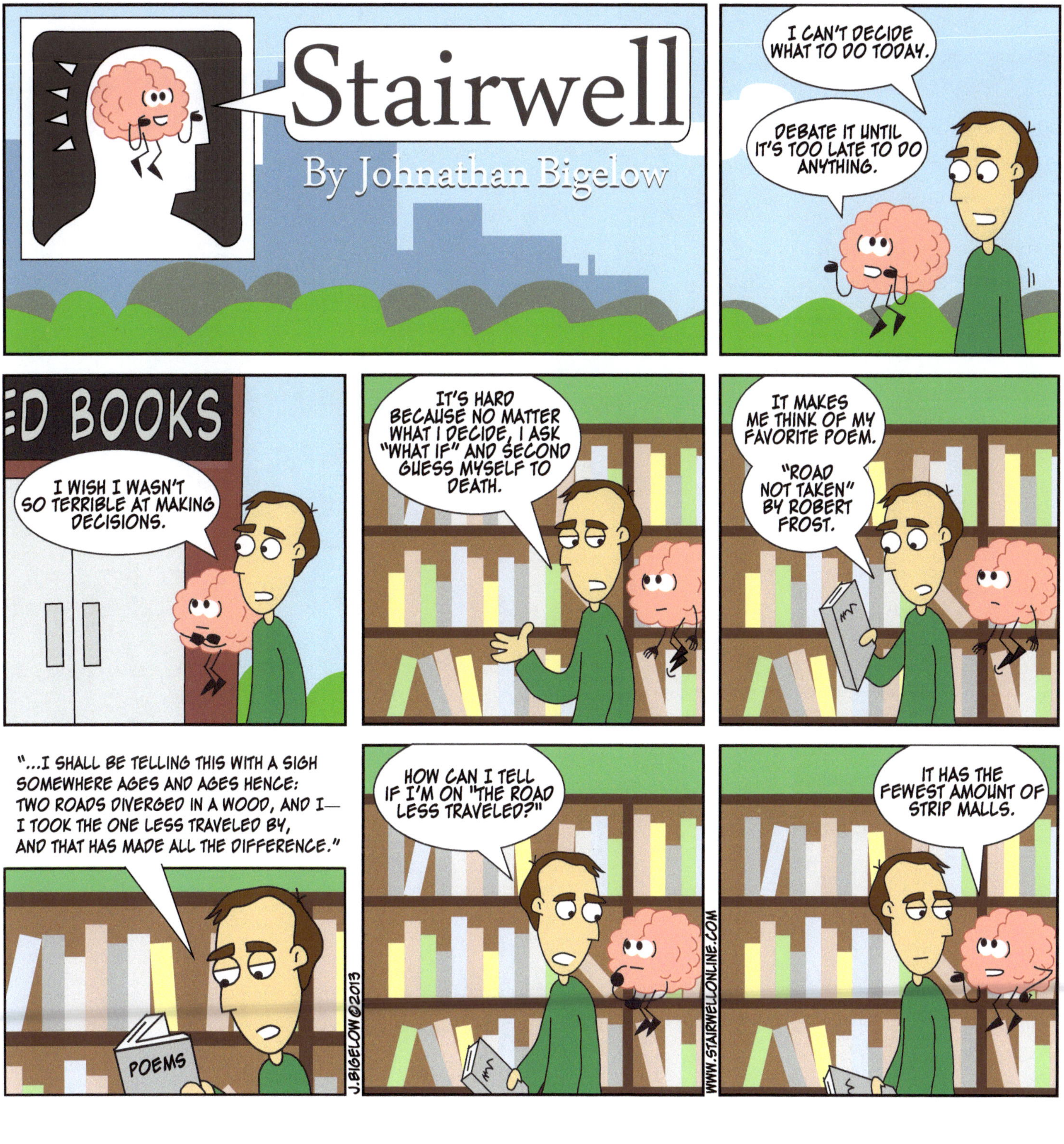
Stairwell
By Johnathan Bigelow
I CAN'T DECIDE WHAT TO DO TODAY.
DEBATE IT UNTIL IT'S TOO LATE TO DO ANYTHING.
ED BOOKS
I WISH I WASN'T SO TERRIBLE AT MAKING DECISIONS.
IT'S HARD BECAUSE NO MATTER WHAT I DECIDE, I ASK "WHAT IF" AND SECOND GUESS MYSELF TO DEATH.
IT MAKES ME THINK OF MY FAVORITE POEM.
"ROAD NOT TAKEN" BY ROBERT FROST.
"...I SHALL BE TELLING THIS WITH A SIGH
SOMEWHERE AGES AND AGES HENCE:
TWO ROADS DIVERGED IN A WOOD, AND I—
I TOOK THE ONE LESS TRAVELED BY,
AND THAT HAS MADE ALL THE DIFFERENCE."
POEMS
J.BIGELOW ©2013
HOW CAN I TELL IF I'M ON "THE ROAD LESS TRAVELED?"
WWW.STAIRWELLONLINE.COM
IT HAS THE FEWEST AMOUNT OF STRIP MALLS.

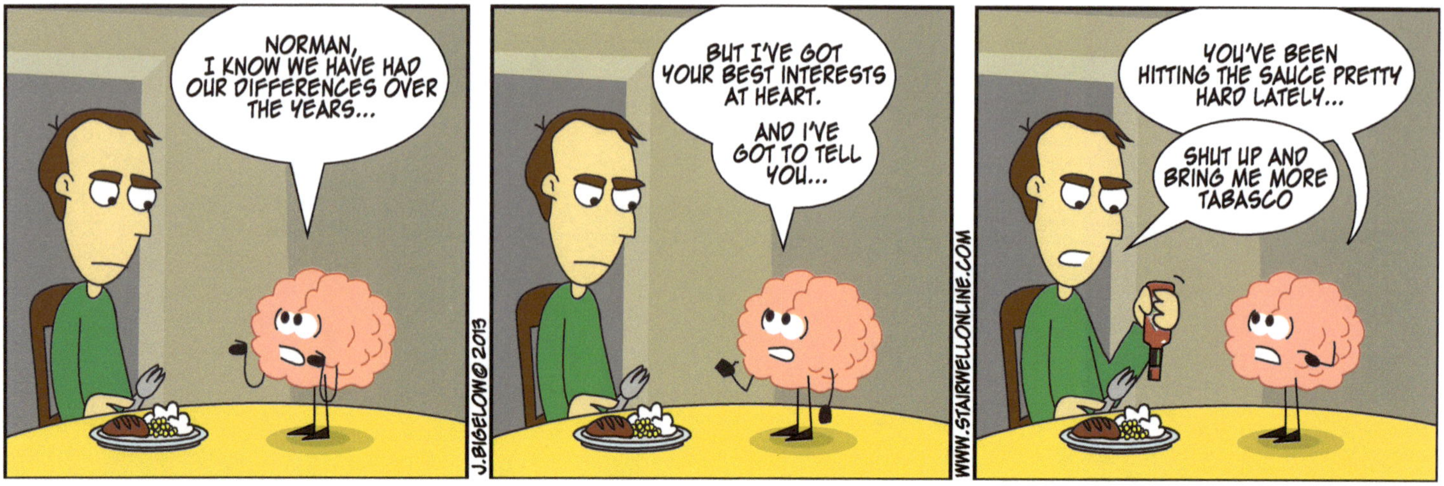
NORMAN,
I KNOW WE HAVE HAD OUR DIFFERENCES OVER THE YEARS...
J.BIGELOW©2013
BUT I'VE GOT YOUR BEST INTERESTS AT HEART.
AND I'VE GOT TO TELL YOU...
WWW.STAIRWELLONLINE.COM
YOU'VE BEEN HITTING THE SAUCE PRETTY HARD LATELY...
SHUT UP AND BRING ME MORE TABASCO

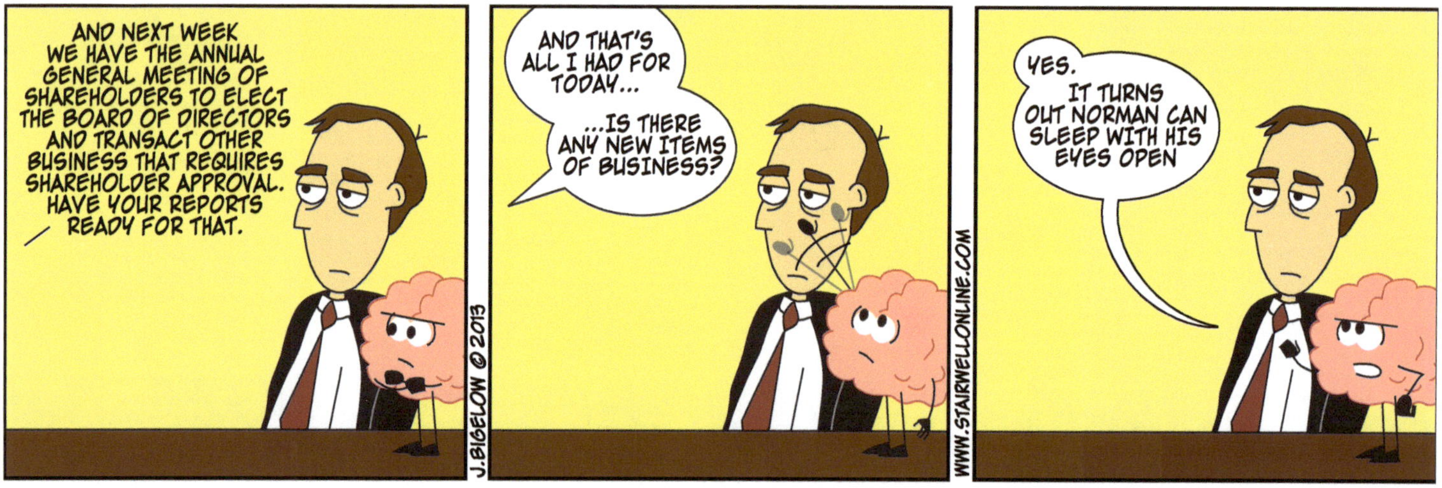
AND NEXT WEEK WE HAVE THE ANNUAL GENERAL MEETING OF SHAREHOLDERS TO ELECT THE BOARD OF DIRECTORS AND TRANSACT OTHER BUSINESS THAT REQUIRES SHAREHOLDER APPROVAL. HAVE YOUR REPORTS READY FOR THAT.
J.BIGELOW © 2013
AND THAT'S ALL I HAD FOR TODAY...
...IS THERE ANY NEW ITEMS OF BUSINESS?
WWW.STAIRWELLONLINE.COM
YES.
IT TURNS OUT NORMAN CAN SLEEP WITH HIS EYES OPEN

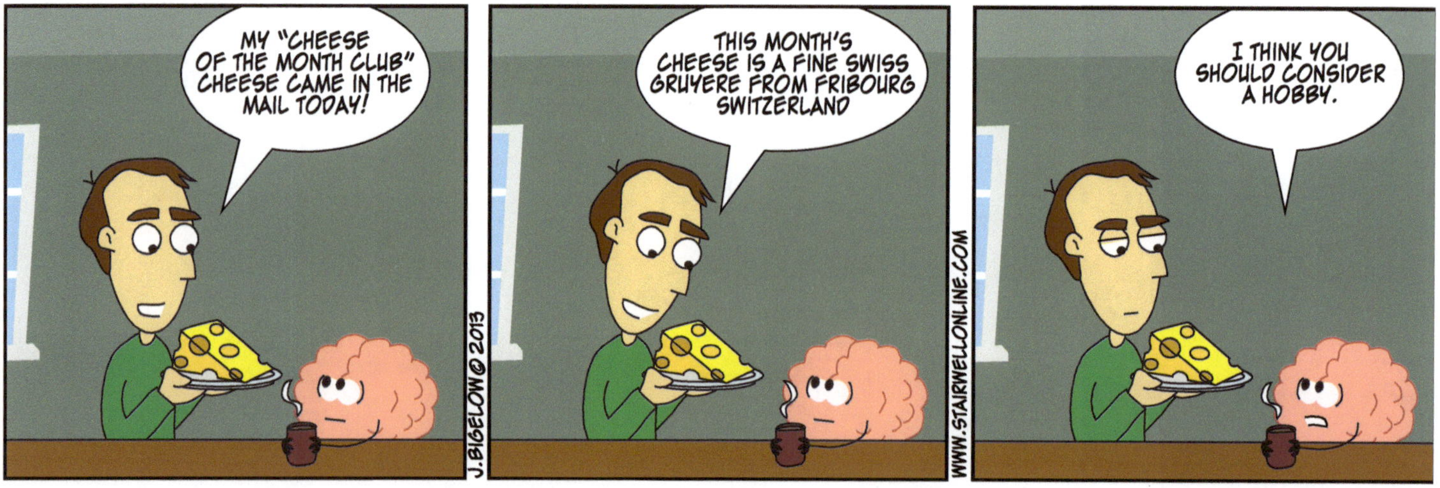
MY "CHEESE OF THE MONTH CLUB" CHEESE CAME IN THE MAIL TODAY!
J.BIGELOW©2013
THIS MONTH'S CHEESE IS A FINE SWISS GRUYERE FROM FRIBOURG SWITZERLAND
WWW.STAIRWELLONLINE.COM
I THINK YOU SHOULD CONSIDER A HOBBY.

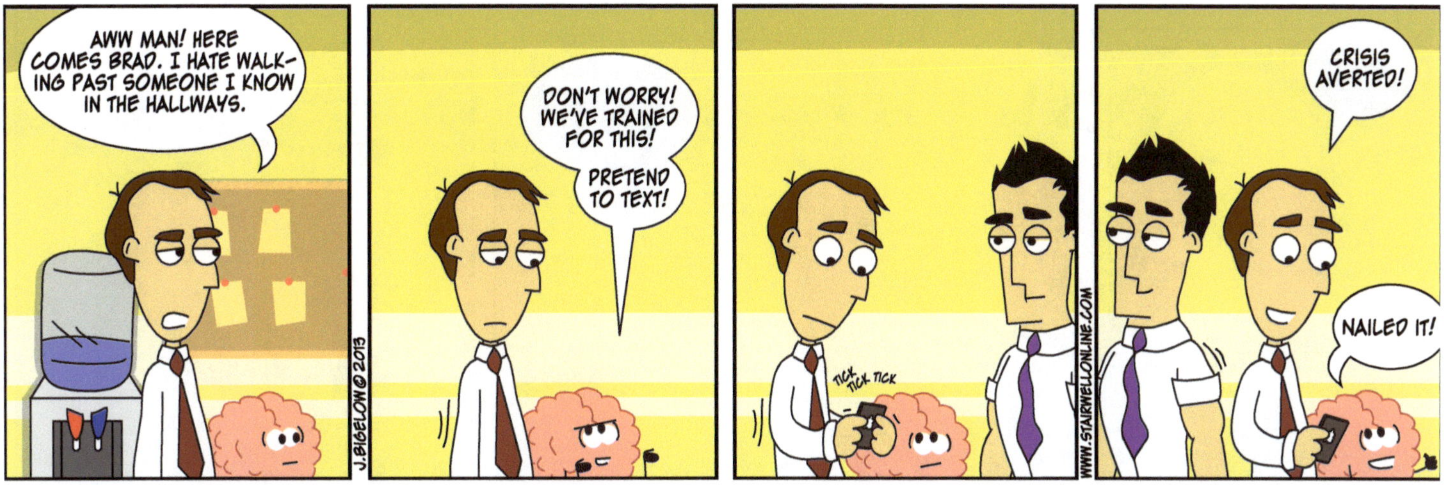
AWW MAN! HERE COMES BRAD. I HATE WALKING PAST SOMEONE I KNOW IN THE HALLWAYS.
J.BIGELOW © 2013
DON'T WORRY! WE'VE TRAINED FOR THIS!
PRETEND TO TEXT!
TICK TICK TICK
WWW.STAIRWELLONLINE.COM
CRISIS AVERTED!
NAILED IT!

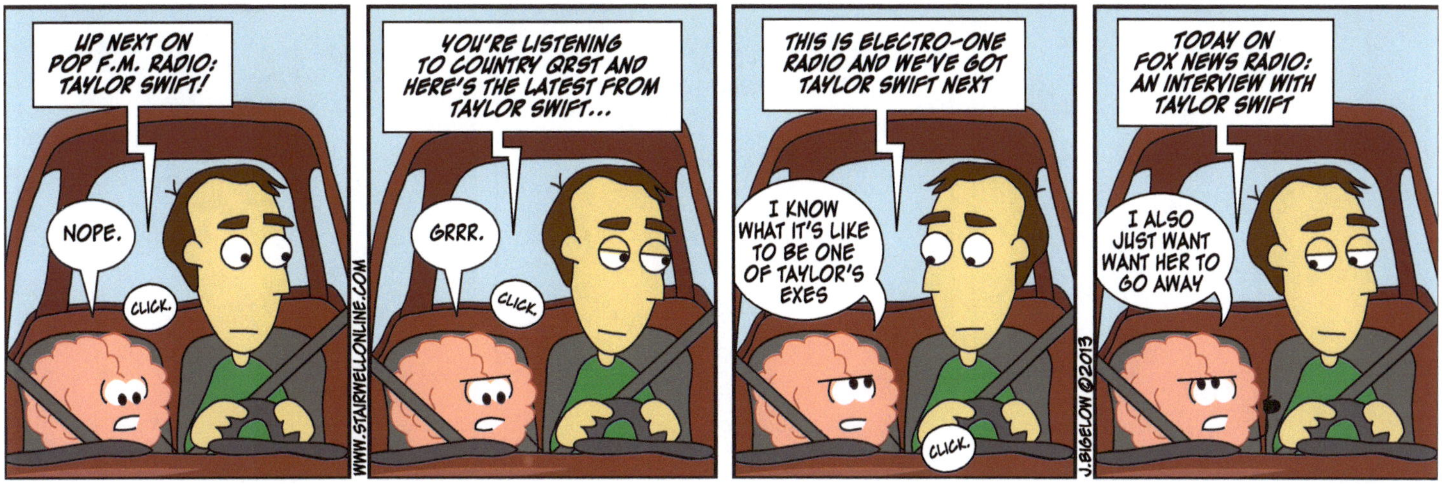
UP NEXT ON POP F.M. RADIO: TAYLOR SWIFT!
NOPE.
CLICK.
WWW.STAIRWELLONLINE.COM
YOU'RE LISTENING TO COUNTRY QRST AND HERE'S THE LATEST FROM TAYLOR SWIFT...
GRRR.
CLICK.
THIS IS ELECTRO-ONE RADIO AND WE'VE GOT TAYLOR SWIFT NEXT
I KNOW WHAT IT'S LIKE TO BE ONE OF TAYLOR'S EXES
CLICK.
J.BIGELOW © 2013
TODAY ON FOX NEWS RADIO: AN INTERVIEW WITH TAYLOR SWIFT
I ALSO JUST WANT WANT HER TO GO AWAY

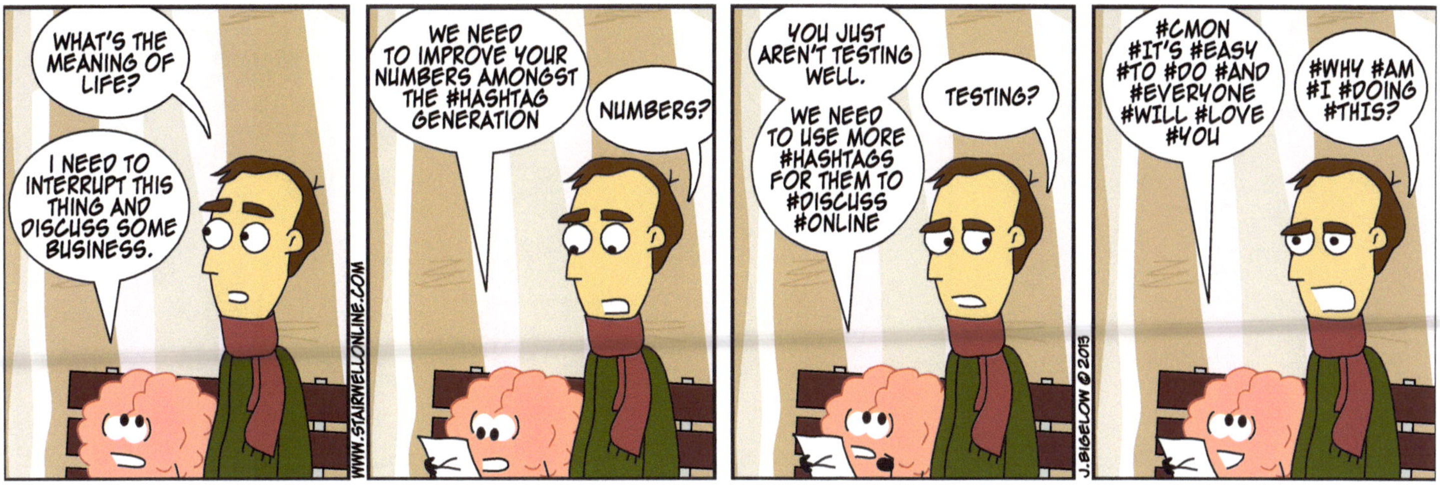
WHAT'S THE MEANING OF LIFE?
I NEED TO INTERRUPT THIS THING AND DISCUSS SOME BUSINESS.
WWW.STAIRWELLONLINE.COM
WE NEED TO IMPROVE YOUR NUMBERS AMONGST THE #HASHTAG GENERATION
NUMBERS?
YOU JUST AREN'T TESTING WELL.
WE NEED TO USE MORE #HASHTAGS FOR THEM TO #DISCUSS #ONLINE
TESTING?
J.BIGELOW © 2013
#CMON #IT'S #EASY #TO #DO #AND #EVERYONE #WILL #LOVE #YOU
#WHY #AM #I #DOING #THIS?

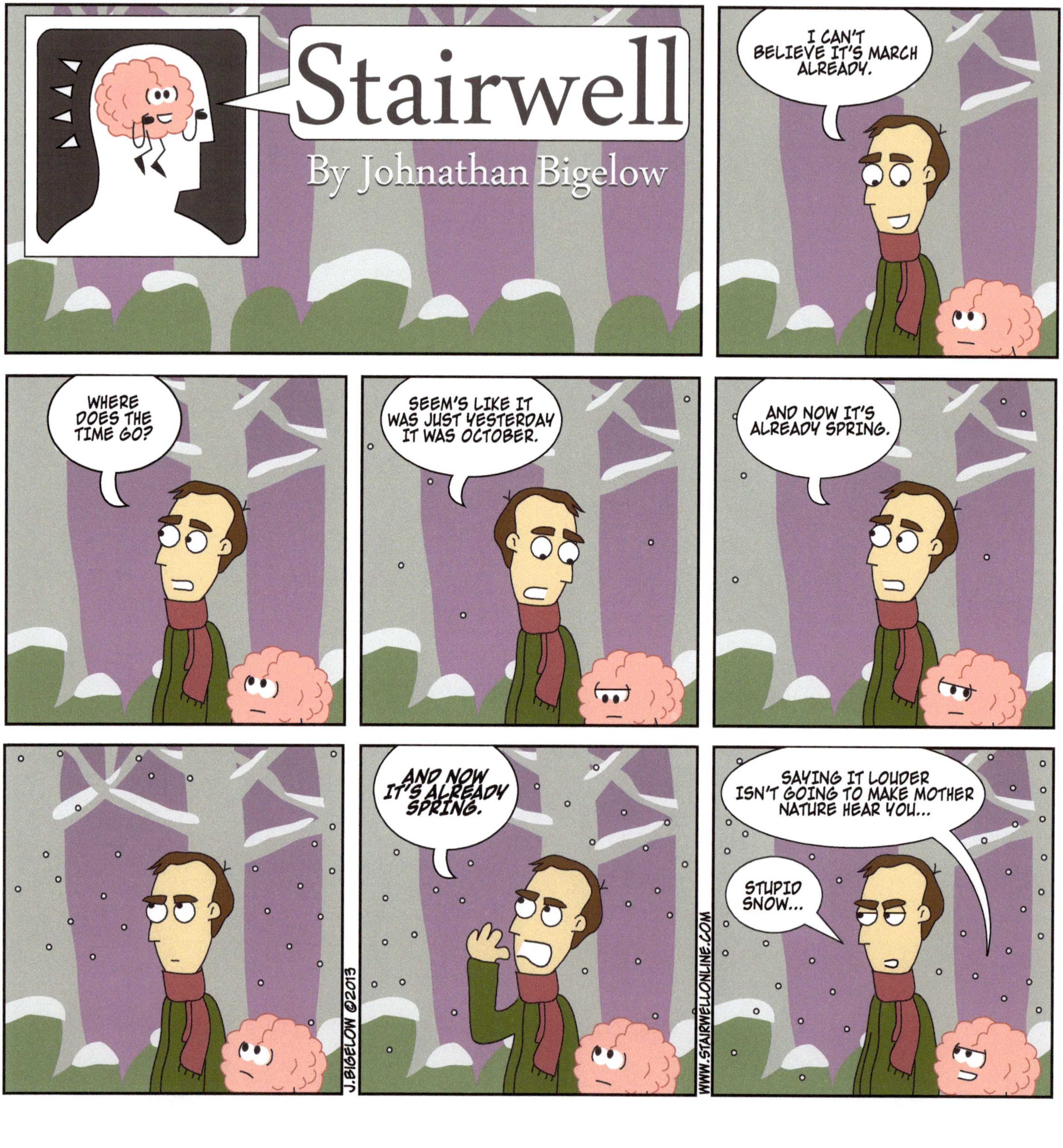
Stairwell
By Johnathan Bigelow
I CAN'T BELIEVE IT'S MARCH ALREADY.
WHERE DOES THE TIME GO?
SEEM'S LIKE IT WAS JUST YESTERDAY IT WAS OCTOBER.
AND NOW IT'S ALREADY SPRING.
J.BIGELOW ©2013
AND NOW IT'S ALREADY SPRING.
WWW.STAIRWELLONLINE.COM
SAYING IT LOUDER ISN'T GOING TO MAKE MOTHER NATURE HEAR YOU...
STUPID SNOW...

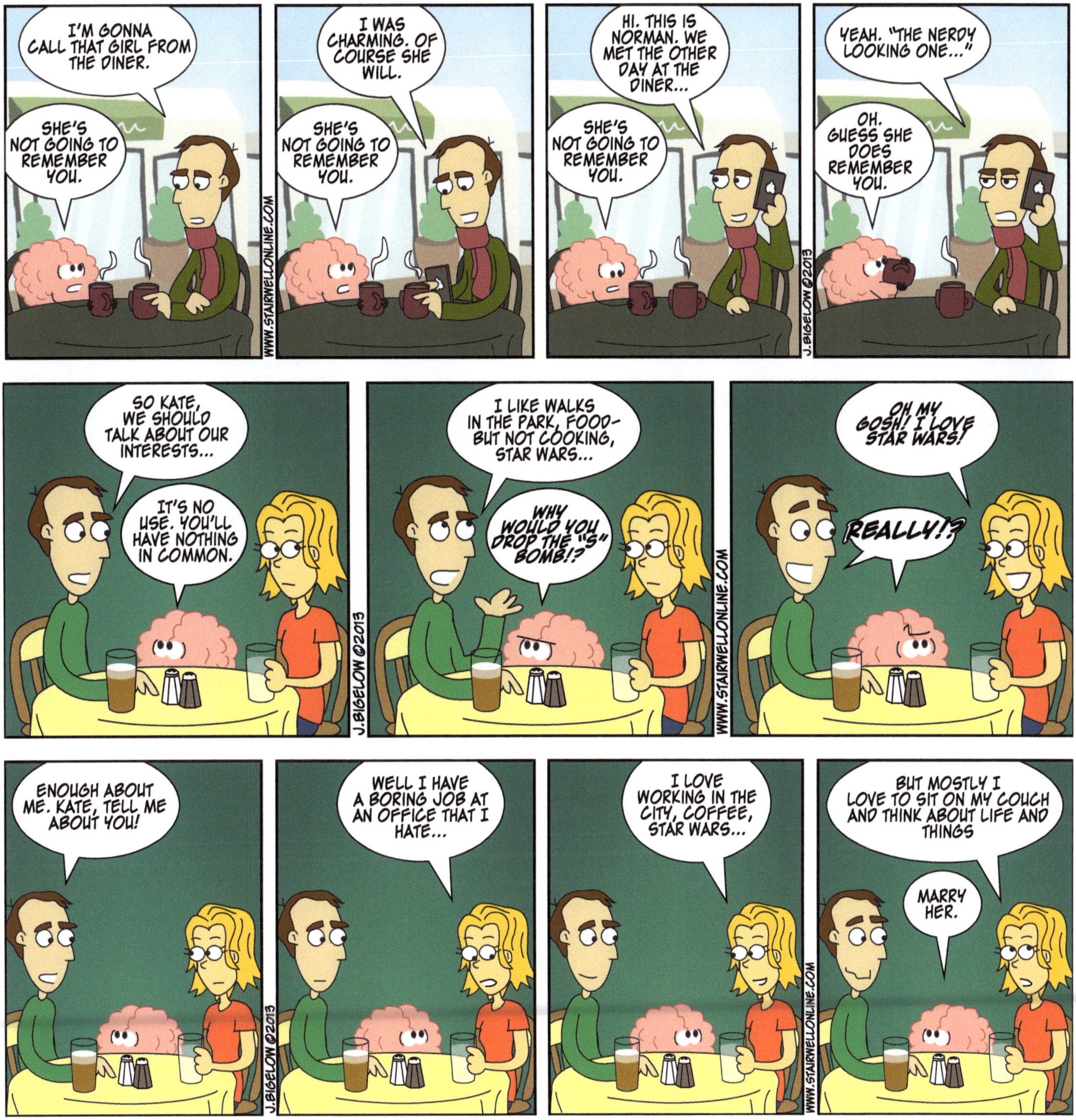
I'M GONNA CALL THAT GIRL FROM THE DINER.
SHE'S NOT GOING TO REMEMBER YOU.
WWW.STAIRWELLONLINE.COM
I WAS CHARMING. OF COURSE SHE WILL.
SHE'S NOT GOING TO REMEMBER YOU.
HI. THIS IS NORMAN. WE MET THE OTHER DAY AT THE DINER...
SHE'S NOT GOING TO REMEMBER YOU.
J. BIGELOW ©2013
YEAH. "THE NERDY LOOKING ONE..."
OH. GUESS SHE DOES REMEMBER YOU.
SO KATE, WE SHOULD TALK ABOUT OUR INTERESTS...
IT'S NO USE. YOU'LL HAVE NOTHING IN COMMON.
J. BIGELOW ©2013
I LIKE WALKS IN THE PARK, FOOD-BUT NOT COOKING, STAR WARS...
WHY WOULD YOU DROP THE "S" BOMB!?
WWW.STAIRWELLONLINE.COM
OH MY GOSH! I LOVE STAR WARS!
REALLY!?
ENOUGH ABOUT ME. KATE, TELL ME ABOUT YOU!
J. BIGELOW ©2013
WELL I HAVE A BORING JOB AT AN OFFICE THAT I HATE...
I LOVE WORKING IN THE CITY, COFFEE, STAR WARS...
WWW.STAIRWELLONLINE.COM
BUT MOSTLY I LOVE TO SIT ON MY COUCH AND THINK ABOUT LIFE AND THINGS
MARRY HER.

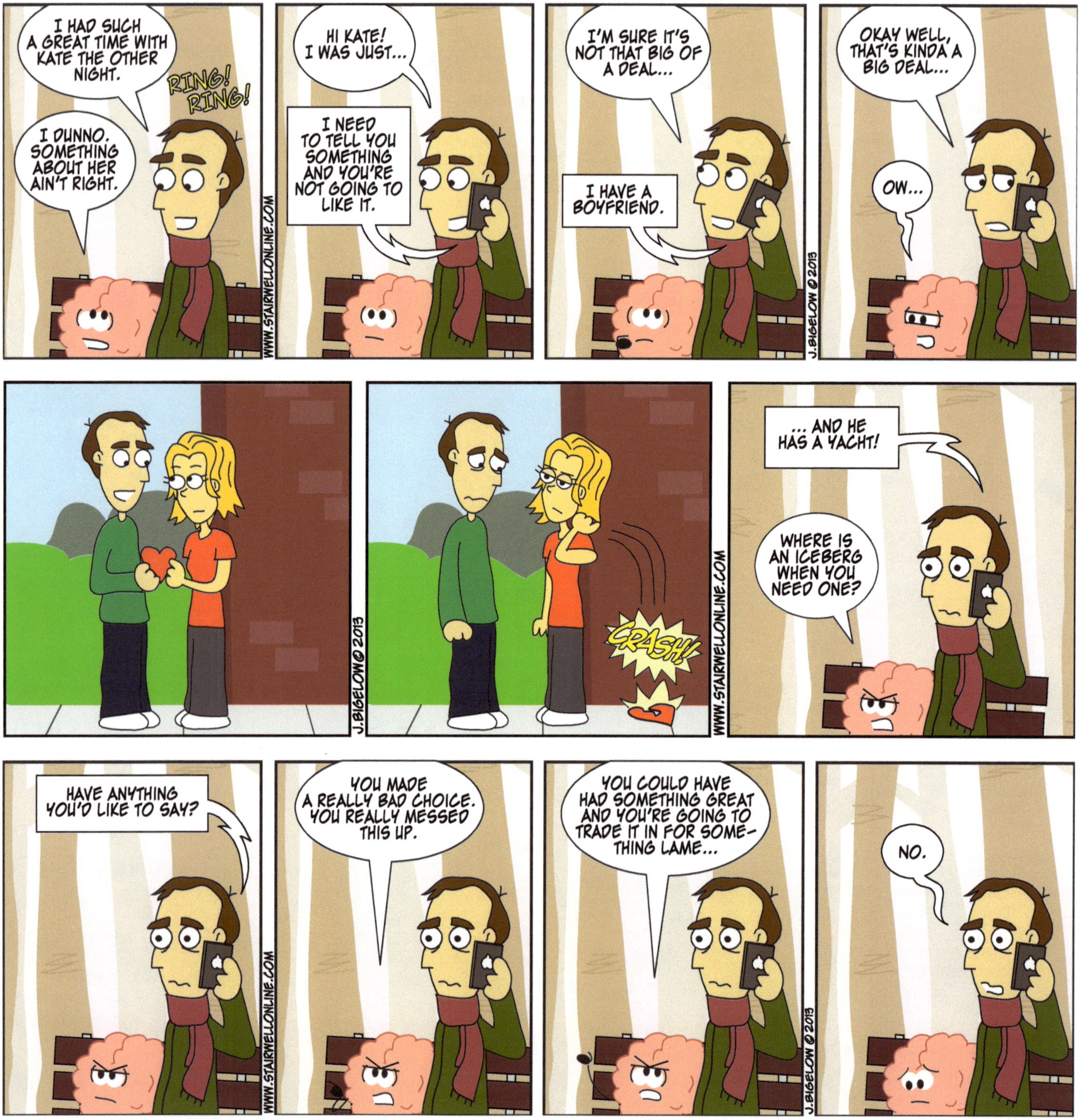

I HAD SUCH A GREAT TIME WITH KATE THE OTHER NIGHT.
RING! RING!
I DUNNO. SOMETHING ABOUT HER AIN'T RIGHT.
WWW.STAIRWELLONLINE.COM
HI KATE! I WAS JUST...
I NEED TO TELL YOU SOMETHING AND YOU'RE NOT GOING TO LIKE IT.
I'M SURE IT'S NOT THAT BIG OF A DEAL...
I HAVE A BOYFRIEND.
J. BIGELOW © 2013
OKAY WELL, THAT'S KINDA A BIG DEAL...
OW...
J. BIGELOW © 2013
CRASH!
WWW.STAIRWELLONLINE.COM
... AND HE HAS A YACHT!
WHERE IS AN ICEBERG WHEN YOU NEED ONE?
HAVE ANYTHING YOU'D LIKE TO SAY?
WWW.STAIRWELLONLINE.COM
YOU MADE A REALLY BAD CHOICE. YOU REALLY MESSED THIS UP.
YOU COULD HAVE HAD SOMETHING GREAT AND YOU'RE GOING TO TRADE IT IN FOR SOMETHING LAME...
J. BIGELOW © 2013
NO.

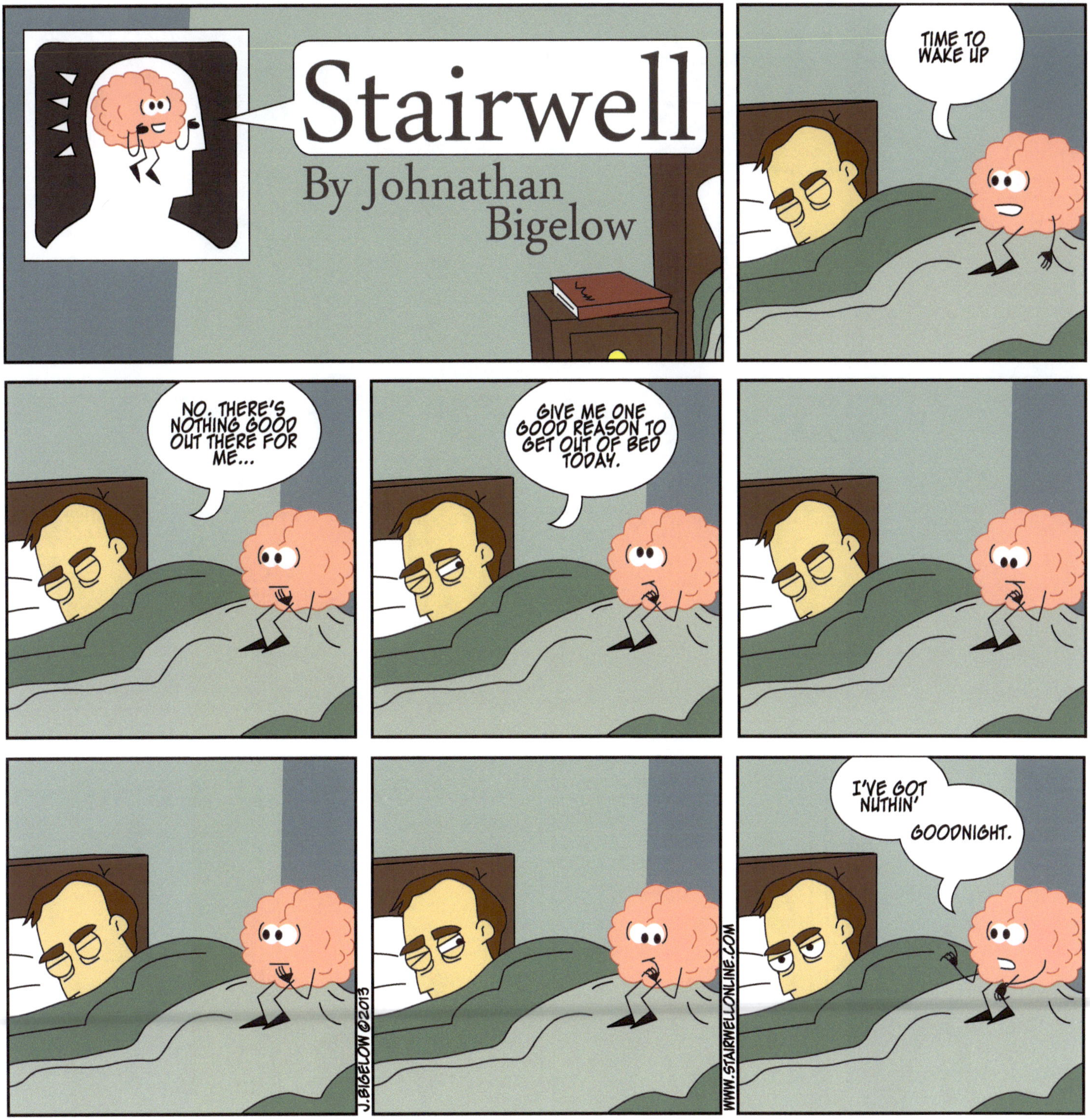
Stairwell
By Johnathan Bigelow
TIME TO WAKE UP
NO. THERE'S NOTHING GOOD OUT THERE FOR ME...
GIVE ME ONE GOOD REASON TO GET OUT OF BED TODAY.
J.BIGELOW ©2013
WWW.STAIRWELLONLINE.COM
I'VE GOT NUTHIN'
GOODNIGHT.

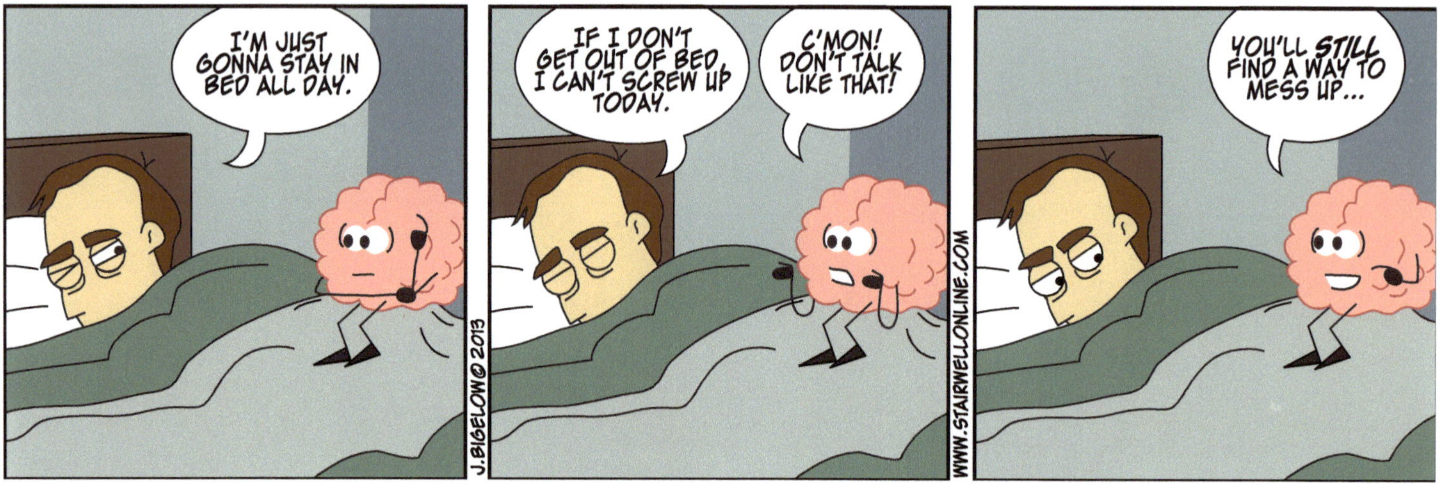
I'M JUST GONNA STAY IN BED ALL DAY.
IF I DON'T GET OUT OF BED I CAN'T SCREW UP TODAY.
C'MON! DON'T TALK LIKE THAT!
YOU'LL STILL FIND A WAY TO MESS UP...
J.BIGELOW © 2013
WWW.STAIRWELLONLINE.COM

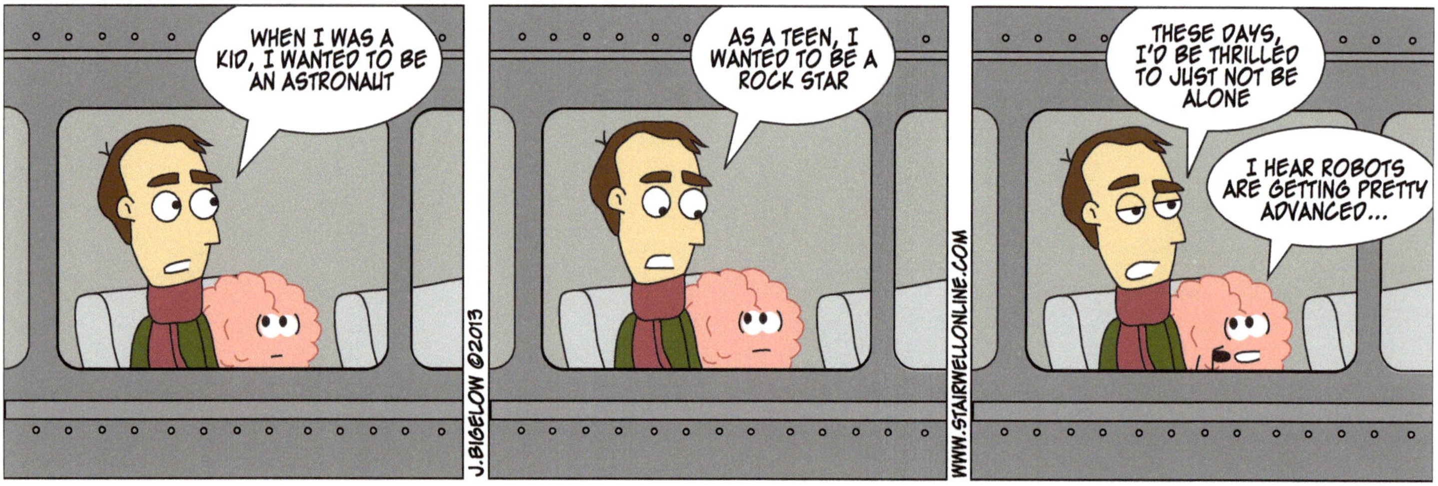
WHEN I WAS A KID, I WANTED TO BE AN ASTRONAUT
AS A TEEN, I WANTED TO BE A ROCK STAR
THESE DAYS, I'D BE THRILLED TO JUST NOT BE ALONE
I HEAR ROBOTS ARE GETTING PRETTY ADVANCED...
J.BIGELOW © 2013
WWW.STAIRWELLONLINE.COM

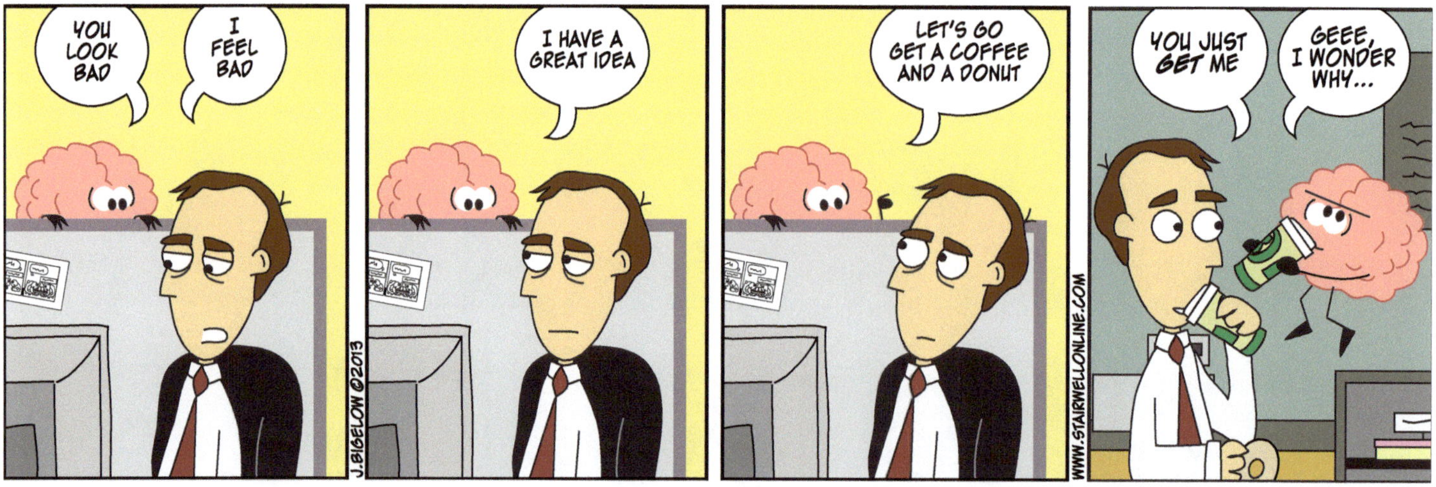
YOU LOOK BAD
I FEEL BAD
I HAVE A GREAT IDEA
LET'S GO GET A COFFEE AND A DONUT
YOU JUST GET ME
GEEE, I WONDER WHY...
J.BIGELOW © 2013
WWW.STAIRWELLONLINE.COM

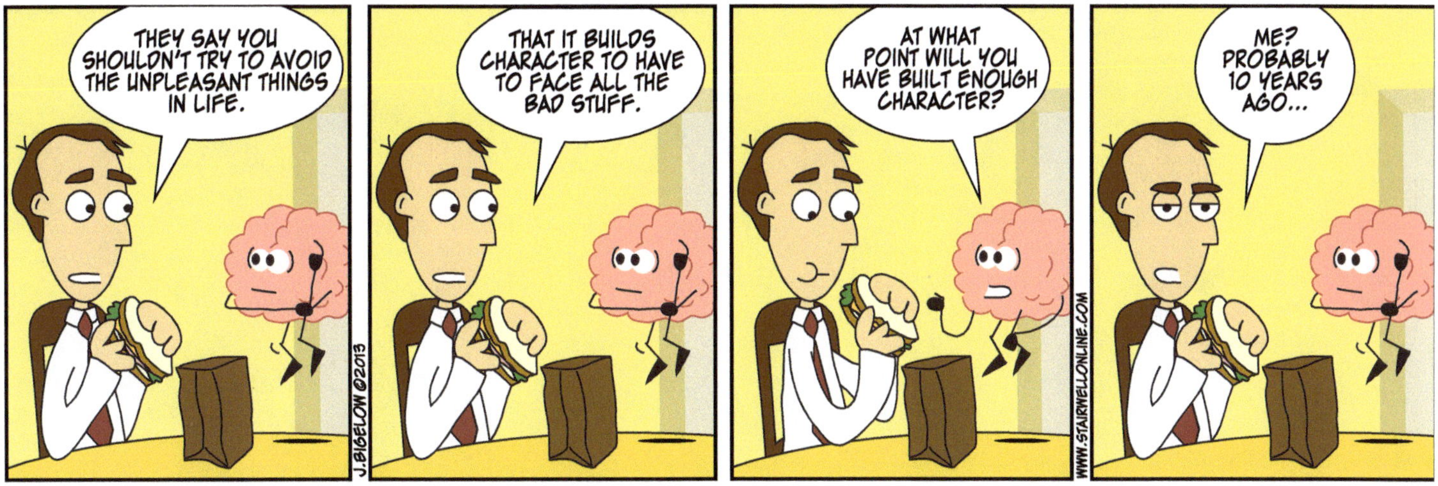
THEY SAY YOU SHOULDN'T TRY TO AVOID THE UNPLEASANT THINGS IN LIFE.
J.BIGELOW ©2013
THAT IT BUILDS CHARACTER TO HAVE TO FACE ALL THE BAD STUFF.
AT WHAT POINT WILL YOU HAVE BUILT ENOUGH CHARACTER?
WWW.STAIRWELLONLINE.COM
ME? PROBABLY 10 YEARS AGO...

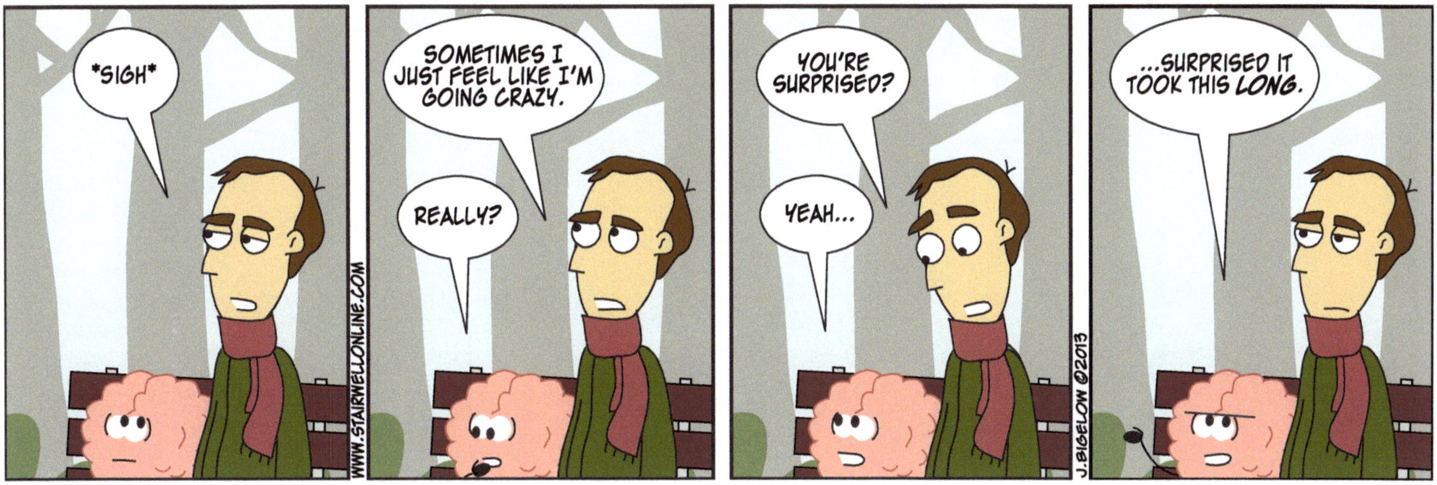
SIGH
WWW.STAIRWELLONLINE.COM
SOMETIMES I JUST FEEL LIKE I'M GOING CRAZY.
REALLY?
YOU'RE SURPRISED?
YEAH...
J.BIGELOW ©2013
...SURPRISED IT TOOK THIS LONG.

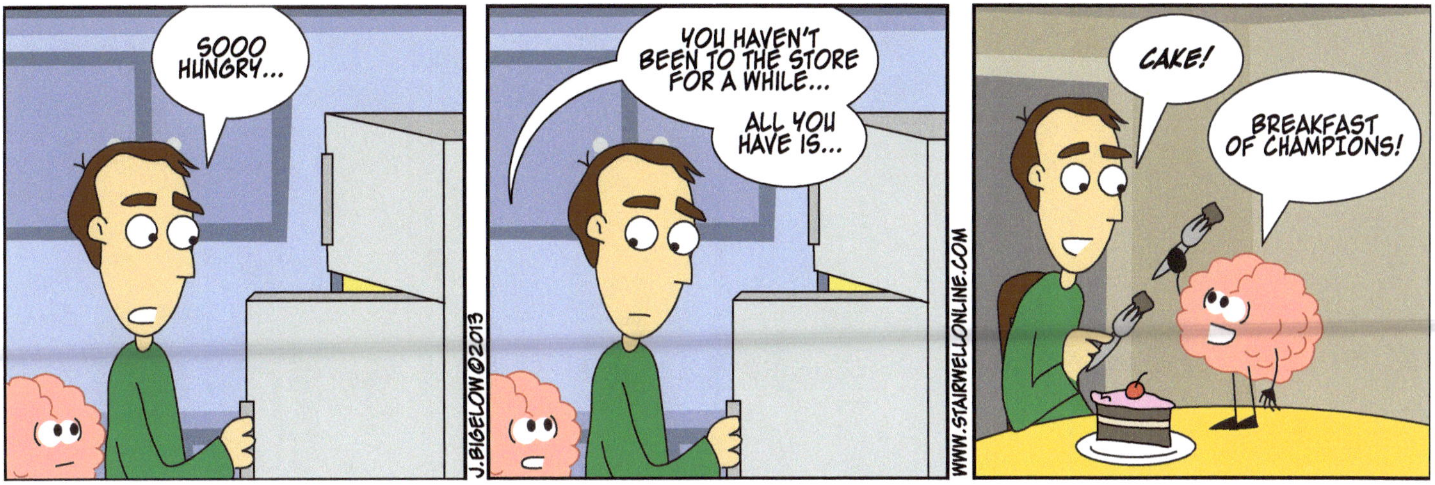
SOOO HUNGRY...
J.BIGELOW ©2013
YOU HAVEN'T BEEN TO THE STORE FOR A WHILE...
ALL YOU HAVE IS...
WWW.STAIRWELLONLINE.COM
CAKE!
BREAKFAST OF CHAMPIONS!

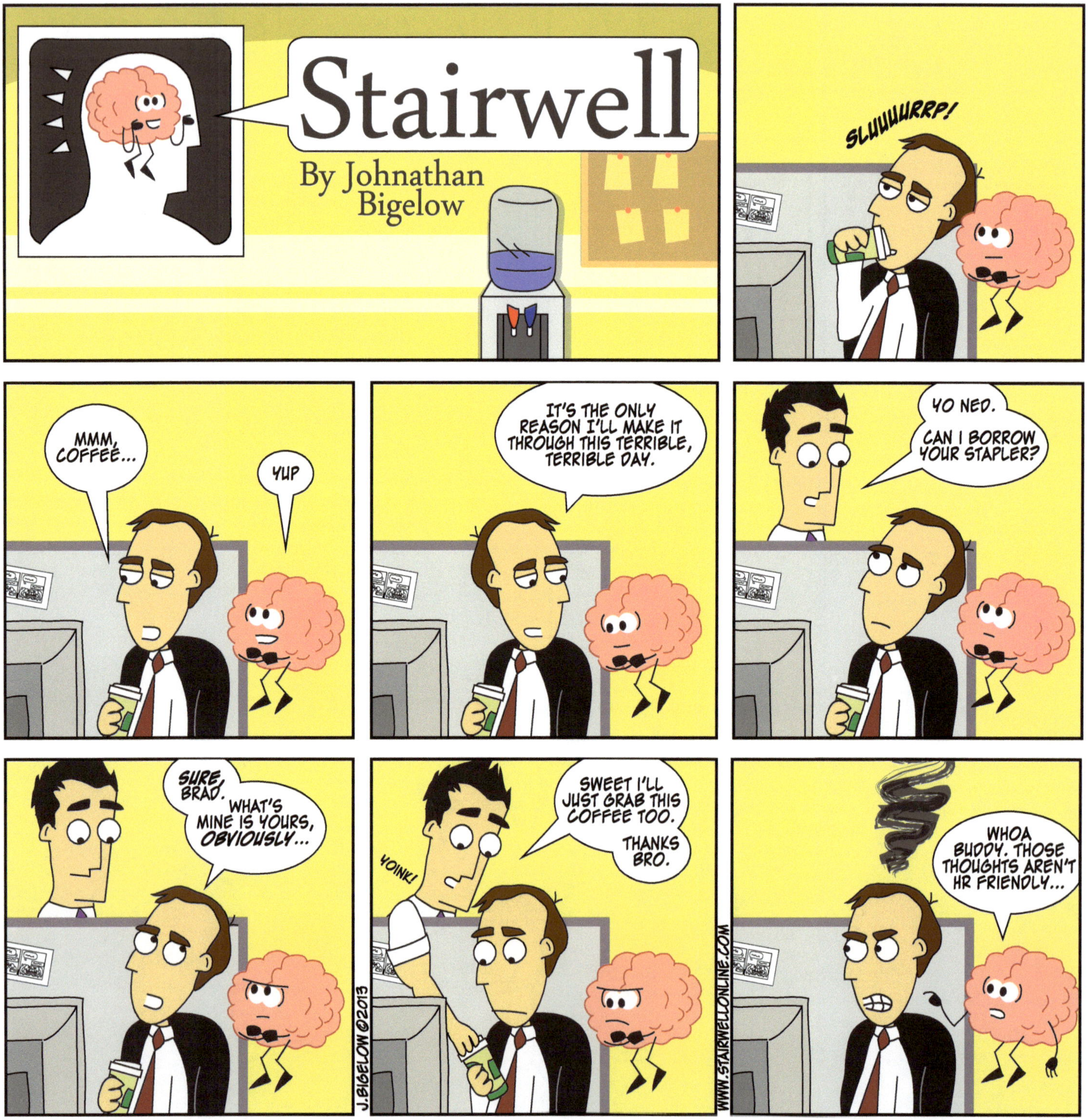
Stairwell
By Johnathan Bigelow
SLUUUURRP!
MMM, COFFEE...
YUP
IT'S THE ONLY REASON I'LL MAKE IT THROUGH THIS TERRIBLE, TERRIBLE DAY.
YO NED.
CAN I BORROW YOUR STAPLER?
SURE, BRAD.
WHAT'S MINE IS YOURS, OBVIOUSLY...
J.BIGELOW ©2013
YOINK!
SWEET I'LL JUST GRAB THIS COFFEE TOO.
THANKS BRO.
WWW.STAIRWELLONLINE.COM
WHOA BUDDY. THOSE THOUGHTS AREN'T HR FRIENDLY...

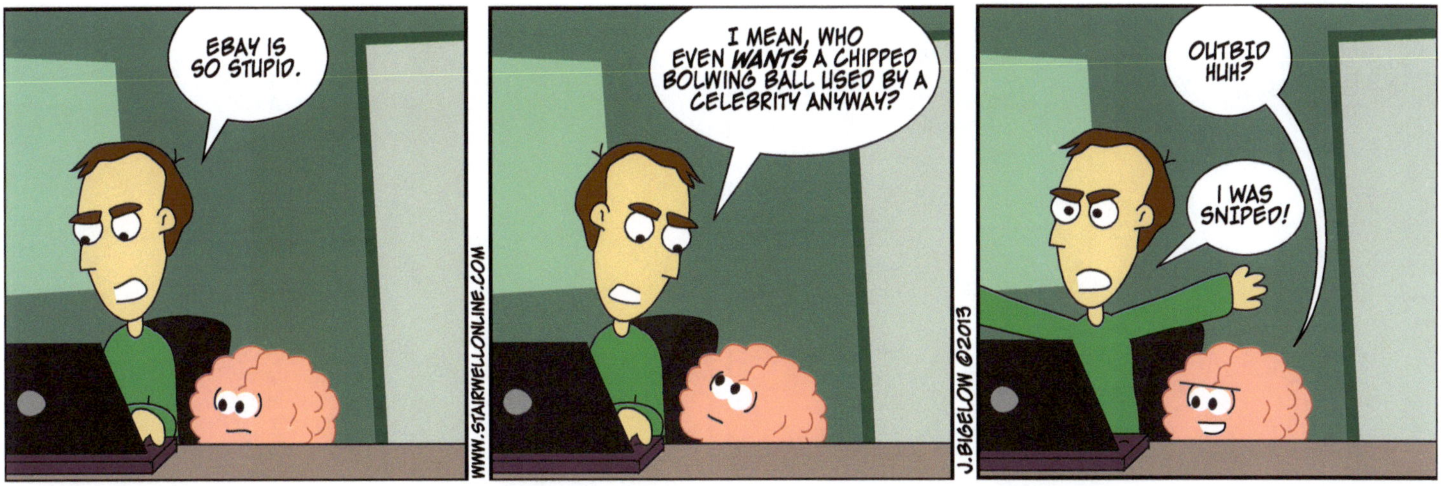
EBAY IS SO STUPID.
I MEAN, WHO EVEN *WANTS* A CHIPPED BOLWING BALL USED BY A CELEBRITY ANYWAY?
WWW.STAIRWELLONLINE.COM
OUTBID HUH?
I WAS SNIPED!
J.BIGELOW ©2013

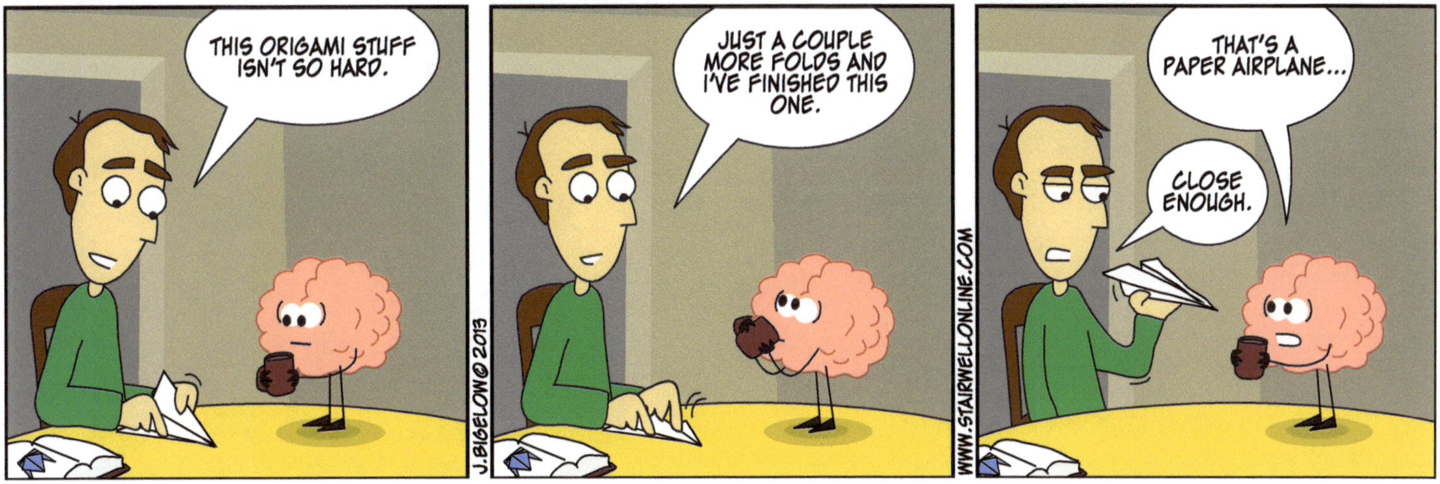
THIS ORIGAMI STUFF ISN'T SO HARD.
J.BIGELOW © 2013
JUST A COUPLE MORE FOLDS AND I'VE FINISHED THIS ONE.
WWW.STAIRWELLONLINE.COM
THAT'S A PAPER AIRPLANE...
CLOSE ENOUGH.

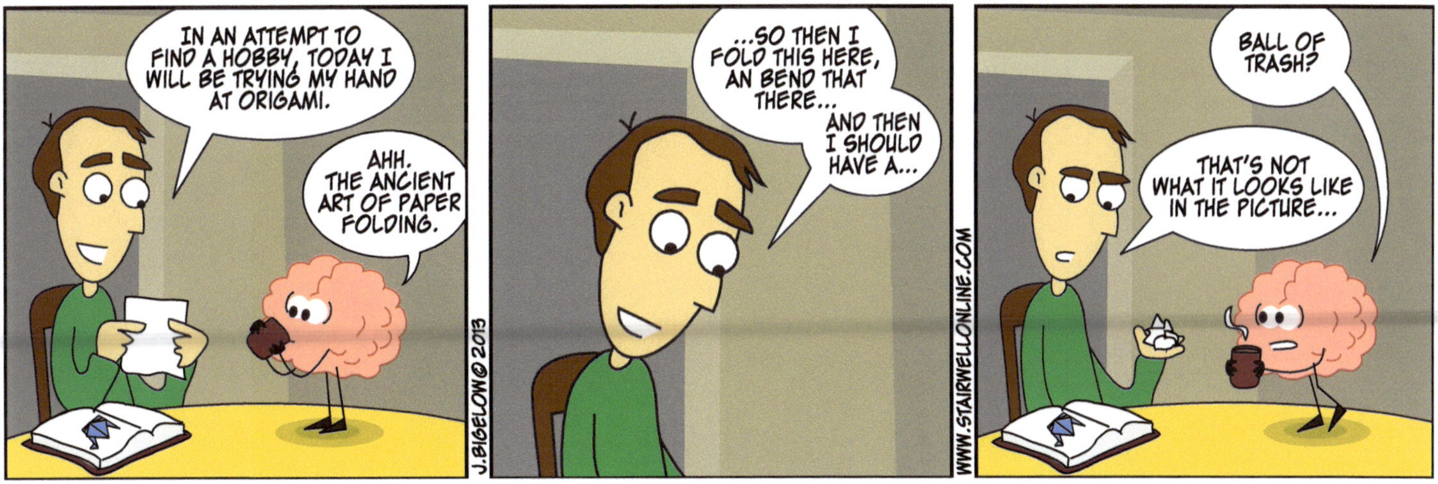
IN AN ATTEMPT TO FIND A HOBBY, TODAY I WILL BE TRYING MY HAND AT ORIGAMI.
AHH. THE ANCIENT ART OF PAPER FOLDING.
J.BIGELOW © 2013
...SO THEN I FOLD THIS HERE, AN BEND THAT THERE...
AND THEN I SHOULD HAVE A...
WWW.STAIRWELLONLINE.COM
BALL OF TRASH?
THAT'S NOT WHAT IT LOOKS LIKE IN THE PICTURE...

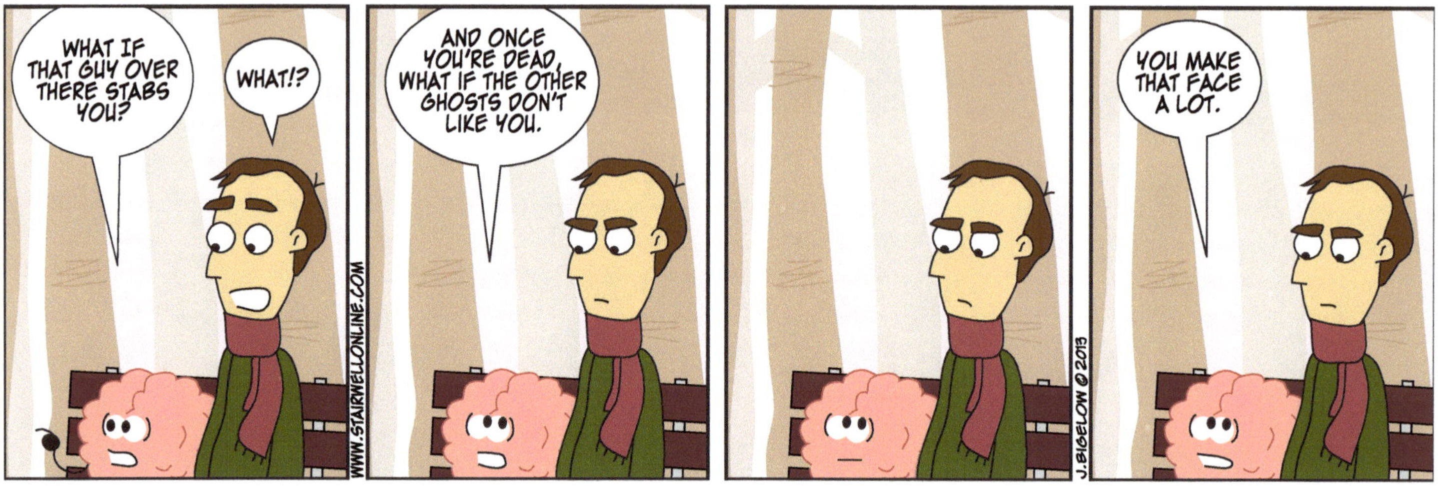
WHAT IF THAT GUY OVER THERE STABS YOU?
WHAT!?
AND ONCE YOU'RE DEAD, WHAT IF THE OTHER GHOSTS DON'T LIKE YOU.
YOU MAKE THAT FACE A LOT.
WWW.STAIRWELLONLINE.COM
J.BIGELOW ©2013

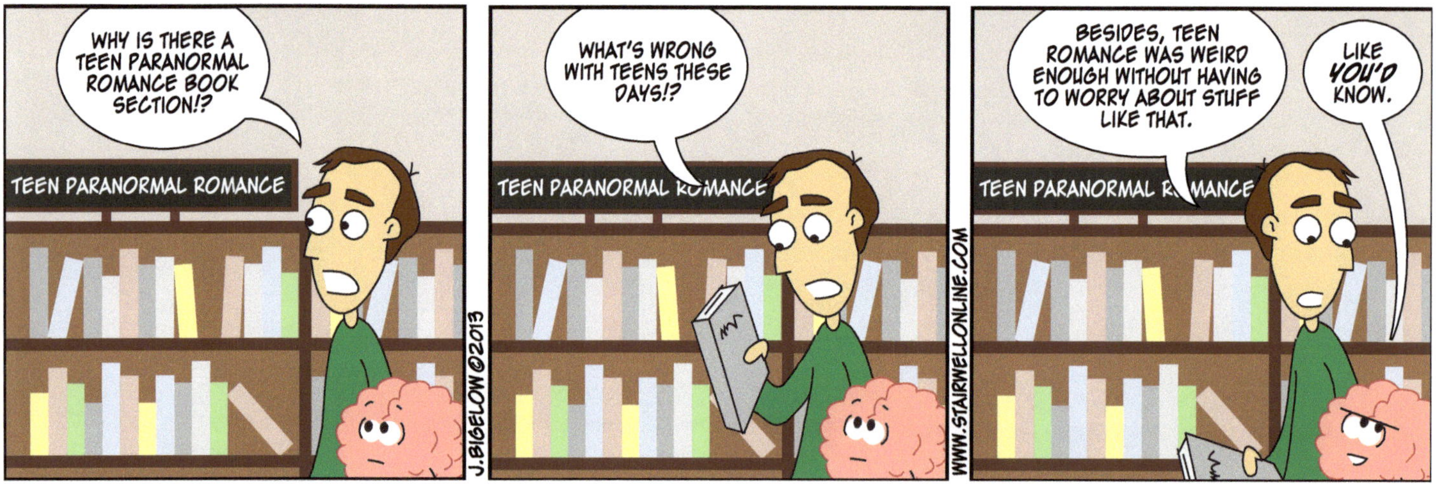
WHY IS THERE A TEEN PARANORMAL ROMANCE BOOK SECTION!?
TEEN PARANORMAL ROMANCE
WHAT'S WRONG WITH TEENS THESE DAYS!?
BESIDES, TEEN ROMANCE WAS WEIRD ENOUGH WITHOUT HAVING TO WORRY ABOUT STUFF LIKE THAT.
LIKE *YOU'D* KNOW.
J.BIGELOW ©2013
WWW.STAIRWELLONLINE.COM

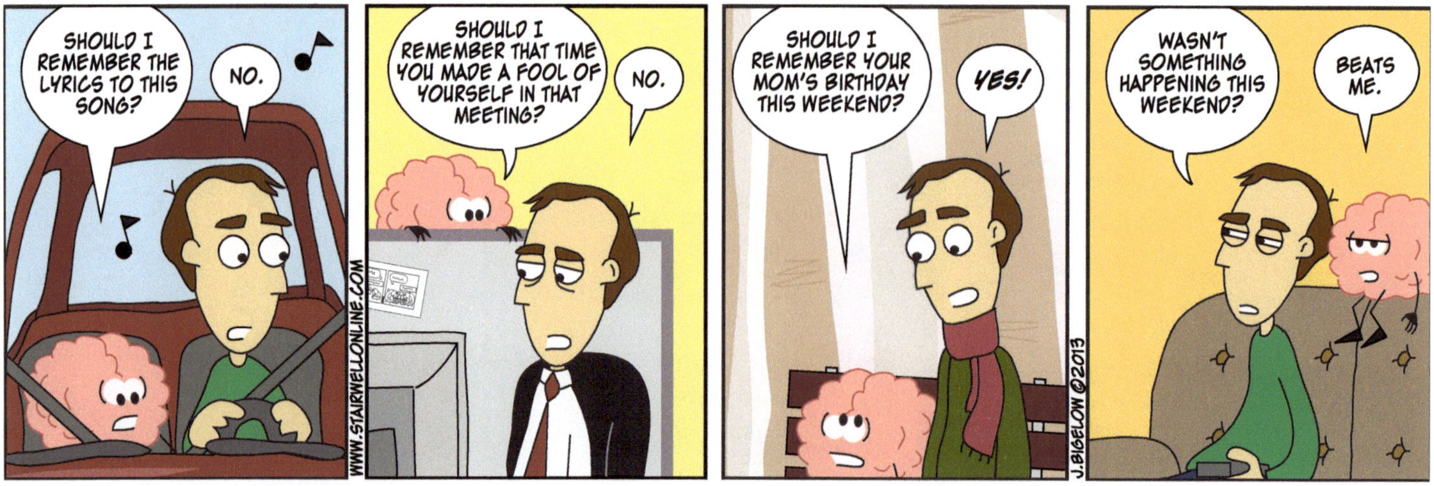
SHOULD I REMEMBER THE LYRICS TO THIS SONG?
NO.
SHOULD I REMEMBER THAT TIME YOU MADE A FOOL OF YOURSELF IN THAT MEETING?
NO.
SHOULD I REMEMBER YOUR MOM'S BIRTHDAY THIS WEEKEND?
YES!
WASN'T SOMETHING HAPPENING THIS WEEKEND?
BEATS ME.
WWW.STAIRWELLONLINE.COM
J.BIGELOW ©2013

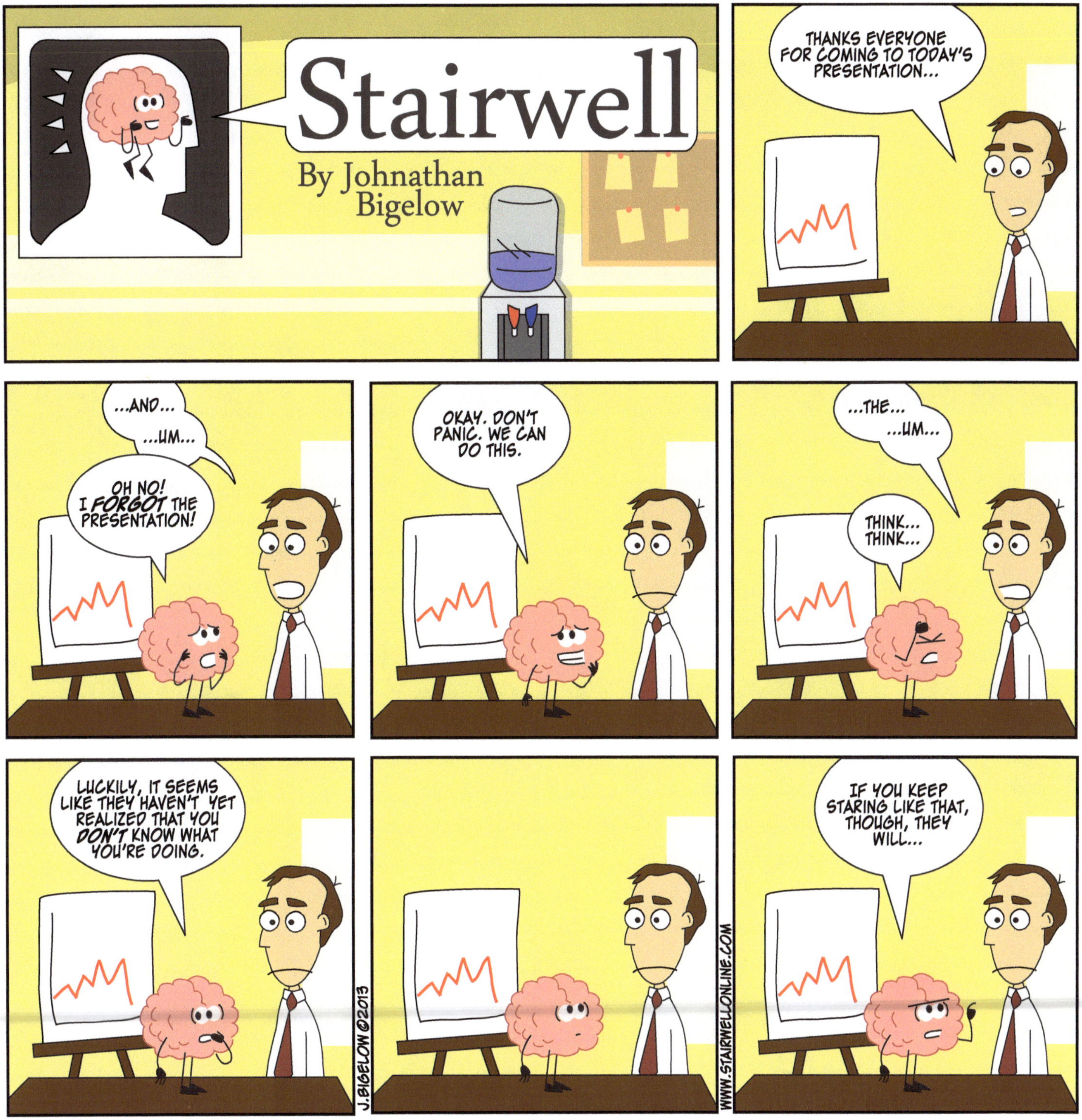
Stairwell
By Johnathan Bigelow
THANKS EVERYONE FOR COMING TO TODAY'S PRESENTATION...
...AND...
...UM...
OH NO! I FORGOT THE PRESENTATION!
OKAY. DON'T PANIC. WE CAN DO THIS.
...THE...
...UM...
THINK... THINK...
LUCKILY, IT SEEMS LIKE THEY HAVEN'T YET REALIZED THAT YOU DON'T KNOW WHAT YOU'RE DOING.
J.BIGELOW ©2013
WWW.STAIRWELLONLINE.COM
IF YOU KEEP STARING LIKE THAT, THOUGH, THEY WILL...

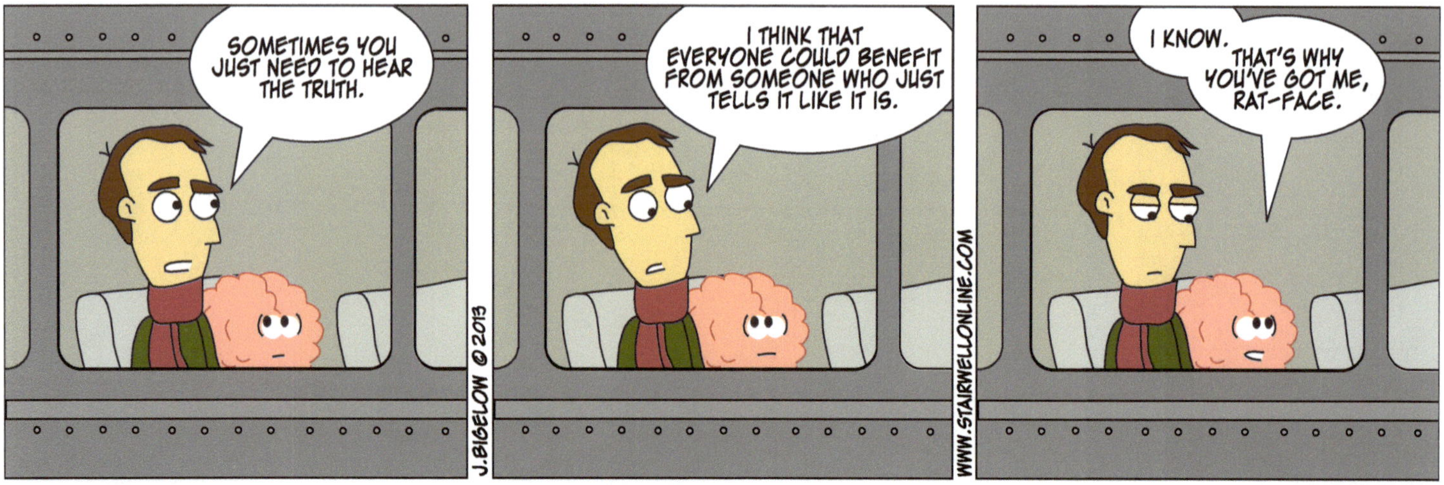
SOMETIMES YOU JUST NEED TO HEAR THE TRUTH.
J.BIGELOW ©2013
I THINK THAT EVERYONE COULD BENEFIT FROM SOMEONE WHO JUST TELLS IT LIKE IT IS.
WWW.STAIRWELLONLINE.COM
I KNOW.
THAT'S WHY YOU'VE GOT ME, RAT-FACE.

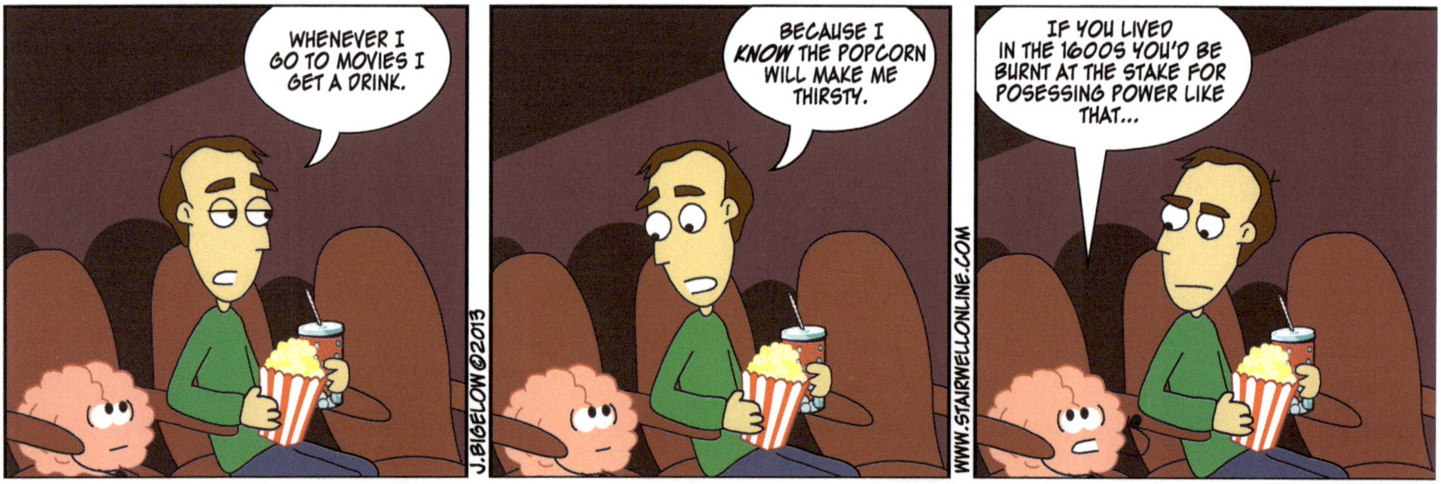
WHENEVER I GO TO MOVIES I GET A DRINK.
J.BIGELOW ©2013
BECAUSE I *KNOW* THE POPCORN WILL MAKE ME THIRSTY.
WWW.STAIRWELLONLINE.COM
IF YOU LIVED IN THE 1600S YOU'D BE BURNT AT THE STAKE FOR POSESSING POWER LIKE THAT...

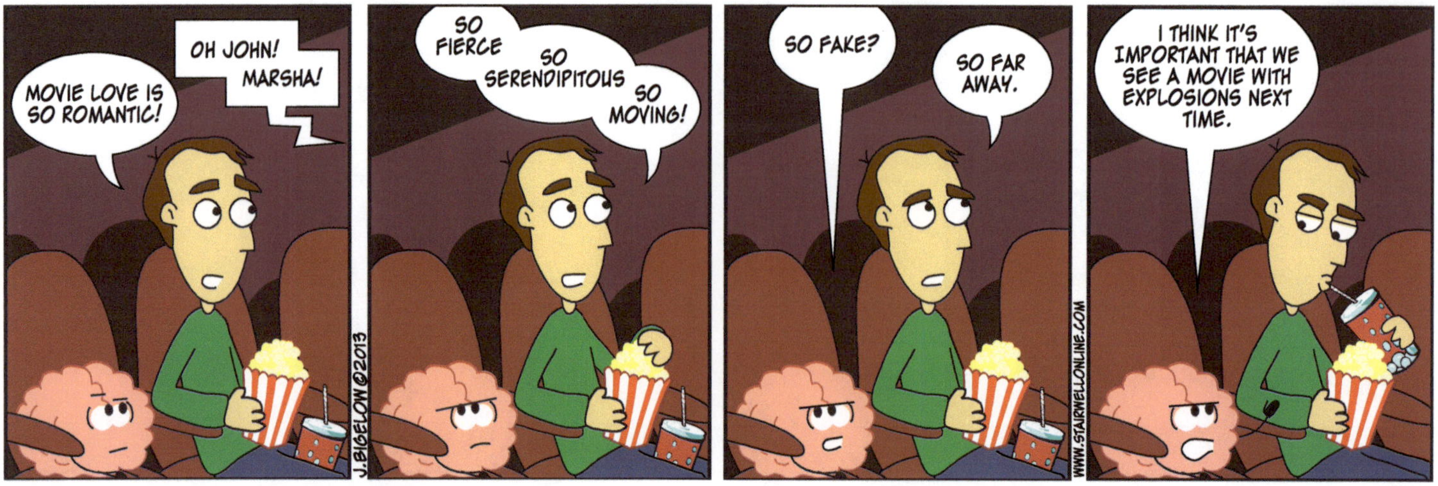
OH JOHN!
MARSHA!
MOVIE LOVE IS SO ROMANTIC!
J.BIGELOW ©2013
SO FIERCE
SO SERENDIPITOUS
SO MOVING!
SO FAKE?
SO FAR AWAY.
WWW.STAIRWELLONLINE.COM
I THINK IT'S IMPORTANT THAT WE SEE A MOVIE WITH EXPLOSIONS NEXT TIME.

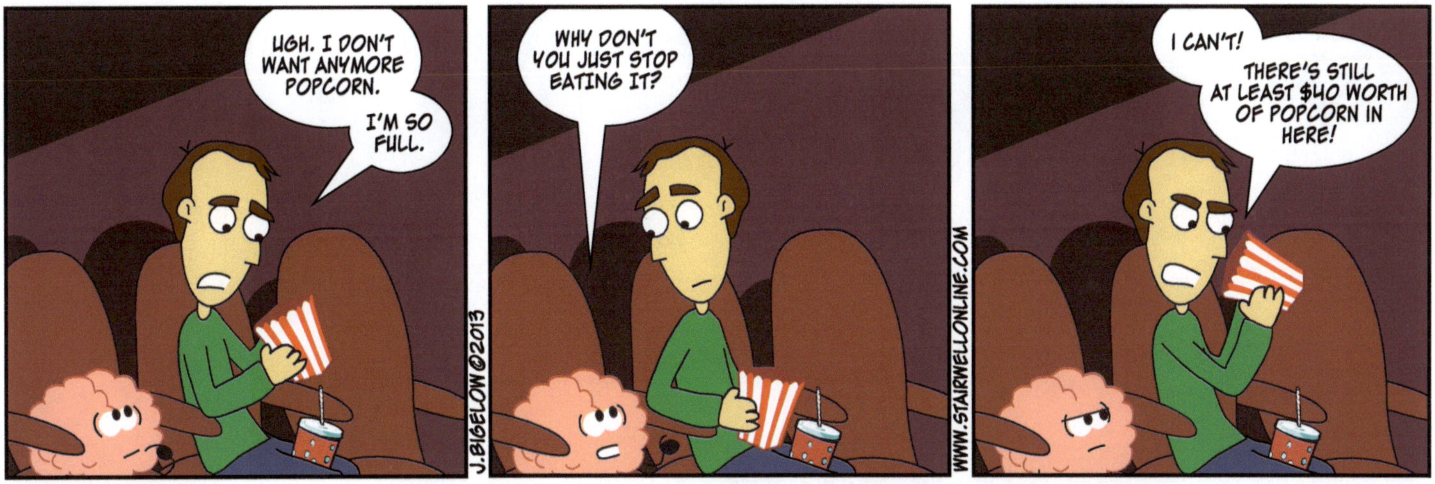
UGH. I DON'T WANT ANYMORE POPCORN.
I'M SO FULL.
J.BIGELOW ©2013
WHY DON'T YOU JUST STOP EATING IT?
WWW.STAIRWELLONLINE.COM
I CAN'T!
THERE'S STILL AT LEAST $40 WORTH OF POPCORN IN HERE!

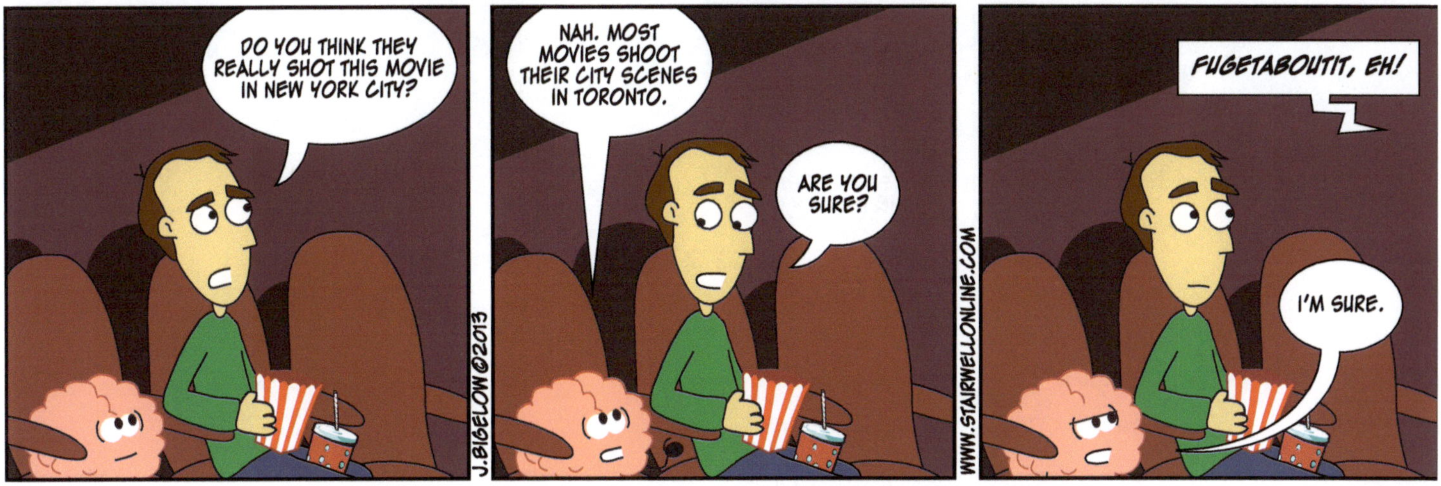
DO YOU THINK THEY REALLY SHOT THIS MOVIE IN NEW YORK CITY?
J.BIGELOW ©2013
NAH. MOST MOVIES SHOOT THEIR CITY SCENES IN TORONTO.
ARE YOU SURE?
WWW.STAIRWELLONLINE.COM
FUGETABOUTIT, EH!
I'M SURE.

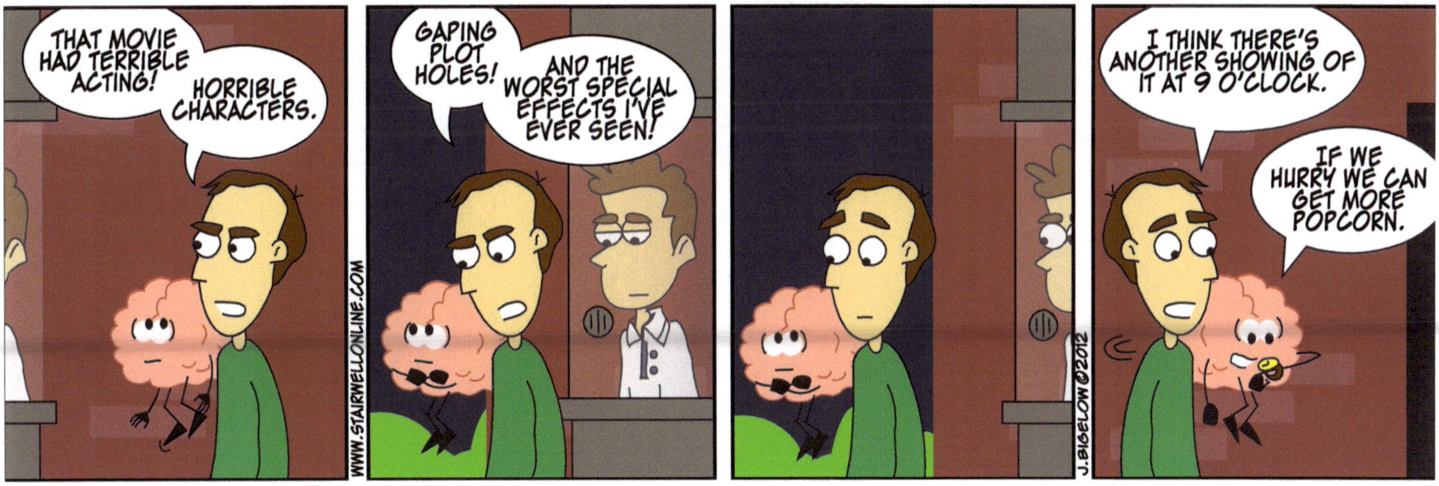
THAT MOVIE HAD TERRIBLE ACTING!
HORRIBLE CHARACTERS.
WWW.STAIRWELLONLINE.COM
GAPING PLOT HOLES!
AND THE WORST SPECIAL EFFECTS I'VE EVER SEEN!
J.BIGELOW ©2012
I THINK THERE'S ANOTHER SHOWING OF IT AT 9 O'CLOCK.
IF WE HURRY WE CAN GET MORE POPCORN.

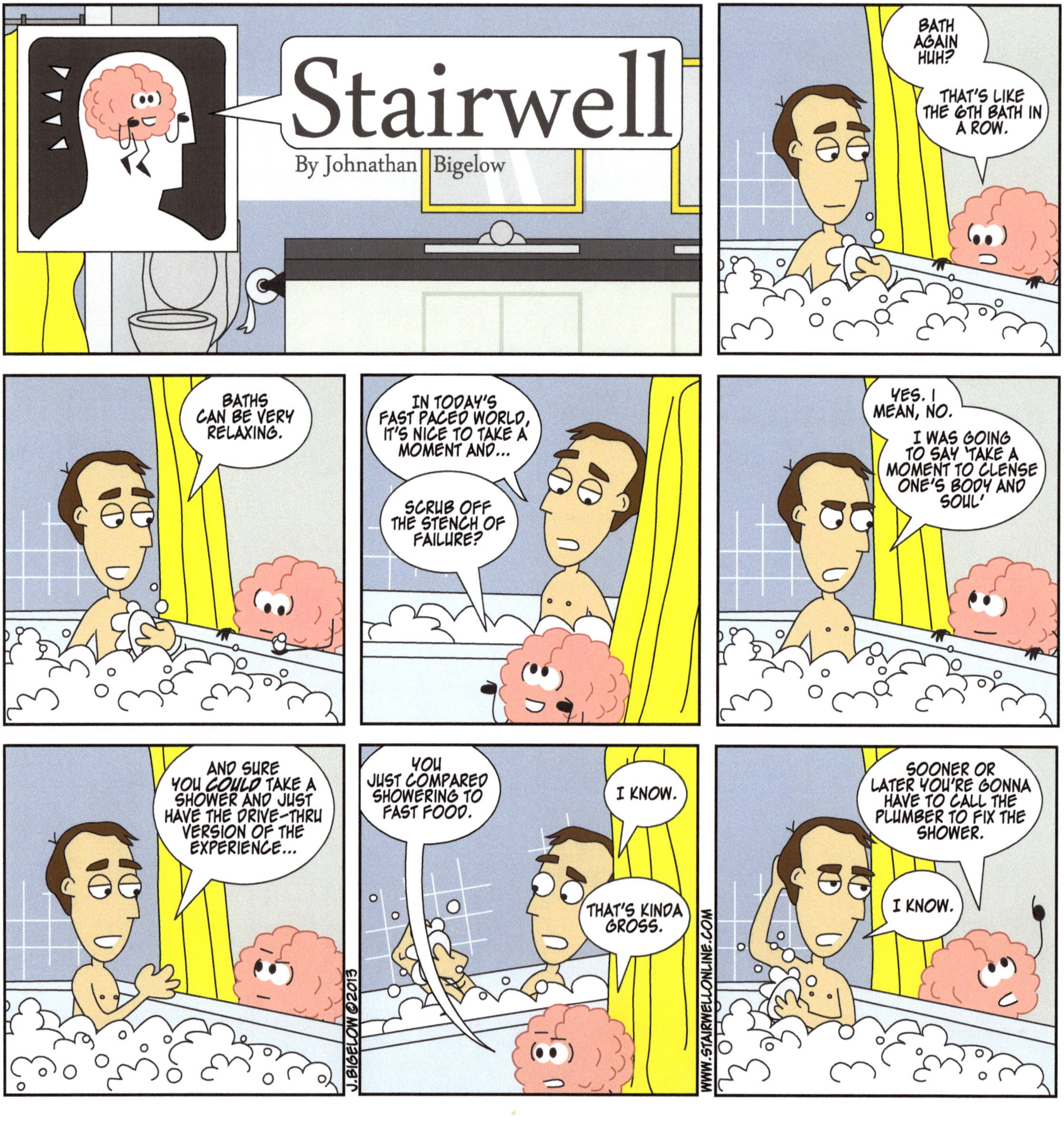
Stairwell
By Johnathan Bigelow
BATH AGAIN HUH?
THAT'S LIKE THE 6TH BATH IN A ROW.
BATHS CAN BE VERY RELAXING.
IN TODAY'S FAST PACED WORLD, IT'S NICE TO TAKE A MOMENT AND...
SCRUB OFF THE STENCH OF FAILURE?
YES. I MEAN, NO.
I WAS GOING TO SAY 'TAKE A MOMENT TO CLENSE ONE'S BODY AND SOUL'
AND SURE YOU *COULD* TAKE A SHOWER AND JUST HAVE THE DRIVE-THRU VERSION OF THE EXPERIENCE...
J.BIGELOW ©2013
YOU JUST COMPARED SHOWERING TO FAST FOOD.
I KNOW.
THAT'S KINDA GROSS.
WWW.STAIRWELLONLINE.COM
SOONER OR LATER YOU'RE GONNA HAVE TO CALL THE PLUMBER TO FIX THE SHOWER.
I KNOW.

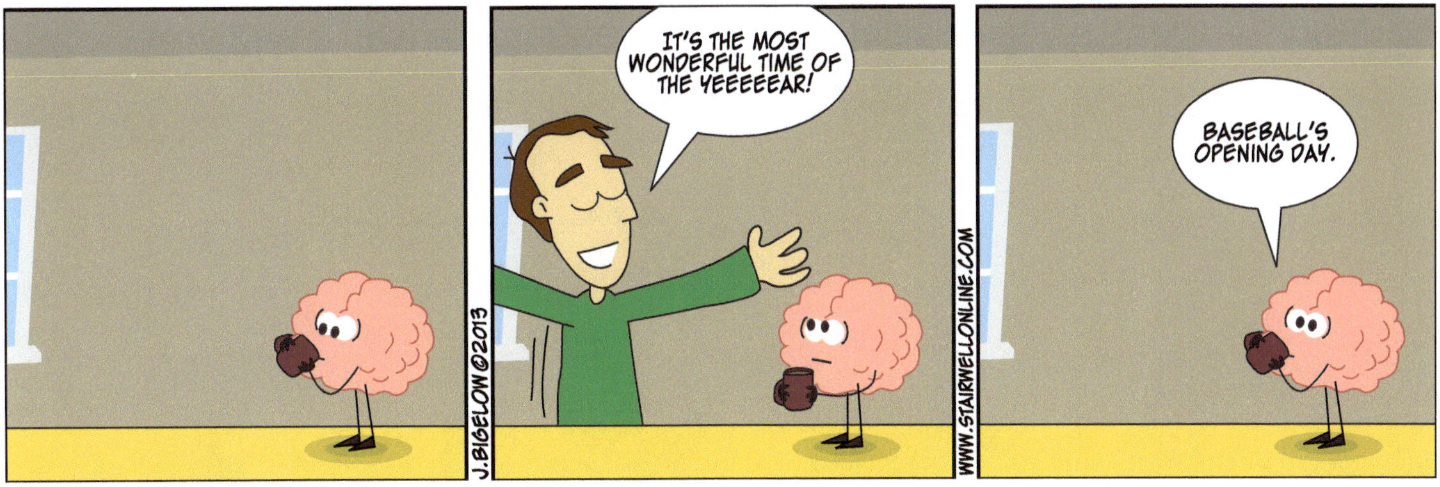
J.BIGELOW ©2013
IT'S THE MOST WONDERFUL TIME OF THE YEEEEEAR!
WWW.STAIRWELLONLINE.COM
BASEBALL'S OPENING DAY.

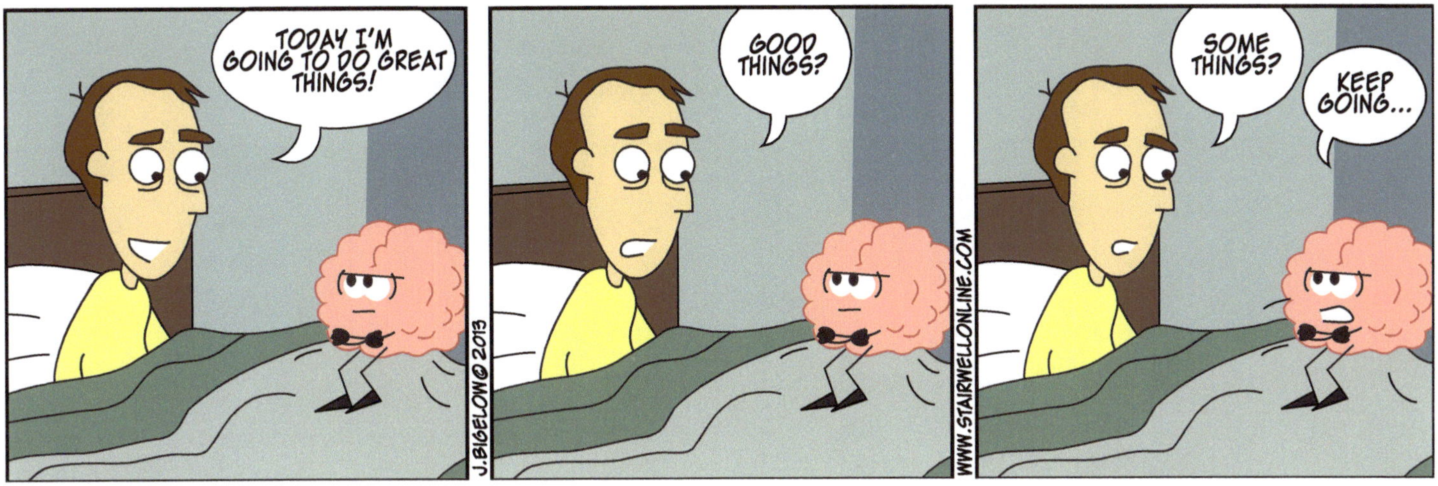
TODAY I'M GOING TO DO GREAT THINGS!
J.BIGELOW © 2013
GOOD THINGS?
WWW.STAIRWELLONLINE.COM
SOME THINGS?
KEEP GOING...

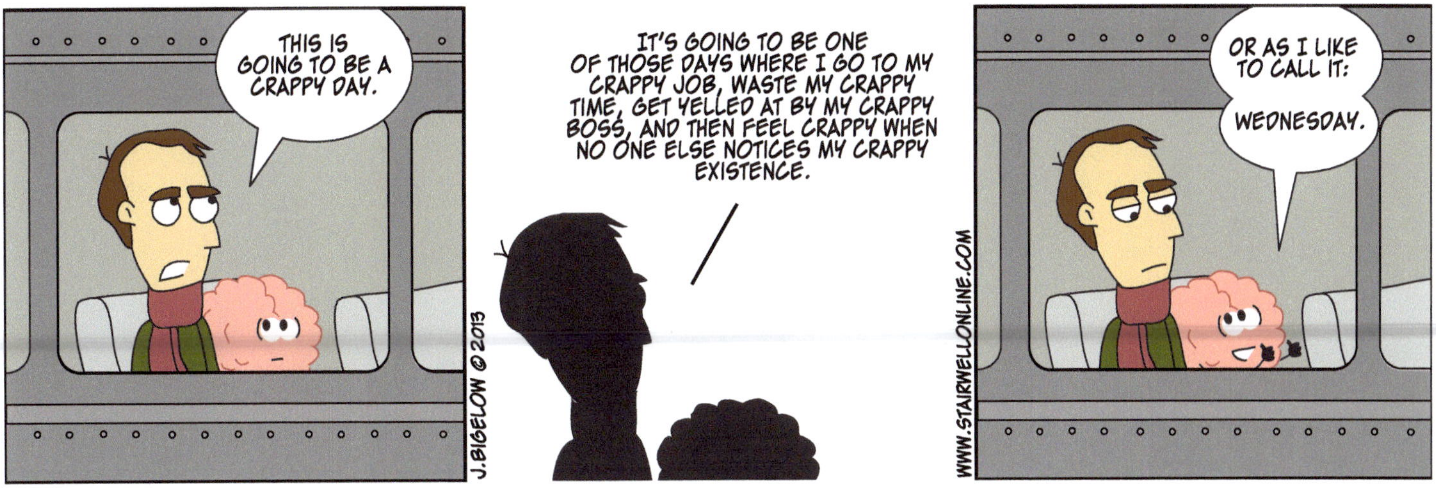
THIS IS GOING TO BE A CRAPPY DAY.
J.BIGELOW © 2013
IT'S GOING TO BE ONE OF THOSE DAYS WHERE I GO TO MY CRAPPY JOB, WASTE MY CRAPPY TIME, GET YELLED AT BY MY CRAPPY BOSS, AND THEN FEEL CRAPPY WHEN NO ONE ELSE NOTICES MY CRAPPY EXISTENCE.
WWW.STAIRWELLONLINE.COM
OR AS I LIKE TO CALL IT:
WEDNESDAY.

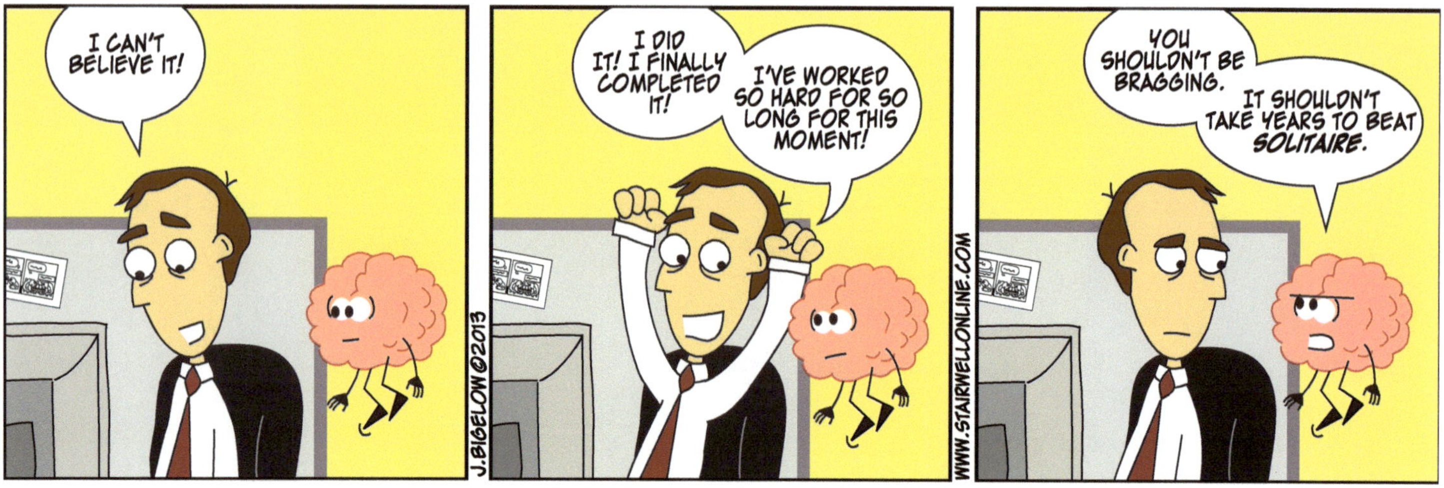
I CAN'T BELIEVE IT!
J.BIGELOW ©2013
I DID IT! I FINALLY COMPLETED IT!
I'VE WORKED SO HARD FOR SO LONG FOR THIS MOMENT!
WWW.STAIRWELLONLINE.COM
YOU SHOULDN'T BE BRAGGING.
IT SHOULDN'T TAKE YEARS TO BEAT *SOLITAIRE*.

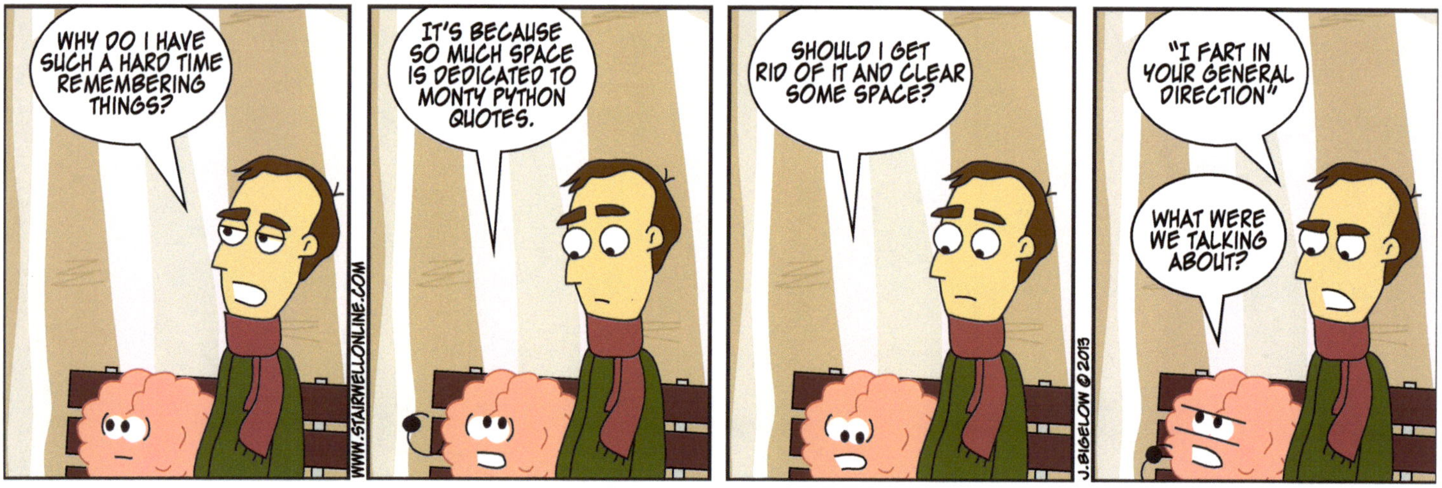
WHY DO I HAVE SUCH A HARD TIME REMEMBERING THINGS?
WWW.STAIRWELLONLINE.COM
IT'S BECAUSE SO MUCH SPACE IS DEDICATED TO MONTY PYTHON QUOTES.
SHOULD I GET RID OF IT AND CLEAR SOME SPACE?
J.BIGELOW ©2013
"I FART IN YOUR GENERAL DIRECTION"
WHAT WERE WE TALKING ABOUT?

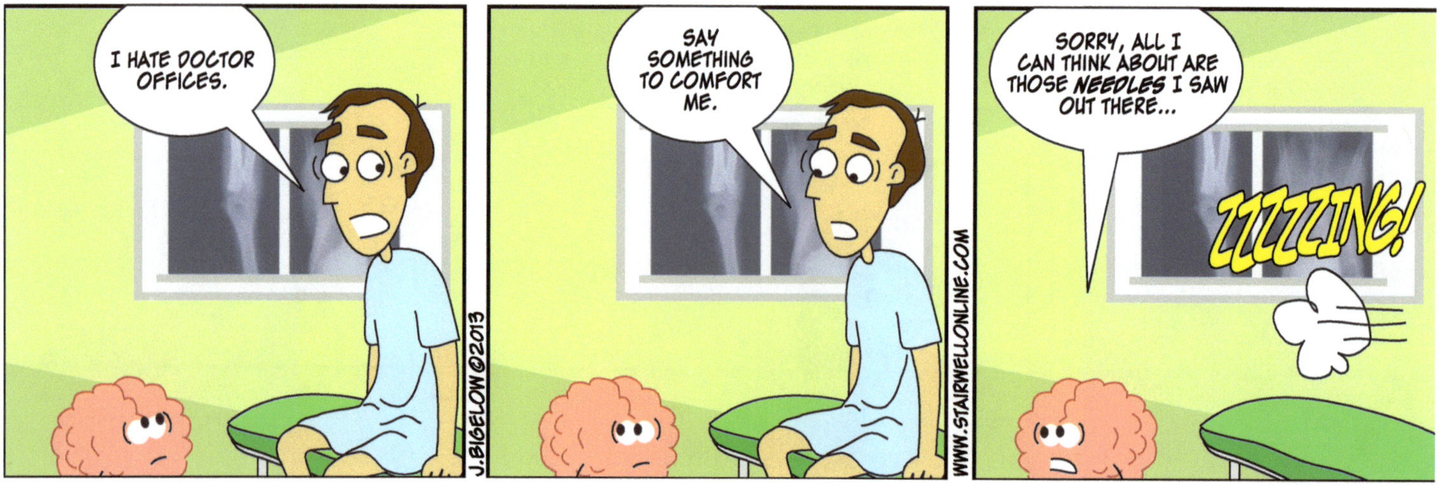
I HATE DOCTOR OFFICES.
J.BIGELOW ©2013
SAY SOMETHING TO COMFORT ME.
WWW.STAIRWELLONLINE.COM
SORRY, ALL I CAN THINK ABOUT ARE THOSE *NEEDLES* I SAW OUT THERE...
ZZZZZING!

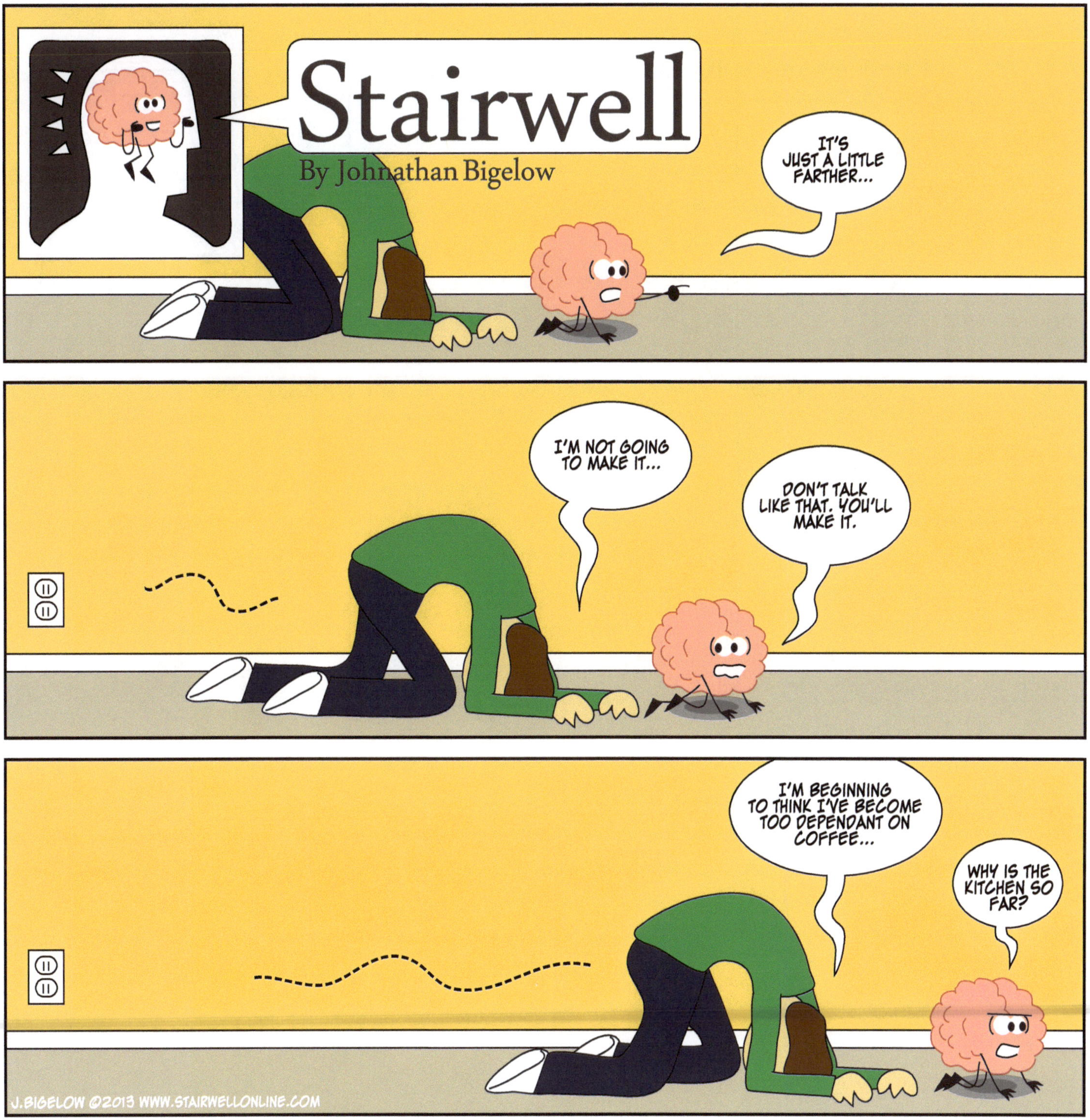
Stairwell
By Johnathan Bigelow
IT'S JUST A LITTLE FARTHER...
I'M NOT GOING TO MAKE IT...
DON'T TALK LIKE THAT. YOU'LL MAKE IT.
I'M BEGINNING TO THINK I'VE BECOME TOO DEPENDANT ON COFFEE...
WHY IS THE KITCHEN SO FAR?
J.BIGELOW ©2013 WWW.STAIRWELLONLINE.COM

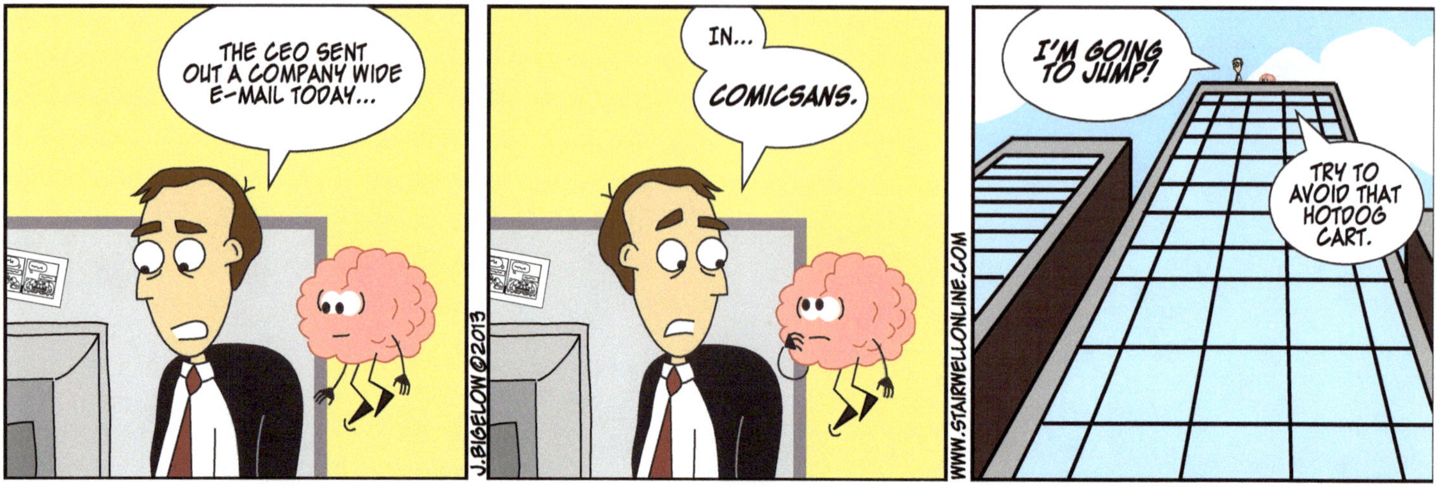
THE CEO SENT OUT A COMPANY WIDE E-MAIL TODAY...
IN...
COMICSANS.
J.BIGELOW ©2013
WWW.STAIRWELLONLINE.COM
I'M GOING TO JUMP!
TRY TO AVOID THAT HOTDOG CART.

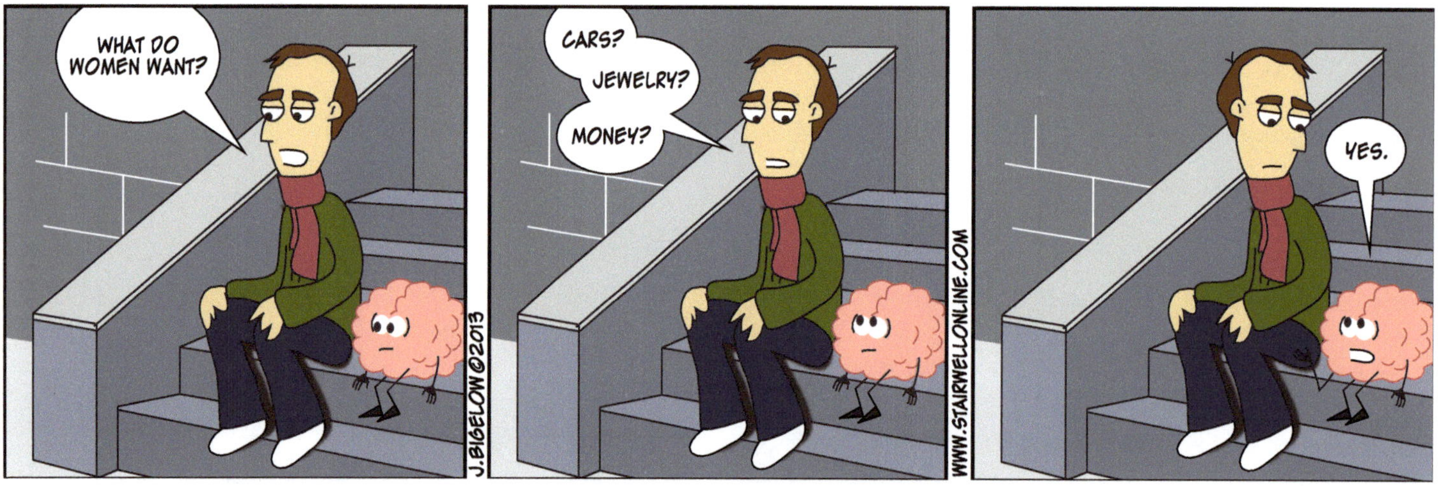
WHAT DO WOMEN WANT?
J.BIGELOW ©2013
CARS?
JEWELRY?
MONEY?
WWW.STAIRWELLONLINE.COM
YES.

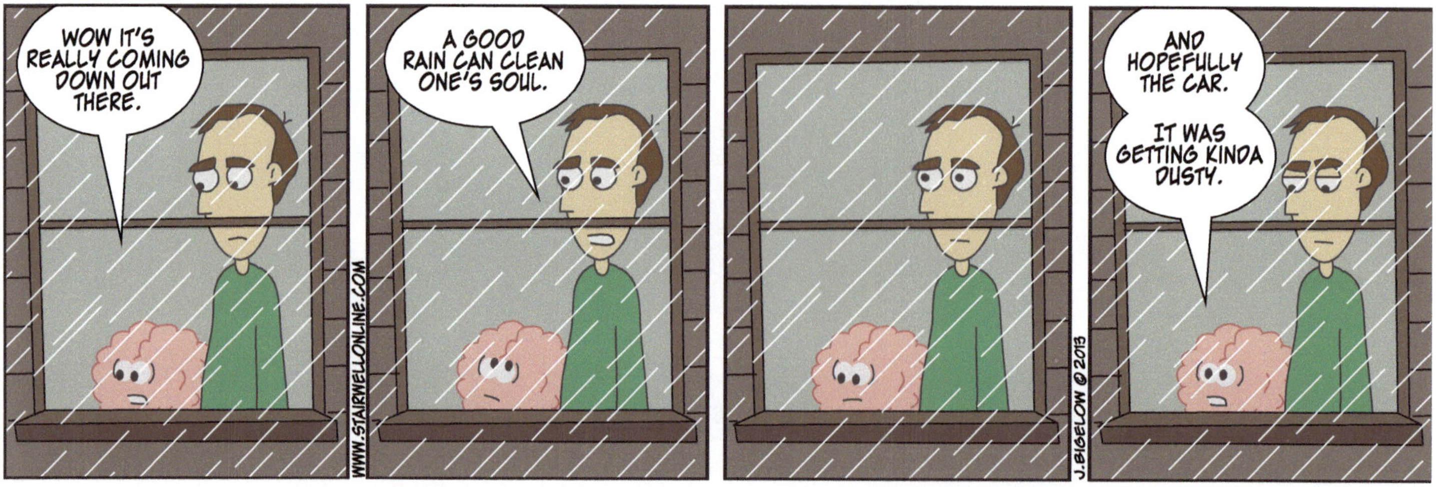
WOW IT'S REALLY COMING DOWN OUT THERE.
WWW.STAIRWELLONLINE.COM
A GOOD RAIN CAN CLEAN ONE'S SOUL.
J.BIGELOW ©2013
AND HOPEFULLY THE CAR.
IT WAS GETTING KINDA DUSTY.

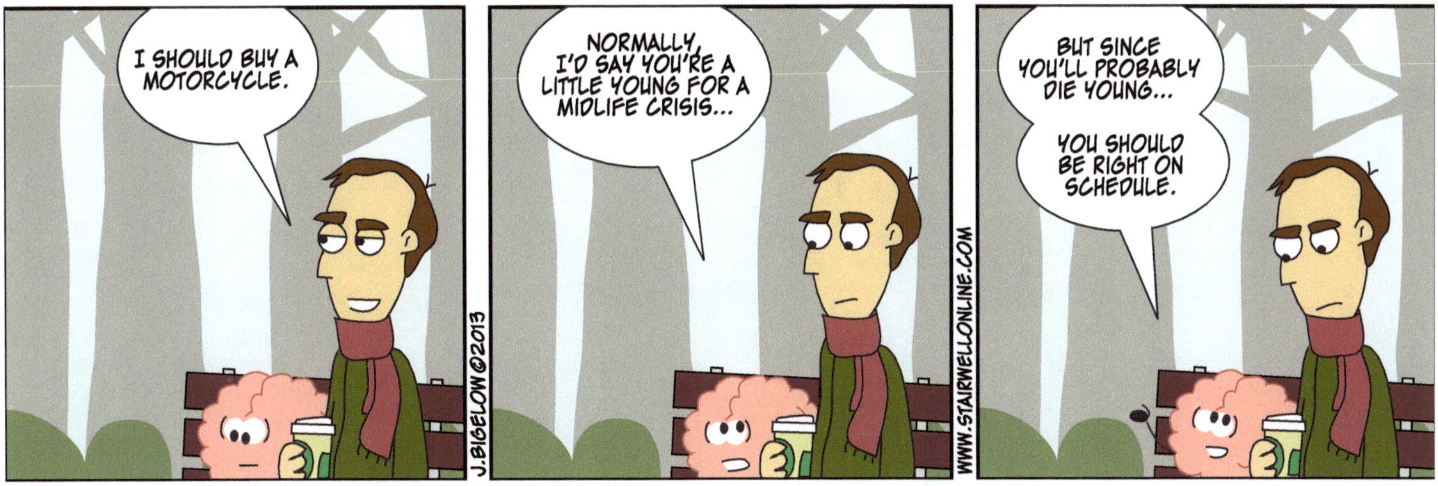
I SHOULD BUY A MOTORCYCLE.
J.BIGELOW ©2013
NORMALLY, I'D SAY YOU'RE A LITTLE YOUNG FOR A MIDLIFE CRISIS...
WWW.STAIRWELLONLINE.COM
BUT SINCE YOU'LL PROBABLY DIE YOUNG...
YOU SHOULD BE RIGHT ON SCHEDULE.

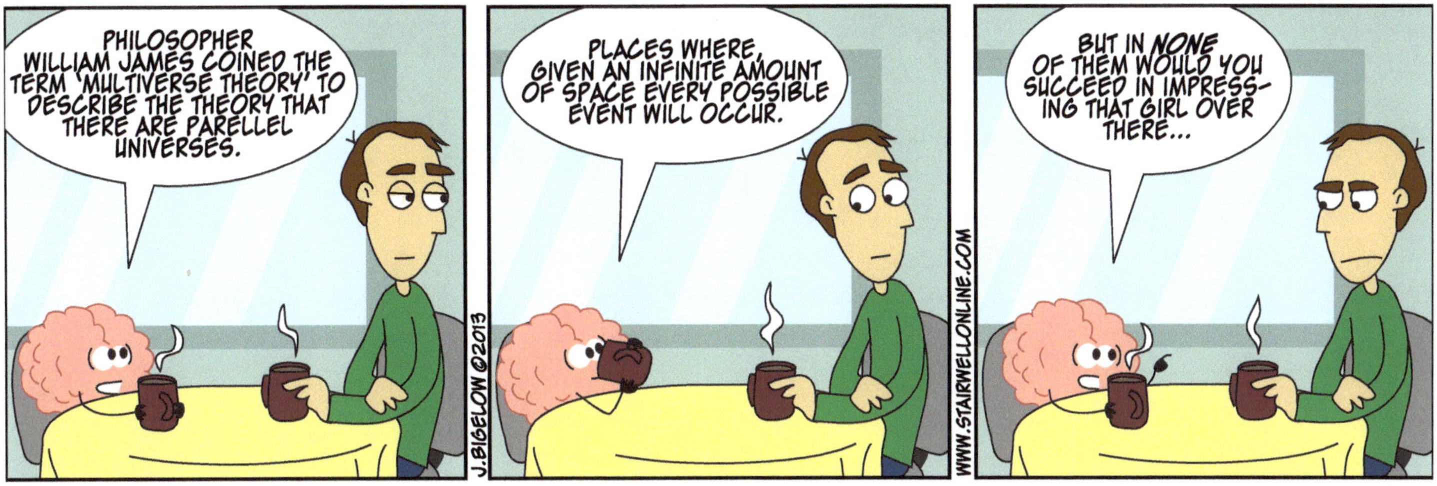
PHILOSOPHER WILLIAM JAMES COINED THE TERM 'MULTIVERSE THEORY' TO DESCRIBE THE THEORY THAT THERE ARE PARELLEL UNIVERSES.
J.BIGELOW ©2013
PLACES WHERE, GIVEN AN INFINITE AMOUNT OF SPACE EVERY POSSIBLE EVENT WILL OCCUR.
WWW.STAIRWELLONLINE.COM
BUT IN *NONE* OF THEM WOULD YOU SUCCEED IN IMPRESS-ING THAT GIRL OVER THERE...

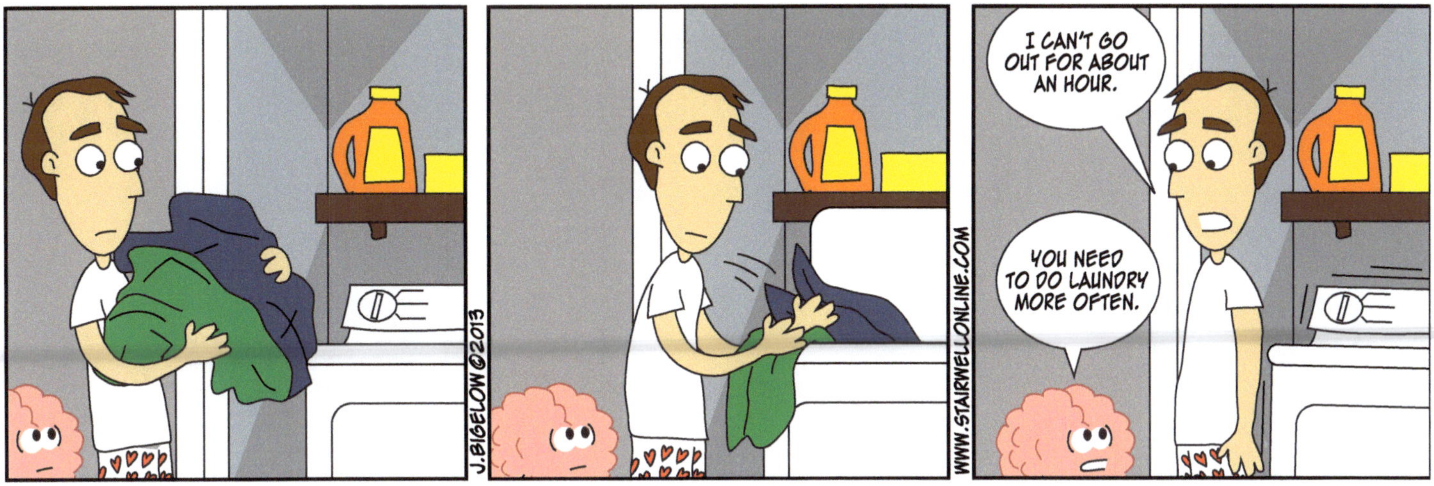
J.BIGELOW ©2013
WWW.STAIRWELLONLINE.COM
I CAN'T GO OUT FOR ABOUT AN HOUR.
YOU NEED TO DO LAUNDRY MORE OFTEN.

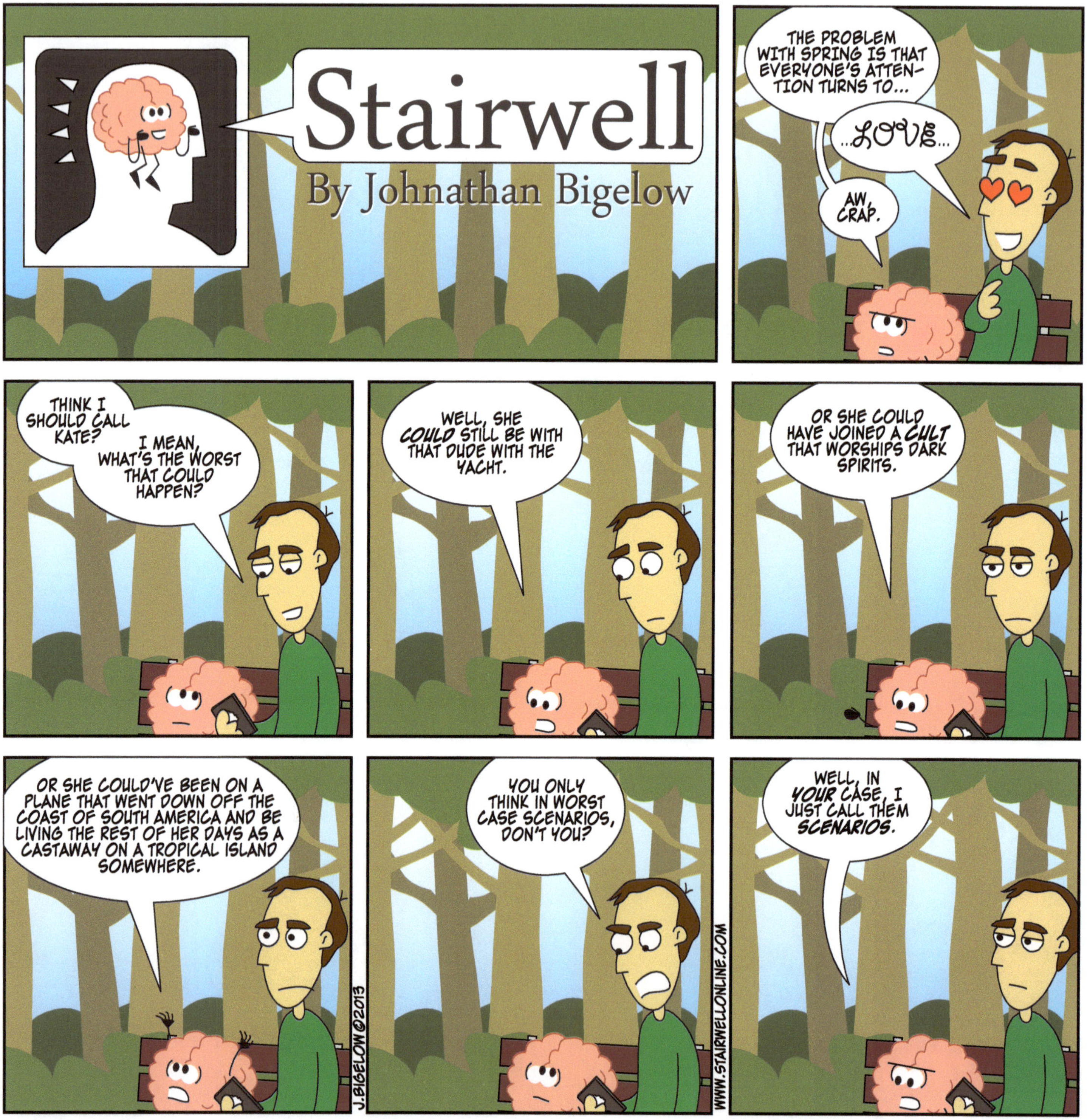
Stairwell
By Johnathan Bigelow
THE PROBLEM WITH SPRING IS THAT EVERYONE'S ATTENTION TURNS TO...
...LOVE...
AW, CRAP.
THINK I SHOULD CALL KATE?
I MEAN, WHAT'S THE WORST THAT COULD HAPPEN?
WELL, SHE *COULD* STILL BE WITH THAT DUDE WITH THE YACHT.
OR SHE COULD HAVE JOINED A *CULT* THAT WORSHIPS DARK SPIRITS.
OR SHE COULD'VE BEEN ON A PLANE THAT WENT DOWN OFF THE COAST OF SOUTH AMERICA AND BE LIVING THE REST OF HER DAYS AS A CASTAWAY ON A TROPICAL ISLAND SOMEWHERE.
J.BIGELOW ©2013
YOU ONLY THINK IN WORST CASE SCENARIOS, DON'T YOU?
WWW.STAIRWELLONLINE.COM
WELL, IN *YOUR* CASE, I JUST CALL THEM *SCENARIOS*.

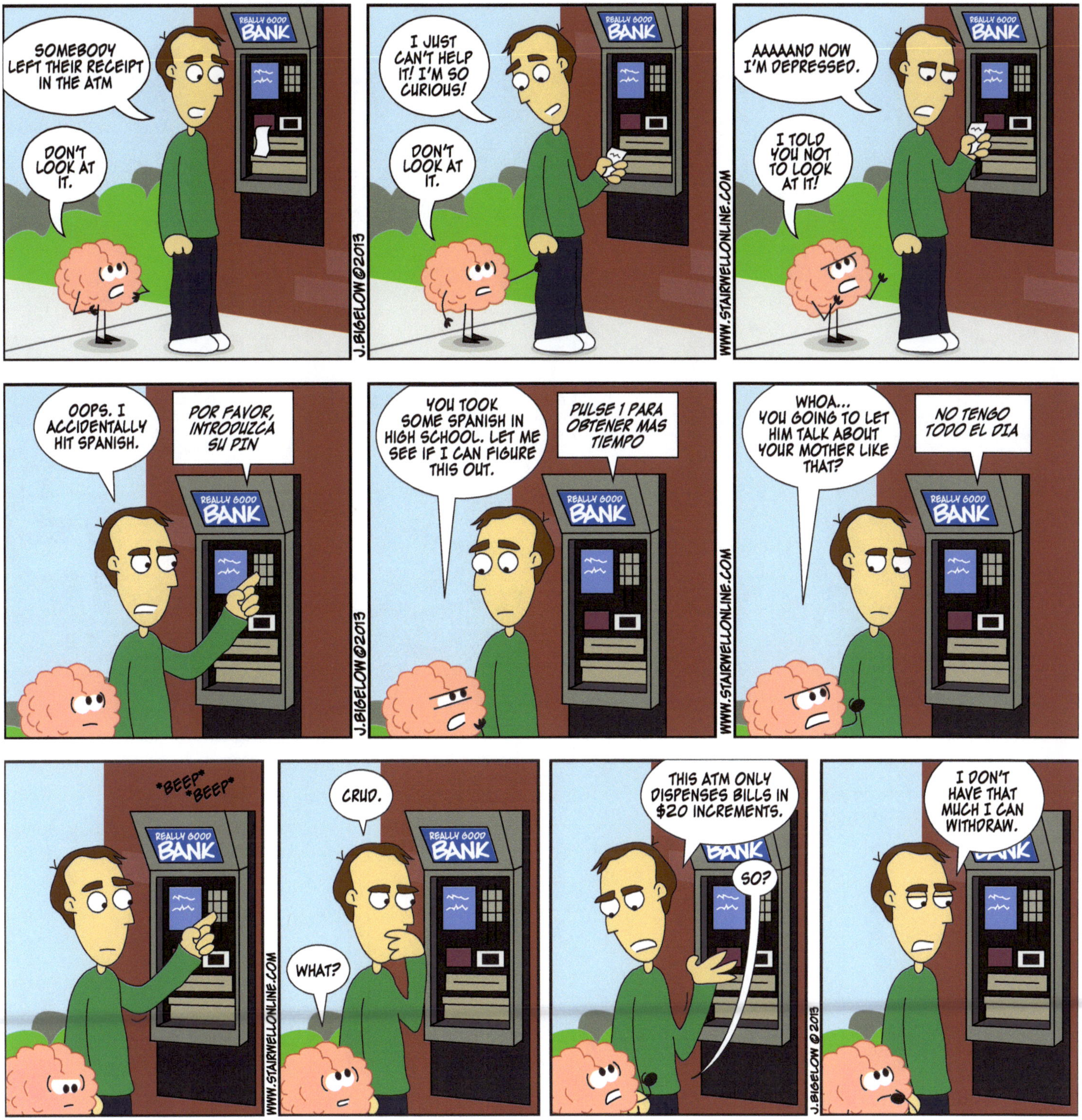

SOMEBODY LEFT THEIR RECEIPT IN THE ATM
DON'T LOOK AT IT.
REALLY GOOD BANK
I JUST CAN'T HELP IT! I'M SO CURIOUS!
DON'T LOOK AT IT.
J.BIGELOW ©2013
AAAAAND NOW I'M DEPRESSED.
I TOLD YOU NOT TO LOOK AT IT!
WWW.STAIRWELLONLINE.COM
OOPS. I ACCIDENTALLY HIT SPANISH.
POR FAVOR, INTRODUZCA SU PIN
YOU TOOK SOME SPANISH IN HIGH SCHOOL. LET ME SEE IF I CAN FIGURE THIS OUT.
PULSE 1 PARA OBTENER MAS TIEMPO
WHOA... YOU GOING TO LET HIM TALK ABOUT YOUR MOTHER LIKE THAT?
NO TENGO TODO EL DIA
BEEP *BEEP*
CRUD.
WHAT?
THIS ATM ONLY DISPENSES BILLS IN $20 INCREMENTS.
SO?
I DON'T HAVE THAT MUCH I CAN WITHDRAW.

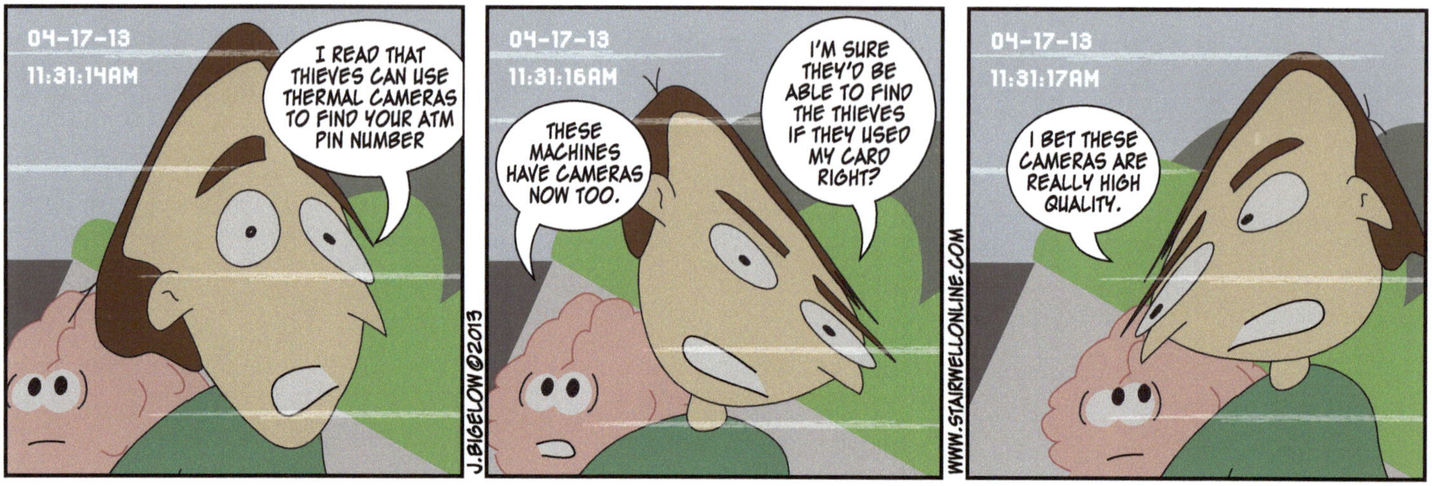
04-17-13
11:31:14AM
I READ THAT THIEVES CAN USE THERMAL CAMERAS TO FIND YOUR ATM PIN NUMBER
04-17-13
11:31:16AM
THESE MACHINES HAVE CAMERAS NOW TOO.
I'M SURE THEY'D BE ABLE TO FIND THE THIEVES IF THEY USED MY CARD RIGHT?
04-17-13
11:31:17AM
I BET THESE CAMERAS ARE REALLY HIGH QUALITY.
J.BIGELOW ©2013
WWW.STAIRWELLONLINE.COM

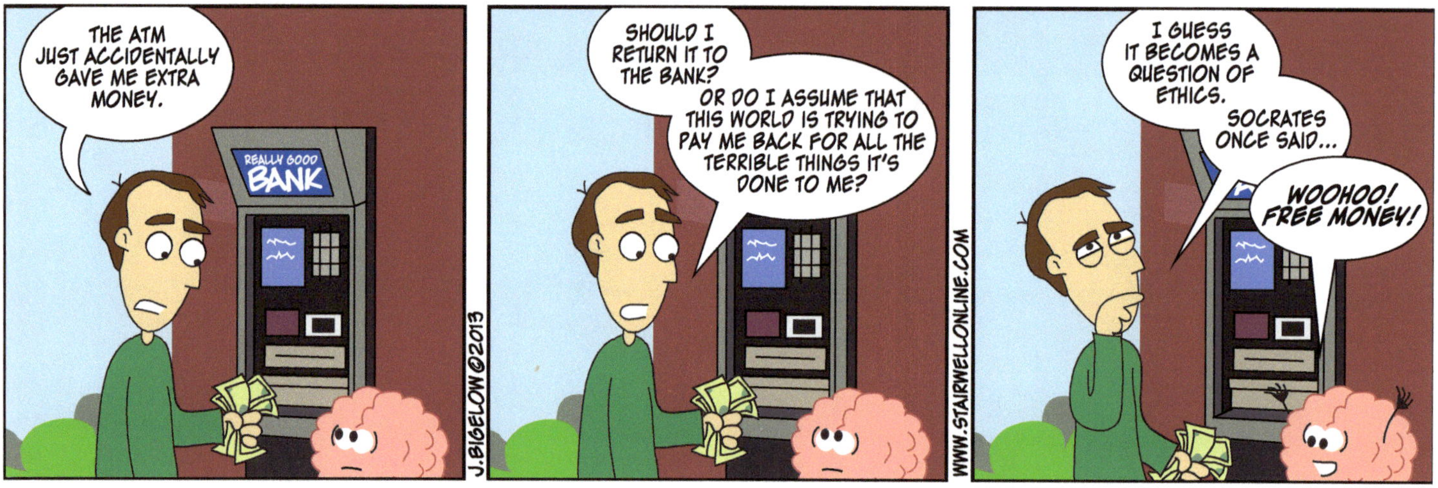
THE ATM JUST ACCIDENTALLY GAVE ME EXTRA MONEY.
REALLY GOOD BANK
SHOULD I RETURN IT TO THE BANK?
OR DO I ASSUME THAT THIS WORLD IS TRYING TO PAY ME BACK FOR ALL THE TERRIBLE THINGS IT'S DONE TO ME?
I GUESS IT BECOMES A QUESTION OF ETHICS.
SOCRATES ONCE SAID...
WOOHOO! FREE MONEY!
J.BIGELOW ©2013
WWW.STAIRWELLONLINE.COM

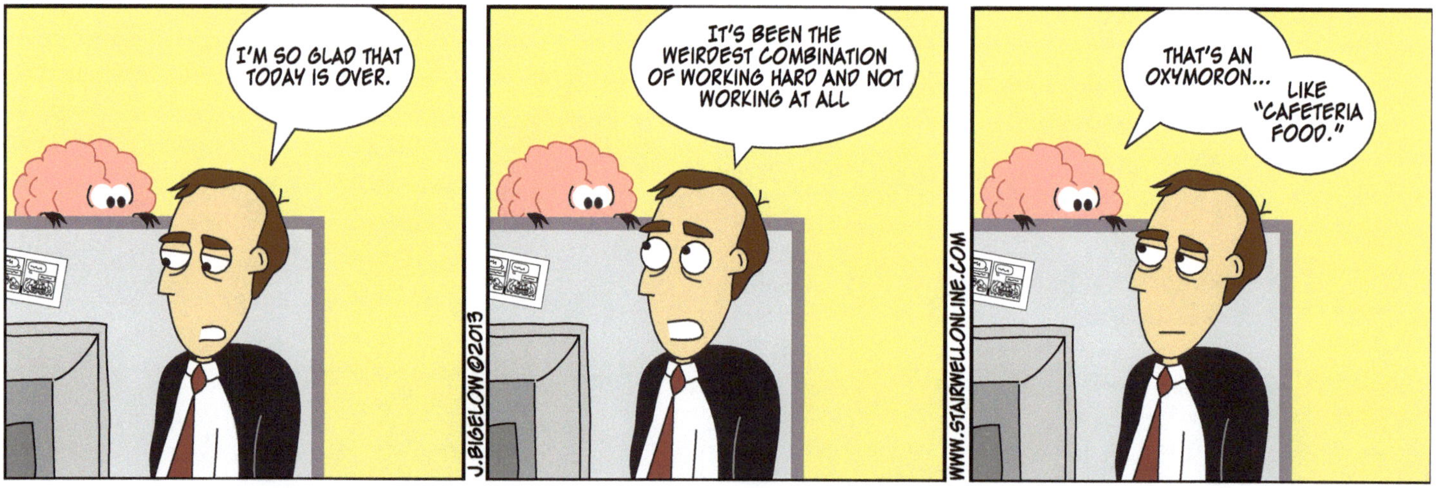
I'M SO GLAD THAT TODAY IS OVER.
IT'S BEEN THE WEIRDEST COMBINATION OF WORKING HARD AND NOT WORKING AT ALL
THAT'S AN OXYMORON...
LIKE "CAFETERIA FOOD."
J.BIGELOW ©2013
WWW.STAIRWELLONLINE.COM

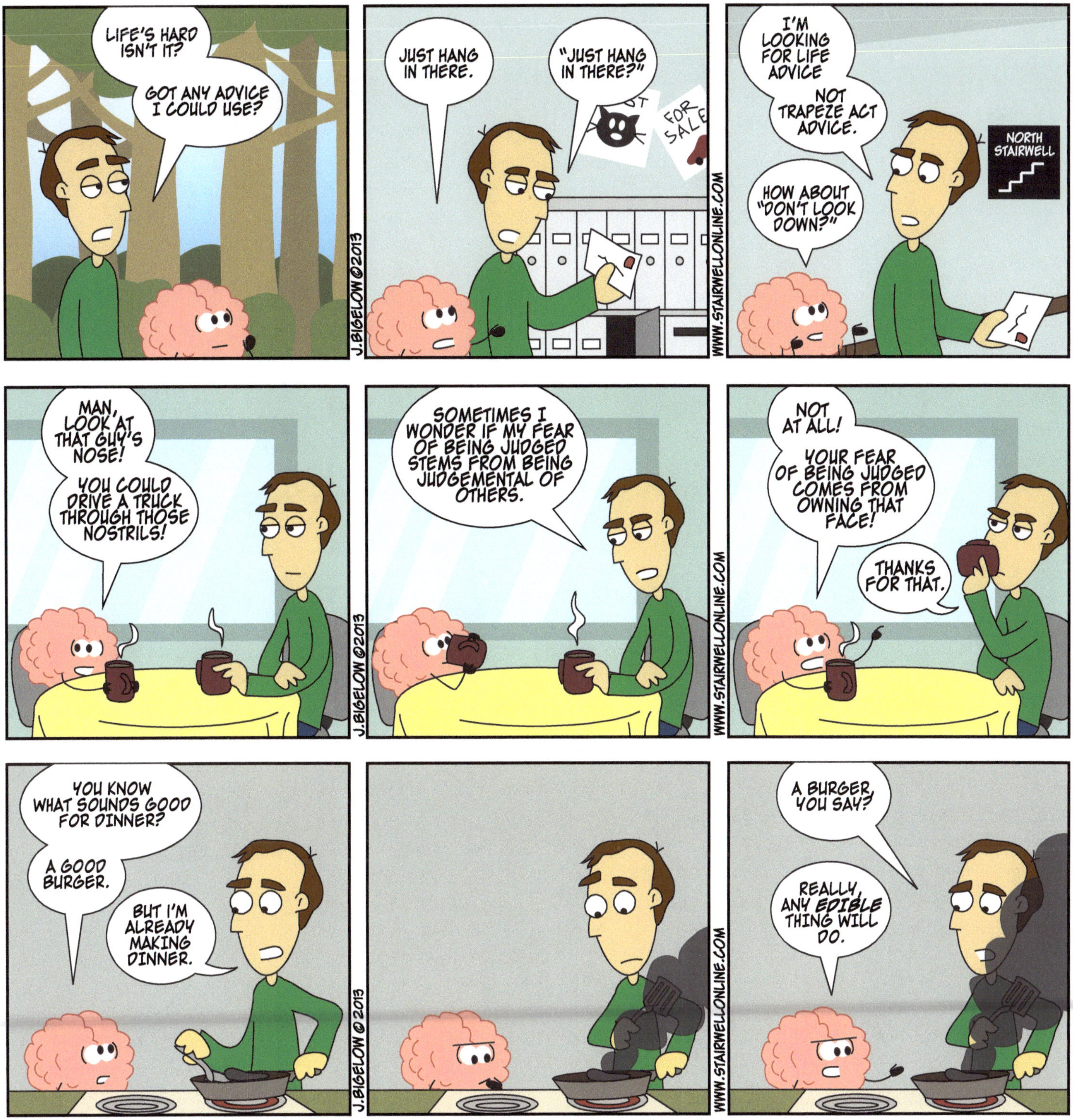
LIFE'S HARD ISN'T IT?
GOT ANY ADVICE I COULD USE?
JUST HANG IN THERE.
"JUST HANG IN THERE?"
FOR SALE
J.BIGELOW ©2013
I'M LOOKING FOR LIFE ADVICE
NOT TRAPEZE ACT ADVICE.
HOW ABOUT "DON'T LOOK DOWN?"
NORTH STAIRWELL
WWW.STAIRWELLONLINE.COM
MAN, LOOK AT THAT GUY'S NOSE!
YOU COULD DRIVE A TRUCK THROUGH THOSE NOSTRILS!
SOMETIMES I WONDER IF MY FEAR OF BEING JUDGED STEMS FROM BEING JUDGEMENTAL OF OTHERS.
J.BIGELOW ©2013
NOT AT ALL!
YOUR FEAR OF BEING JUDGED COMES FROM OWNING THAT FACE!
THANKS FOR THAT.
WWW.STAIRWELLONLINE.COM
YOU KNOW WHAT SOUNDS GOOD FOR DINNER?
A GOOD BURGER.
BUT I'M ALREADY MAKING DINNER.
J.BIGELOW ©2013
A BURGER, YOU SAY?
REALLY, ANY EDIBLE THING WILL DO.
WWW.STAIRWELLONLINE.COM

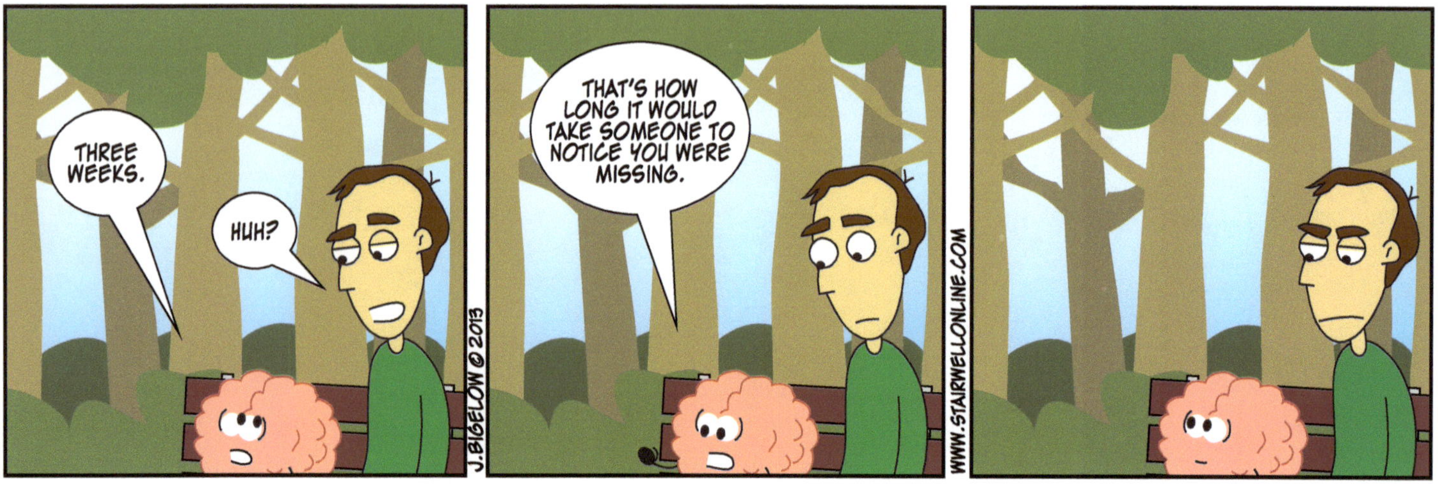
THREE WEEKS.
HUH?
J.BIGELOW © 2013
THAT'S HOW LONG IT WOULD TAKE SOMEONE TO NOTICE YOU WERE MISSING.
WWW.STAIRWELLONLINE.COM

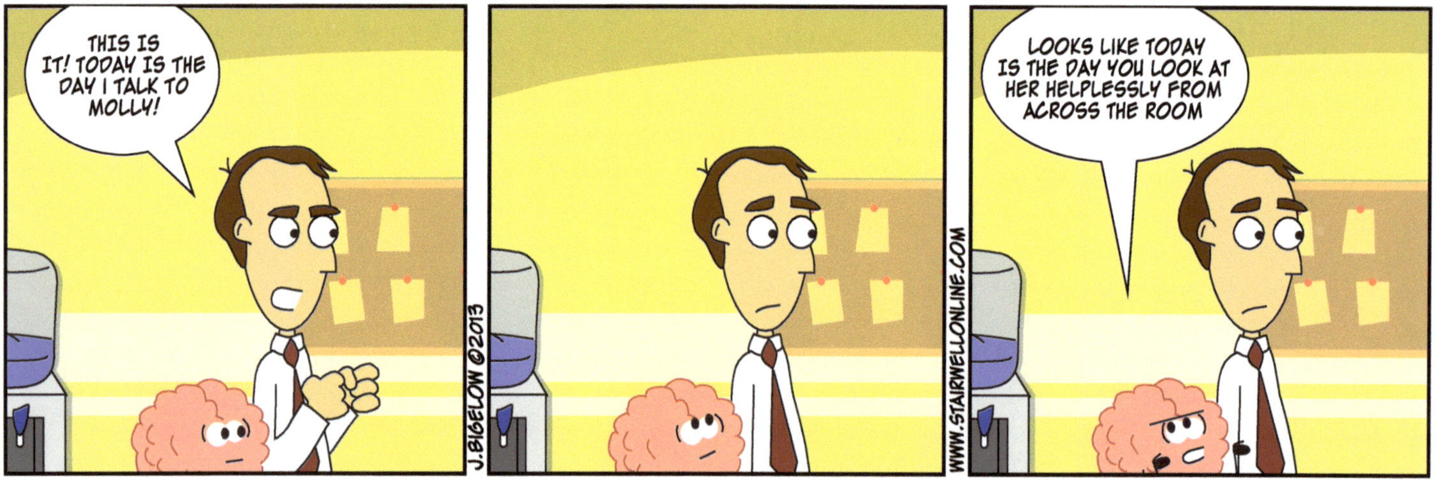
THIS IS IT! TODAY IS THE DAY I TALK TO MOLLY!
J.BIGELOW © 2013
WWW.STAIRWELLONLINE.COM
LOOKS LIKE TODAY IS THE DAY YOU LOOK AT HER HELPLESSLY FROM ACROSS THE ROOM

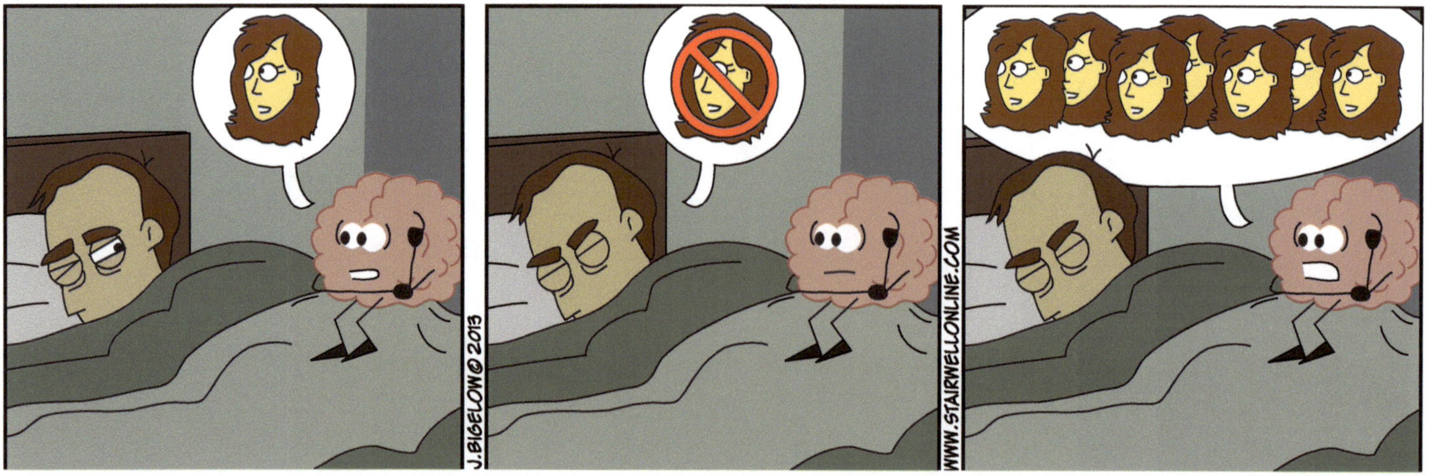
J.BIGELOW © 2013
WWW.STAIRWELLONLINE.COM

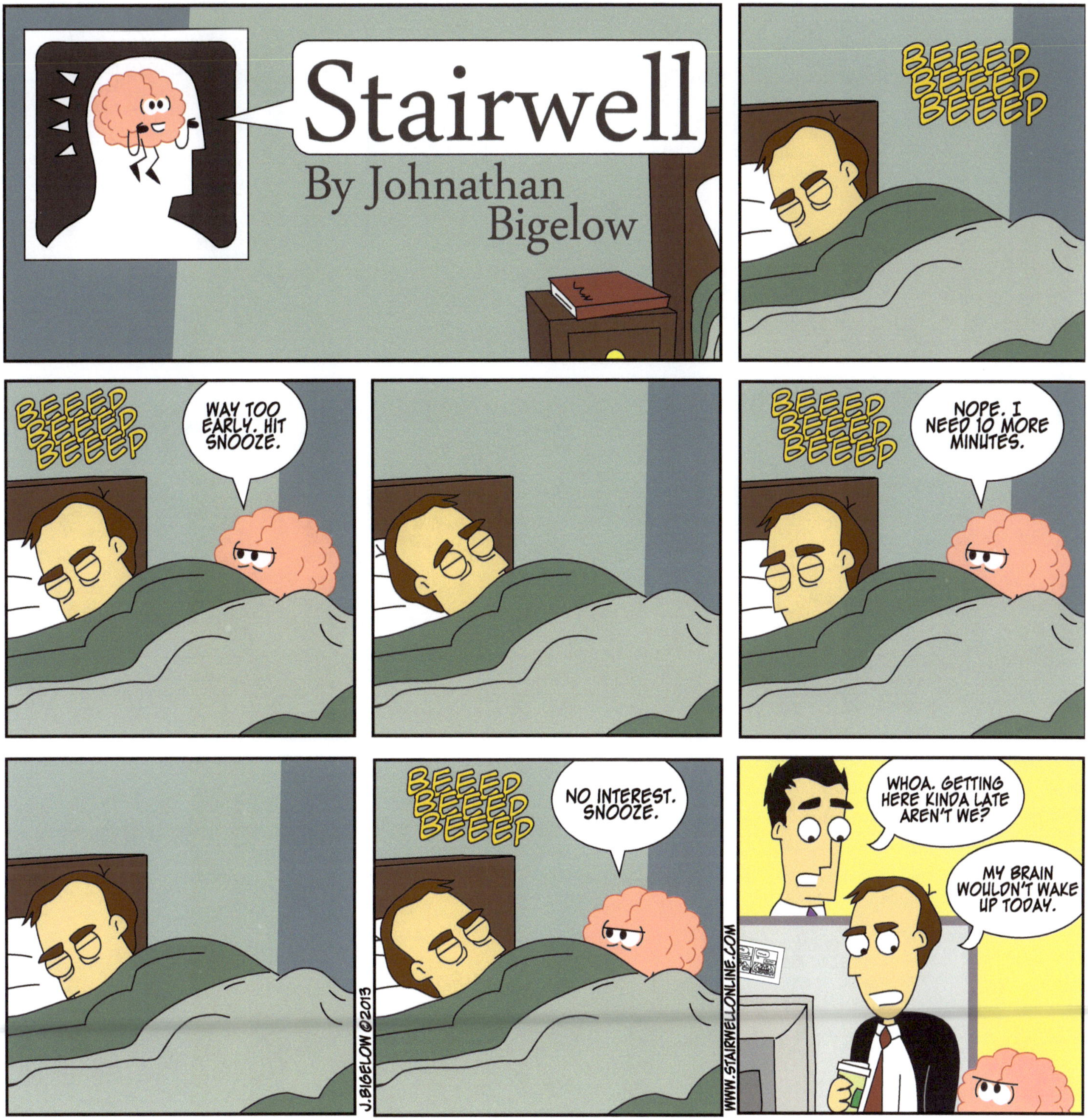
Stairwell
By Johnathan Bigelow
BEEEP BEEEP BEEEP
BEEEP BEEEP BEEEP
WAY TOO EARLY. HIT SNOOZE.
BEEEP BEEEP BEEEP
NOPE. I NEED 10 MORE MINUTES.
J.BIGELOW ©2013
BEEEP BEEEP BEEEP
NO INTEREST. SNOOZE.
WWW.STAIRWELLONLINE.COM
WHOA. GETTING HERE KINDA LATE AREN'T WE?
MY BRAIN WOULDN'T WAKE UP TODAY.

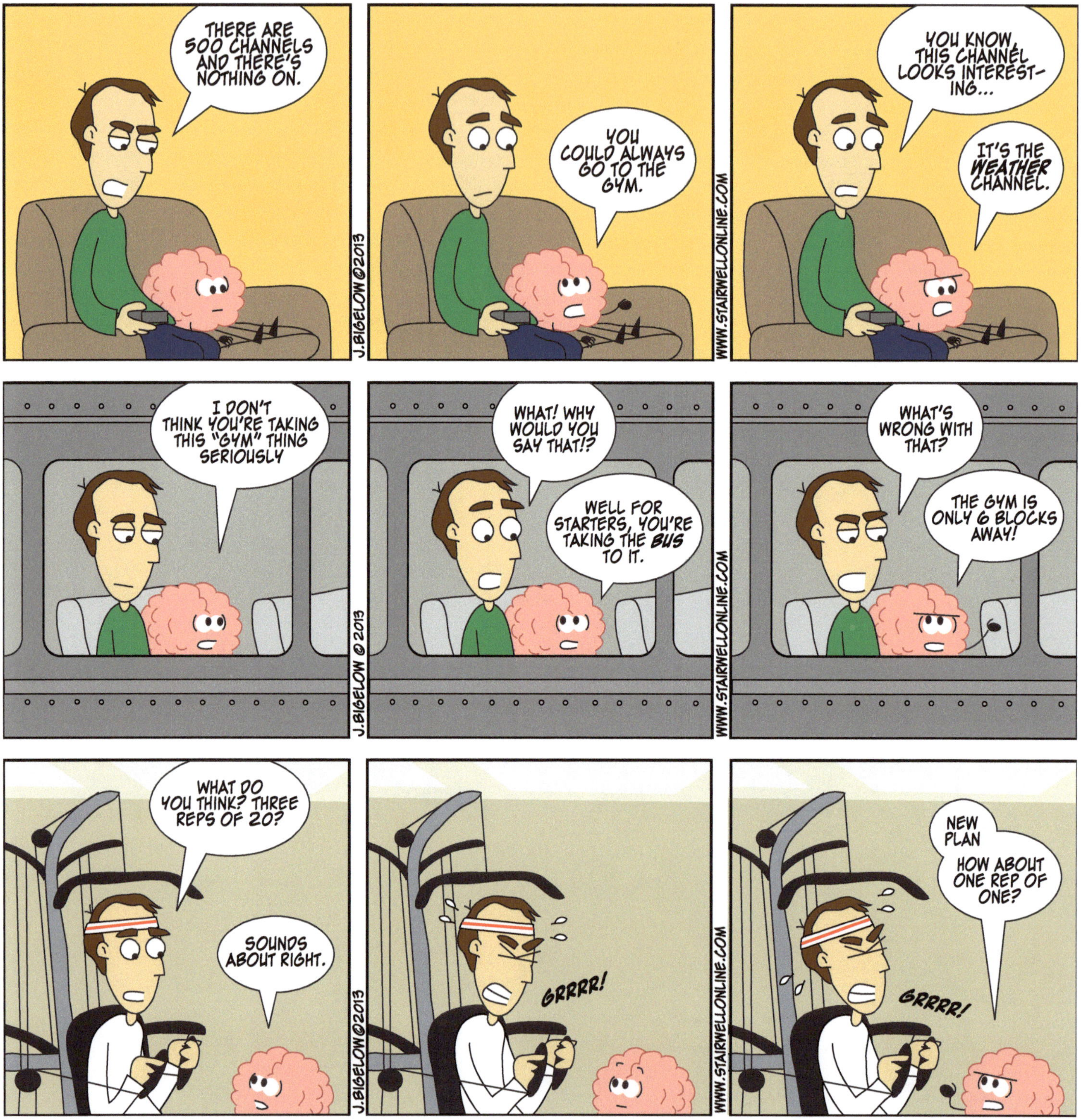
THERE ARE 500 CHANNELS AND THERE'S NOTHING ON.
YOU COULD ALWAYS GO TO THE GYM.
YOU KNOW, THIS CHANNEL LOOKS INTEREST-ING...
IT'S THE WEATHER CHANNEL.
J.BIGELOW ©2013
WWW.STAIRWELLONLINE.COM
I DON'T THINK YOU'RE TAKING THIS "GYM" THING SERIOUSLY
WHAT! WHY WOULD YOU SAY THAT!?
WELL FOR STARTERS, YOU'RE TAKING THE BUS TO IT.
WHAT'S WRONG WITH THAT?
THE GYM IS ONLY 6 BLOCKS AWAY!
J.BIGELOW © 2013
WWW.STAIRWELLONLINE.COM
WHAT DO YOU THINK? THREE REPS OF 20?
SOUNDS ABOUT RIGHT.
GRRRR!
NEW PLAN
HOW ABOUT ONE REP OF ONE?
GRRRR!
J.BIGELOW ©2013
WWW.STAIRWELLONLINE.COM

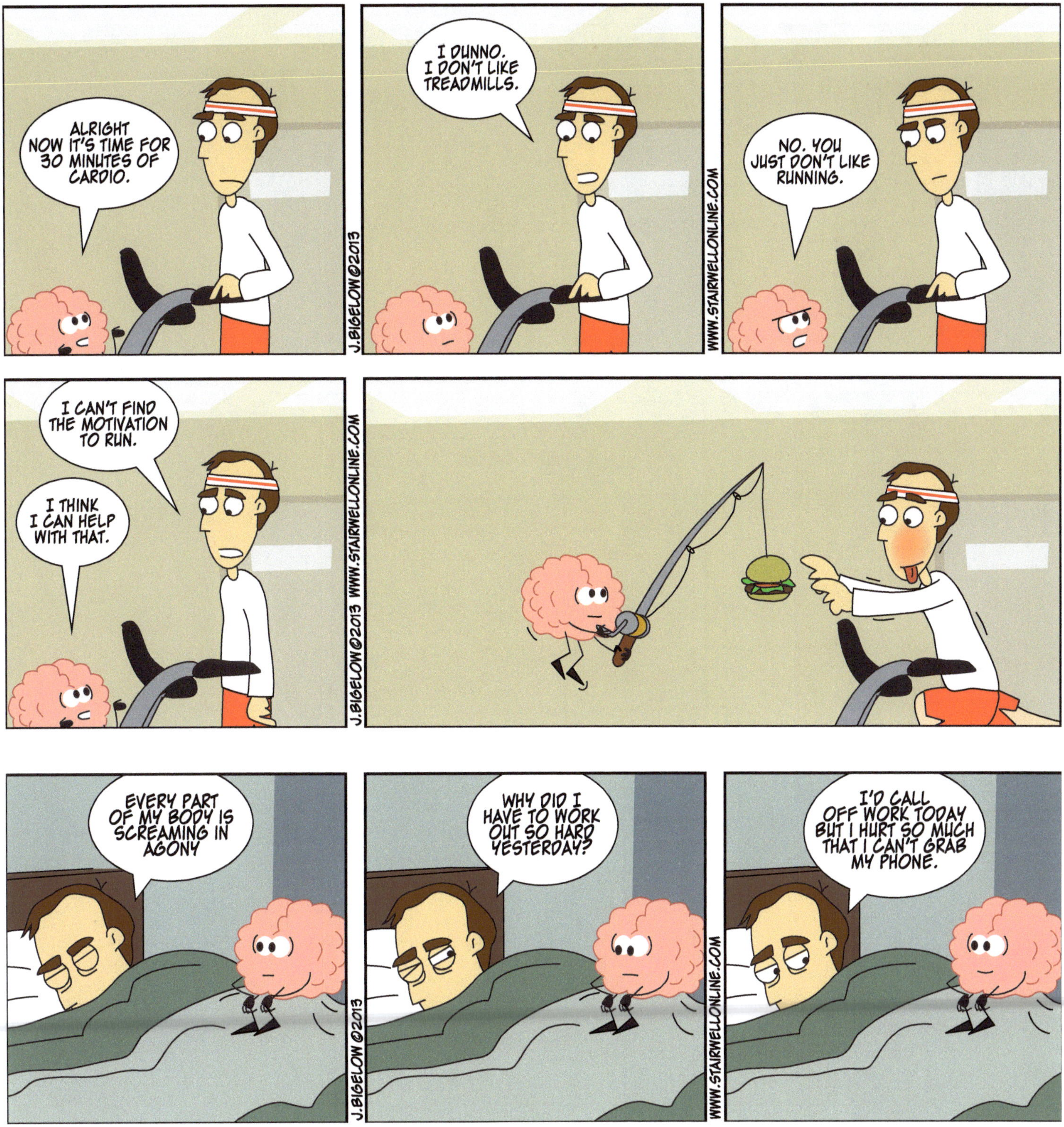
ALRIGHT NOW IT'S TIME FOR 30 MINUTES OF CARDIO.
I DUNNO. I DON'T LIKE TREADMILLS.
NO. YOU JUST DON'T LIKE RUNNING.
I CAN'T FIND THE MOTIVATION TO RUN.
I THINK I CAN HELP WITH THAT.
EVERY PART OF MY BODY IS SCREAMING IN AGONY
WHY DID I HAVE TO WORK OUT SO HARD YESTERDAY?
I'D CALL OFF WORK TODAY BUT I HURT SO MUCH THAT I CAN'T GRAB MY PHONE.
J.BIGELOW ©2013
WWW.STAIRWELLONLINE.COM

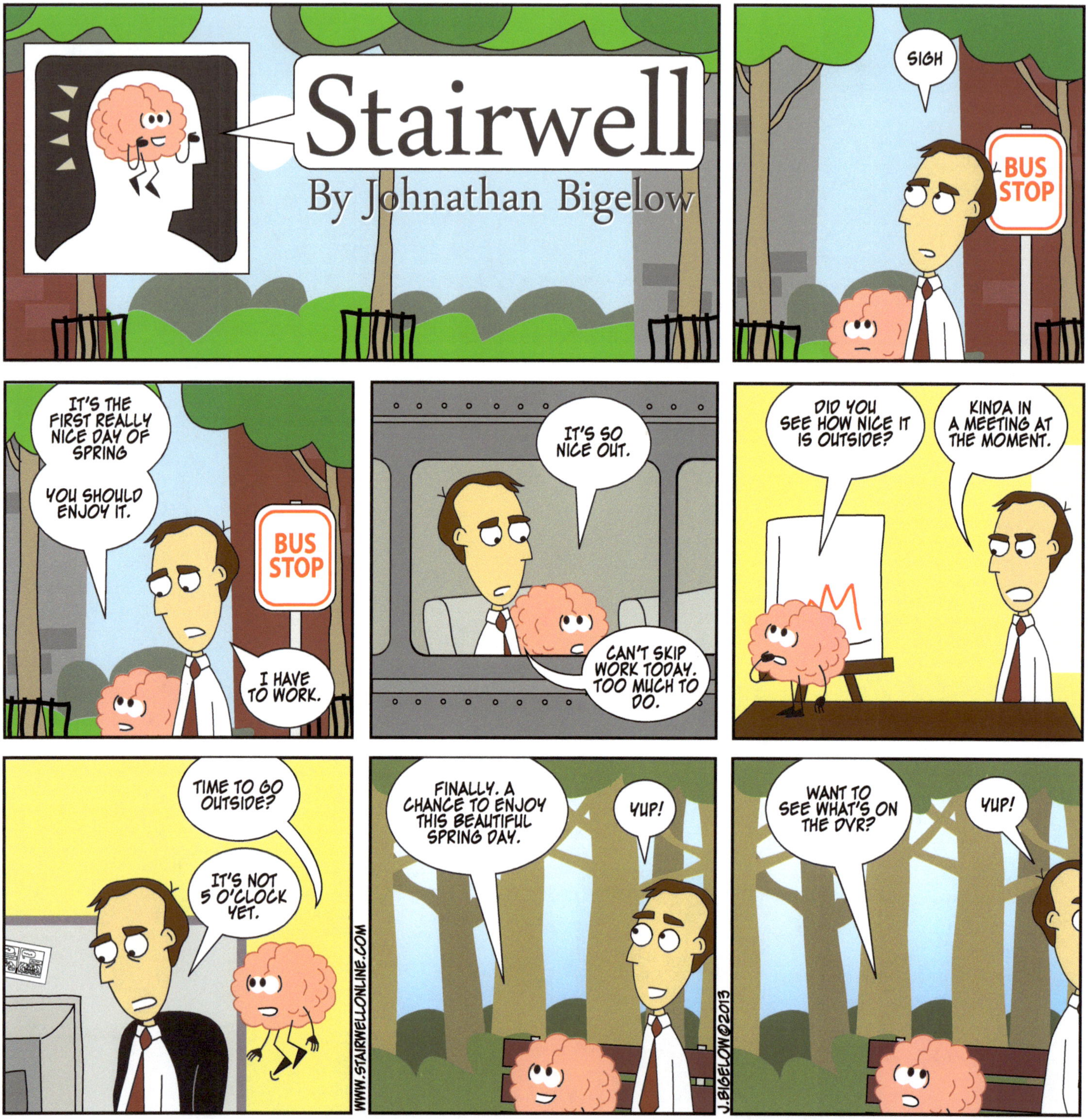
Stairwell
By Johnathan Bigelow
SIGH
BUS STOP
IT'S THE FIRST REALLY NICE DAY OF SPRING
YOU SHOULD ENJOY IT.
I HAVE TO WORK.
BUS STOP
IT'S SO NICE OUT.
CAN'T SKIP WORK TODAY. TOO MUCH TO DO.
DID YOU SEE HOW NICE IT IS OUTSIDE?
KINDA IN A MEETING AT THE MOMENT.
TIME TO GO OUTSIDE?
IT'S NOT 5 O'CLOCK YET.
WWW.STAIRWELLONLINE.COM
FINALLY. A CHANCE TO ENJOY THIS BEAUTIFUL SPRING DAY.
YUP!
J.BIGELOW©2013
WANT TO SEE WHAT'S ON THE DVR?
YUP!

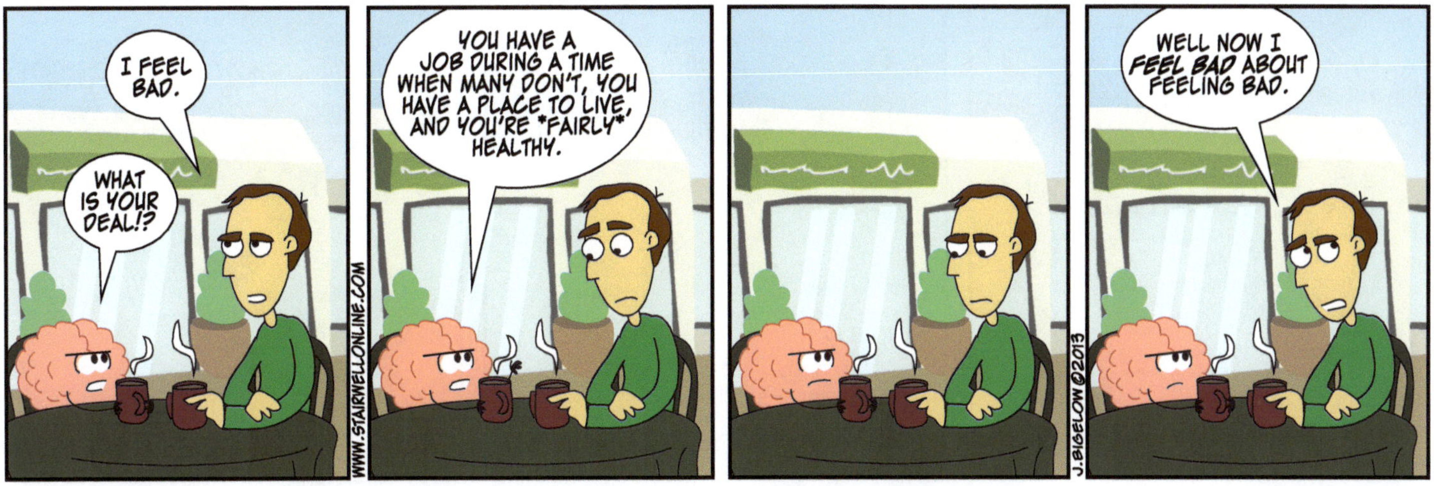
I FEEL BAD.
WHAT IS YOUR DEAL!?
YOU HAVE A JOB DURING A TIME WHEN MANY DON'T, YOU HAVE A PLACE TO LIVE, AND YOU'RE *FAIRLY* HEALTHY.
WWW.STAIRWELLONLINE.COM
WELL NOW I FEEL BAD ABOUT FEELING BAD.
J.BIGELOW ©2013

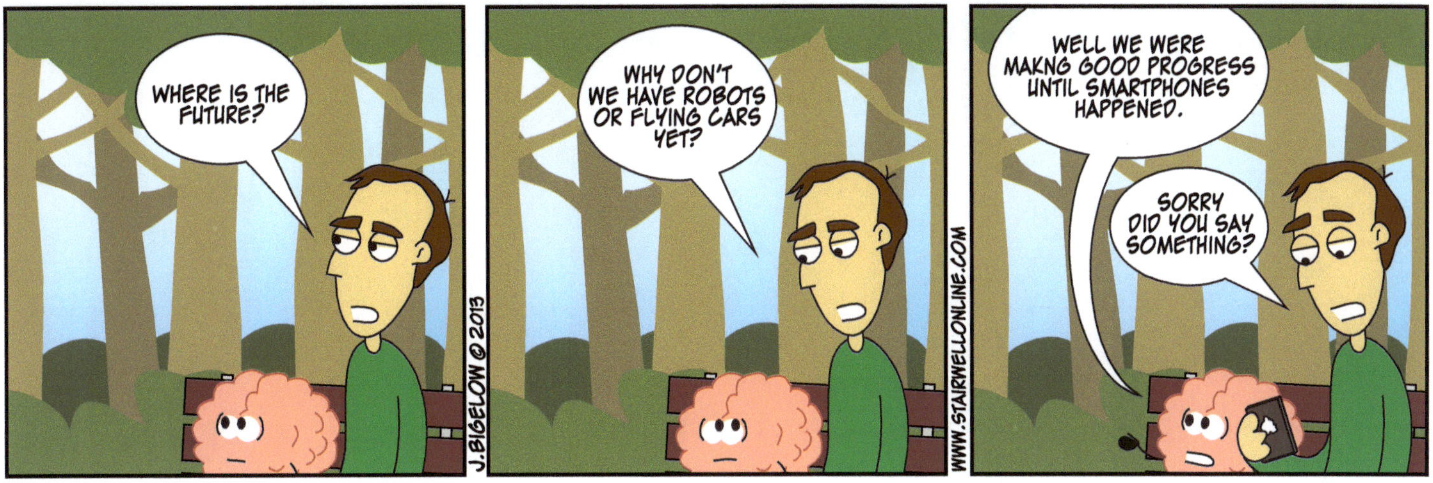
WHERE IS THE FUTURE?
J.BIGELOW ©2013
WHY DON'T WE HAVE ROBOTS OR FLYING CARS YET?
WWW.STAIRWELLONLINE.COM
WELL WE WERE MAKNG GOOD PROGRESS UNTIL SMARTPHONES HAPPENED.
SORRY DID YOU SAY SOMETHING?

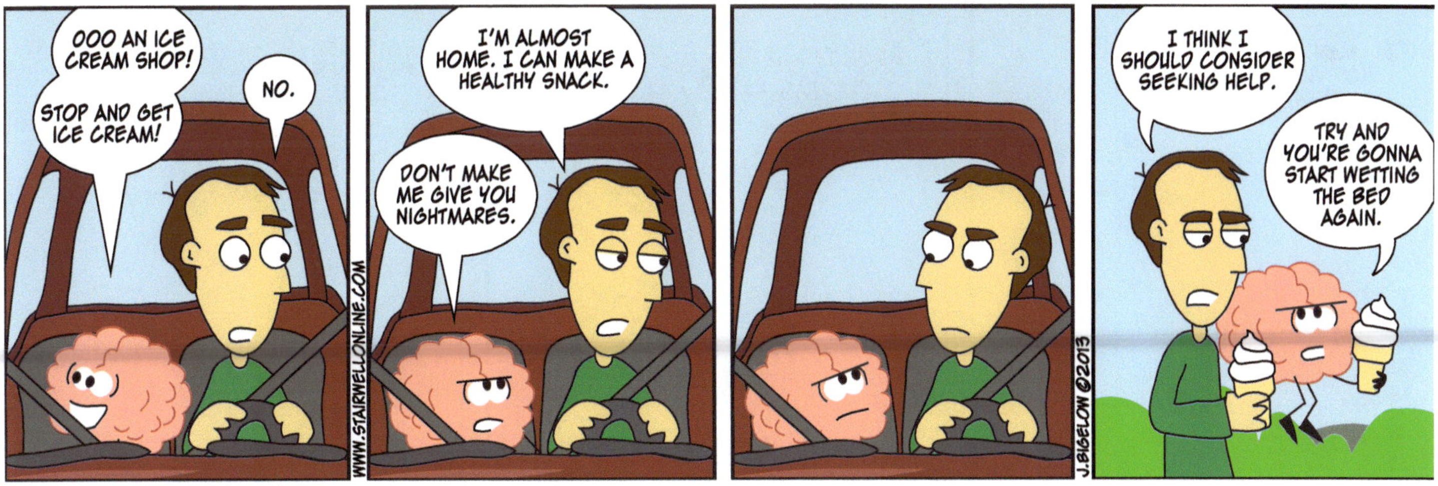
OOO AN ICE CREAM SHOP!
NO.
STOP AND GET ICE CREAM!
WWW.STAIRWELLONLINE.COM
I'M ALMOST HOME. I CAN MAKE A HEALTHY SNACK.
DON'T MAKE ME GIVE YOU NIGHTMARES.
J.BIGELOW ©2013
I THINK I SHOULD CONSIDER SEEKING HELP.
TRY AND YOU'RE GONNA START WETTING THE BED AGAIN.

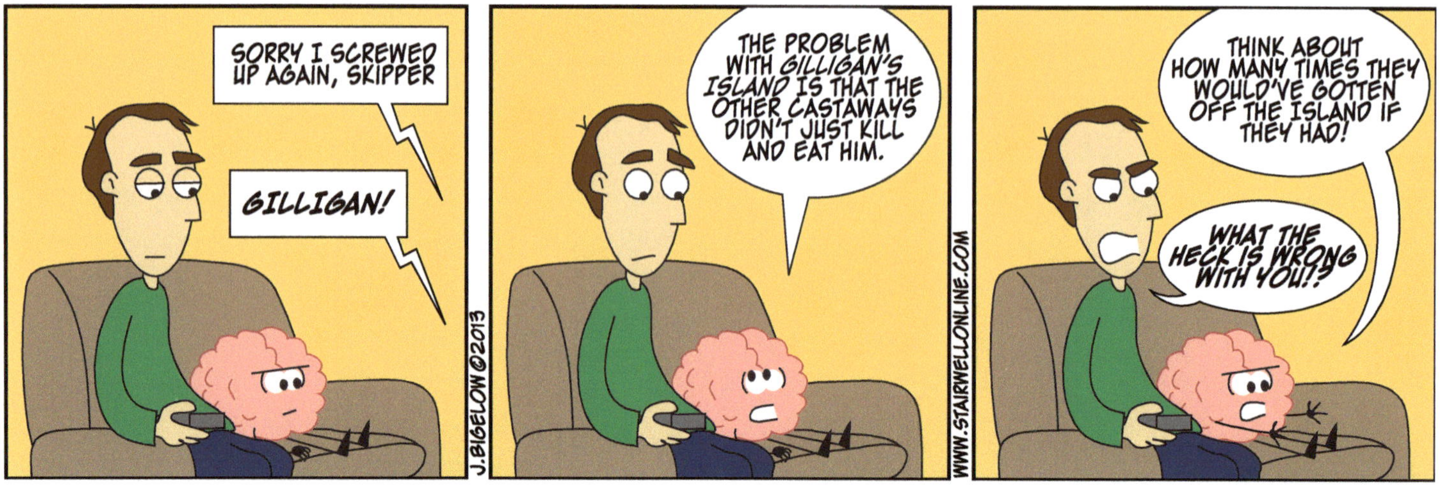
SORRY I SCREWED UP AGAIN, SKIPPER
GILLIGAN!
THE PROBLEM WITH *GILLIGAN'S ISLAND* IS THAT THE OTHER CASTAWAYS DIDN'T JUST KILL AND EAT HIM.
J.BIGELOW ©2013
THINK ABOUT HOW MANY TIMES THEY WOULD'VE GOTTEN OFF THE ISLAND IF THEY HAD!
WHAT THE HECK IS WRONG WITH YOU!?
WWW.STAIRWELLONLINE.COM

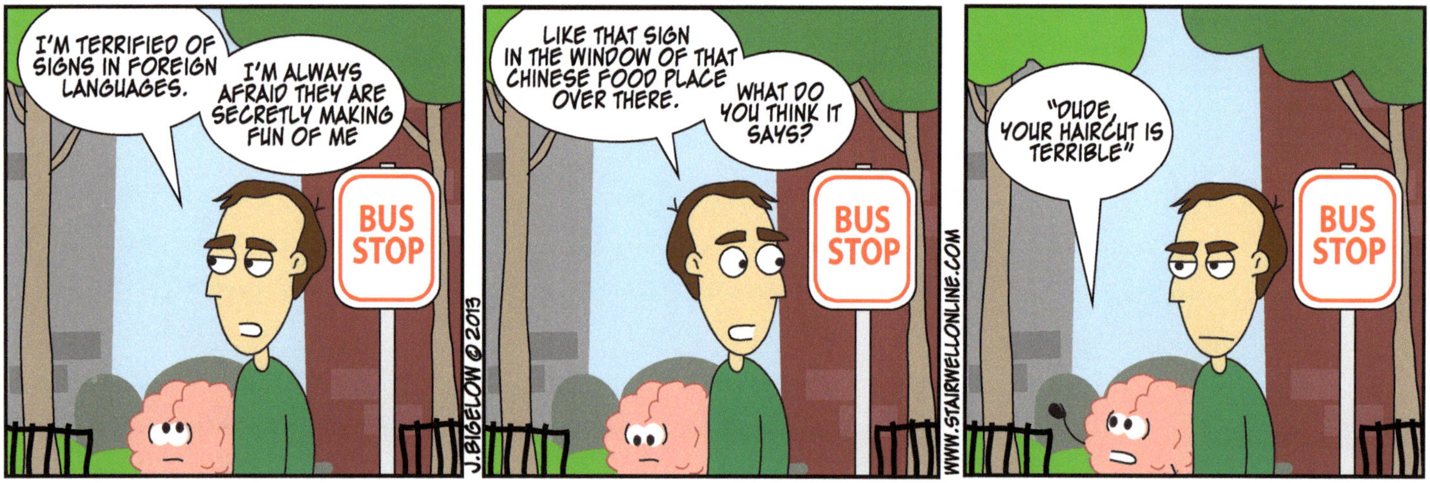
I'M TERRIFIED OF SIGNS IN FOREIGN LANGUAGES.
I'M ALWAYS AFRAID THEY ARE SECRETLY MAKING FUN OF ME
BUS STOP
LIKE THAT SIGN IN THE WINDOW OF THAT CHINESE FOOD PLACE OVER THERE.
WHAT DO YOU THINK IT SAYS?
BUS STOP
J.BIGELOW ©2013
"DUDE, YOUR HAIRCUT IS TERRIBLE"
BUS STOP
WWW.STAIRWELLONLINE.COM

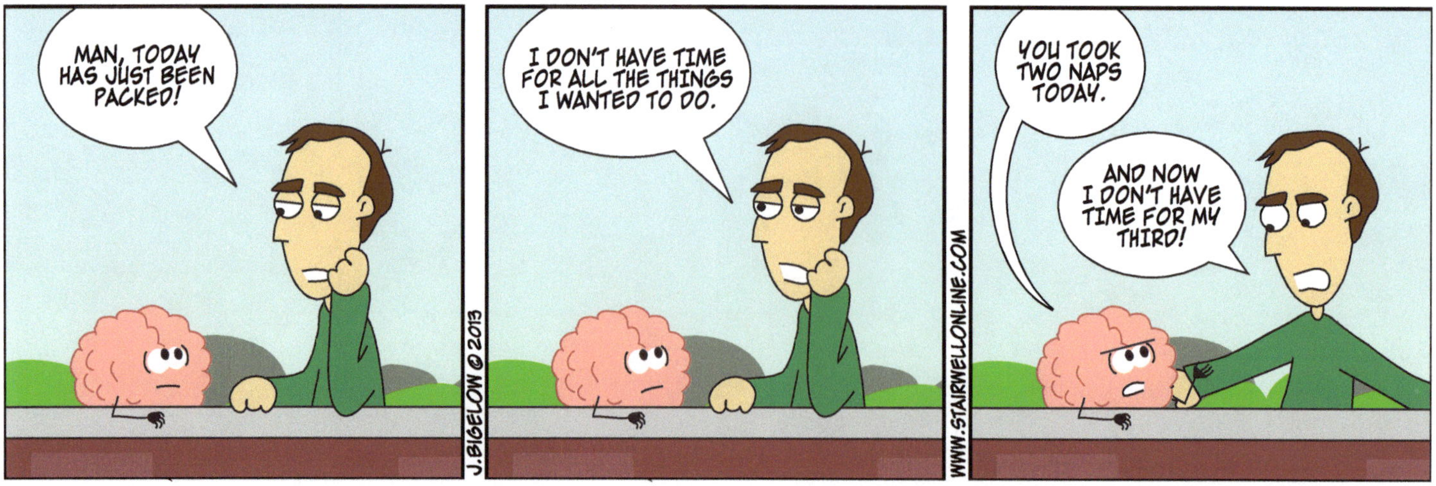
MAN, TODAY HAS JUST BEEN PACKED!
I DON'T HAVE TIME FOR ALL THE THINGS I WANTED TO DO.
J.BIGELOW ©2013
YOU TOOK TWO NAPS TODAY.
AND NOW I DON'T HAVE TIME FOR MY THIRD!
WWW.STAIRWELLONLINE.COM

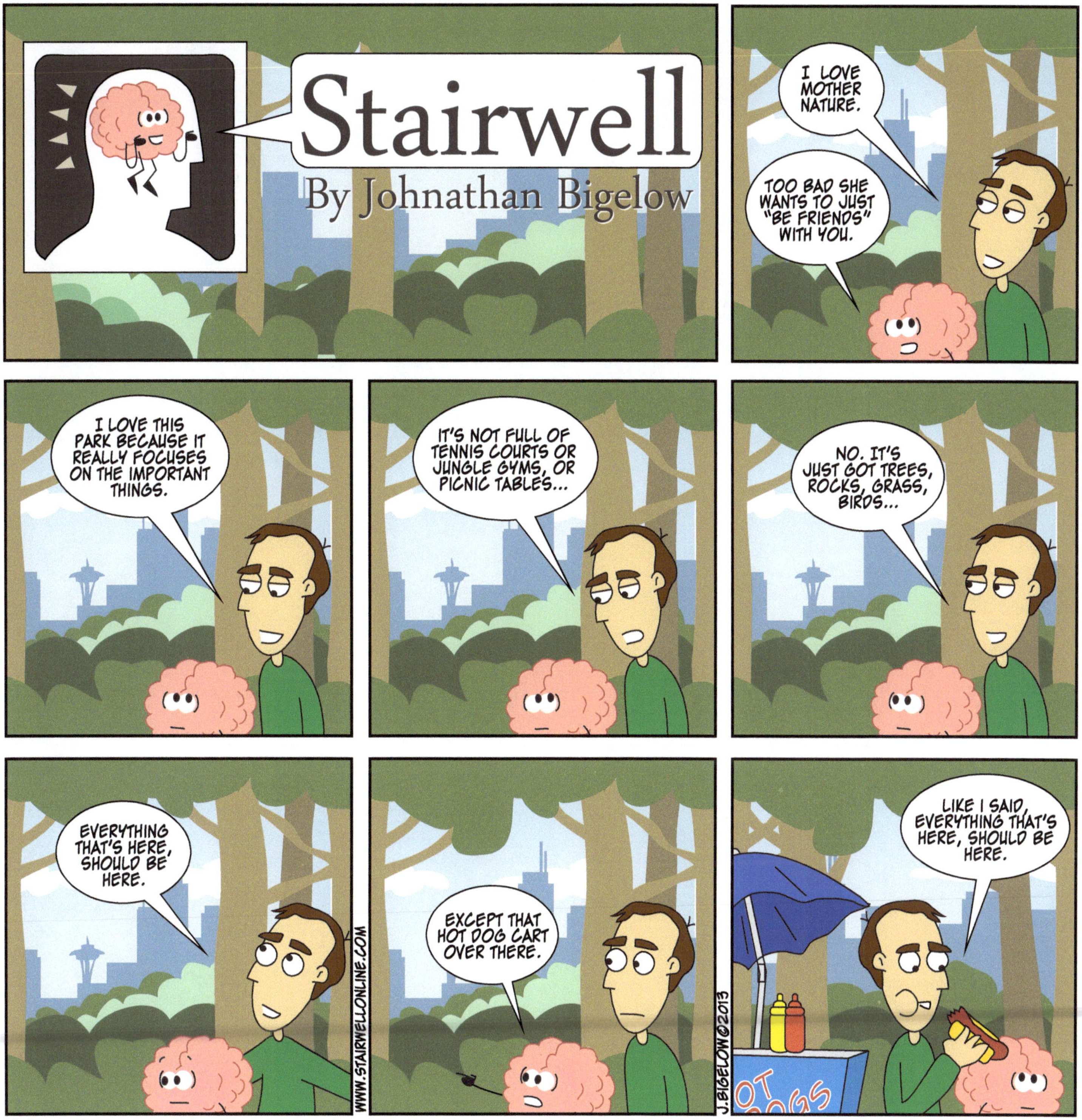
Stairwell
By Johnathan Bigelow
I LOVE MOTHER NATURE.
TOO BAD SHE WANTS TO JUST "BE FRIENDS" WITH YOU.
I LOVE THIS PARK BECAUSE IT REALLY FOCUSES ON THE IMPORTANT THINGS.
IT'S NOT FULL OF TENNIS COURTS OR JUNGLE GYMS, OR PICNIC TABLES...
NO. IT'S JUST GOT TREES, ROCKS, GRASS, BIRDS...
EVERYTHING THAT'S HERE, SHOULD BE HERE.
WWW.STAIRWELLONLINE.COM
EXCEPT THAT HOT DOG CART OVER THERE.
J.BIGELOW©2013
LIKE I SAID, EVERYTHING THAT'S HERE, SHOULD BE HERE.

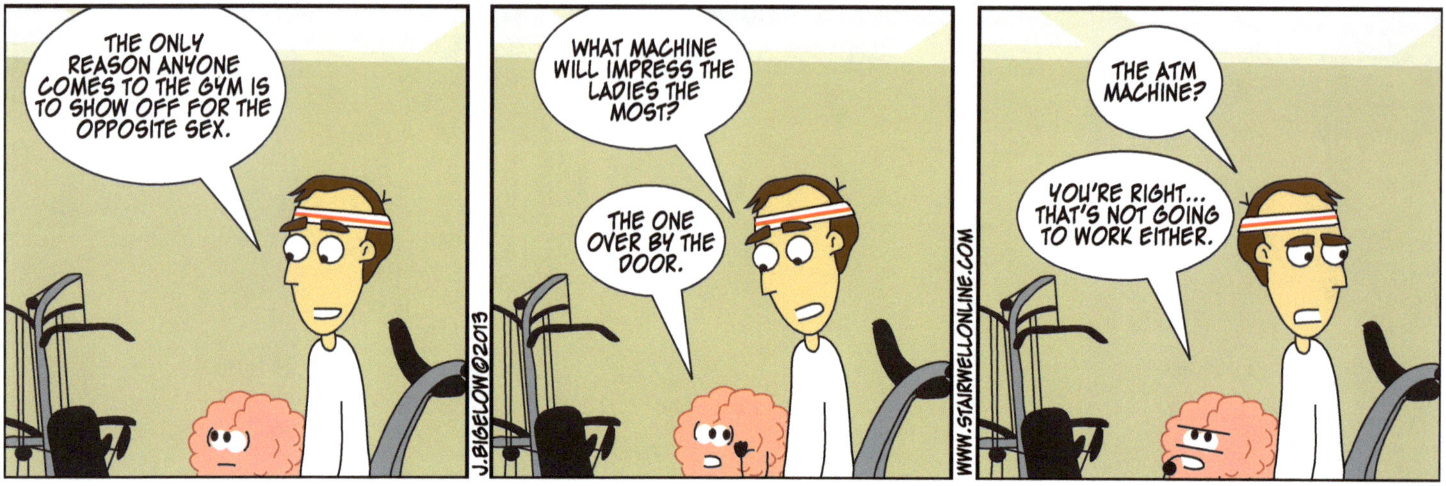
THE ONLY REASON ANYONE COMES TO THE GYM IS TO SHOW OFF FOR THE OPPOSITE SEX.
J.BIGELOW ©2013
WHAT MACHINE WILL IMPRESS THE LADIES THE MOST?
THE ONE OVER BY THE DOOR.
WWW.STAIRWELLONLINE.COM
THE ATM MACHINE?
YOU'RE RIGHT... THAT'S NOT GOING TO WORK EITHER.

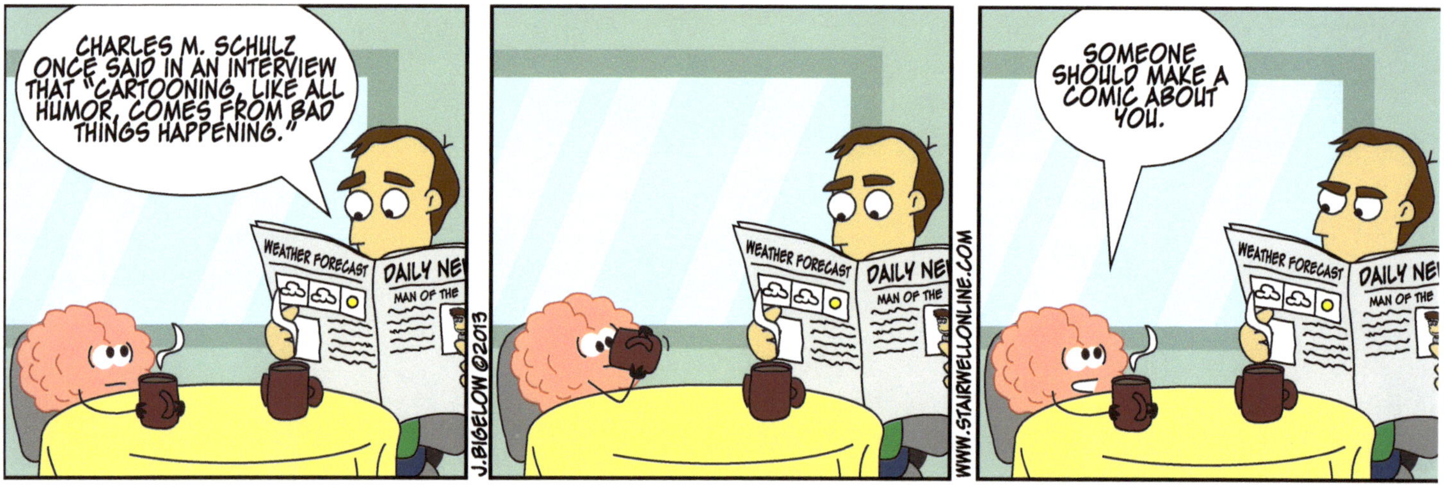
CHARLES M. SCHULZ ONCE SAID IN AN INTERVIEW THAT "CARTOONING, LIKE ALL HUMOR, COMES FROM BAD THINGS HAPPENING."
WEATHER FORECAST
DAILY NE
MAN OF THE
J.BIGELOW ©2013
WWW.STAIRWELLONLINE.COM
SOMEONE SHOULD MAKE A COMIC ABOUT YOU.

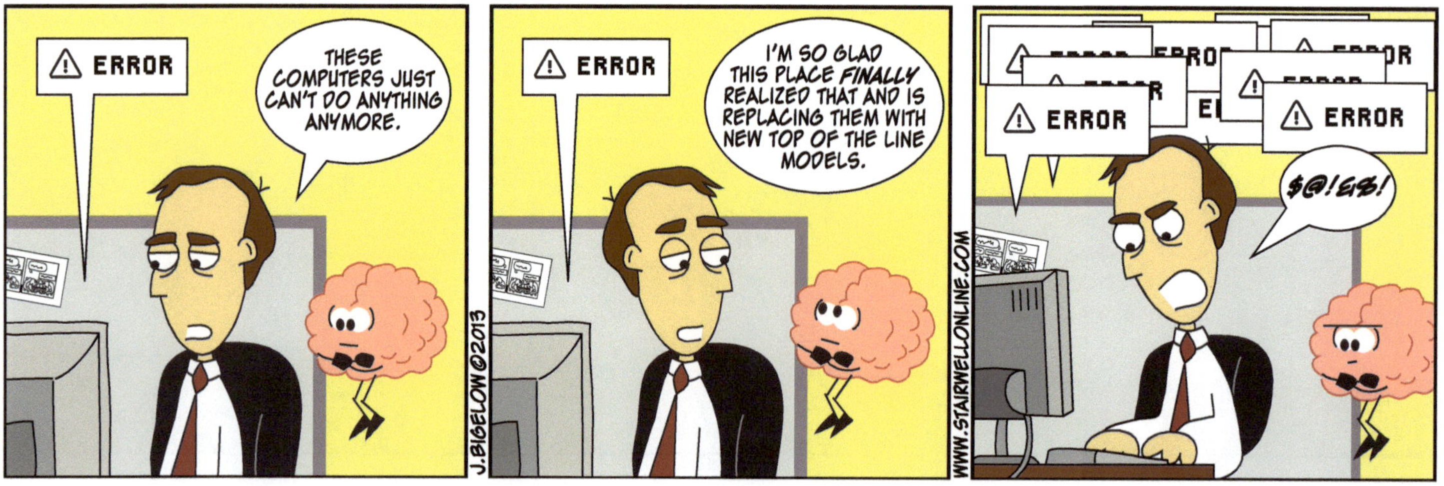
ERROR
THESE COMPUTERS JUST CAN'T DO ANYTHING ANYMORE.
J.BIGELOW ©2013
ERROR
I'M SO GLAD THIS PLACE FINALLY REALIZED THAT AND IS REPLACING THEM WITH NEW TOP OF THE LINE MODELS.
WWW.STAIRWELLONLINE.COM
ERROR
ERROR
$@!&$!

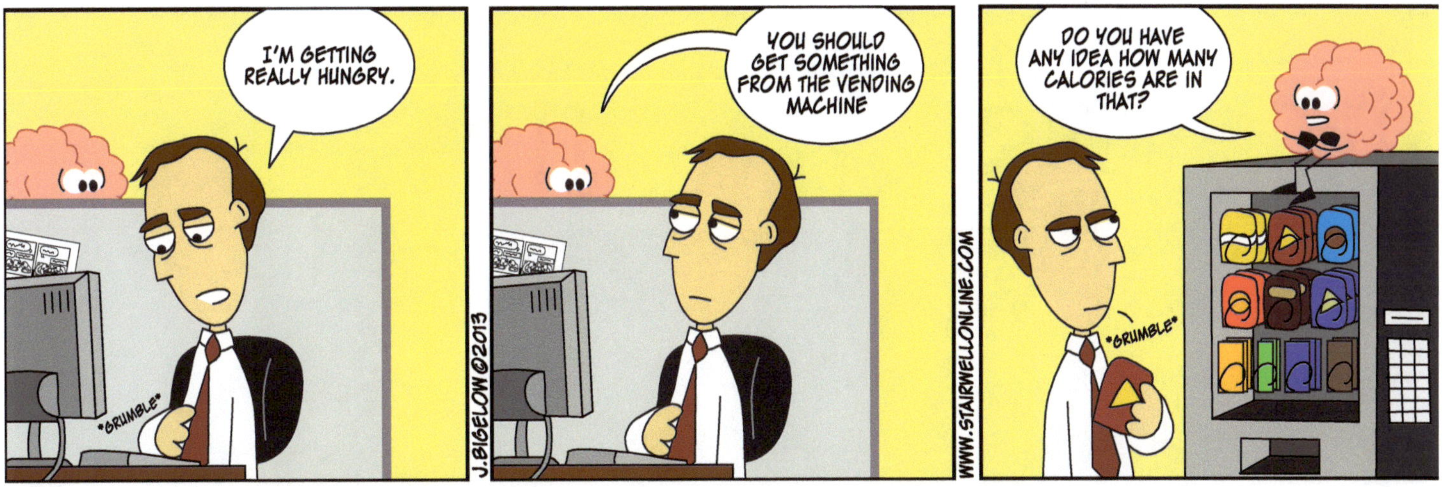
I'M GETTING REALLY HUNGRY.
GRUMBLE
J.BIGELOW ©2013
YOU SHOULD GET SOMETHING FROM THE VENDING MACHINE
WWW.STAIRWELLONLINE.COM
DO YOU HAVE ANY IDEA HOW MANY CALORIES ARE IN THAT?
GRUMBLE

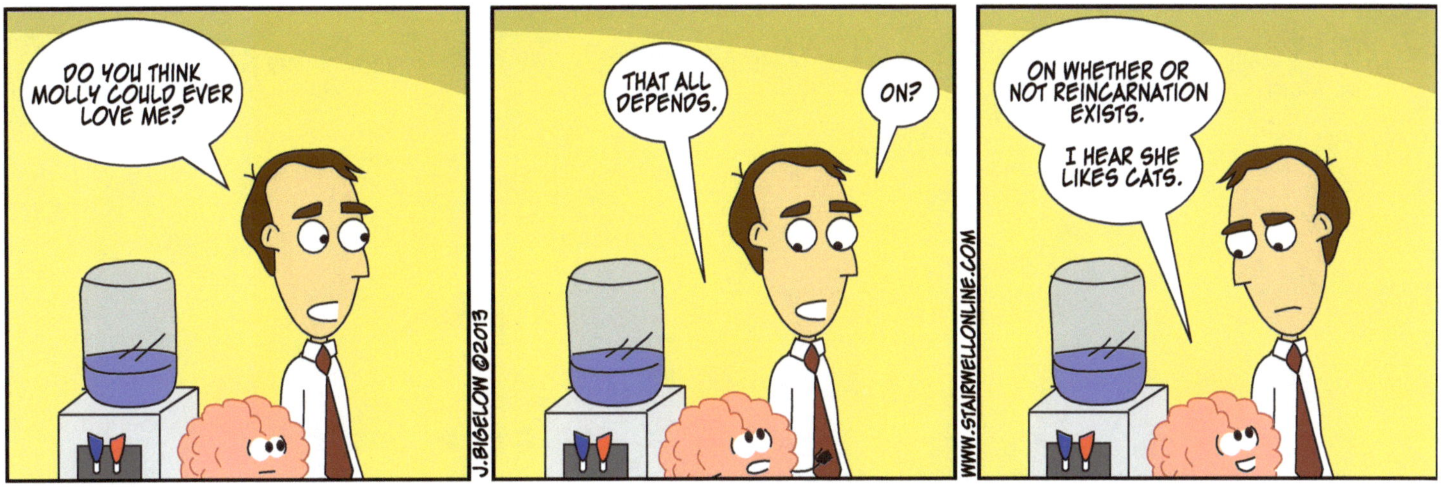
DO YOU THINK MOLLY COULD EVER LOVE ME?
J.BIGELOW ©2013
THAT ALL DEPENDS.
ON?
WWW.STAIRWELLONLINE.COM
ON WHETHER OR NOT REINCARNATION EXISTS.
I HEAR SHE LIKES CATS.

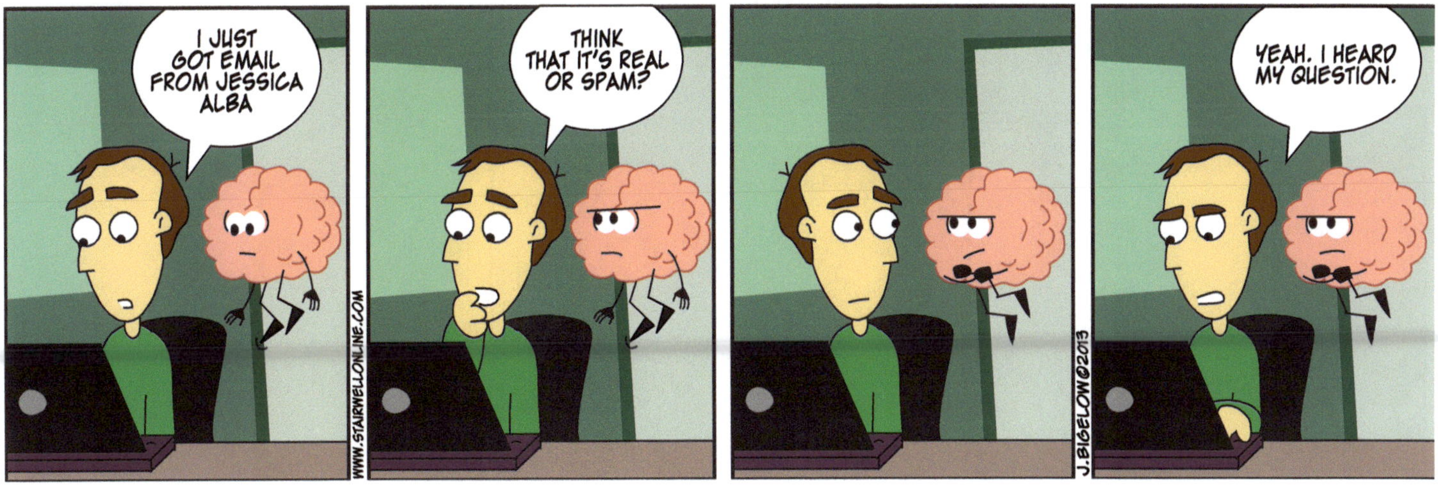
I JUST GOT EMAIL FROM JESSICA ALBA
WWW.STAIRWELLONLINE.COM
THINK THAT IT'S REAL OR SPAM?
J.BIGELOW ©2013
YEAH. I HEARD MY QUESTION.

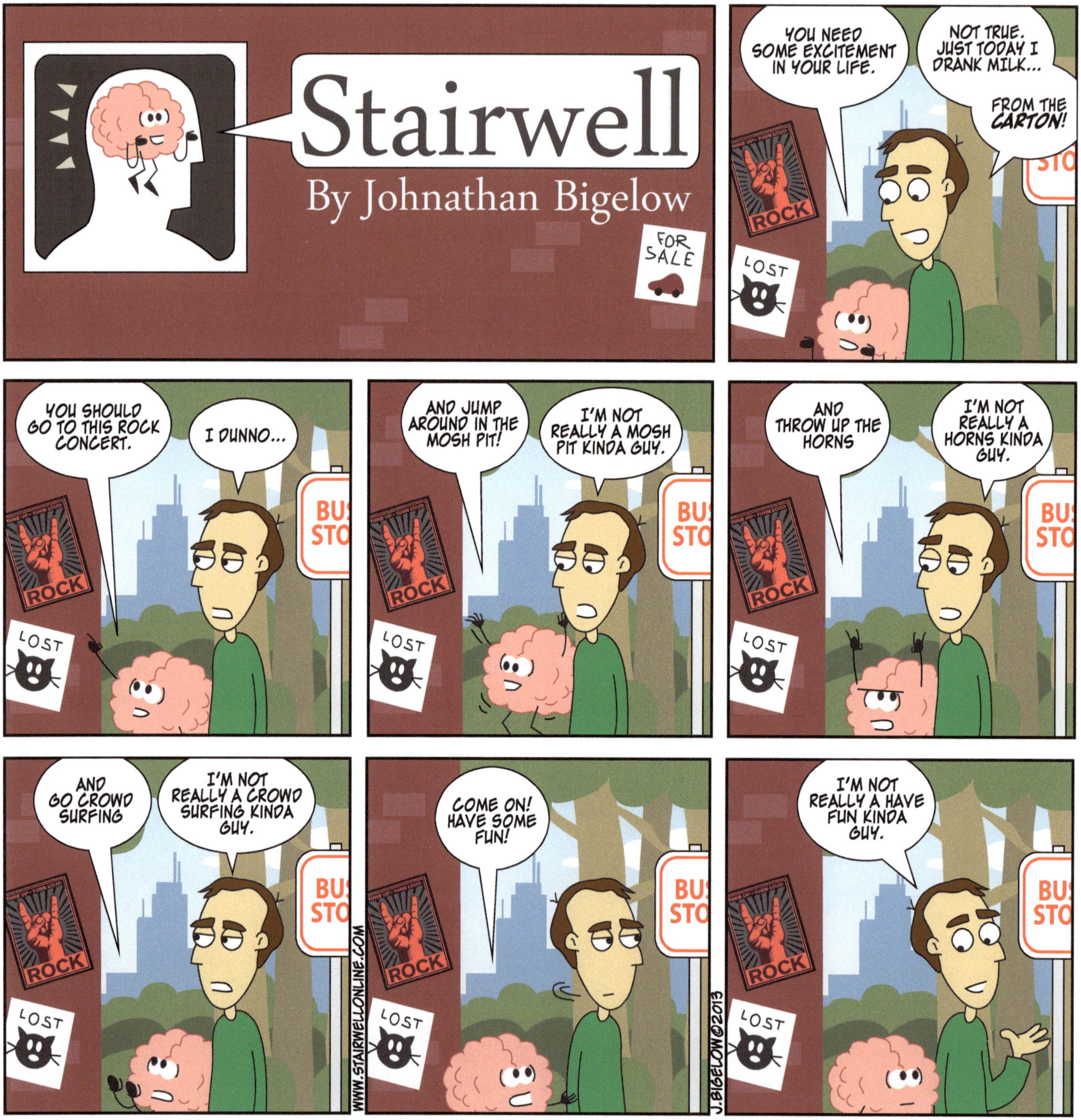
Stairwell
By Johnathan Bigelow
FOR SALE
YOU NEED SOME EXCITEMENT IN YOUR LIFE.
NOT TRUE. JUST TODAY I DRANK MILK...
FROM THE CARTON!
TUNE UP • TURN LOUD
ROCK
LOST
YOU SHOULD GO TO THIS ROCK CONCERT.
I DUNNO...
BUS STO
AND JUMP AROUND IN THE MOSH PIT!
I'M NOT REALLY A MOSH PIT KINDA GUY.
AND THROW UP THE HORNS
I'M NOT REALLY A HORNS KINDA GUY.
AND GO CROWD SURFING
I'M NOT REALLY A CROWD SURFING KINDA GUY.
WWW.STAIRWELLONLINE.COM
COME ON! HAVE SOME FUN!
J.BIGELOW©2013
I'M NOT REALLY A HAVE FUN KINDA GUY.

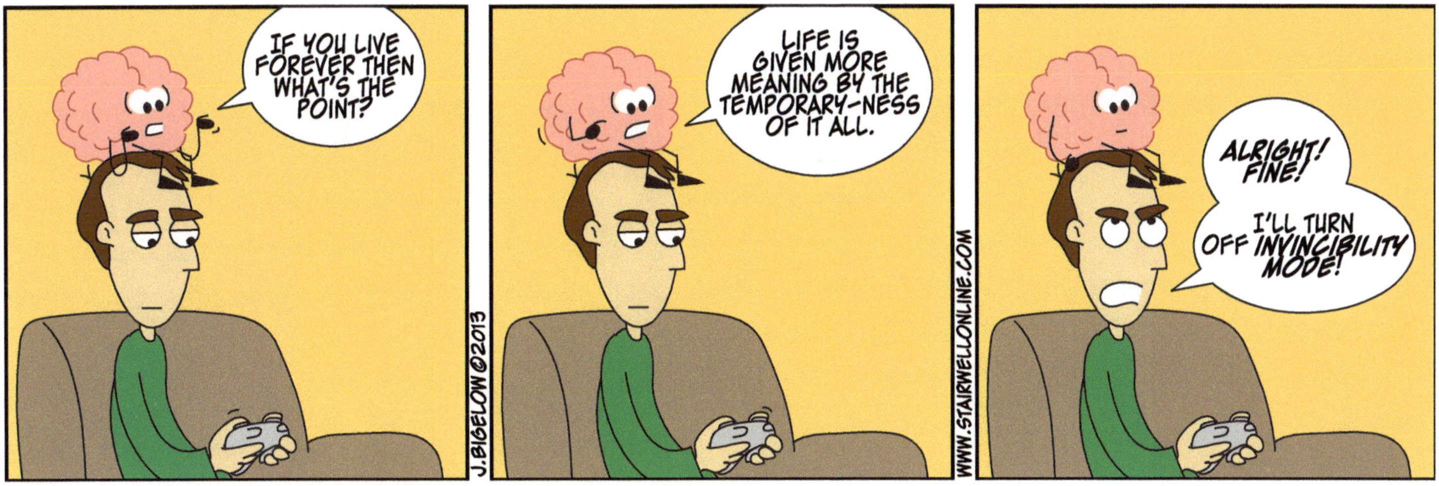
IF YOU LIVE FOREVER THEN WHAT'S THE POINT?
LIFE IS GIVEN MORE MEANING BY THE TEMPORARY-NESS OF IT ALL.
J.BIGELOW ©2013
ALRIGHT! FINE!
I'LL TURN OFF INVINCIBILITY MODE!
WWW.STAIRWELLONLINE.COM

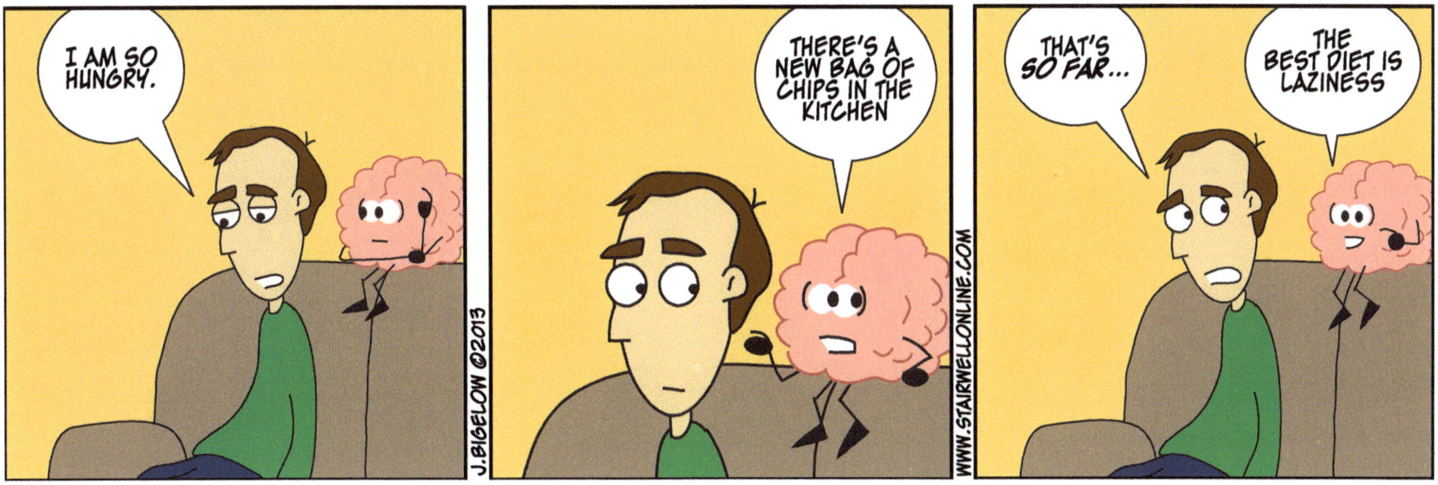
I AM SO HUNGRY.
THERE'S A NEW BAG OF CHIPS IN THE KITCHEN
J.BIGELOW ©2013
THAT'S SO FAR...
THE BEST DIET IS LAZINESS
WWW.STAIRWELLONLINE.COM

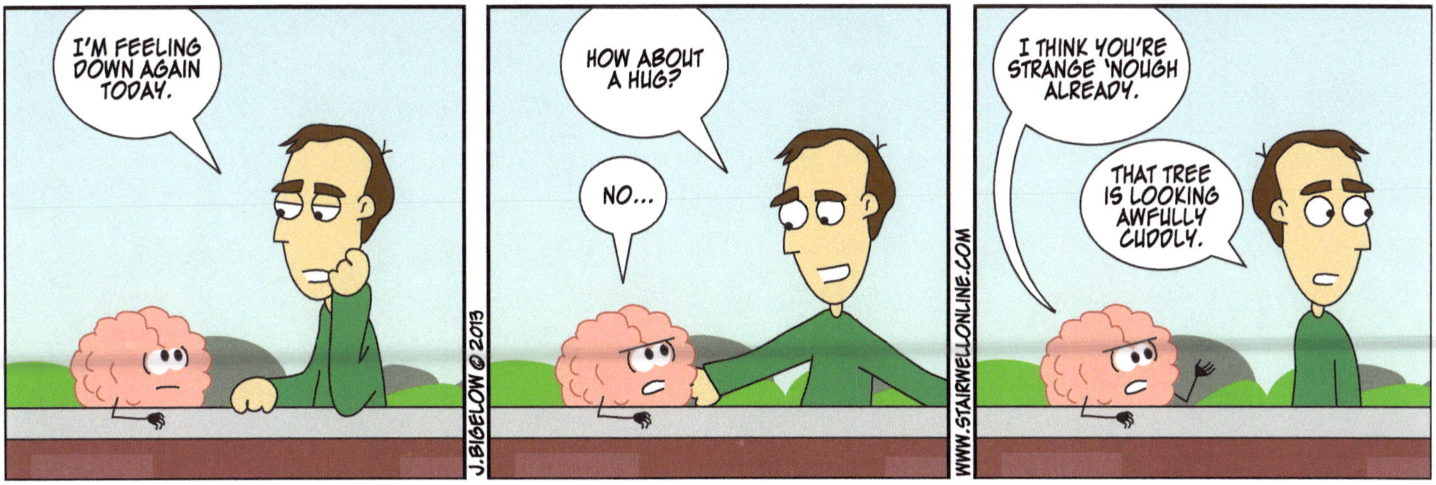
I'M FEELING DOWN AGAIN TODAY.
HOW ABOUT A HUG?
NO...
J.BIGELOW ©2013
THAT TREE IS LOOKING AWFULLY CUDDLY.
I THINK YOU'RE STRANGE 'NOUGH ALREADY.
WWW.STAIRWELLONLINE.COM

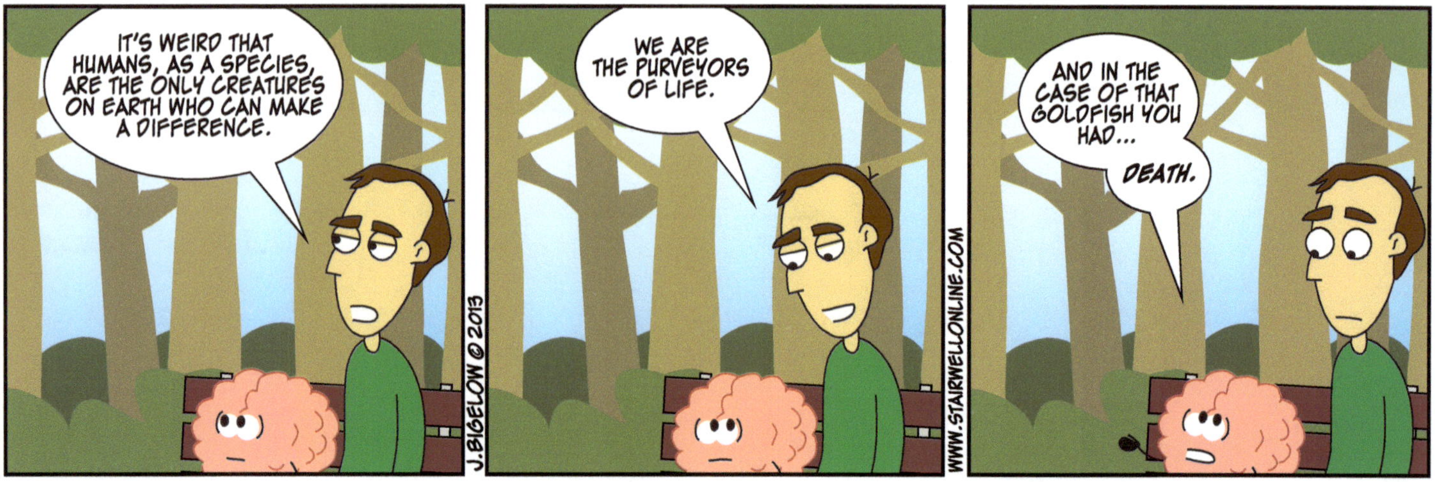
IT'S WEIRD THAT HUMANS, AS A SPECIES, ARE THE ONLY CREATURES ON EARTH WHO CAN MAKE A DIFFERENCE.
J.BIGELOW © 2013
WE ARE THE PURVEYORS OF LIFE.
WWW.STAIRWELLONLINE.COM
AND IN THE CASE OF THAT GOLDFISH YOU HAD...
DEATH.

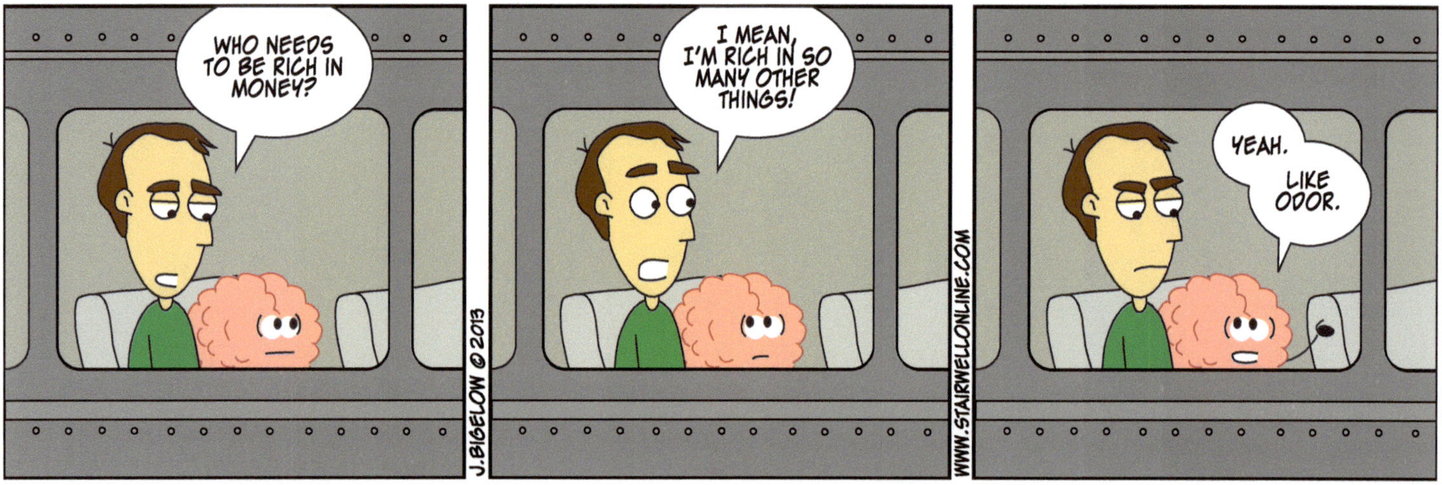
WHO NEEDS TO BE RICH IN MONEY?
J.BIGELOW © 2013
I MEAN, I'M RICH IN SO MANY OTHER THINGS!
WWW.STAIRWELLONLINE.COM
YEAH.
LIKE ODOR.

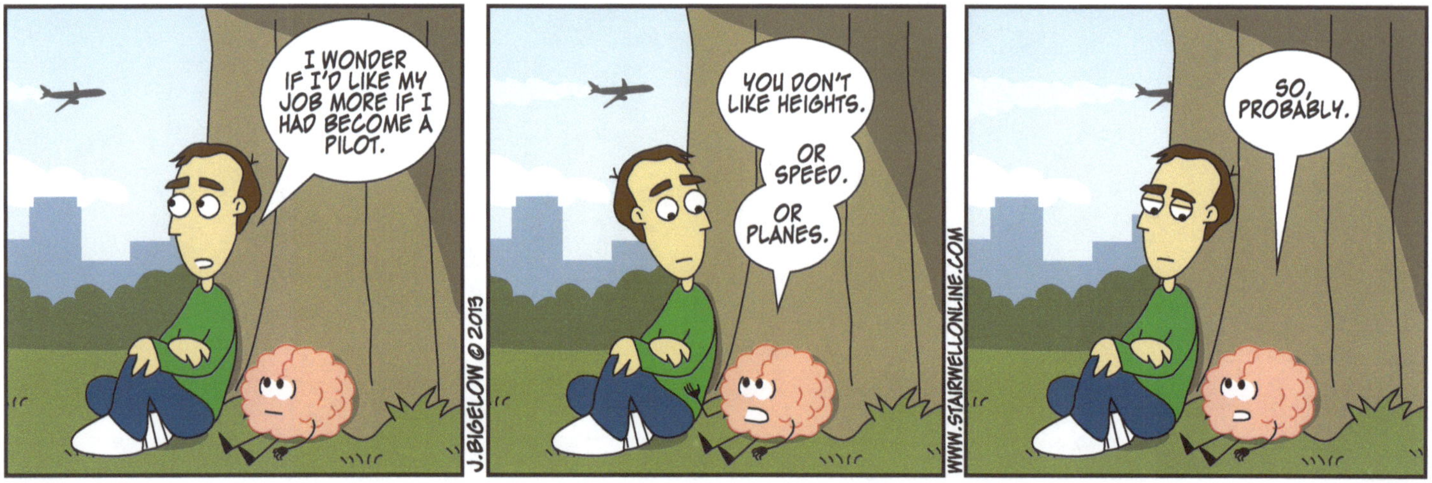
I WONDER IF I'D LIKE MY JOB MORE IF I HAD BECOME A PILOT.
J.BIGELOW © 2013
YOU DON'T LIKE HEIGHTS.
OR SPEED.
OR PLANES.
WWW.STAIRWELLONLINE.COM
SO, PROBABLY.

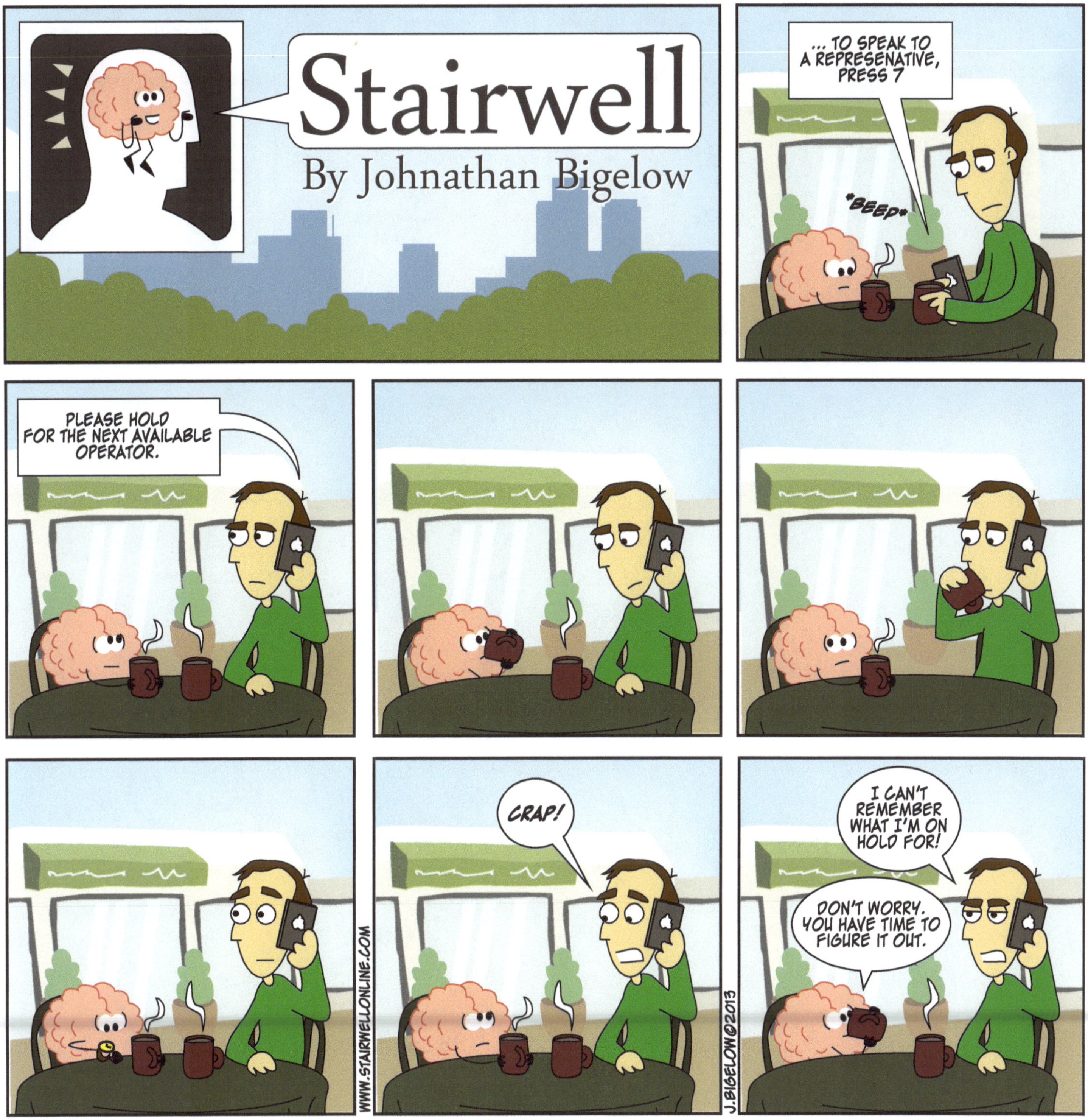
Stairwell
By Johnathan Bigelow
... TO SPEAK TO A REPRESENATIVE, PRESS 7
BEEP
PLEASE HOLD FOR THE NEXT AVAILABLE OPERATOR.
WWW.STAIRWELLONLINE.COM
CRAP!
J.BIGELOW©2013
I CAN'T REMEMBER WHAT I'M ON HOLD FOR!
DON'T WORRY. YOU HAVE TIME TO FIGURE IT OUT.

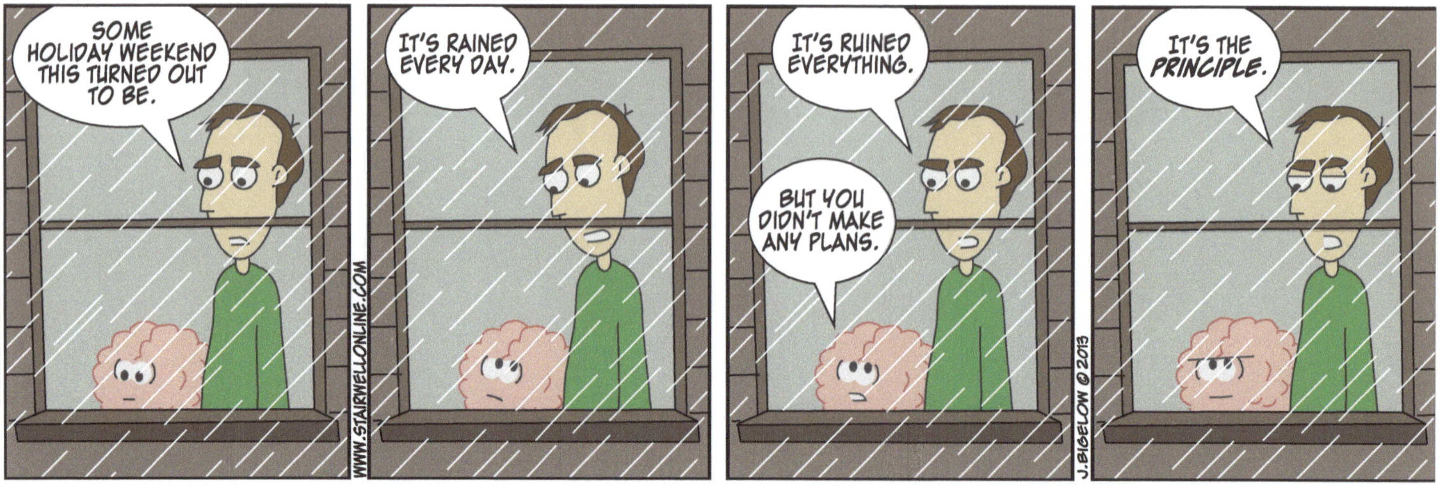
SOME HOLIDAY WEEKEND THIS TURNED OUT TO BE.
IT'S RAINED EVERY DAY.
IT'S RUINED EVERYTHING.
BUT YOU DIDN'T MAKE ANY PLANS.
IT'S THE *PRINCIPLE*.
WWW.STAIRWELLONLINE.COM
J.BIGELOW © 2013

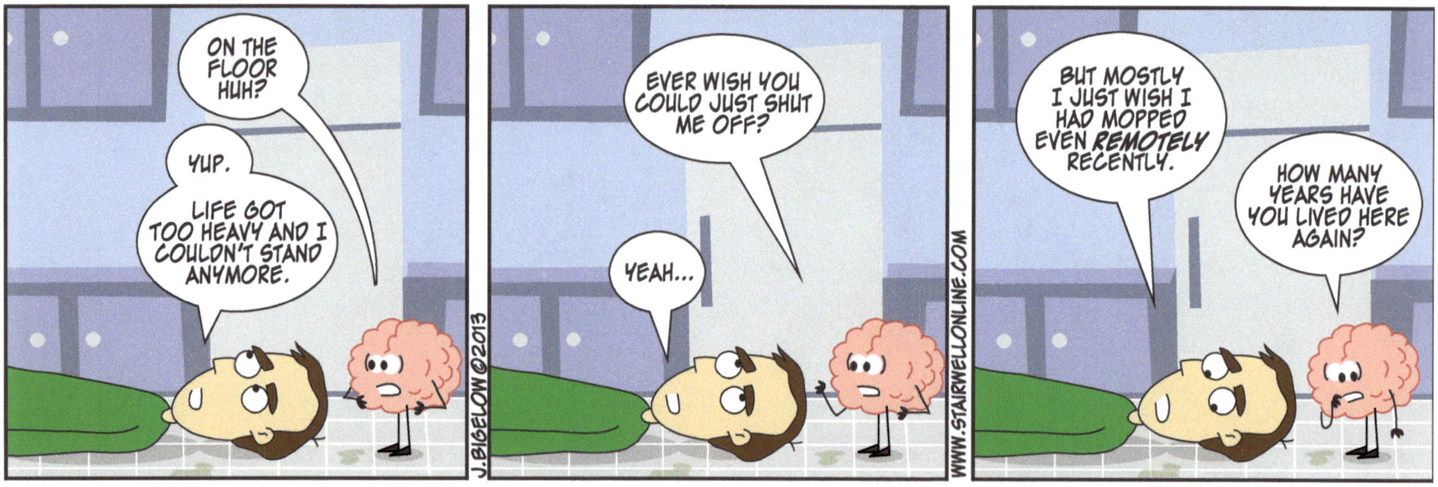
ON THE FLOOR HUH?
YUP.
LIFE GOT TOO HEAVY AND I COULDN'T STAND ANYMORE.
J.BIGELOW ©2013
EVER WISH YOU COULD JUST SHUT ME OFF?
YEAH...
WWW.STAIRWELLONLINE.COM
BUT MOSTLY I JUST WISH I HAD MOPPED EVEN *REMOTELY* RECENTLY.
HOW MANY YEARS HAVE YOU LIVED HERE AGAIN?

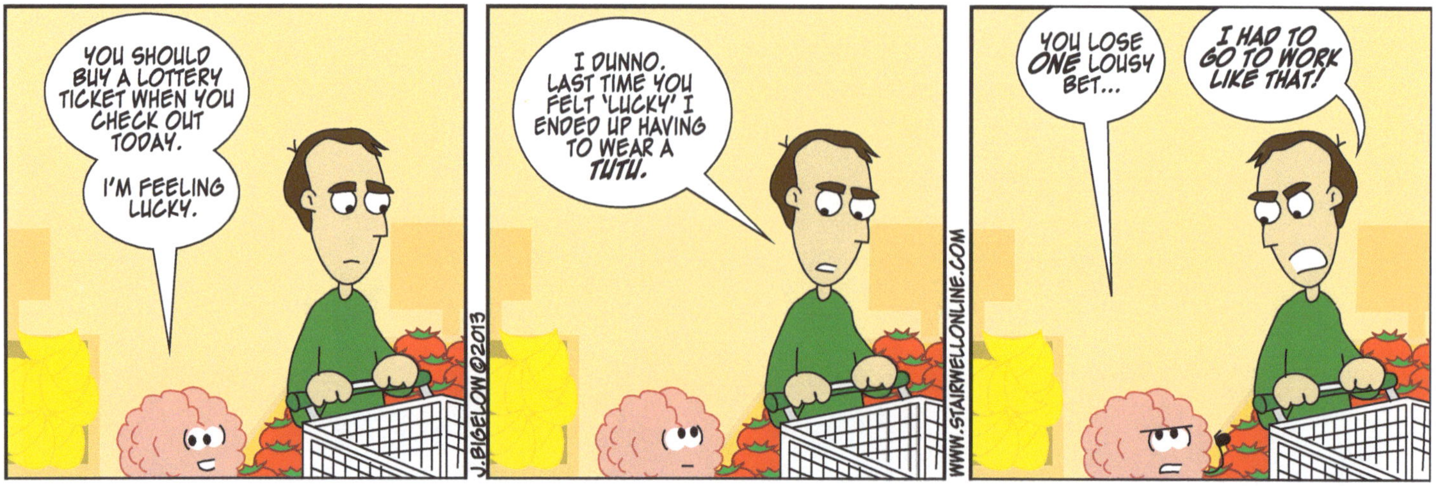
YOU SHOULD BUY A LOTTERY TICKET WHEN YOU CHECK OUT TODAY.
I'M FEELING LUCKY.
J.BIGELOW ©2013
I DUNNO. LAST TIME YOU FELT 'LUCKY' I ENDED UP HAVING TO WEAR A *TUTU*.
WWW.STAIRWELLONLINE.COM
YOU LOSE *ONE* LOUSY BET...
I HAD TO GO TO WORK LIKE THAT!

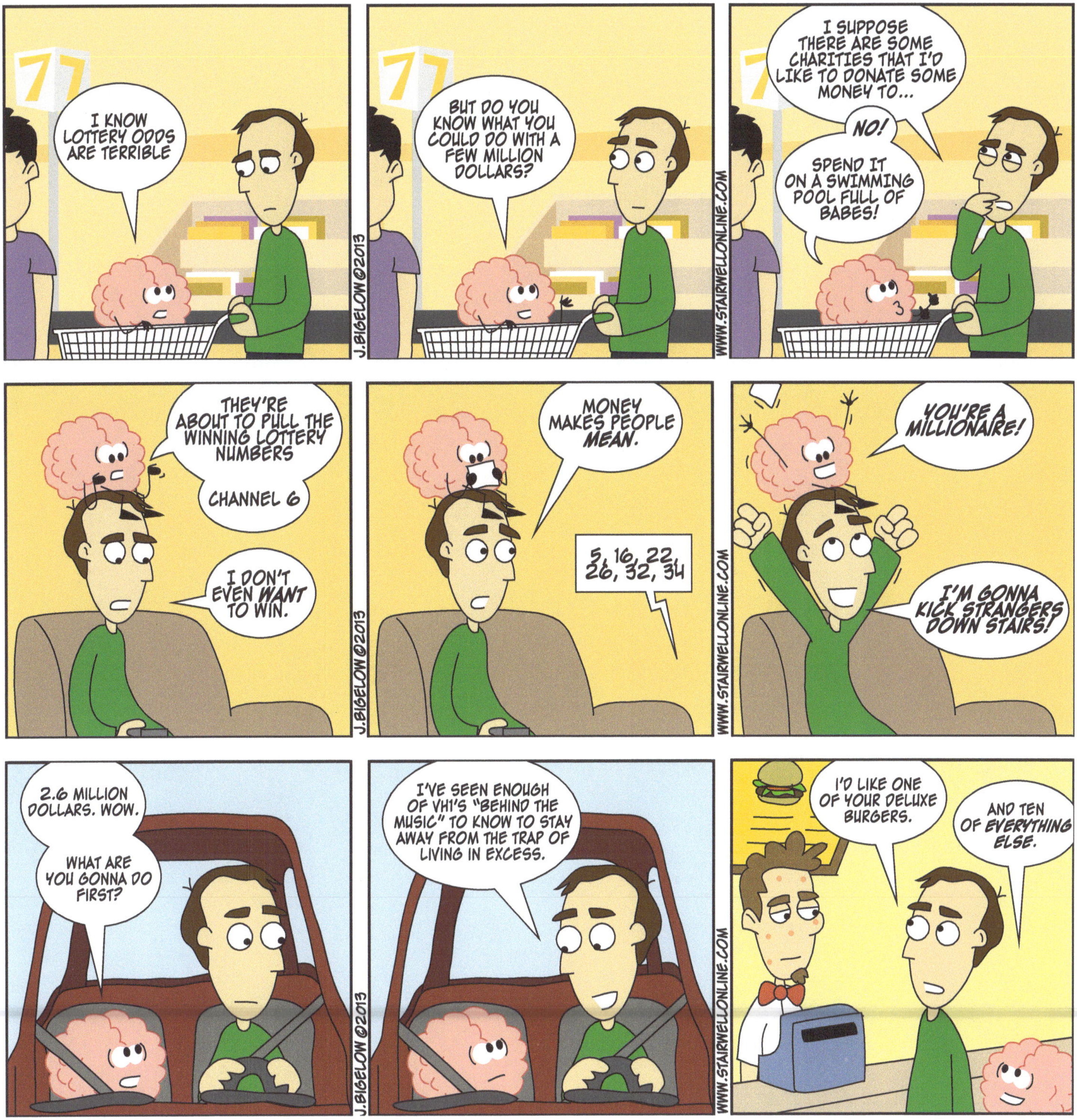
7
I KNOW LOTTERY ODDS ARE TERRIBLE
BUT DO YOU KNOW WHAT YOU COULD DO WITH A FEW MILLION DOLLARS?
J.BIGELOW ©2013
I SUPPOSE THERE ARE SOME CHARITIES THAT I'D LIKE TO DONATE SOME MONEY TO...
NO!
SPEND IT ON A SWIMMING POOL FULL OF BABES!
WWW.STAIRWELLONLINE.COM
THEY'RE ABOUT TO PULL THE WINNING LOTTERY NUMBERS
CHANNEL 6
I DON'T EVEN WANT TO WIN.
J.BIGELOW ©2013
MONEY MAKES PEOPLE MEAN.
5, 16, 22, 26, 32, 34
WWW.STAIRWELLONLINE.COM
YOU'RE A MILLIONAIRE!
I'M GONNA KICK STRANGERS DOWN STAIRS!
2.6 MILLION DOLLARS. WOW.
WHAT ARE YOU GONNA DO FIRST?
J.BIGELOW ©2013
I'VE SEEN ENOUGH OF VH1'S "BEHIND THE MUSIC" TO KNOW TO STAY AWAY FROM THE TRAP OF LIVING IN EXCESS.
WWW.STAIRWELLONLINE.COM
I'D LIKE ONE OF YOUR DELUXE BURGERS.
AND TEN OF EVERYTHING ELSE.

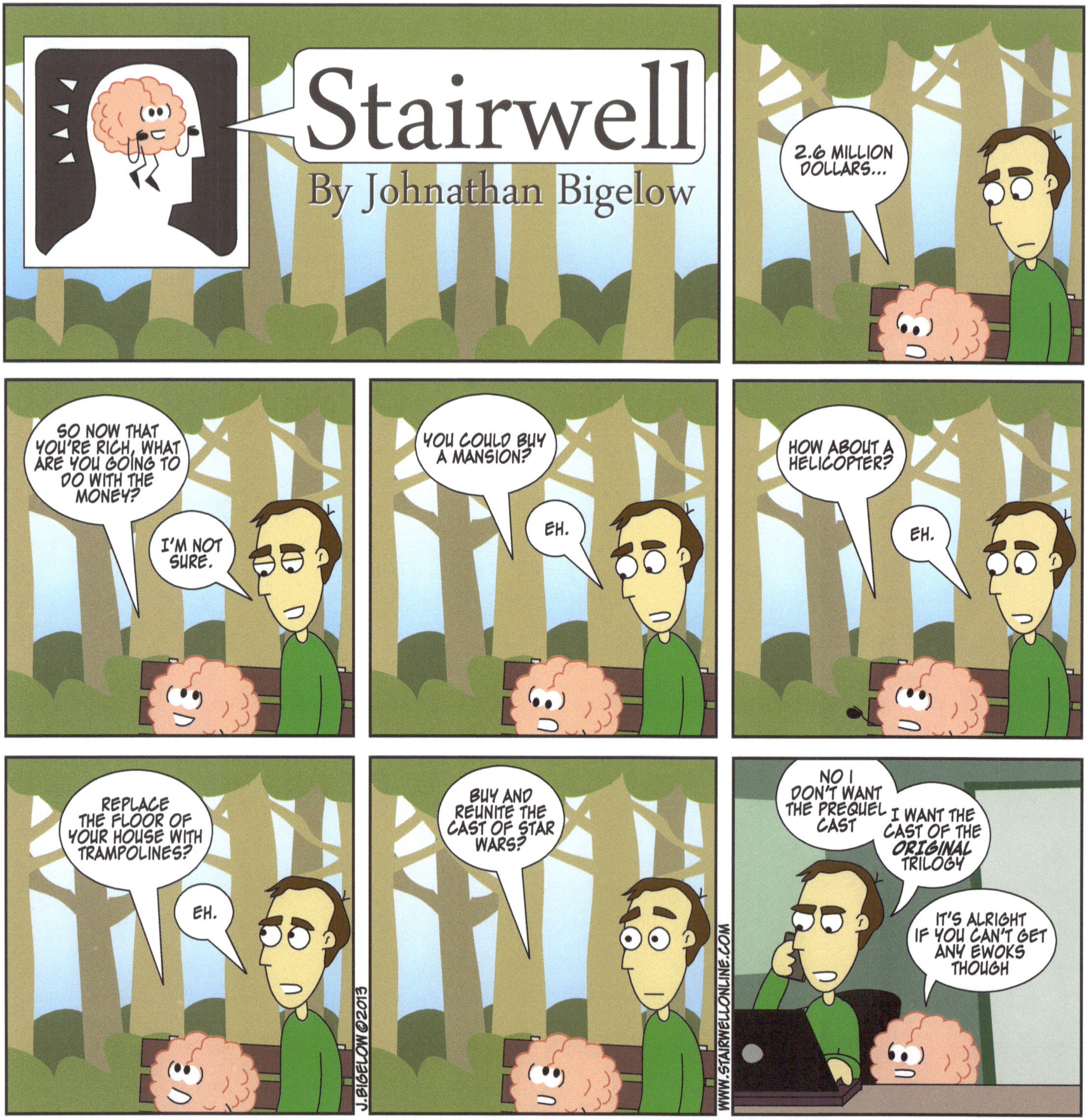
Stairwell
By Johnathan Bigelow
2.6 MILLION DOLLARS...
SO NOW THAT YOU'RE RICH, WHAT ARE YOU GOING TO DO WITH THE MONEY?
I'M NOT SURE.
YOU COULD BUY A MANSION?
EH.
HOW ABOUT A HELICOPTER?
EH.
REPLACE THE FLOOR OF YOUR HOUSE WITH TRAMPOLINES?
EH.
J.BIGELOW ©2013
BUY AND REUNITE THE CAST OF STAR WARS?
WWW.STAIRWELLONLINE.COM
NO I DON'T WANT THE PREQUEL CAST
I WANT THE CAST OF THE *ORIGINAL* TRILOGY
IT'S ALRIGHT IF YOU CAN'T GET ANY EWOKS THOUGH

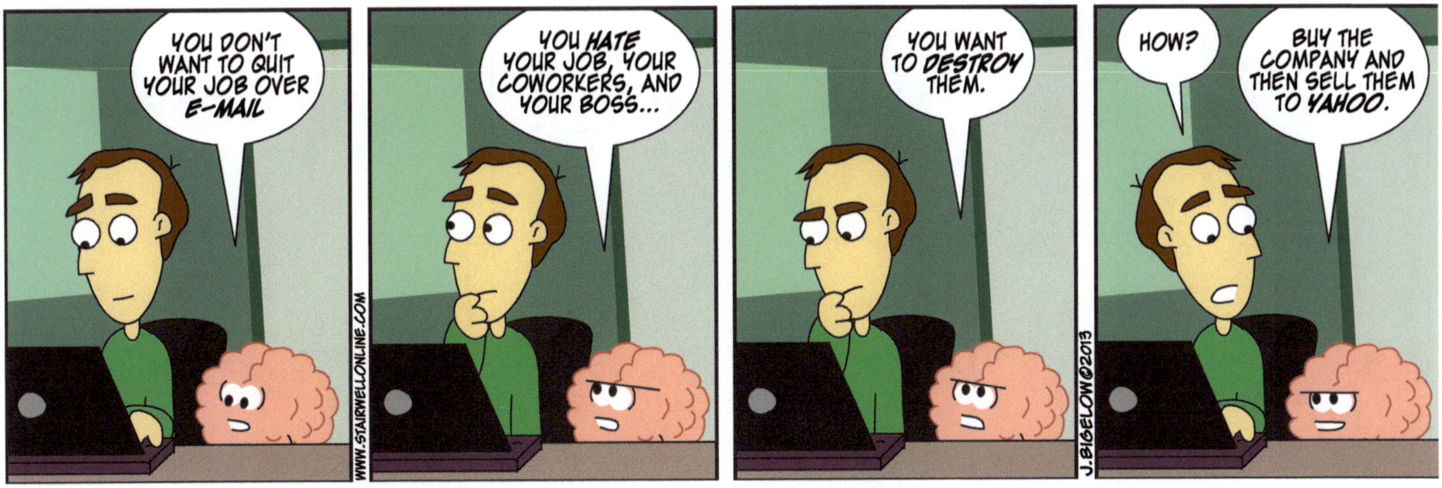
YOU DON'T WANT TO QUIT YOUR JOB OVER *E-MAIL*
WWW.STAIRWELLONLINE.COM
YOU *HATE* YOUR JOB, YOUR COWORKERS, AND YOUR BOSS...
YOU WANT TO *DESTROY* THEM.
J.BIGELOW ©2013
HOW?
BUY THE COMPANY AND THEN SELL THEM TO *YAHOO*.

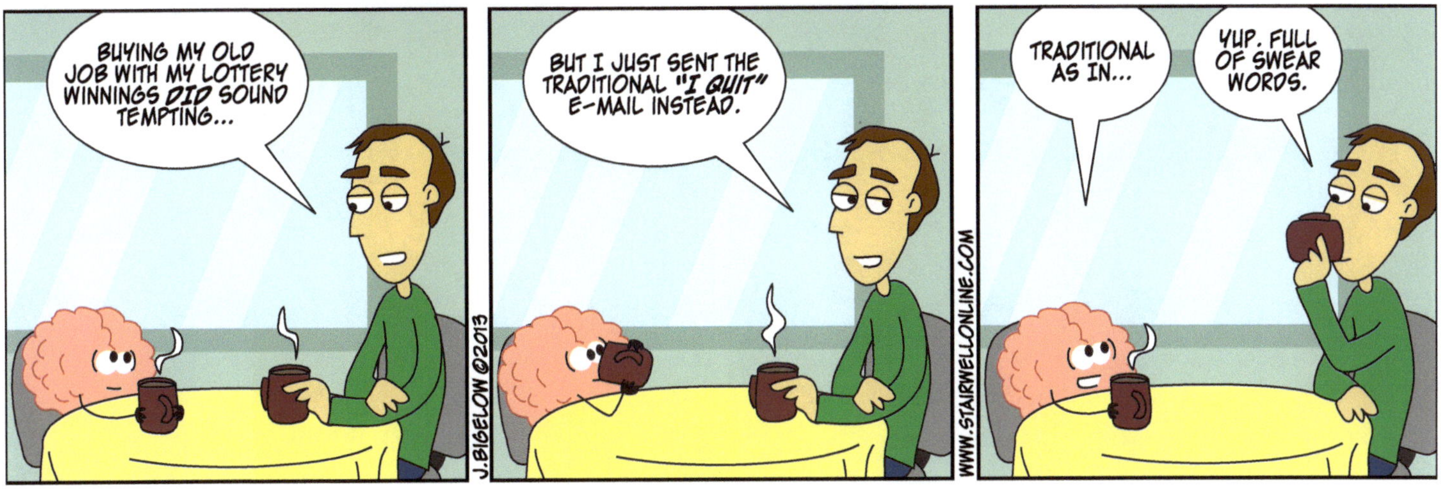
BUYING MY OLD JOB WITH MY LOTTERY WINNINGS *DID* SOUND TEMPTING...
J.BIGELOW ©2013
BUT I JUST SENT THE TRADITIONAL *"I QUIT"* E-MAIL INSTEAD.
WWW.STAIRWELLONLINE.COM
TRADITIONAL AS IN...
YUP. FULL OF SWEAR WORDS.

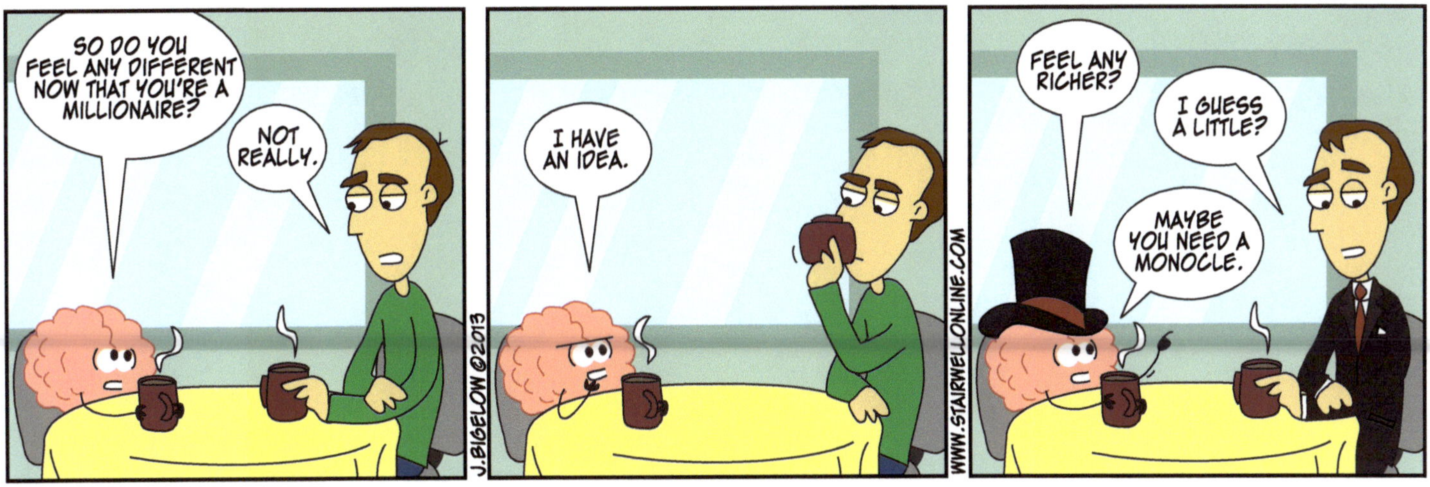
SO DO YOU FEEL ANY DIFFERENT NOW THAT YOU'RE A MILLIONAIRE?
NOT REALLY.
J.BIGELOW ©2013
I HAVE AN IDEA.
WWW.STAIRWELLONLINE.COM
FEEL ANY RICHER?
I GUESS A LITTLE?
MAYBE YOU NEED A MONOCLE.

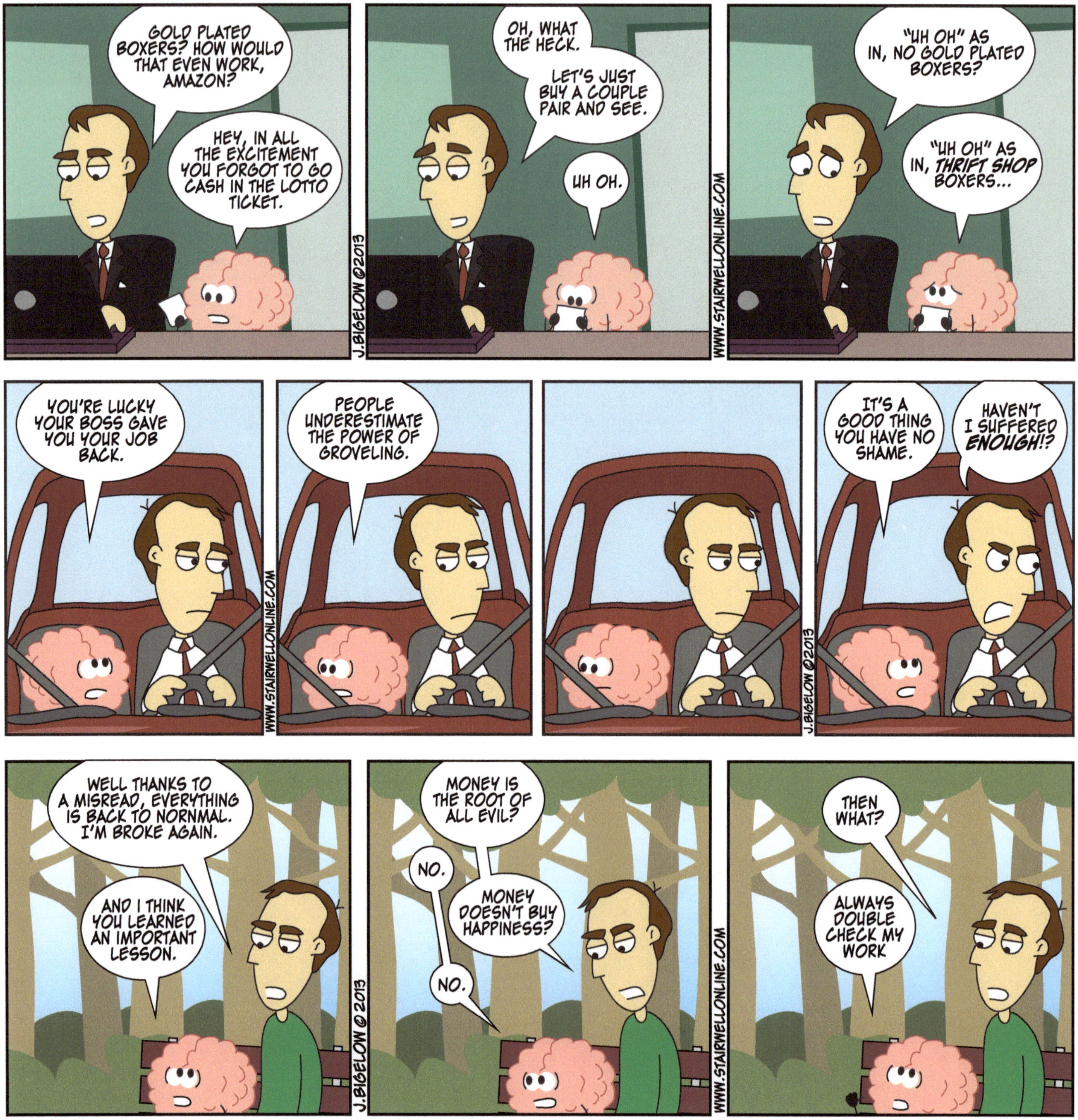
GOLD PLATED BOXERS? HOW WOULD THAT EVEN WORK, AMAZON?
HEY, IN ALL THE EXCITEMENT YOU FORGOT TO GO CASH IN THE LOTTO TICKET.
J. BIGELOW ©2013
OH, WHAT THE HECK.
LET'S JUST BUY A COUPLE PAIR AND SEE.
UH OH.
WWW.STAIRWELLONLINE.COM
"UH OH" AS IN, NO GOLD PLATED BOXERS?
"UH OH" AS IN, THRIFT SHOP BOXERS...
YOU'RE LUCKY YOUR BOSS GAVE YOU YOUR JOB BACK.
WWW.STAIRWELLONLINE.COM
PEOPLE UNDERESTIMATE THE POWER OF GROVELING.
J. BIGELOW ©2013
IT'S A GOOD THING YOU HAVE NO SHAME.
HAVEN'T I SUFFERED ENOUGH!?
WELL THANKS TO A MISREAD, EVERYTHING IS BACK TO NORNMAL. I'M BROKE AGAIN.
AND I THINK YOU LEARNED AN IMPORTANT LESSON.
J. BIGELOW © 2013
MONEY IS THE ROOT OF ALL EVIL?
NO.
MONEY DOESN'T BUY HAPPINESS?
NO.
WWW.STAIRWELLONLINE.COM
THEN WHAT?
ALWAYS DOUBLE CHECK MY WORK

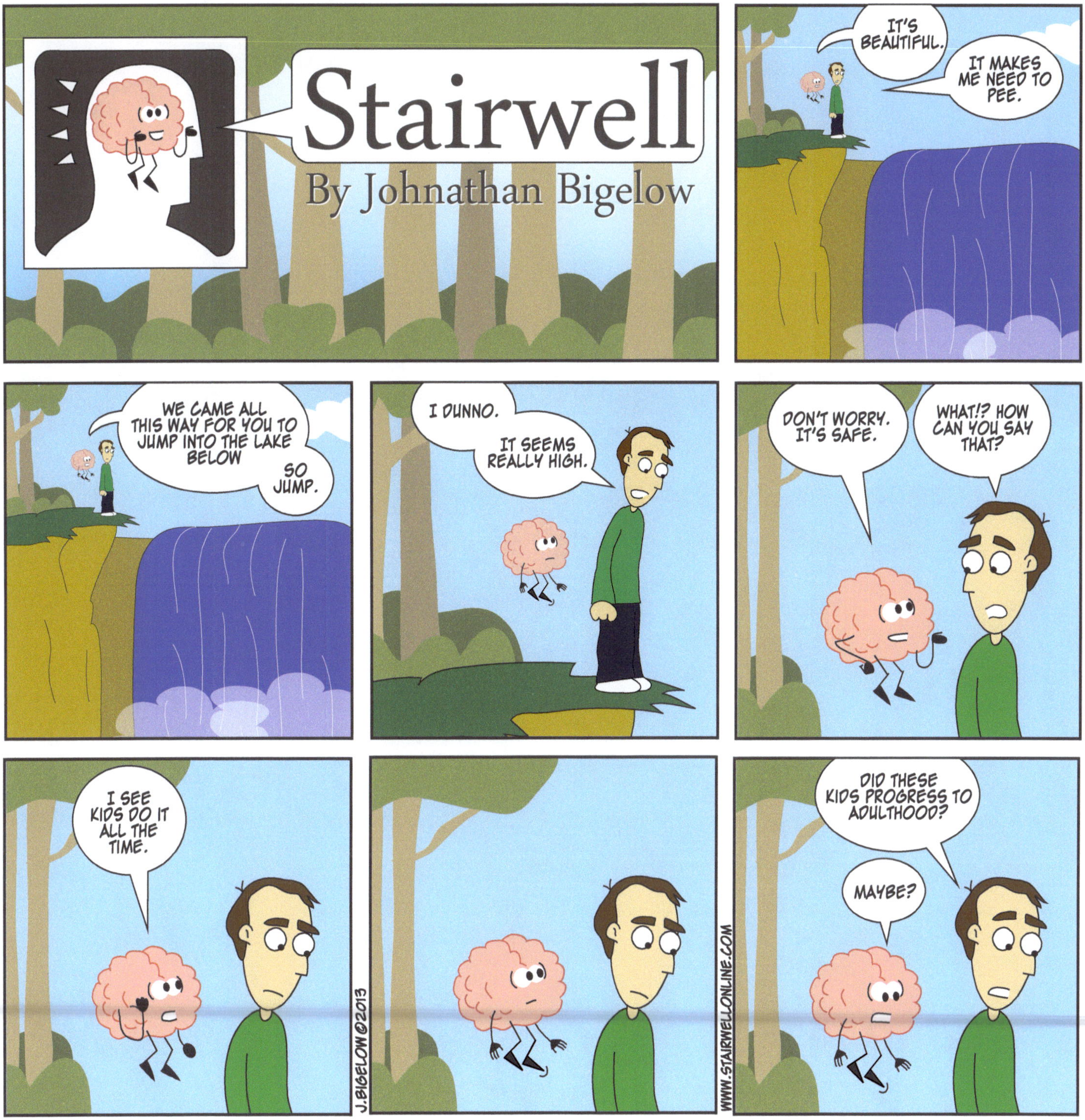
Stairwell
By Johnathan Bigelow
IT'S BEAUTIFUL.
IT MAKES ME NEED TO PEE.
WE CAME ALL THIS WAY FOR YOU TO JUMP INTO THE LAKE BELOW
SO JUMP.
I DUNNO.
IT SEEMS REALLY HIGH.
DON'T WORRY. IT'S SAFE.
WHAT!? HOW CAN YOU SAY THAT?
I SEE KIDS DO IT ALL THE TIME.
J.BIGELOW ©2013
WWW.STAIRWELLONLINE.COM
DID THESE KIDS PROGRESS TO ADULTHOOD?
MAYBE?

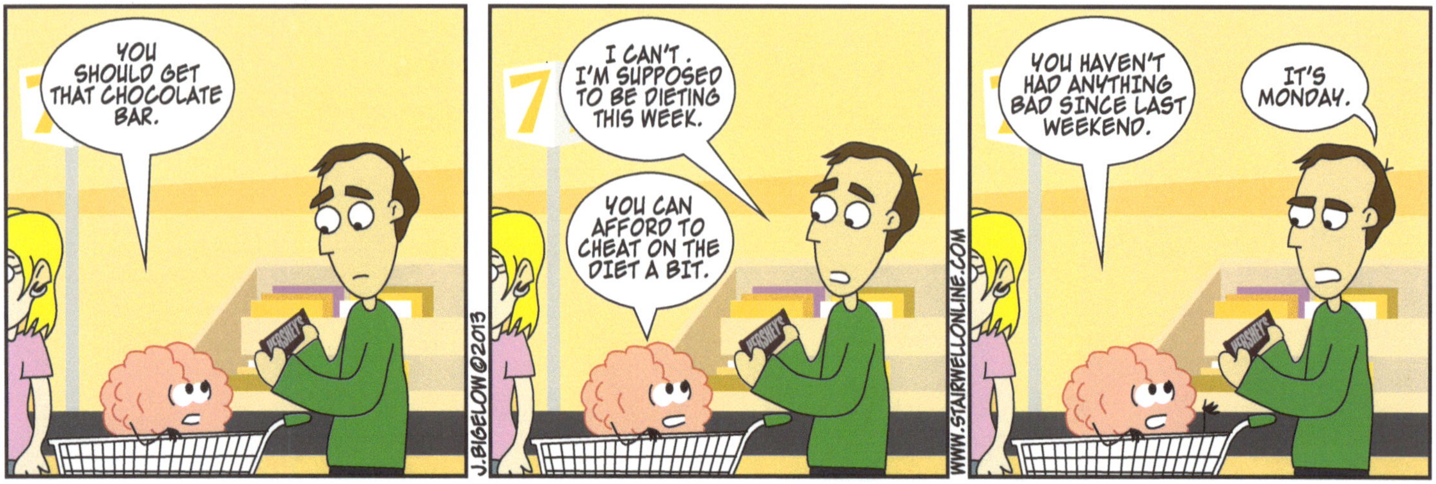
YOU SHOULD GET THAT CHOCOLATE BAR.
I CAN'T. I'M SUPPOSED TO BE DIETING THIS WEEK.
YOU CAN AFFORD TO CHEAT ON THE DIET A BIT.
YOU HAVEN'T HAD ANYTHING BAD SINCE LAST WEEKEND.
IT'S MONDAY.
J. BIGELOW ©2013
WWW.STAIRWELLONLINE.COM

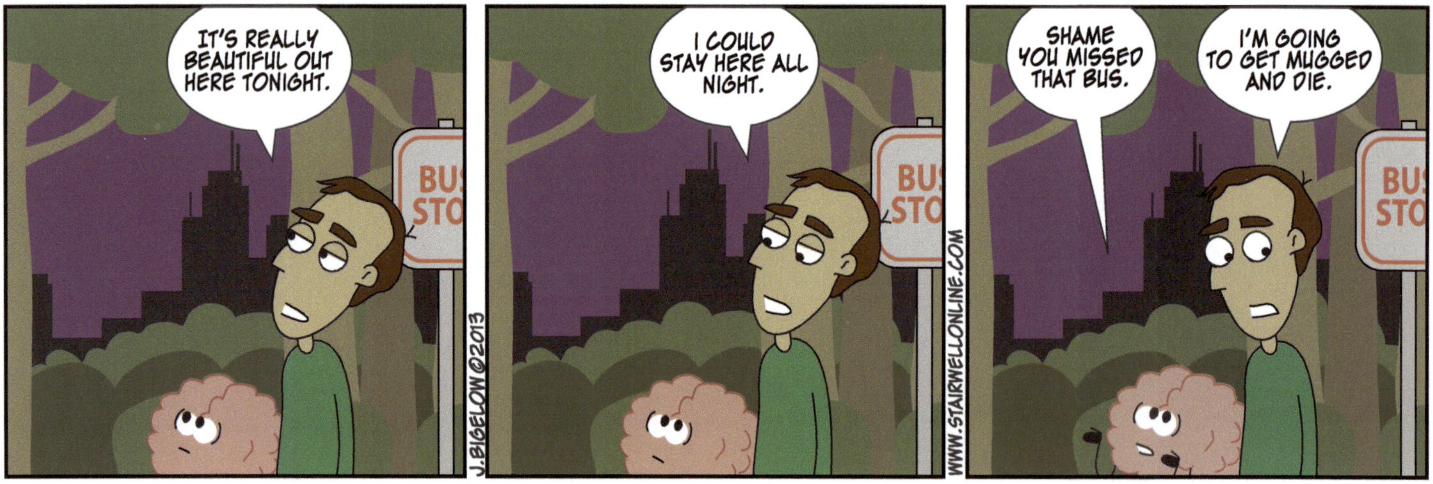
IT'S REALLY BEAUTIFUL OUT HERE TONIGHT.
I COULD STAY HERE ALL NIGHT.
SHAME YOU MISSED THAT BUS.
I'M GOING TO GET MUGGED AND DIE.
J. BIGELOW ©2013
WWW.STAIRWELLONLINE.COM

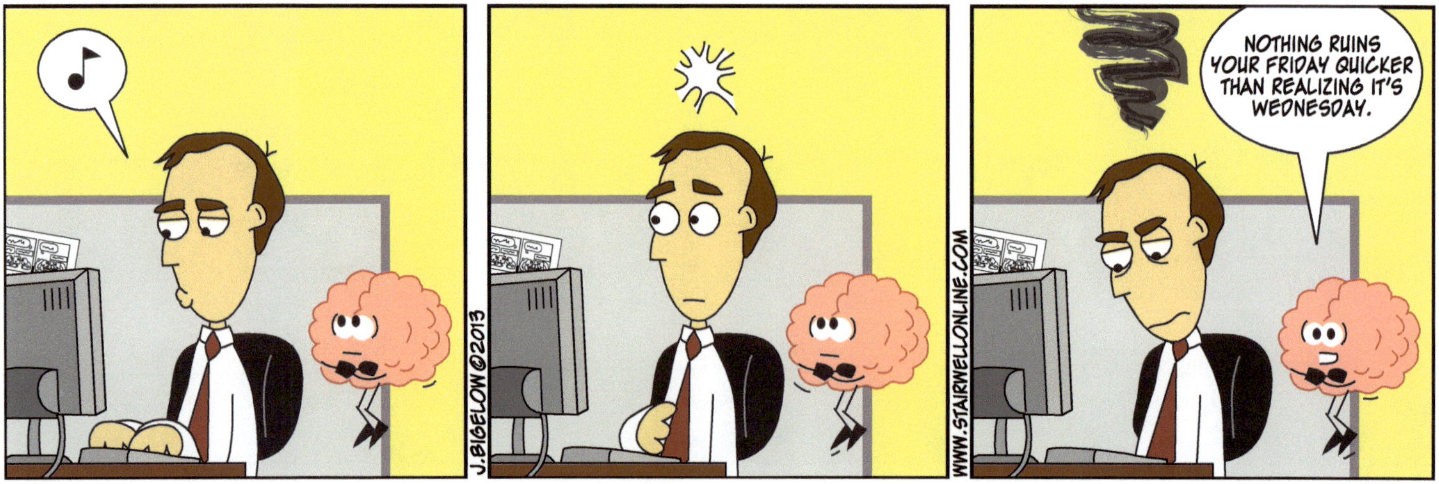
NOTHING RUINS YOUR FRIDAY QUICKER THAN REALIZING IT'S WEDNESDAY.
J. BIGELOW ©2013
WWW.STAIRWELLONLINE.COM

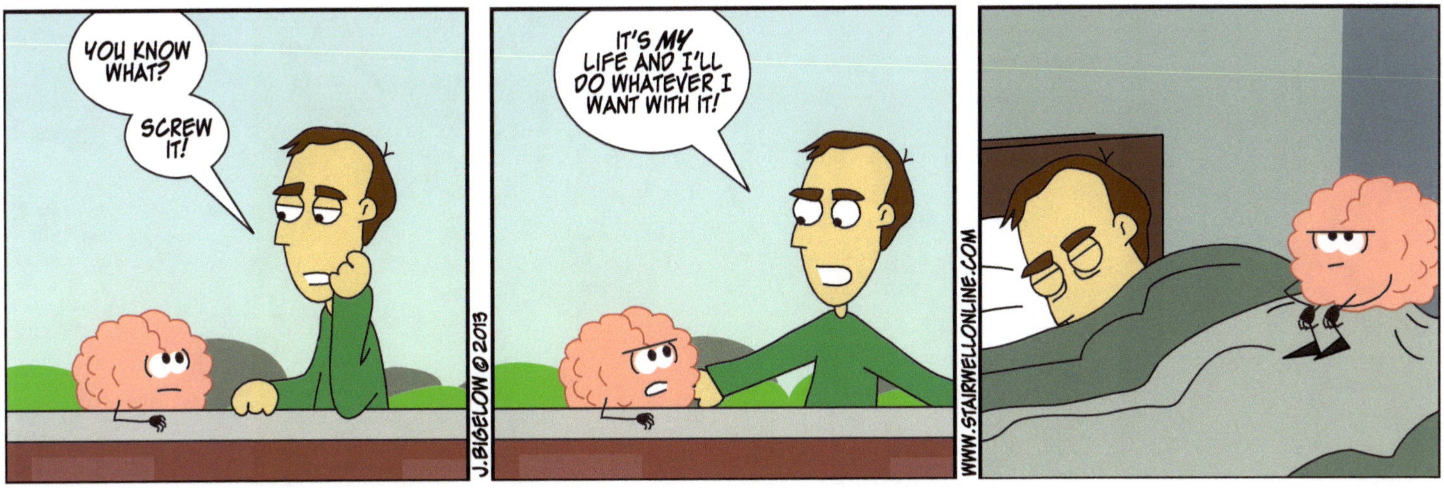
YOU KNOW WHAT?
SCREW IT!
IT'S MY LIFE AND I'LL DO WHATEVER I WANT WITH IT!
J.BIGELOW © 2013
WWW.STAIRWELLONLINE.COM

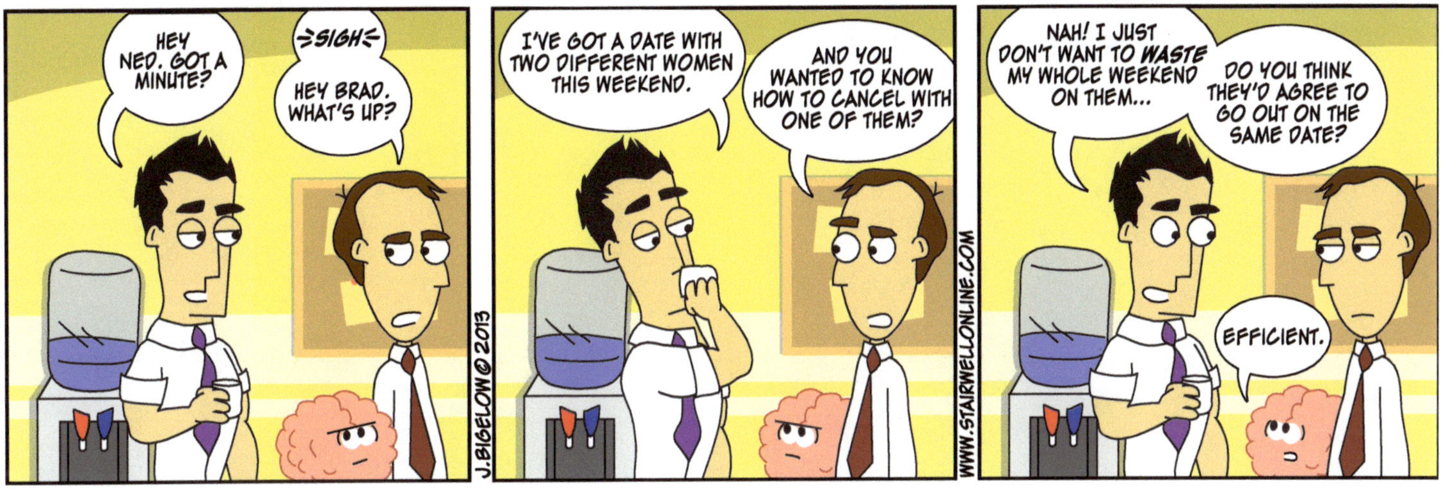
HEY NED. GOT A MINUTE?
≥SIGH≤
HEY BRAD. WHAT'S UP?
J.BIGELOW © 2013
I'VE GOT A DATE WITH TWO DIFFERENT WOMEN THIS WEEKEND.
AND YOU WANTED TO KNOW HOW TO CANCEL WITH ONE OF THEM?
WWW.STAIRWELLONLINE.COM
NAH! I JUST DON'T WANT TO WASTE MY WHOLE WEEKEND ON THEM...
DO YOU THINK THEY'D AGREE TO GO OUT ON THE SAME DATE?
EFFICIENT.

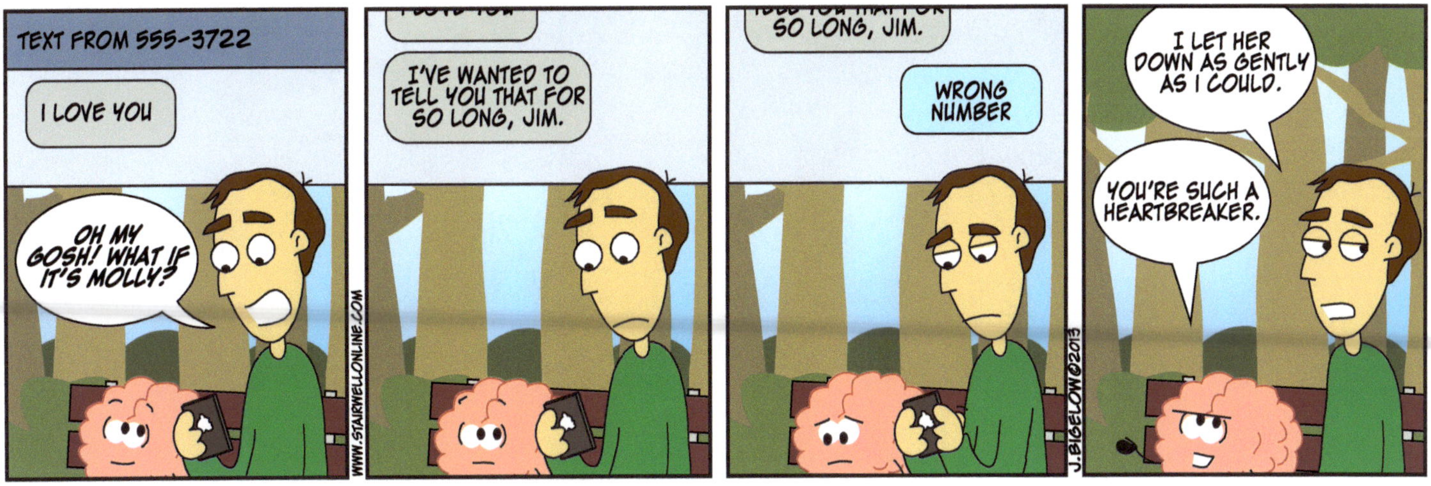
TEXT FROM 555-3722
I LOVE YOU
OH MY GOSH! WHAT IF IT'S MOLLY?
WWW.STAIRWELLONLINE.COM
I'VE WANTED TO TELL YOU THAT FOR SO LONG, JIM.
SO LONG, JIM.
WRONG NUMBER
J.BIGELOW©2013
I LET HER DOWN AS GENTLY AS I COULD.
YOU'RE SUCH A HEARTBREAKER.

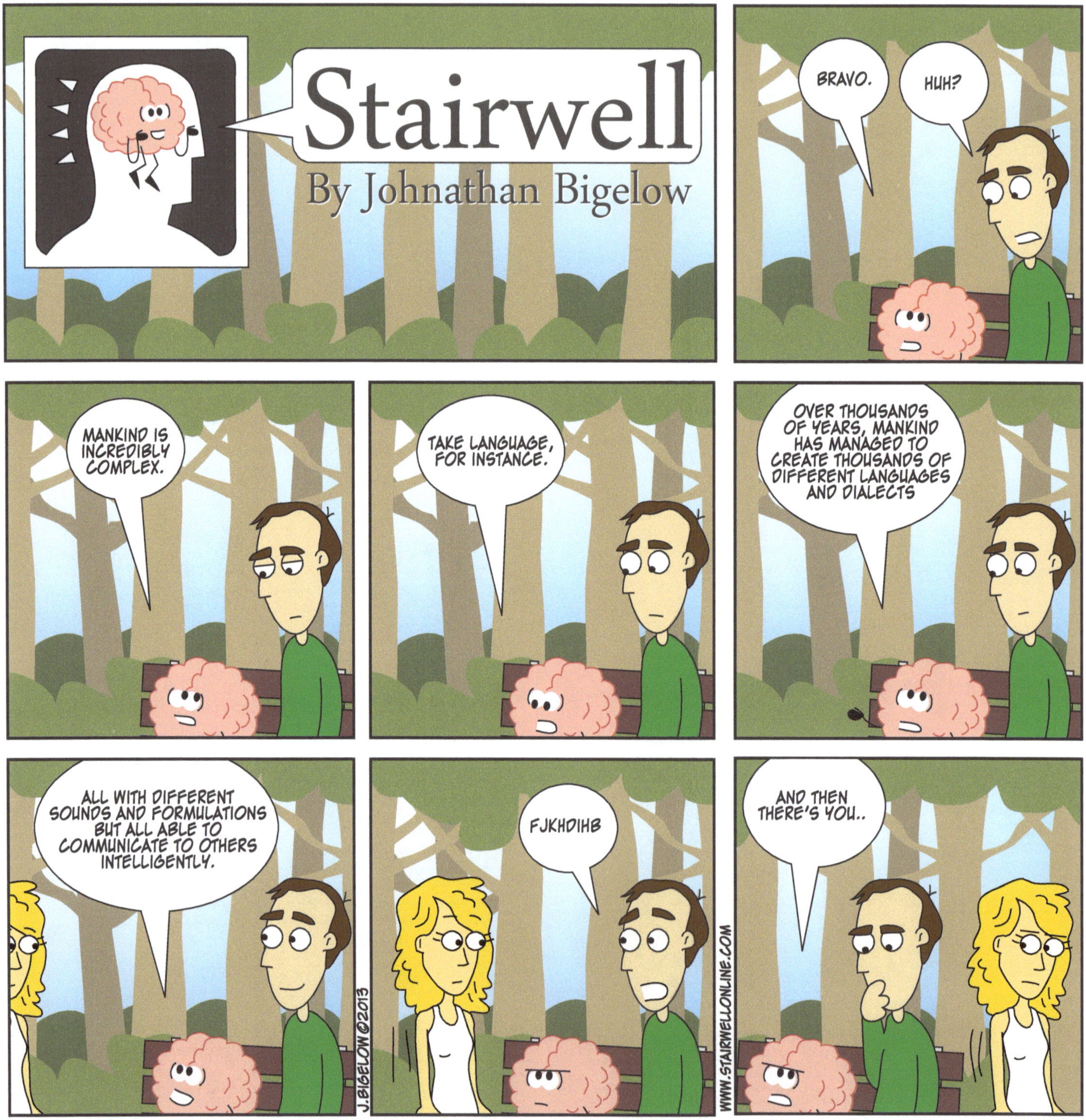
Stairwell
By Johnathan Bigelow
BRAVO.
HUH?
MANKIND IS INCREDIBLY COMPLEX.
TAKE LANGUAGE, FOR INSTANCE.
OVER THOUSANDS OF YEARS, MANKIND HAS MANAGED TO CREATE THOUSANDS OF DIFFERENT LANGUAGES AND DIALECTS
ALL WITH DIFFERENT SOUNDS AND FORMULATIONS BUT ALL ABLE TO COMMUNICATE TO OTHERS INTELLIGENTLY.
J.BIGELOW ©2013
FJKHDIHB
WWW.STAIRWELLONLINE.COM
AND THEN THERE'S YOU..

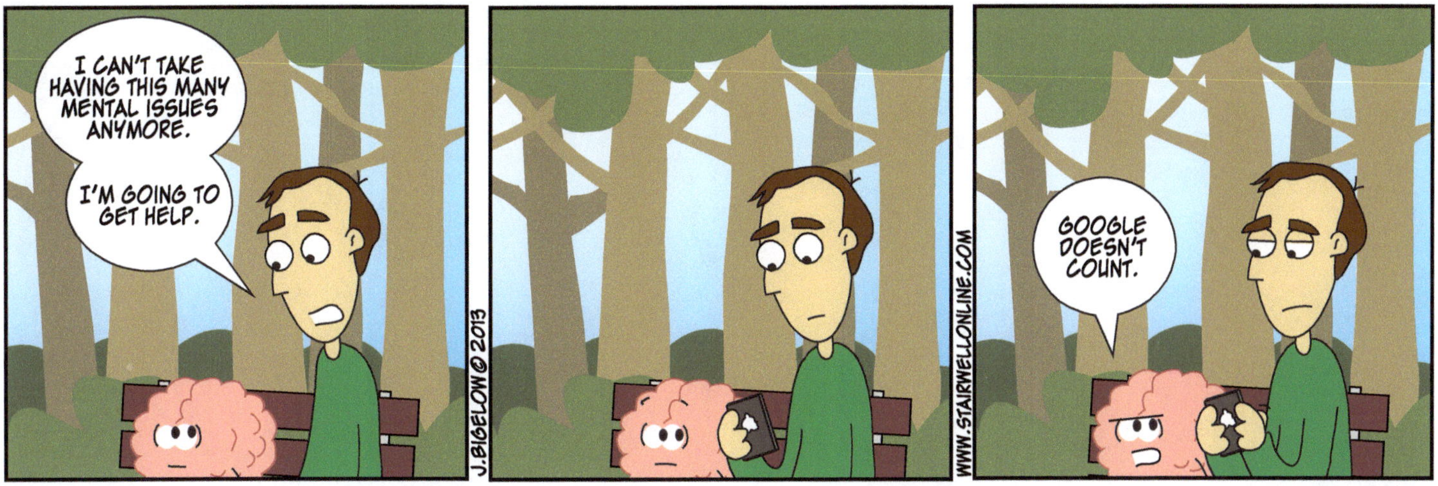
I CAN'T TAKE HAVING THIS MANY MENTAL ISSUES ANYMORE.
I'M GOING TO GET HELP.
J.BIGELOW © 2013
GOOGLE DOESN'T COUNT.
WWW.STAIRWELLONLINE.COM

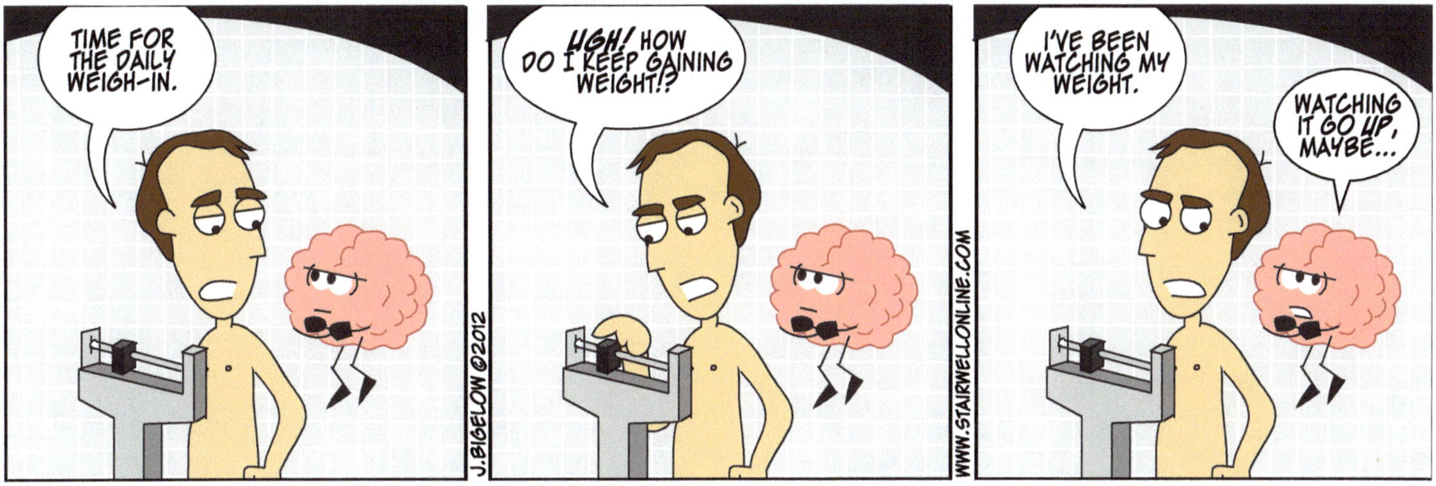
TIME FOR THE DAILY WEIGH-IN.
J.BIGELOW © 2012
UGH! HOW DO I KEEP GAINING WEIGHT!?
WWW.STAIRWELLONLINE.COM
I'VE BEEN WATCHING MY WEIGHT.
WATCHING IT GO UP, MAYBE...

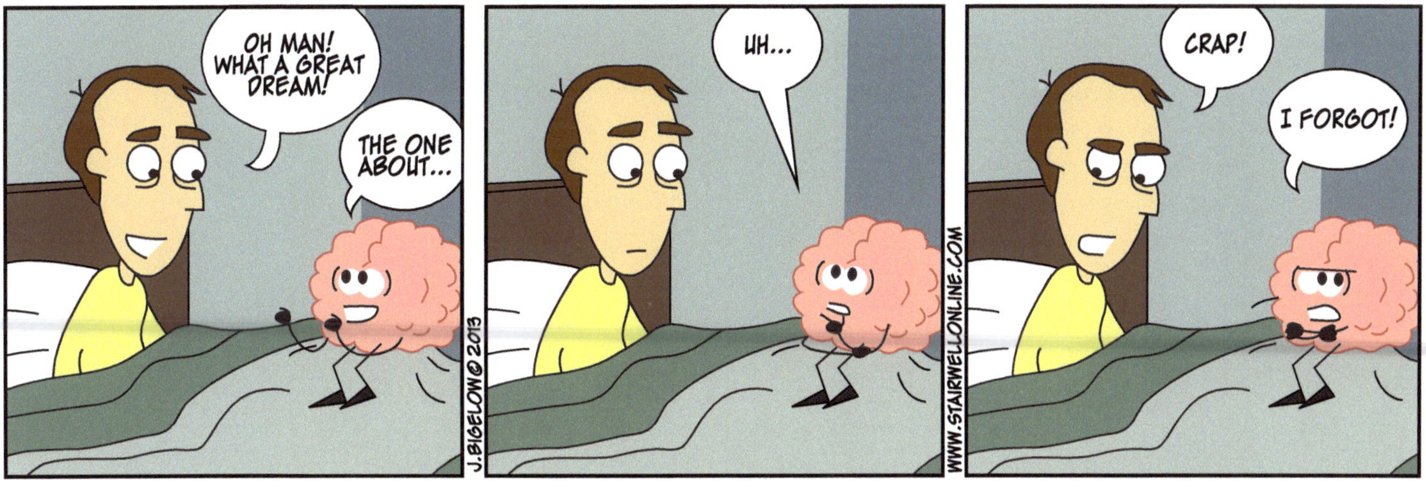
OH MAN! WHAT A GREAT DREAM!
THE ONE ABOUT...
J.BIGELOW © 2013
UH...
WWW.STAIRWELLONLINE.COM
CRAP!
I FORGOT!

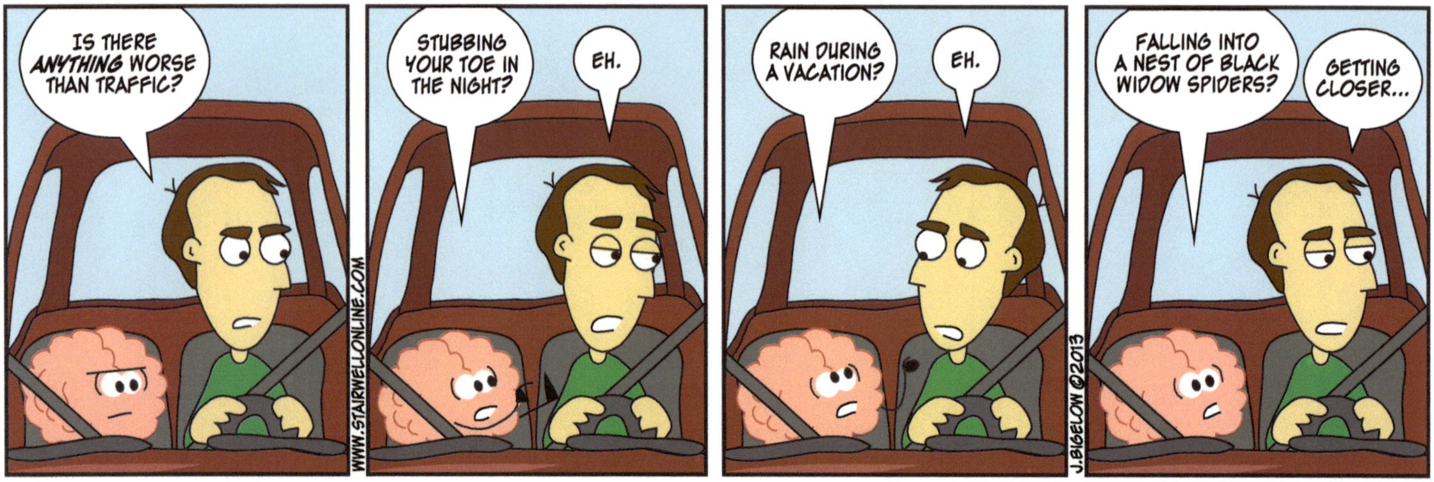
IS THERE ANYTHING WORSE THAN TRAFFIC?
STUBBING YOUR TOE IN THE NIGHT?
EH.
RAIN DURING A VACATION?
EH.
FALLING INTO A NEST OF BLACK WIDOW SPIDERS?
GETTING CLOSER...
WWW.STAIRWELLONLINE.COM
J.BIGELOW ©2013

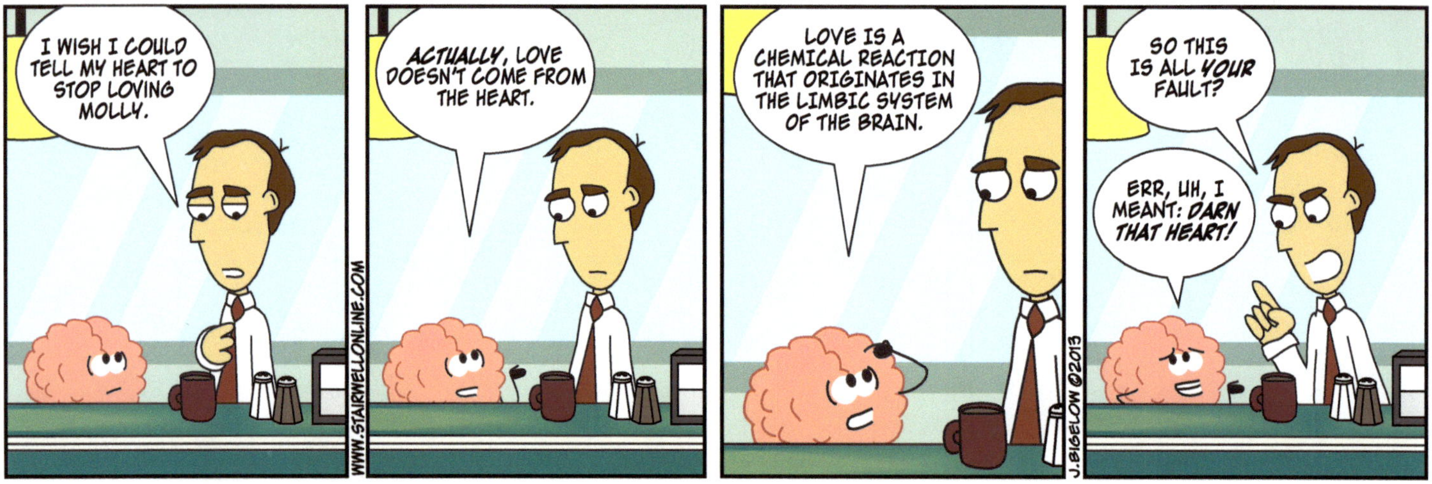
I WISH I COULD TELL MY HEART TO STOP LOVING MOLLY.
ACTUALLY, LOVE DOESN'T COME FROM THE HEART.
LOVE IS A CHEMICAL REACTION THAT ORIGINATES IN THE LIMBIC SYSTEM OF THE BRAIN.
SO THIS IS ALL YOUR FAULT?
ERR, UH, I MEANT: DARN THAT HEART!
WWW.STAIRWELLONLINE.COM
J.BIGELOW ©2013

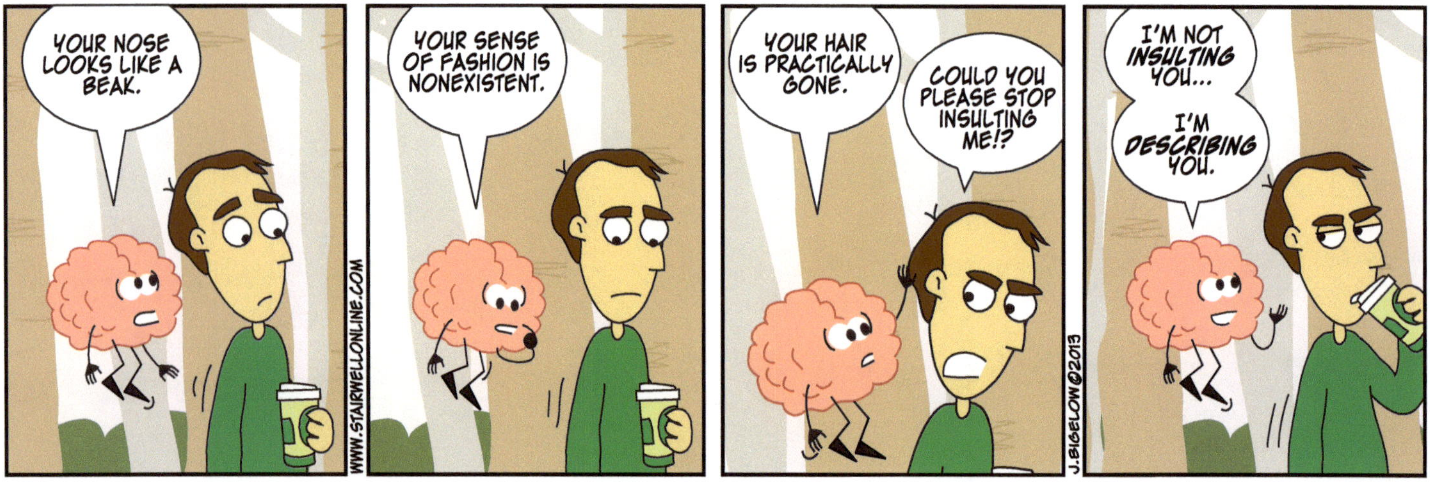
YOUR NOSE LOOKS LIKE A BEAK.
YOUR SENSE OF FASHION IS NONEXISTENT.
YOUR HAIR IS PRACTICALLY GONE.
COULD YOU PLEASE STOP INSULTING ME!?
I'M NOT INSULTING YOU...
I'M DESCRIBING YOU.
WWW.STAIRWELLONLINE.COM
J.BIGELOW ©2013

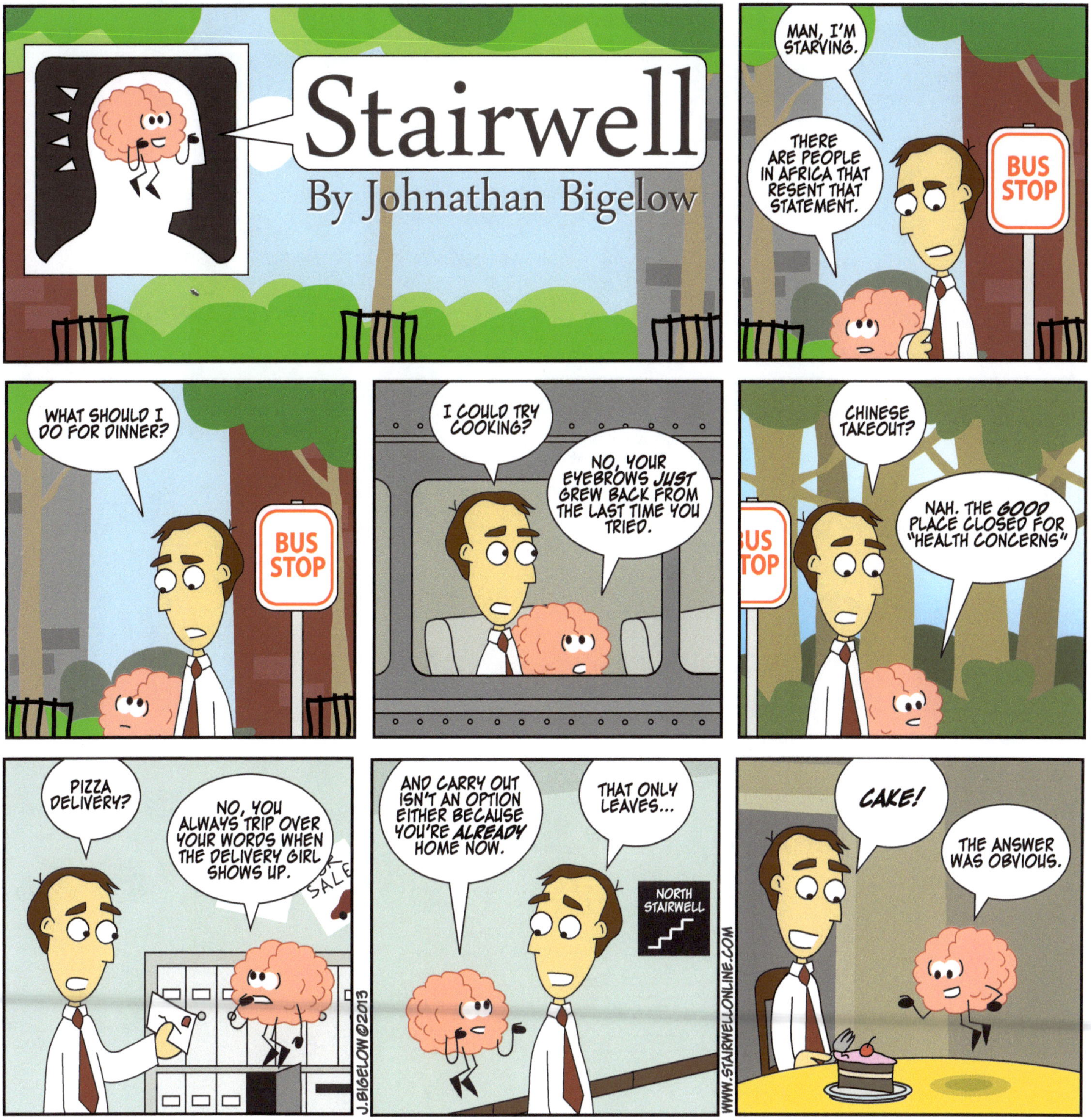
Stairwell
By Johnathan Bigelow
MAN, I'M STARVING.
THERE ARE PEOPLE IN AFRICA THAT RESENT THAT STATEMENT.
BUS STOP
WHAT SHOULD I DO FOR DINNER?
BUS STOP
I COULD TRY COOKING?
NO, YOUR EYEBROWS JUST GREW BACK FROM THE LAST TIME YOU TRIED.
CHINESE TAKEOUT?
NAH. THE GOOD PLACE CLOSED FOR "HEALTH CONCERNS"
PIZZA DELIVERY?
NO, YOU ALWAYS TRIP OVER YOUR WORDS WHEN THE DELIVERY GIRL SHOWS UP.
J.BIGELOW ©2013
AND CARRY OUT ISN'T AN OPTION EITHER BECAUSE YOU'RE ALREADY HOME NOW.
THAT ONLY LEAVES...
NORTH STAIRWELL
WWW.STAIRWELLONLINE.COM
CAKE!
THE ANSWER WAS OBVIOUS.

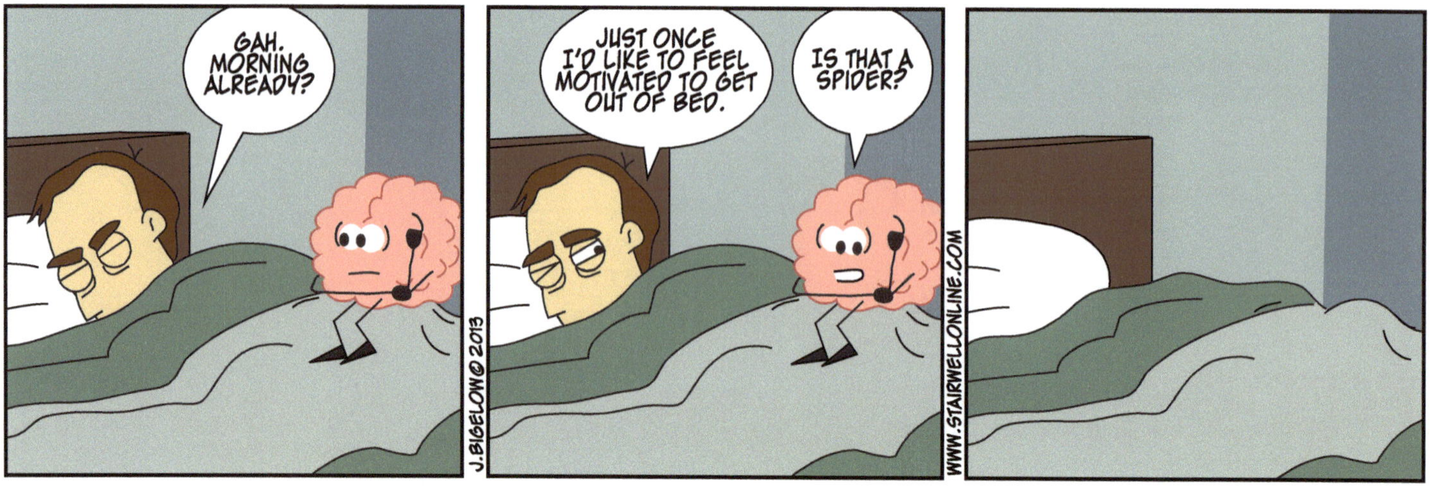
GAH. MORNING ALREADY?
JUST ONCE I'D LIKE TO FEEL MOTIVATED TO GET OUT OF BED.
IS THAT A SPIDER?
J.BIGELOW © 2013
WWW.STAIRWELLONLINE.COM

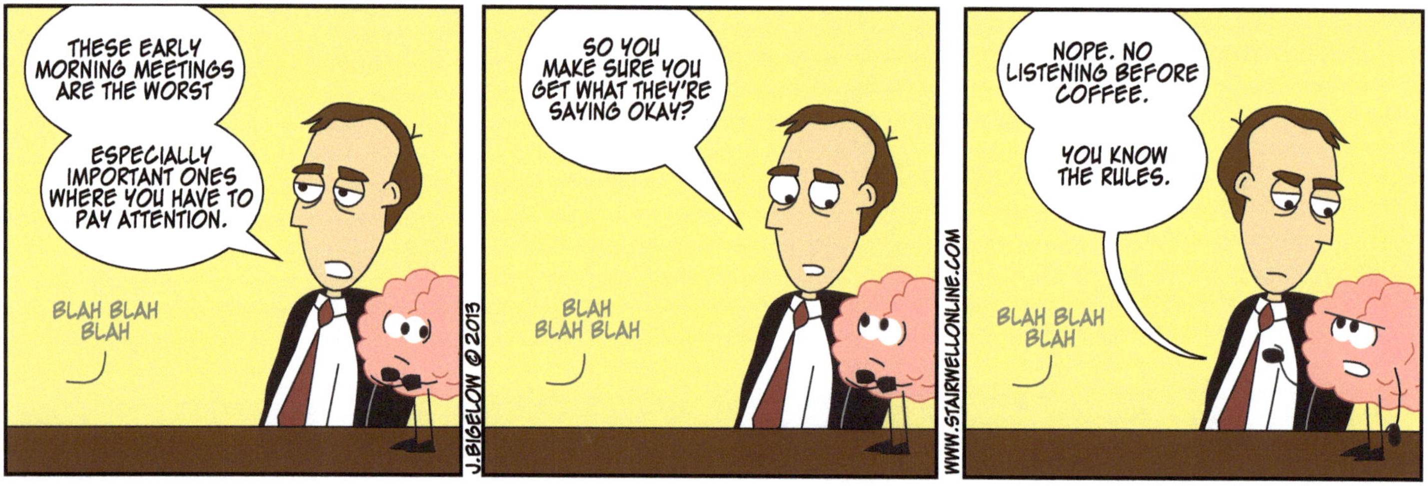
THESE EARLY MORNING MEETINGS ARE THE WORST
ESPECIALLY IMPORTANT ONES WHERE YOU HAVE TO PAY ATTENTION.
BLAH BLAH BLAH
SO YOU MAKE SURE YOU GET WHAT THEY'RE SAYING OKAY?
BLAH BLAH BLAH
NOPE. NO LISTENING BEFORE COFFEE.
YOU KNOW THE RULES.
BLAH BLAH BLAH
J.BIGELOW © 2013
WWW.STAIRWELLONLINE.COM

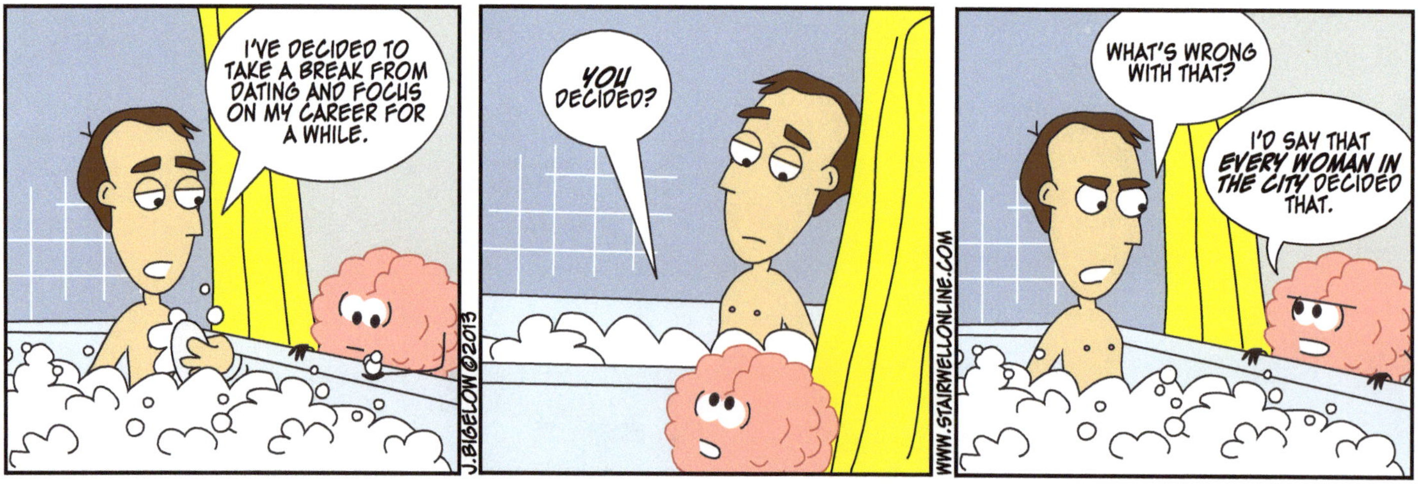
I'VE DECIDED TO TAKE A BREAK FROM DATING AND FOCUS ON MY CAREER FOR A WHILE.
YOU DECIDED?
WHAT'S WRONG WITH THAT?
I'D SAY THAT ***EVERY WOMAN IN THE CITY*** DECIDED THAT.
J.BIGELOW © 2013
WWW.STAIRWELLONLINE.COM

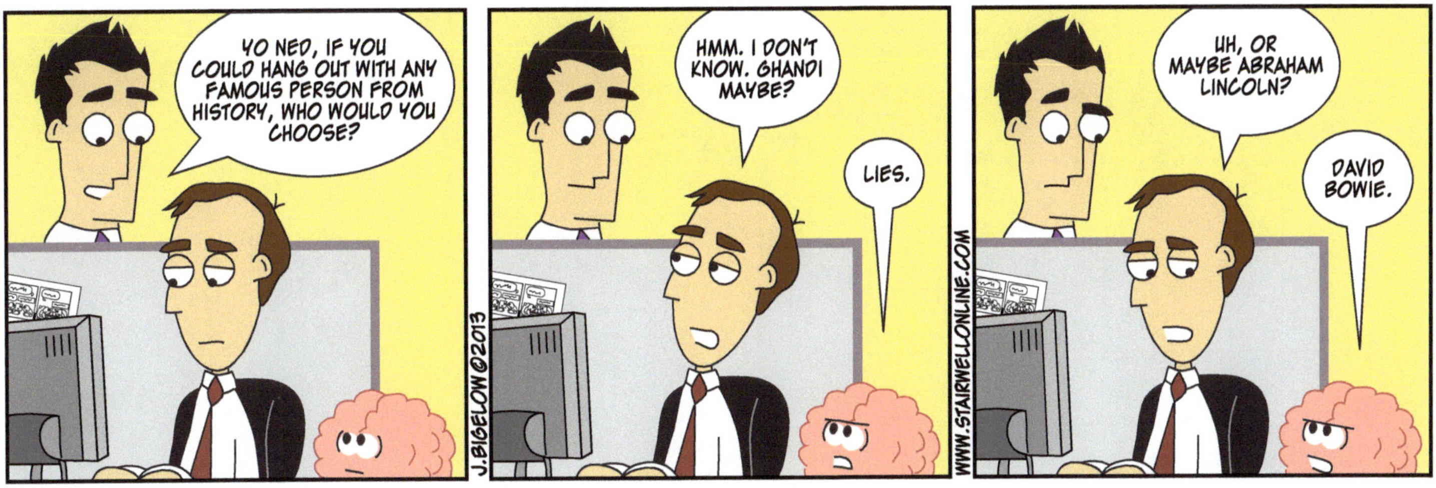
YO NED, IF YOU COULD HANG OUT WITH ANY FAMOUS PERSON FROM HISTORY, WHO WOULD YOU CHOOSE?
J.BIGELOW ©2013
HMM. I DON'T KNOW. GHANDI MAYBE?
LIES.
WWW.STAIRWELLONLINE.COM
UH, OR MAYBE ABRAHAM LINCOLN?
DAVID BOWIE.

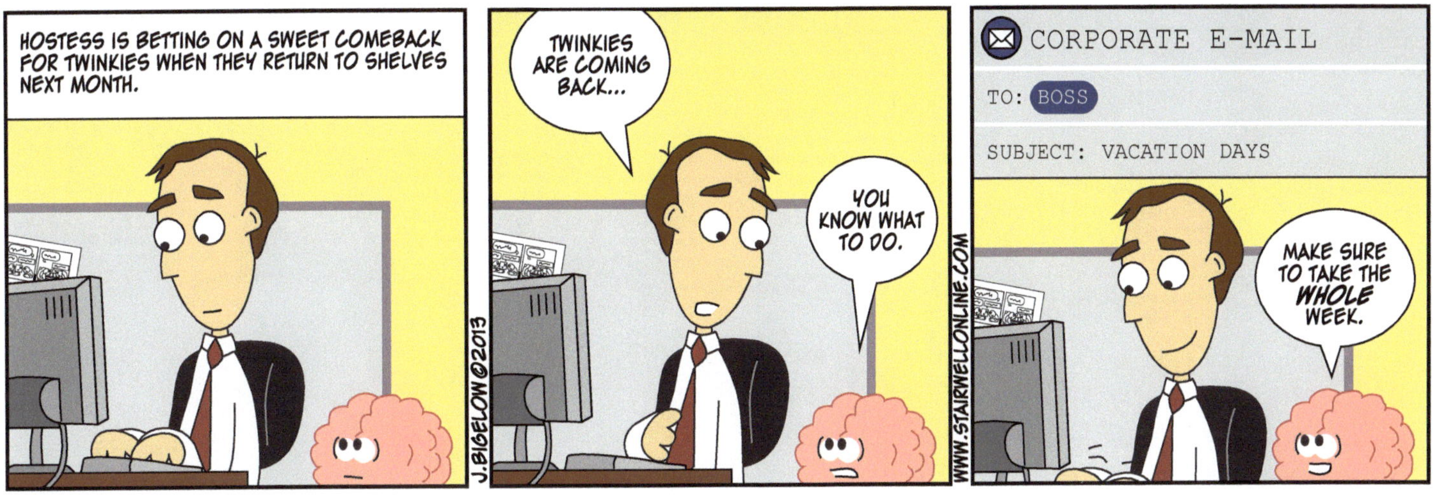
HOSTESS IS BETTING ON A SWEET COMEBACK FOR TWINKIES WHEN THEY RETURN TO SHELVES NEXT MONTH.
J.BIGELOW ©2013
TWINKIES ARE COMING BACK...
YOU KNOW WHAT TO DO.
WWW.STAIRWELLONLINE.COM
CORPORATE E-MAIL
TO: BOSS
SUBJECT: VACATION DAYS
MAKE SURE TO TAKE THE *WHOLE* WEEK.

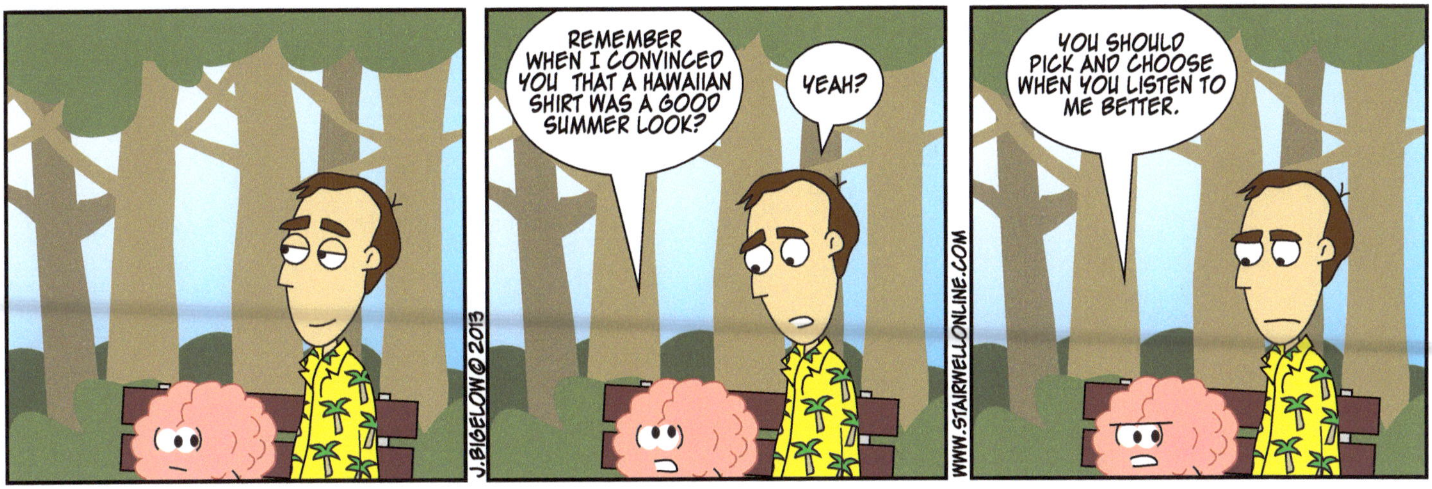
J.BIGELOW ©2013
REMEMBER WHEN I CONVINCED YOU THAT A HAWAIIAN SHIRT WAS A GOOD SUMMER LOOK?
YEAH?
WWW.STAIRWELLONLINE.COM
YOU SHOULD PICK AND CHOOSE WHEN YOU LISTEN TO ME BETTER.

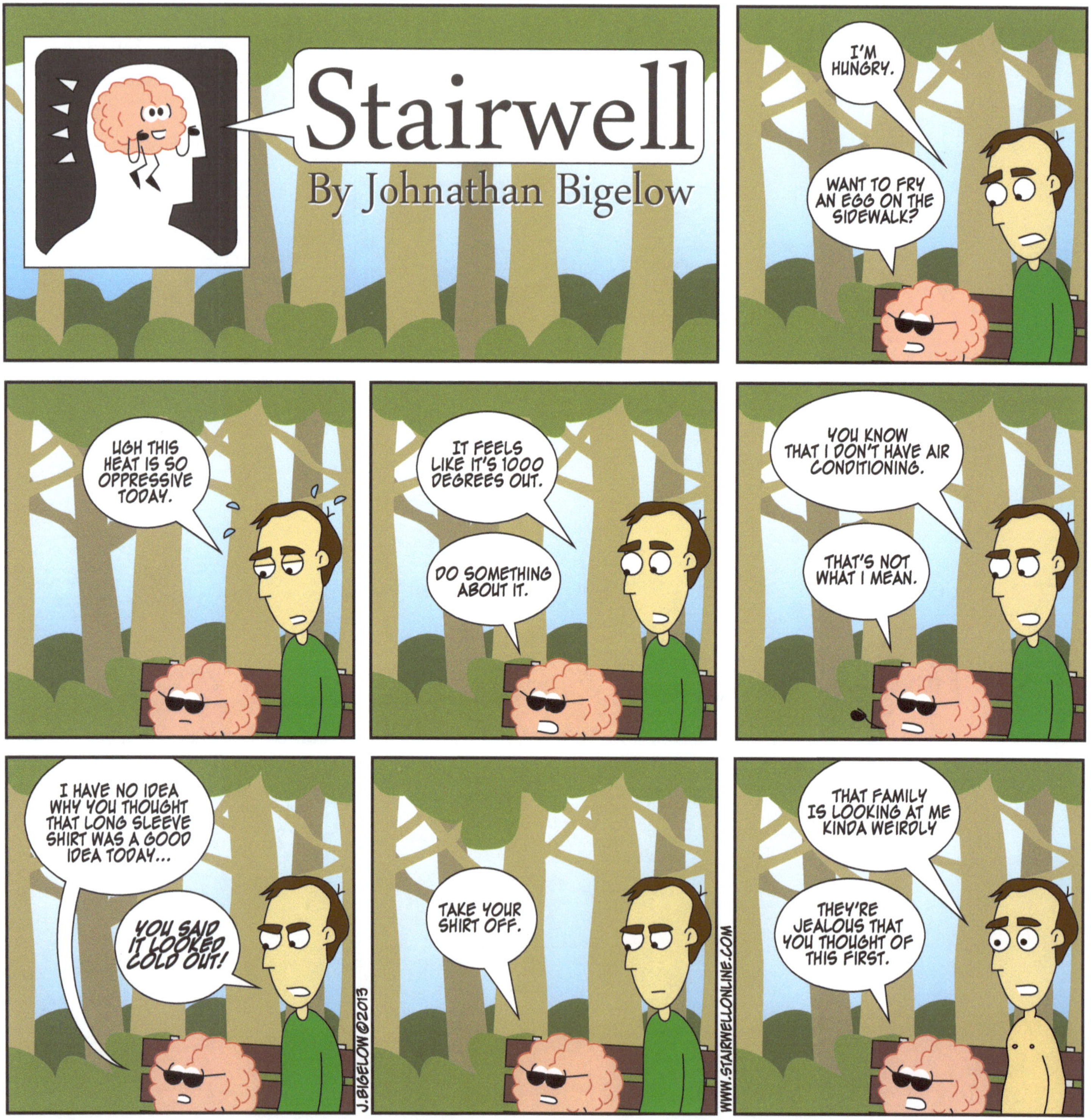
Stairwell
By Johnathan Bigelow
I'M HUNGRY.
WANT TO FRY AN EGG ON THE SIDEWALK?
UGH THIS HEAT IS SO OPPRESSIVE TODAY.
IT FEELS LIKE IT'S 1000 DEGREES OUT.
DO SOMETHING ABOUT IT.
YOU KNOW THAT I DON'T HAVE AIR CONDITIONING.
THAT'S NOT WHAT I MEAN.
I HAVE NO IDEA WHY YOU THOUGHT THAT LONG SLEEVE SHIRT WAS A GOOD IDEA TODAY...
YOU SAID IT LOOKED COLD OUT!
J.BIGELOW ©2013
TAKE YOUR SHIRT OFF.
WWW.STAIRWELLONLINE.COM
THAT FAMILY IS LOOKING AT ME KINDA WEIRDLY
THEY'RE JEALOUS THAT YOU THOUGHT OF THIS FIRST.

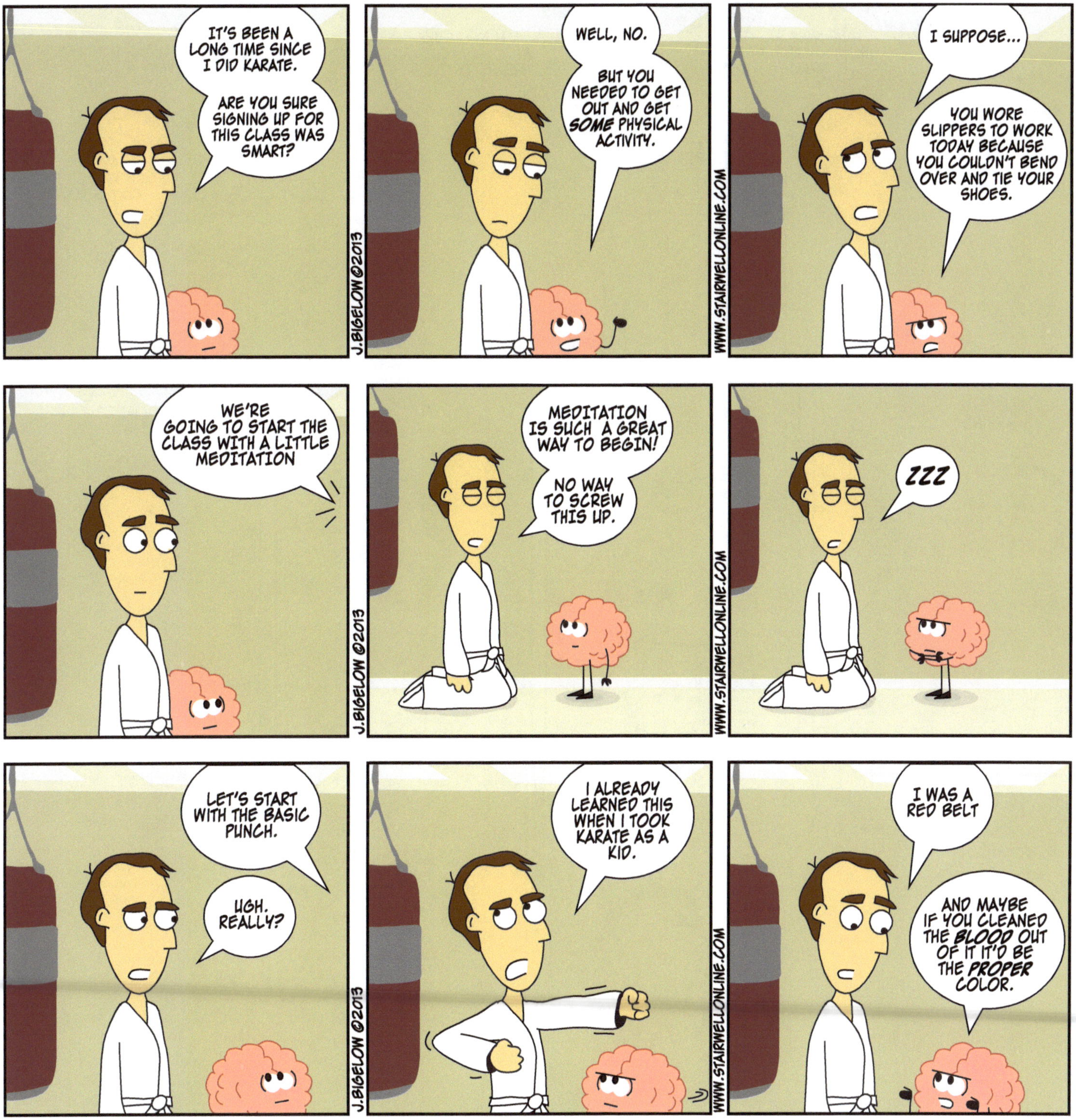

IT'S BEEN A LONG TIME SINCE I DID KARATE.
ARE YOU SURE SIGNING UP FOR THIS CLASS WAS SMART?
J.BIGELOW ©2013
WELL, NO.
BUT YOU NEEDED TO GET OUT AND GET SOME PHYSICAL ACTIVITY.
WWW.STAIRWELLONLINE.COM
I SUPPOSE...
YOU WORE SLIPPERS TO WORK TODAY BECAUSE YOU COULDN'T BEND OVER AND TIE YOUR SHOES.
WE'RE GOING TO START THE CLASS WITH A LITTLE MEDITATION
J.BIGELOW ©2013
MEDITATION IS SUCH A GREAT WAY TO BEGIN!
NO WAY TO SCREW THIS UP.
WWW.STAIRWELLONLINE.COM
ZZZ
LET'S START WITH THE BASIC PUNCH.
UGH. REALLY?
J.BIGELOW ©2013
I ALREADY LEARNED THIS WHEN I TOOK KARATE AS A KID.
WWW.STAIRWELLONLINE.COM
I WAS A RED BELT
AND MAYBE IF YOU CLEANED THE BLOOD OUT OF IT IT'D BE THE PROPER COLOR.

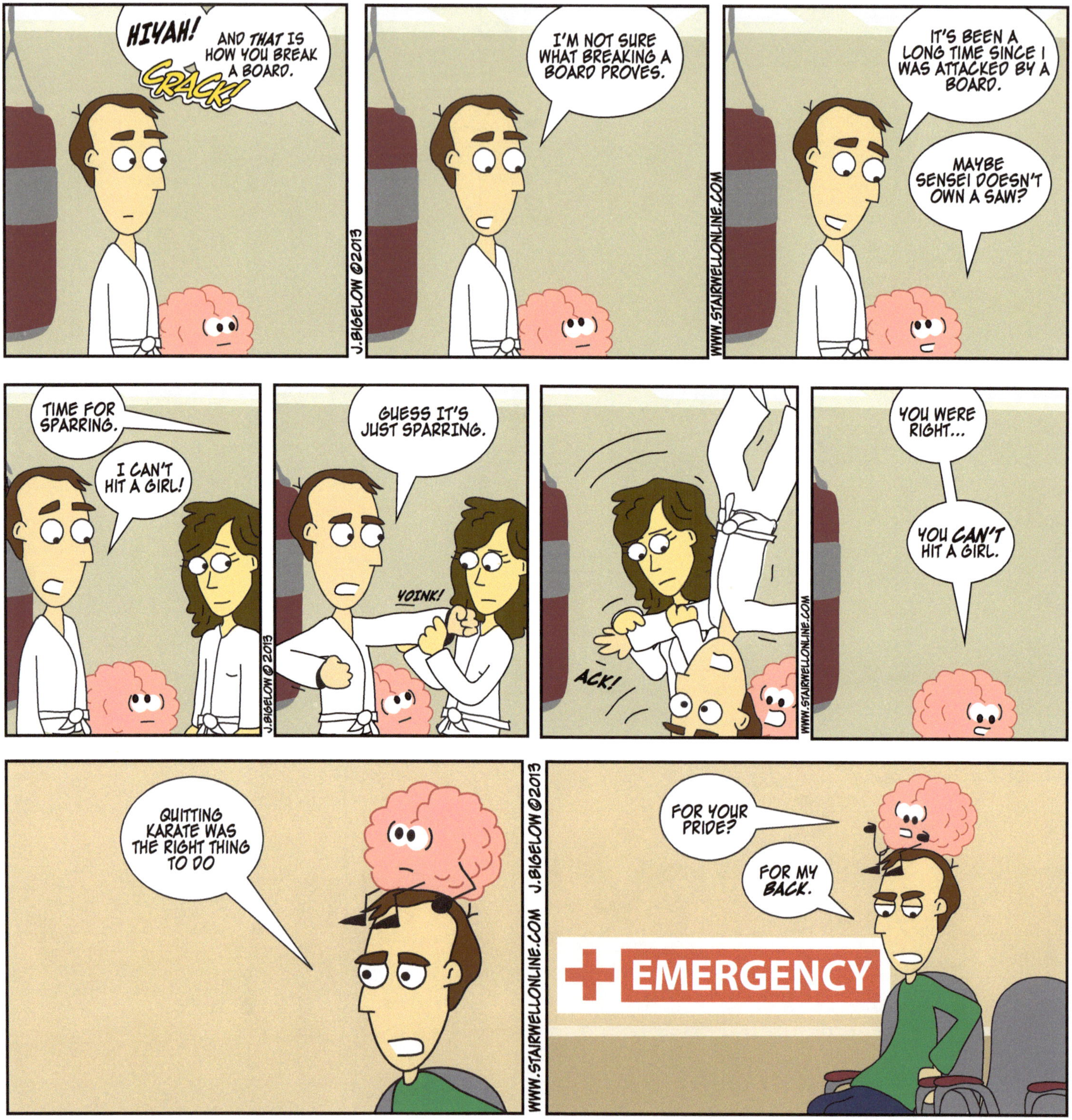
HIYAH!
CRACK!
AND *THAT* IS HOW YOU BREAK A BOARD.
J.BIGELOW ©2013
I'M NOT SURE WHAT BREAKING A BOARD PROVES.
WWW.STAIRWELLONLINE.COM
IT'S BEEN A LONG TIME SINCE I WAS ATTACKED BY A BOARD.
MAYBE SENSEI DOESN'T OWN A SAW?
TIME FOR SPARRING.
I CAN'T HIT A GIRL!
J.BIGELOW © 2013
GUESS IT'S JUST SPARRING.
YOINK!
ACK!
WWW.STAIRWELLONLINE.COM
YOU WERE RIGHT...
YOU *CAN'T* HIT A GIRL.
QUITTING KARATE WAS THE RIGHT THING TO DO
WWW.STAIRWELLONLINE.COM J.BIGELOW ©2013
FOR YOUR PRIDE?
FOR MY *BACK*.
EMERGENCY

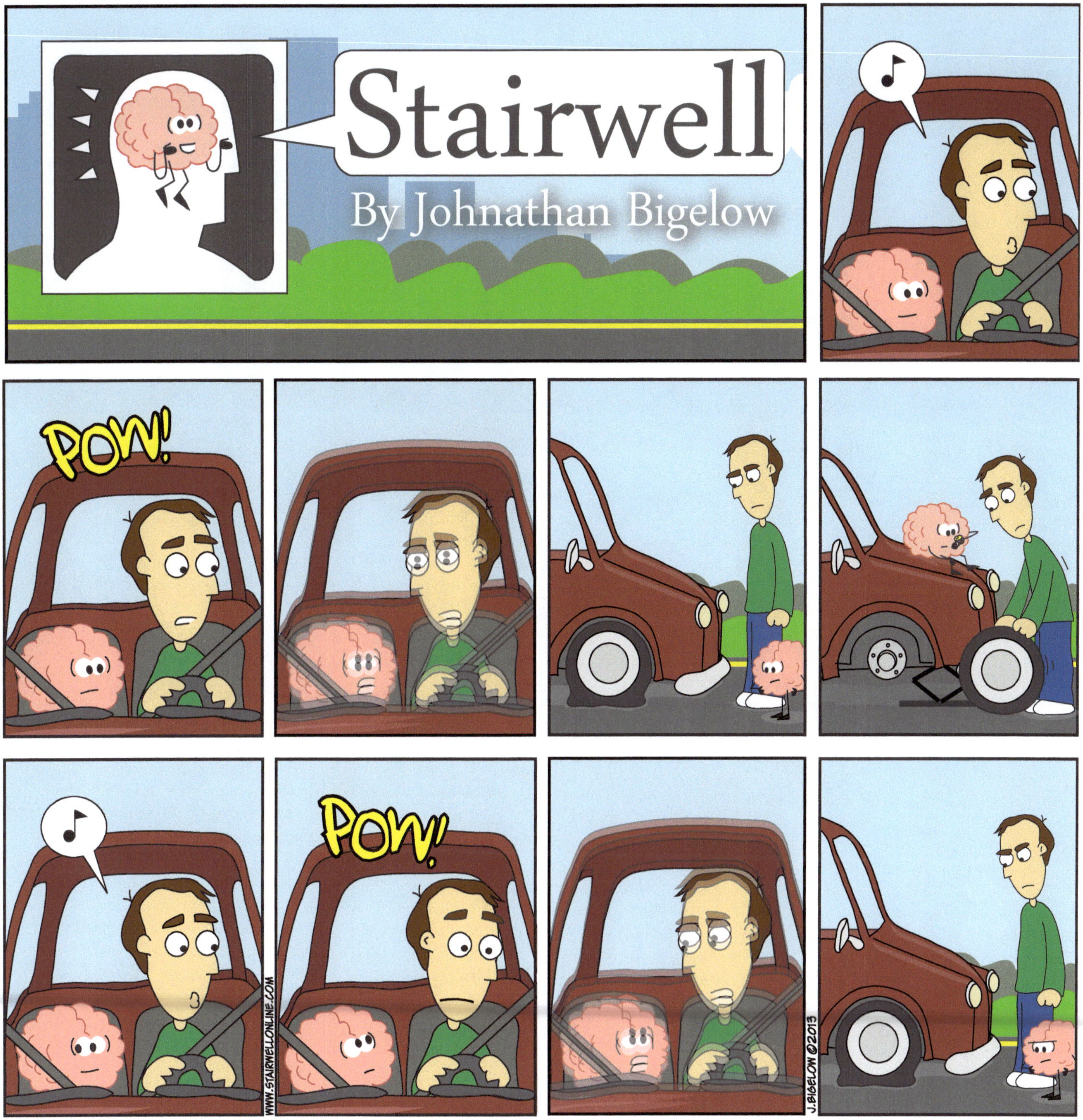
Stairwell
By Johnathan Bigelow
POW!
POW!
WWW.STAIRWELLONLINE.COM
J.BIGELOW ©2013

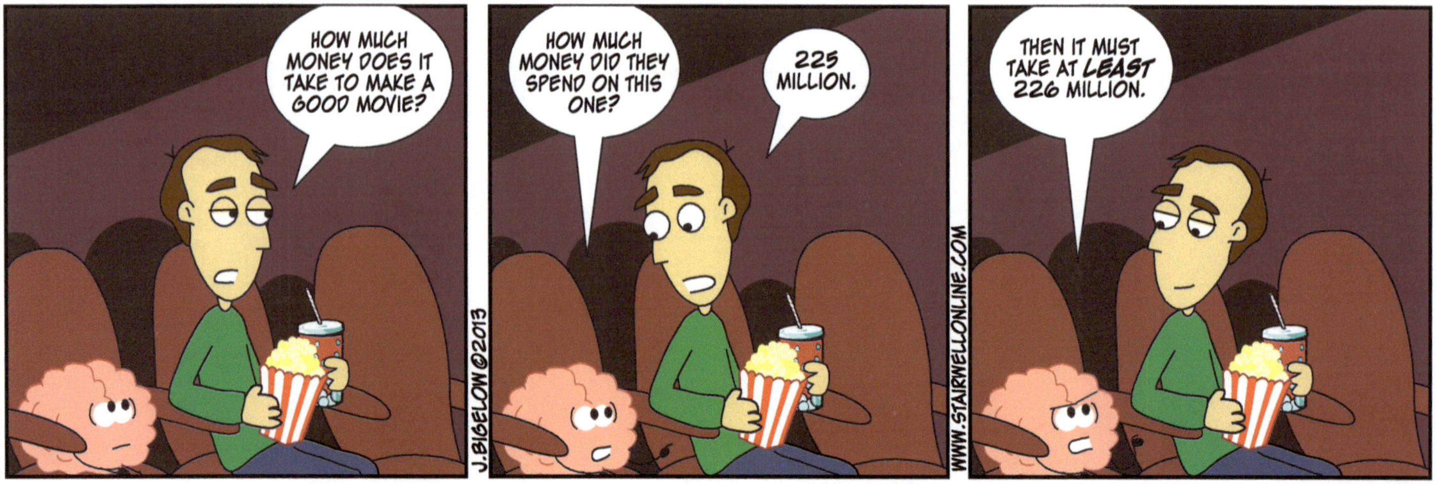
HOW MUCH MONEY DOES IT TAKE TO MAKE A GOOD MOVIE?
HOW MUCH MONEY DID THEY SPEND ON THIS ONE?
225 MILLION.
J.BIGELOW ©2013
THEN IT MUST TAKE AT **LEAST** 226 MILLION.
WWW.STAIRWELLONLINE.COM

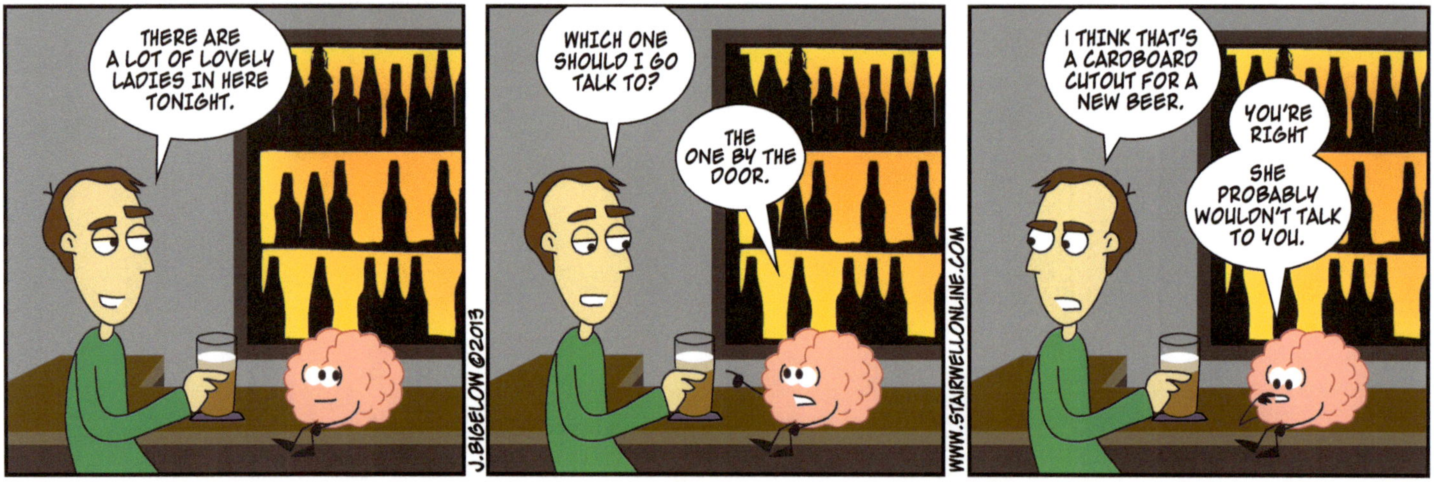
THERE ARE A LOT OF LOVELY LADIES IN HERE TONIGHT.
WHICH ONE SHOULD I GO TALK TO?
THE ONE BY THE DOOR.
J.BIGELOW ©2013
I THINK THAT'S A CARDBOARD CUTOUT FOR A NEW BEER.
YOU'RE RIGHT
SHE PROBABLY WOULDN'T TALK TO YOU.
WWW.STAIRWELLONLINE.COM

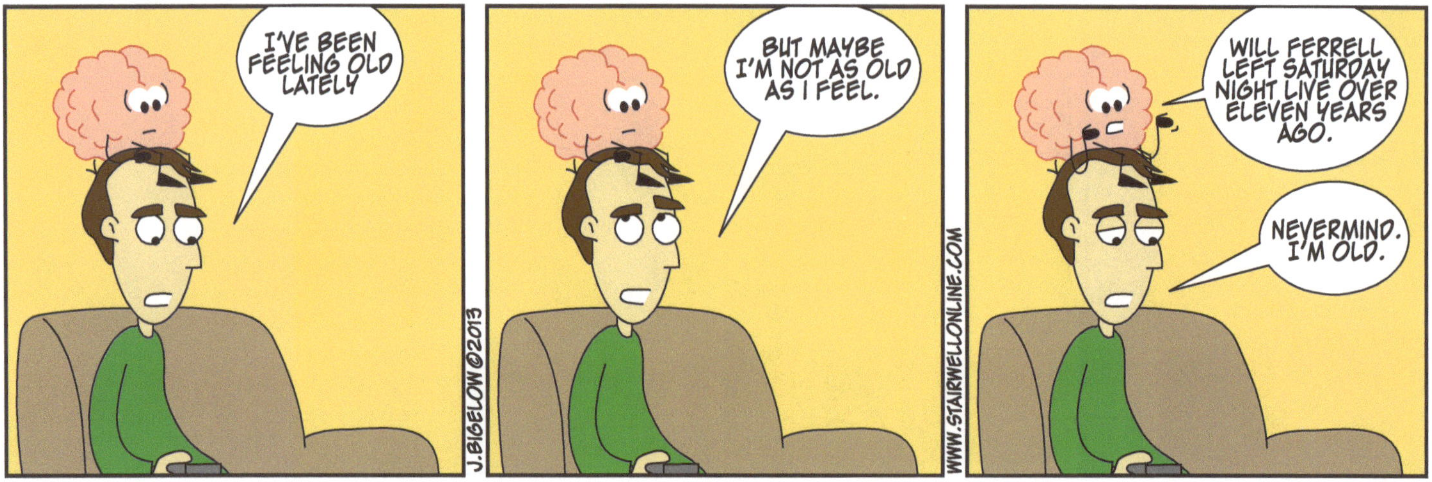
I'VE BEEN FEELING OLD LATELY
BUT MAYBE I'M NOT AS OLD AS I FEEL.
J.BIGELOW ©2013
WILL FERRELL LEFT SATURDAY NIGHT LIVE OVER ELEVEN YEARS AGO.
NEVERMIND. I'M OLD.
WWW.STAIRWELLONLINE.COM

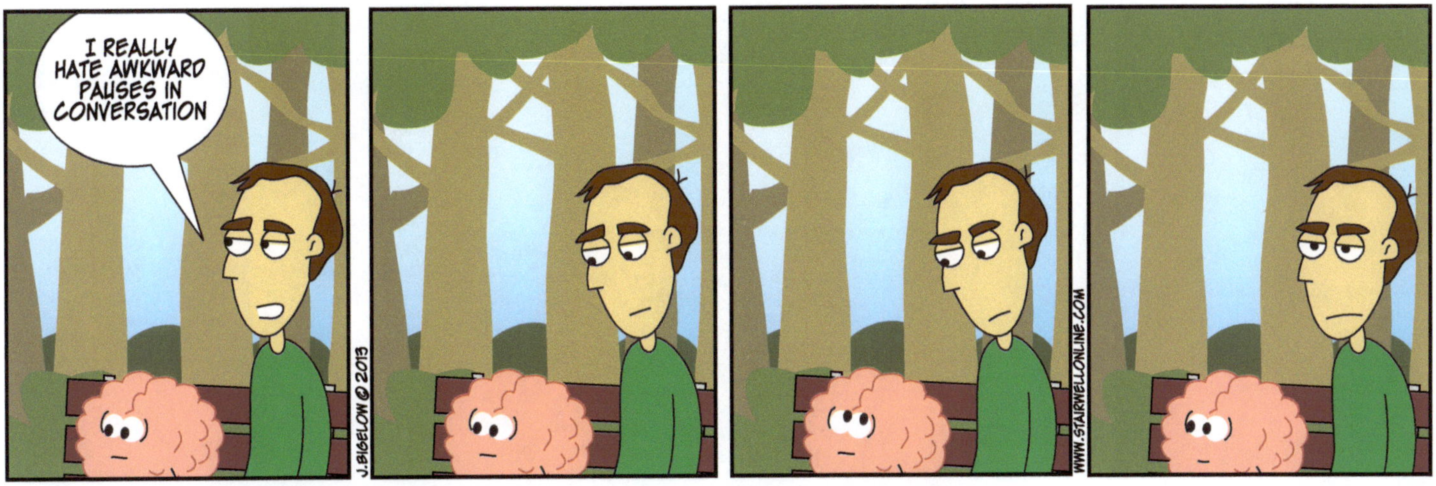
I REALLY HATE AWKWARD PAUSES IN CONVERSATION
J.BIGELOW ©2013
WWW.STAIRWELLONLINE.COM

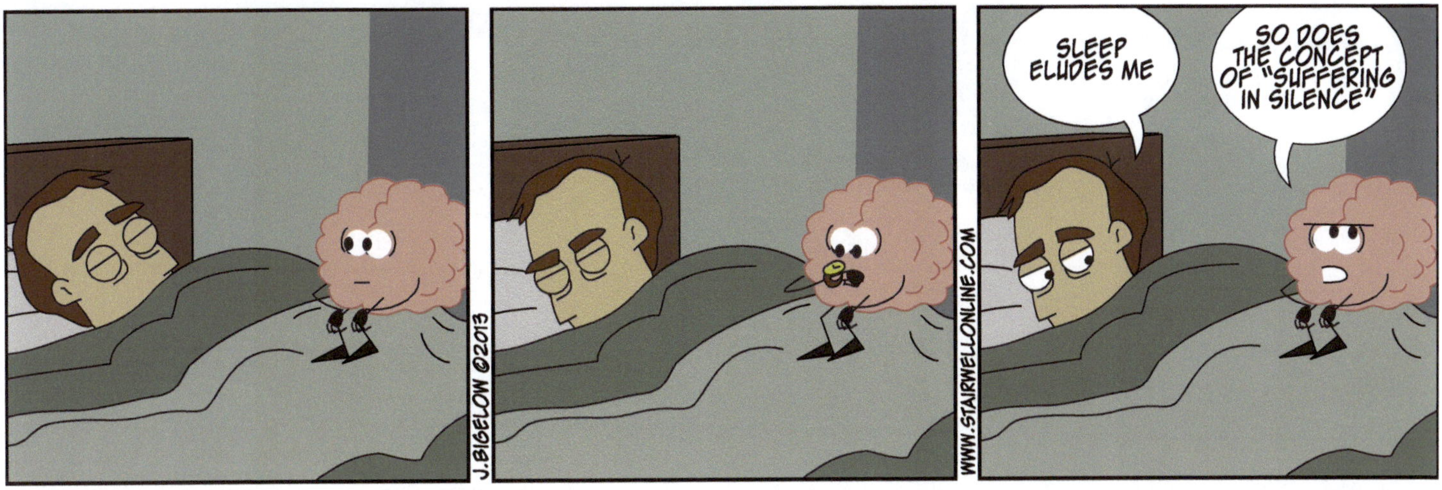
J.BIGELOW ©2013
WWW.STAIRWELLONLINE.COM
SLEEP ELUDES ME
SO DOES THE CONCEPT OF "SUFFERING IN SILENCE"

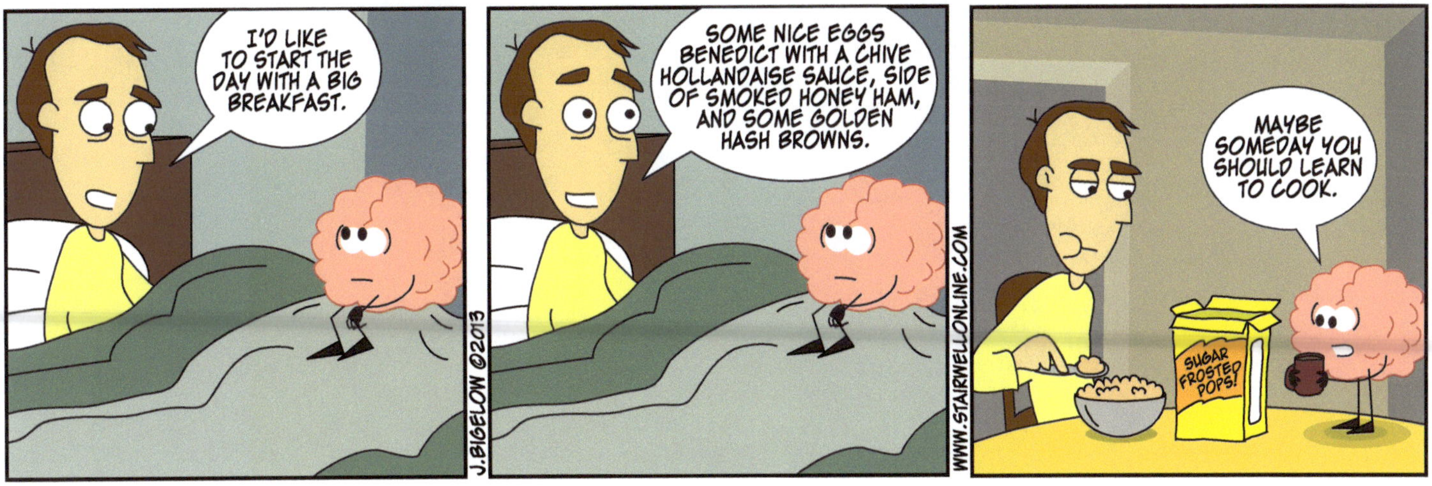
I'D LIKE TO START THE DAY WITH A BIG BREAKFAST.
J.BIGELOW ©2013
SOME NICE EGGS BENEDICT WITH A CHIVE HOLLANDAISE SAUCE, SIDE OF SMOKED HONEY HAM, AND SOME GOLDEN HASH BROWNS.
WWW.STAIRWELLONLINE.COM
MAYBE SOMEDAY YOU SHOULD LEARN TO COOK.
SUGAR FROSTED POPS!

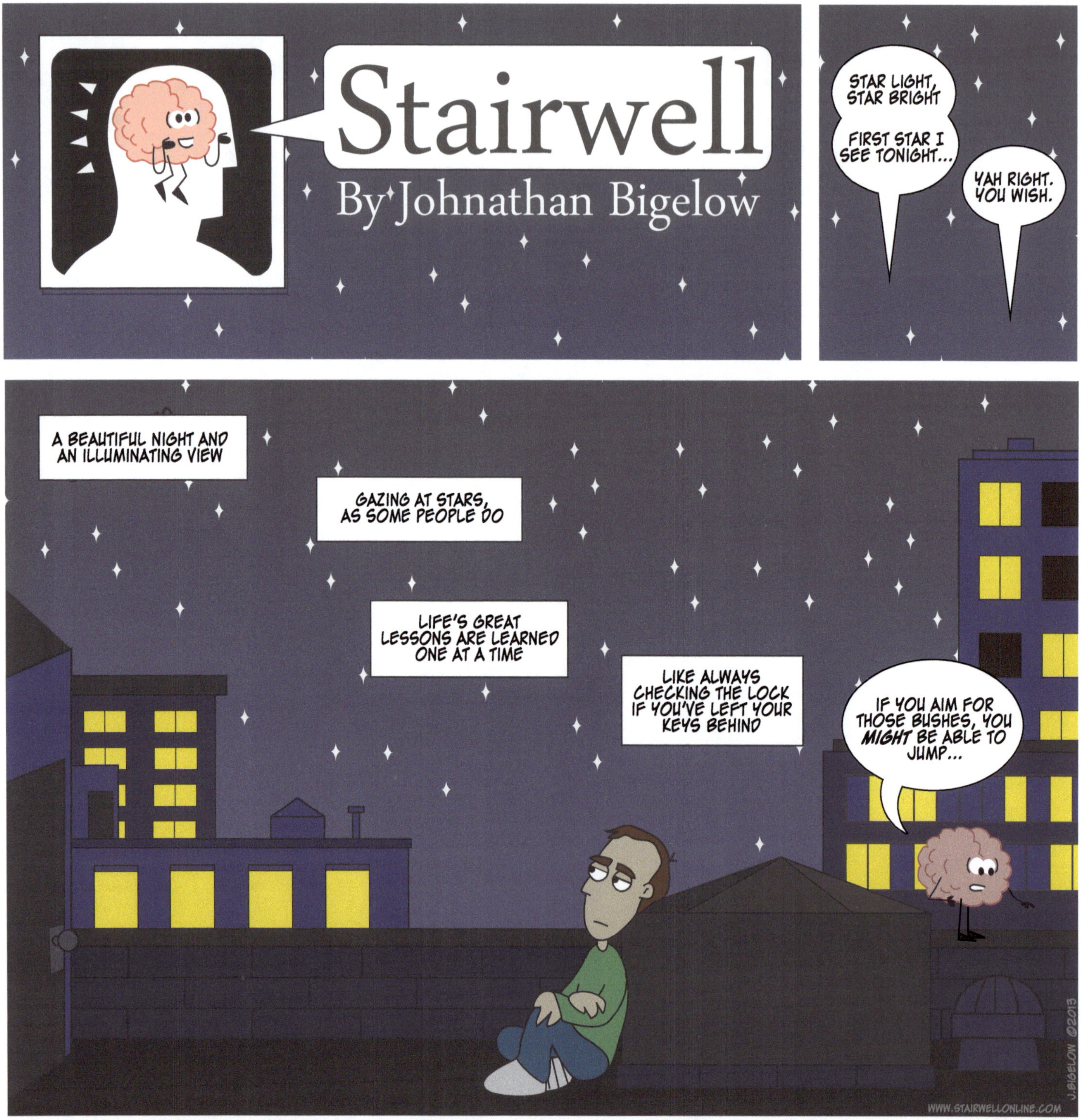
Stairwell
By Johnathan Bigelow
STAR LIGHT, STAR BRIGHT
FIRST STAR I SEE TONIGHT...
YAH RIGHT. YOU WISH.
A BEAUTIFUL NIGHT AND AN ILLUMINATING VIEW
GAZING AT STARS, AS SOME PEOPLE DO
LIFE'S GREAT LESSONS ARE LEARNED ONE AT A TIME
LIKE ALWAYS CHECKING THE LOCK IF YOU'VE LEFT YOUR KEYS BEHIND
IF YOU AIM FOR THOSE BUSHES, YOU *MIGHT* BE ABLE TO JUMP...
J.BIGELOW ©2013
WWW.STAIRWELLONLINE.COM

BONUS MATERIAL

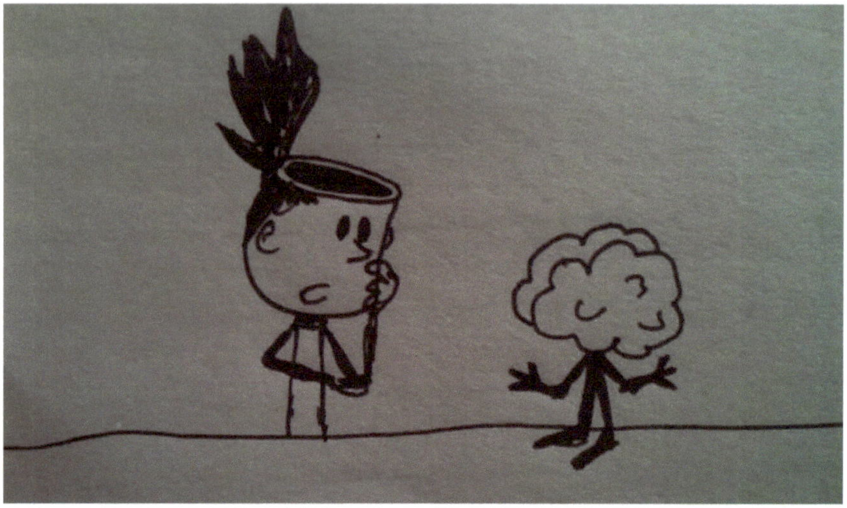

This is the original idea sketch. I drew this at work while I was doodling. It's drawn on a bit of Post-It note. After this doodle sparked my imaginiation, I started to develop a strip where a man's head would literally open up and the brain would pop out and talk to him. This proved to be very odd and I switched to what the strip is today.

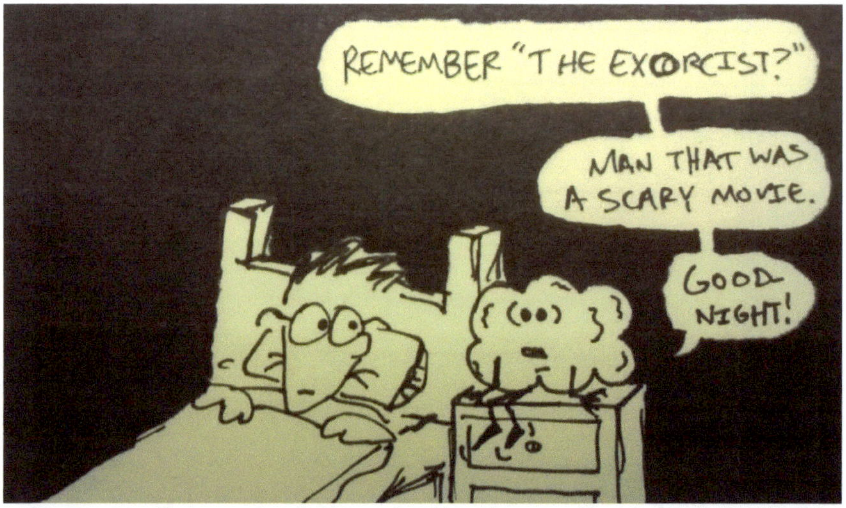
REMEMBER "THE EXORCIST?"
MAN THAT WAS A SCARY MOVIE.
GOOD NIGHT!

This was the first concept comic strip. Also done on Post-It. Look familiar? It became the first strip that ever appeared on the Stairwell website and in this book. Norman in the original idea was going to be a kinda nerdy guy. The brain? Apparently supposed to be used chewing gum.

BONUS MATERIAL

In the original drafts of Stairwell, Norman was a background character that I had drawn in my other comic strip "A Rusty Life." He had spikey hair which I had to axe for two reasons. Reason one: He looked too "cool." No one was going to believe that this guy was an "everyman." Reason two: The spikey hair took too much panel real estate.

First Draft:

REMEMBER "THE EXORCIST" MOVIE?
MAN, THAT WAS A SCARY MOVIE...
ANYWAY. GOODNIGHT!
WWW.THINKINGOUTLOUD.COM ©2012
CRAP.

Published:

REMEMBER "THE EXORCIST" MOVIE?
MAN, THAT WAS A SCARY FILM...
J.BIGELOW ©2012
ANYWAY. GOODNIGHT!
WWW.STAIRWELLONLINE.COM
CRAP.

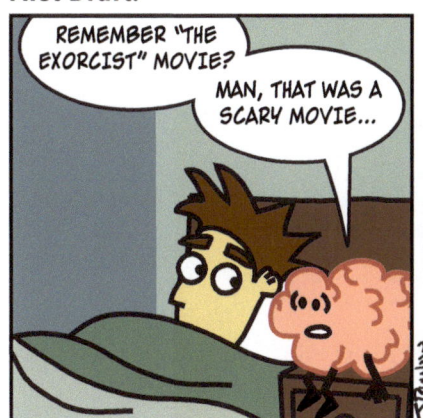

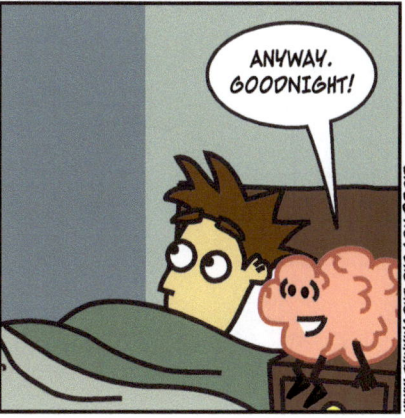

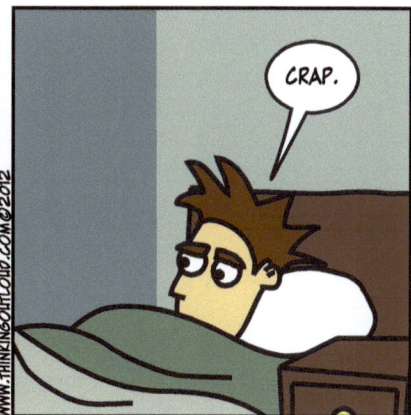

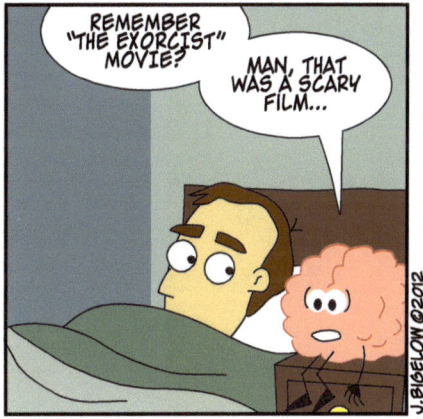

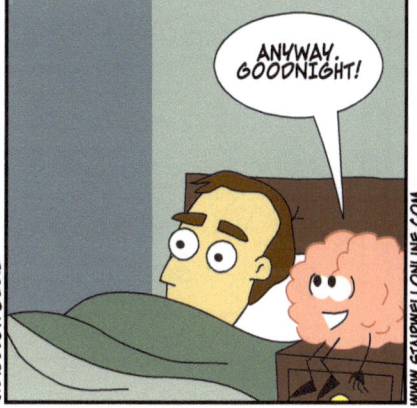

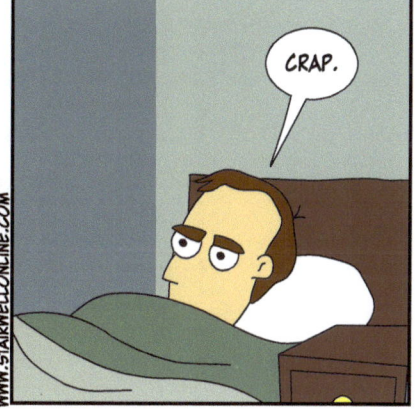

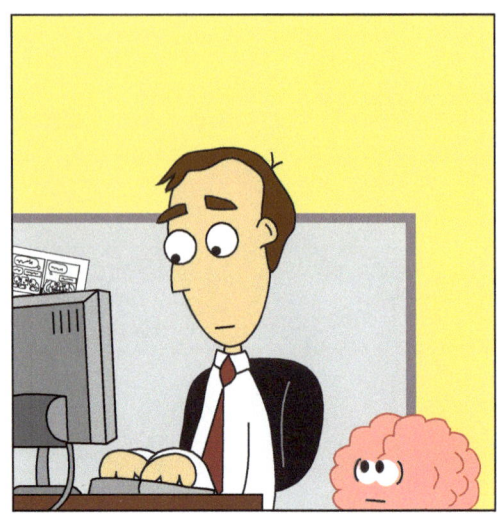

Did you know that the comic on Norman's cubicle wall is real? Not only is it real, but it's a strip from one of my previous comic projects: There and In Between.

I BUILT A ROBOT WIFE.
AFFIRMITIVE.
I BET YOU'RE GOING TO HAVE FUN TONIGHT.
I SURE AM.
AFFIRMITIVE.
J.BIGELOW
THAT NIGHT:
BABY, YOU SUNK MY BATTLESHIP!
AFFIRMITIVE.

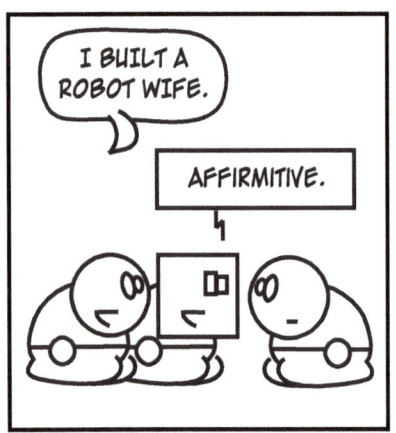

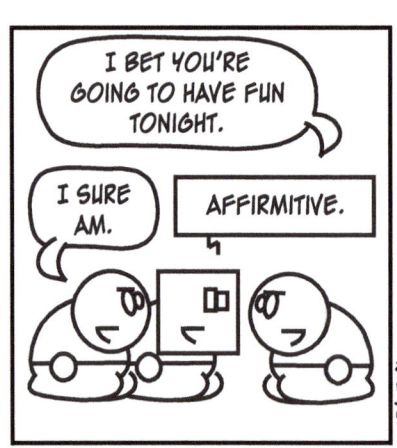

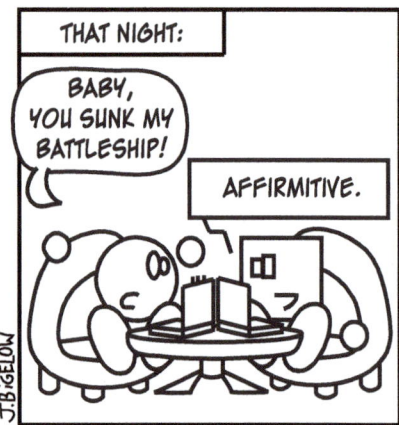

Also by Johnathan Bigelow:

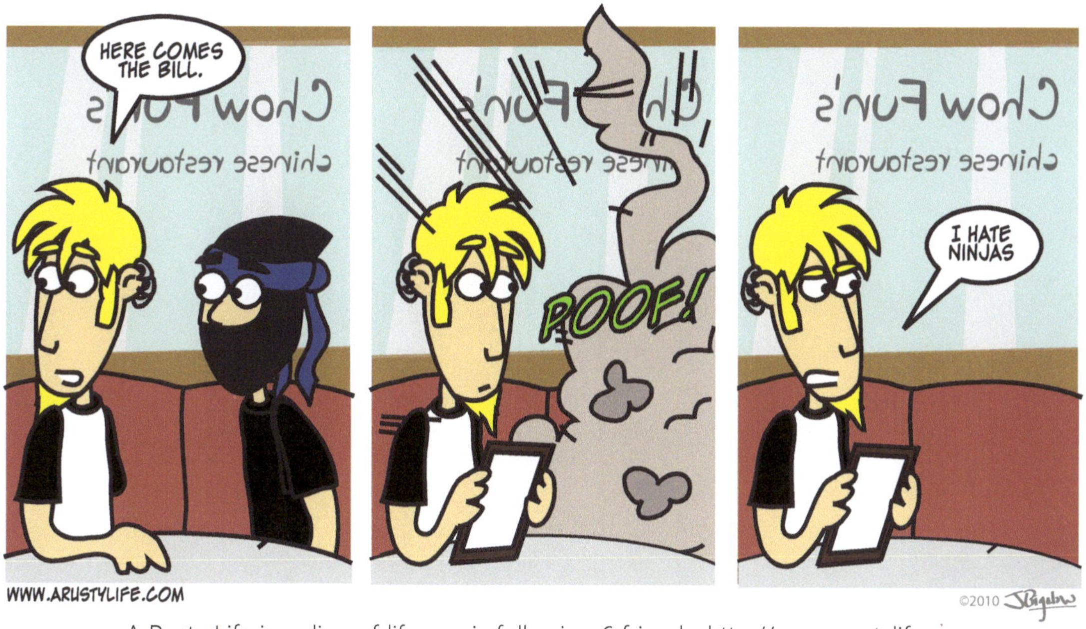
HERE COMES THE BILL.
POOF!
I HATE NINJAS
WWW.ARUSTYLIFE.COM
©2010 J.Bigelow

A Rusty Life is a slice-of-life comic following 6 friends. http://www.arustylife.com

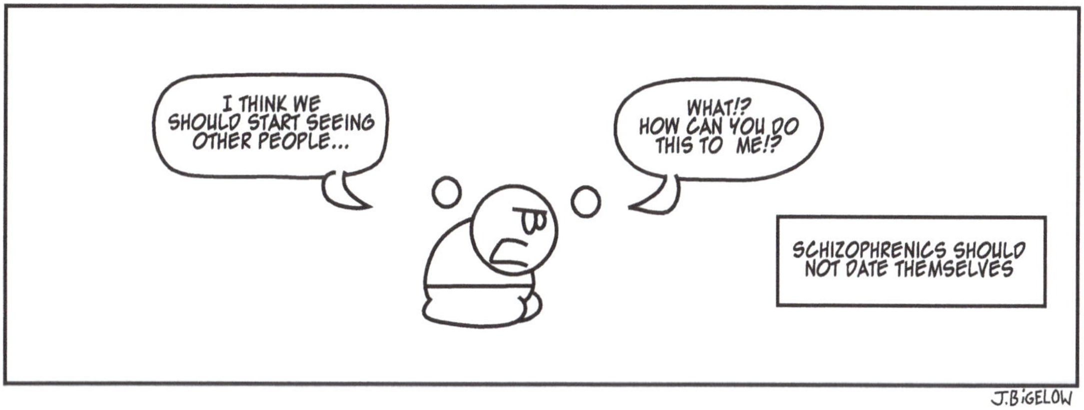
I THINK WE SHOULD START SEEING OTHER PEOPLE...
WHAT!? HOW CAN YOU DO THIS TO ME!?
SCHIZOPHRENICS SHOULD NOT DATE THEMSELVES
J.BIGELOW

There and In Between is a random gag comic. http://www.thereandinbetween.com

www.ingramcontent.com/pod-product-compliance
Lightning Source LLC
Chambersburg PA
CBHW042033150426
43201CB00002B/16